KT-147-609

King

SATELLITES OVER SOUTH ASIA

SATELLITES OVER SOUTH ASIA

Broadcasting, Culture and the Public Interest

DAVID PAGE
WILLIAM CRAWLEY

Sage Publications
New Delhi/Thousand Oaks/London

First published in 2001 by

Sage Publications India Pvt Ltd
M-32 Market, Greater Kailash-I
New Delhi 110 048

Sage Publications Inc.   Sage Publications Ltd
2455 Teller Road   6 Bonhill Street
Thousand Oaks, California 91320 London EC2A 4PU

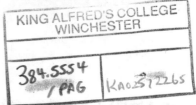

Published by Tejeshwar Singh for Sage Publications India Pvt Ltd, typeset
in 10 pt. Palatino by Asian Telelinks, New Delhi, and printed at Chaman
Enterprises, New Delhi.

Library of Congress Cataloging-in-Publication Data

Page, David, 1944–
    Satellites over South Asia: broadcasting, culture, and the public
interest/David Page, William Crawley.
        p.   cm.
    Includes bibliographical references and index.
    1. Direct broadcast satellite television—Social aspects—Sout Asia.
    2. Direct broadcast satellite television—Social aspects—India. I.
Crawley, William, 1940–II. Title.
    HE8700.66.S64 P34   384.55'2'0954—dc21   2000   00–062690

ISBN: 0–7619–9481–5 (US–Hb)   81–7036–958–4 (India–Hb)
        0–7619–9482–3 (US–Pb)   81–7036–959–2 (India–Pb)

Sage Production Team: Dipika Nath, M.S.V. Namboodiri and Santosh
Rawat

CONTENTS

LIST OF TABLES

LIST OF ABBREVIATIONS

ABC	American Broadcasting Company (part of Disney)
ABNI	Asian Business News International (merged with CNBC Asia)
AIADMK	All India Anna Dravida Munnetra Kazagham
AIDWA	All India Democratic Women's Association
AIR	All India Radio
APL	Ammirati Puris Lintas
ATN	Asia Television Network
BB	Bangladesh Betar (Bangladesh Radio)
BBC	British Broadcasting Corporation
BITV	Business India Television, later TVi
BJP	Bharatiya Janata Party
BTV	Bangladesh Television
CBS	Columbia Broadcasting Service (part of Sony)
CENDIT	Centre for the Development of Instructional Technology (India)
CNBC	Part of the NBC/Dow Jones Group
CNN/CNNI	Cable News Network International (part of Time-Warner)
DANIDA	Danish Development Agency
DART	Doordarshan Audience Research Television (ratings system)
DD	Doordarshan (state TV in India)
DMK	Dravida Munnetra Kazagham
DTH	Direct to Home
EMRA	Electronic Media Regulatory Authority (Pakistan)
ESPN	Entertainment and Sports Programming Network (part of ABC)
ETV	Ekushey TV (Bangladesh)
FGD	Focus Group Discussion
FMCG	Fast Moving Consumer Goods
GEC	Golden Eagle Communications (first owner of Vijay TV)
GEC	General Electric Company

HBO	Home Box Office (part of Time Warner)
HTA	Hindustan Thompson Associates, an affiliate of J. Walter Thompson
IMF	International Monetary Fund
IMRB	Indian Market Research Bureau
INTAM	Indian National Television Audience Measurement (research wing of ORG-MARG)
IRS	Indian Readership Survey
ISRO	Indian Space Research Organisation
ITN	Independent Television News (Sri Lanka)
JJTV	Commercial TV channel (named after Jayaram Jayalalitha)
MBC	Maharaja Broadcasting Corporation (MTV's radio arm in Sri Lanka)
MNC	Multinational Corporation
MRUC	Media Research Users Council (India)
MSO	Multi-System Operator
MSSRF	M.S. Swaminathan Research Foundation
MTV	Music TV (part of Viacom)
MTV	Maharaja Television (Sri Lanka)
NASA	National Aeronautics and Space Administration (USA)
NBC	National Broadcasting Company (partner of Dow Jones, owner of CNBC)
NCAER	National Council of Applied Economic Research (India)
NDTV	New Delhi Television
NRS	National Readership Survey (India)
NTM	Network Television Marketing (Pakistan)
NTV	Nepal Television
O&M	Ogilvy & Mather
ORG/MARG	Indian Market Research Organisation
PBC	Pakistan Broadcasting Corporation (formerly Radio Pakistan)
PTI	Press Trust of India
PTV	Pakistan Television
RPG	R.P. Goenka Group of Companies
SEAC	South East Asia Command
SITE	Satellite Instructional Television Educational Project

SLBC	Sri Lanka Broadcasting Corporation (Radio)
SLFP	Sri Lanka Freedom Party
SLRC	Sri Lanka Rupavahini Corporation (TV)
SMC	Social Marketing Company (Bangladesh)
SET	Sony Entertainment Television
STAR	Satellite Television Asia Region
STN	Shalimar Television Network (Pakistan)
TAM	Television Audience Measurement
TNL	Teleshan Network Lanka
TNT	Turner Network Television (part of Time Warner, now called TCM)
TRP	Television Rating Point
TVi	Television India, formerly Business India TV
UNDP	United Nations Development Programme
UNESCO	United Nations Educational, Scientific and Cultural Organisation
UNI	United News of India
UNICEF	United Nations Children's Fund
UNP	United National Party (Sri Lanka)
UTV	United Television (Indian television software house)
WTO	World Trade Organisation

PREFACE AND ACKNOWLEDGEMENTS

The arrival of satellite television in South Asia brought radical change, not just for the viewing public but also for all those working in the media with an interest in the region. For the BBC World Service, with whose radio services to the region we had worked for twenty years, it brought the need for a radical re-appraisal of strategy. Our own interest in the implications of satellite television for South Asia arose from our involvement in the BBC's efforts to reposition itself to meet the new challenges. We also found ourselves talking about the new media to audiences outside the BBC—in British universities and other broadcasting organisations. By the time we left the BBC, it had become a subject we were both keen to pursue.

At a personal level, we have brought to the study our training as historians and our experience as political analysts and radio broadcasters. In probing the cultural influences of television, we have drawn heavily on the expertise of others. Our emphasis is on exploring the views both of people with special knowledge and members of the public. We have provided the framework of analysis, but we believe the value of the book lies in the cogency and diversity of their views on key issues of public interest raised by the new media.

We declare an interest, as former BBC broadcasters, in public service broadcasting as a valid ideal. However, we do not suppose that ideals and models transfer easily from one country to another. In fact, this book shows clearly that they do not. The ethos of broadcasting tends to reflect the state of civil society at a particular time and place; it is only changed if the society itself wishes to change it. In Britain, the ideal has been under attack since the 1980s from the same commercial ethos which is now being reproduced in South Asia and elsewhere. To that extent, Britain's experience is not without interest. Our aim in this study, however, is not to prescribe British solutions for South Asian problems, but to explore the new issues of national and regional public interest which have emerged in the satellite era.

We have chosen to speak of 'public interest' rather than 'public service'. In South Asia, the concept of public service has been so closely linked to the state's own use of the media that there is little clarity about its meaning. We believe, however, that broadcasting has a key role to play in the development of representative institutions and civil society in South Asia and that public opinion needs to be mobilised to make it more effective in this field.

The book concentrates on the five main countries of South Asia. We have not included in the study either of the two smallest South Asian states—the Maldives and Bhutan. When the project was started, Bhutan had no state television; the trigger for change was to make the 1998 World Cup accessible to football enthusiasts in that deeply traditional society. The Maldives has a single channel state television service, with no indication of any plans to diversify or reform. Though many of the issues we look at seem relevant to the Maldives, for practical reasons we did not attempt to extend our research agenda there.

In writing the book, we were convinced that the phenomenon needed to be examined from a regional perspective. We also knew that it would only be possible to do justice to the subject if we could build a team of research associates with local knowledge and expertise. We were fortunate that the Ford Foundation in New Delhi liked the idea and offered us funding to pursue it. Terry George gave us an encouraging first hearing. David Arnold and Gowher Rizvi, as directors of the Delhi office, have both taken an interest in our progress. However, we owe a special debt to Sharada Ramanathan, the officer for media and culture, who helped us shape our proposal, encouraged us to think of a documentary film on the same themes, attended our workshops, and made a big difference by putting her faith in us.

We are also grateful to Professor James Manor of the Institute of Development Studies at Sussex University who provided us with an institutional base for our activities. John Sanders and Sue Pafford of the IDS Finance Department administered our finances with promptness and understanding.

Our primary debt in writing this book is to the research associates with whom we have worked. Their knowledge and experience have been our guide in interpreting developments in their countries and regions, in saving us from error and in putting us right on nuances of culture or interpretation. Though our names appear on the cover, it is their book as much as ours.

The project began at a workshop in New Delhi in February 1998 at the India International Centre, where we formulated an agreed programme for research over the following six months. We met again in July in the offices of Panos South Asia in Kathmandu to tell each other what we had learnt and to begin the process of interpretation, refinement and further research. Between the two workshops, both of us visited our research associates in their home territories and worked with them on the project. In January 1999, we held three smaller workshops, in Chennai, Delhi and Islamabad, in which early drafts of some of the chapters were discussed. During the writing of the book in 1999, we were in regular touch with the team by e-mail and benefited from their comments as the book took shape. A small amount of additional research was done during this period to take account of new developments.

The research agenda first of all involved the compilation of media profiles of the different South Asian countries. These were descriptive accounts of the state of broadcasting, which covered the legislative framework, the history, operations and reach of public and private broadcasters, and their performance in news and current affairs, entertainment, development, education and health. The profiles also documented reactions to the new satellite media and assessed emerging market trends.

In total, over 400 interviews, which are listed in the bibliography, were conducted by us or our associates over a period of two years. In addition to the interviews with experts, we arranged focus group discussions with six categories of people to gauge public reactions to satellite programmes in a number of key areas of cultural influence: language, dress, music, sport, cultural practices, patterns of consumption, social relations and the impact on women and children. Six district surveys were also carried out—three in India and one each in Bangladesh, Nepal and Sri Lanka—to measure reactions at different levels of society outside the metropolitan cities. In total, 110 discussions were carried out, which are listed by country, region and category in the bibliography, accompanied by a fuller description of the methodology.

India was divided into four regions, which were researched from Delhi (Mohammed Firoz), Calcutta (Anuradha Mukherjee), Chennai (Lata Ramaseshan and Pritham Chakravarty) and

Mumbai. Because of India's size and centrality, we appointed three Indian research associates with specific briefs: the economics of the new media market (Mayank Bhatt), the role of government (Saibal Das Gupta) and the cultural influence of the satellite channels (Deepa Bhatia). Though they worked only on India, their expertise fed into the work of other members of the group. Bangladesh (Afsan Chowdhury), Nepal (Deepak Thapa), Pakistan (Tasneem Ahmar) and Sri Lanka (Santhini Jayawardena) were each researched by one associate.

Several others played an important part in the research process. Kunda Dixit shared his knowledge of Nepal and South Asia and acted as our host during the second workshop. We are thankful to him and the staff of Panos South Asia for making that such a memorable and useful experience. Nilu Damle carried out district surveys in Latur and Varanasi and provided a model for others to follow. M.S.S. Pandian helped to coordinate our research effort in Tamil Nadu after N.V. Sankaran was obliged for personal reasons to withdraw from the team. A.S. Panneerselvan of *Outlook* wrote a background note and conducted some interviews. K. Babu conducted some discussion groups in Madurai. For the chapter on 'Broadcasting and Community', Pritham Chakravarty compiled a report on cable systems in south Chennai and M.J.R. David wrote a brief history of community broadcasting in Sri Lanka. In Pakistan, M.F. Memon contributed a report on the cable systems of Karachi. Subir Bhaumik, with the assistance of Anirban Roy and Shankadweep Choudhury, researched the influence of satellite in Assam, conducting interviews and carrying out discussions with students, university lecturers, editors and politicians.

We thank all these colleagues for the insights and experience they brought to the project, for their assistance, guidance and hospitality to us on visits, and for their patience in responding to a stream of e-mail queries and telephone calls during the writing of the book.

We are very conscious that in writing the book we have been unable to use directly a great deal of excellent material which has been generated by the research. Many of the reports and discussion groups merit publication in their own right. Our plan is to make some of this material available on the Internet.

Nupur Basu has been commissioned to produce a documentary film about the impact of the satellite revolution and the issues raised by the project. We are confident that the film will help to give these issues wider currency. It is being distributed by Television Trust for the Environment, and information about how it can be obtained is provided at the end of the book.

We took advice from many people in setting up the project, recruiting our research associates and completing the work. It is impossible to mention them all but we are specifically grateful to the following:

In Bangladesh: Ataus Samad, Farouk Ahmed Choudhury, Syed Shamsul Haq, Frances Harrison.

In India: Amit Agarwal, M.J. Akbar, Indrani Bagchi, Shailaja Bajpai, Somnath Banerji, Prem Behl, Shekhar Bhatia, Urvashi Butalia, Subhash Chakravarti, Dr. B.S. Chandrasekhar, P.C. Chatterji, Anurag Chaturvedi, Pramit Pal Chaudhuri, Anil Dharkar, Rajeshwar Dayal, Prof. P.S. Deodhar, Sucharita Eashwar, Sheeba George, Bhaskar Ghose, Dipankar Ghosh, Nilanjana Gupta, Shekhar Gupta, Dr. Kiran Karnik, Kumar Ketkar, Smruti Koppikar, Narendra Kumar, Amita Malik, Indira Mansingh, Hima Mehta, Anjan Mitra, Rekha Mody, Eileen Mozoomdar, Ashis Nandy, P. Narayanmoorthy, Sevanti Ninan, Saeed Naqvi, Mahesh Pande, Mrinal Pande, H.Y. Sharada Prasad, Sam Rajappa, N. Ram, Chanchal Sarkar, Ameen Sayani, Bhabani Sengupta, Akhila Sivadas, Kalpana Sharma, Jayashree Shidore, Nandan Unnikrishnan, G.T. Verghese, Prof. J.S. Yadava.

In Nepal: Kanak Mani Dixit, Bharat D. Koirala, Kedar Man Singh, Barbara Adams.

In Pakistan: Zaffar Abbas, H. Aftab Ahmed, Khaled Ahmed, Hameed Asghar, Aslam Azhar, Dr. Mubarak Ali, Zubair Ali, Farhan Bokhari, Roshan Dhunjibhoy, Mushtaq Gazdar, Hameed Haroon, Javed Jabbar, Altamash Kamal, Shahid Malik, Tahir Mirza, Gulrez Mojiz, M.B. Naqvi, Agha Nasir, I.A. Rehman, Khwaja Ijaz Sarwar, Amera Saeed, the late Aziz Siddiqui, Raana Syed.

In Sri Lanka: Hilmy Ahamed, Sharmini Boyle, Elmo Fernando, H.M. Gunasekera, Nalaka Gunawardene, Victor Gunawardene, Amal Jayasinghe, Shirley Perera, Suren de Silva, Jayadeva Uyangoda, Livy Wijemanne.

In the United Kingdom: The late Athar Ali, Hugh Hope-Stone, Naresh Kaushik, Sampath Kumar, the late Alan Macdonald, Nimal and Ranjani Mendis, Graham Mytton, Ashis Ray, Achala Sharma, Anandhi Suryaprakasan.

We would like to thank the staff at the India Office and Oriental Reading Room of the British Library and at the library of the School of Oriental and African Studies; also Anne Davies, then librarian at the World Association of Christian Communication in London. Several organisations invited us to contribute to discussions on the media in Asia. William Crawley is grateful to Elizabeth Smith, Secretary General of the Commonwealth Broadcasting Association, and Vijay Menon and his colleagues at the Asian Media Information and Communication Centre (AMIC) in Singapore for invitations to AMIC/CBA conferences in Singapore in February 1998 and Delhi in April 1999; and to Kenji Miyakage of NHK Public Affairs in Tokyo. David Page would like to thank the Heinrich Boll Foundation for an invitation to a conference in Karachi on globalisation in February 1998 and Panos South Asia for the opportunity to attend a seminar on public service broadcasting in Kathmandu in September 1998.

In our travels to different parts of South Asia, we enjoyed the hospitality of famiiy and friends and benefited from their knowledge of regional politics and media.

William Crawley would like to thank Shafik and Taleya Rahman and F.R. Mahmud Hasan and Shamse Hasan in Dhaka, Natarajan and Nirmala Sundaram in Chennai, and Satish and Anju Bedi in Mumbai. He is also grateful to K.K. Sharma and Bulbul Sharma, Joysree Mukherjee and Dr. Ashok Mukherjee for their hospitality during the eight months he spent in Delhi in 1998 and on numerous occasions before and since; and to Arunabh Mukherjee for help in transcribing interviews.

David Page owes special thanks to Alauddin in Lahore, Ismail and Sarwat Niazi in Islamabad, Sayeed Hasan Khan in Karachi, Mark Tully and Gillian Wright in Delhi, Colonel C.B. Ramesh and Indira Ramesh in Bangalore, Ruma and Samaraditiya Pal in Calcutta, and Roland and Carmen Edirisinghe in Colombo.

Thanks also need to be given to those who read parts or all of the book during the writing stage. Our research associates have seen and commented on the passages relevant to their own research. Professor Anthony D. King made valuable comments on drafts of six of the chapters. David Morley provided useful feedback on the Introduction. Pradip Thomas and M.J.R. David read and commented on Chapter 9. Ijaz Gilani of Gallup Pakistan and Indrani Sen of Hindustan Thompson in Calcutta provided important media research updates as the book went to press. We are also very grateful to Sevanti Ninan and Shailaja Bajpai in Delhi and Stephen Hughes in London, whose comments and criticisms of the completed draft we have attempted to take into account in the final version of the book.

Tejeshwar Singh of Sage has been immensely helpful and supportive in accepting the book for publication and keeping us up to the mark to meet a tight deadline. Thanks too to Dipika Nath and the Sage production team, and to Uzma Mohsin for the cover design. We would also like to acknowledge the encouragement we received from Tim Farmiloe at an earlier stage of the project.

Finally, our sincere thanks to our families and friends, particularly Bonny and Ruth, who have put up with our absences and given us much needed support and encouragement.

Doing the research and producing the book has been a stimulating experience. We have shared the work equally at every stage. William Crawley completed first drafts of Chapters 3, 4, 8 and 10; David Page of the remainder. But the different drafts have changed computers many times since then and the final result is an agreed text which expresses our joint view. Our debts to so many people do not absolve us of the responsibility for the shortcomings that remain.

May 2000   **David Page**
                                                          William Crawley

One

INTRODUCTION

In the town of Biratnagar in the Nepal terai—where the North Indian plains confront the foothills of the Himalayas—students debated the impact of satellite TV on their lives and disagreed strongly among themselves. 'Personally', said one boy, 'I don't like Star Movies and Channel V. The life shown on these channels is far removed from the reality of our own country. Because of these channels, Nepali girls too have started wearing short skirts.' 'I think films are much more dangerous to society', replied a girl. 'Nepali boys are very quick at copying. That's why we see boys wearing earrings, bandanas on their heads and teasing girls. This is all due to films.' 'Our earrings and bandanas have nothing to do with TV,' retorted a boy, 'though the provocative clothes girls wear may be something they have learnt from TV.' 'I would not dare to kiss a girl on the road, just because they do so on TV,' mused another male student. 'But there have been changes in the way I dress and in the way I look at things.'

The young men and women taking part in this discussion were students at a local college. They all still watched Nepali state television or Indian state television, but almost all of them also had access to twenty satellite channels on a local cable system. The charge was Rs. 200 or less than US$ 3 a month. The channels included Channel V and MTV, the youth and music channels, Zee TV, the popular Hindi entertainment channel, three channels from the Star platform offering regional news, movies and sports, plus international news providers CNN and BBC.

Ten years earlier, Biratnagar had a choice only of Indian and Nepali state television channels, and the difference is palpable. 'Nepal TV programmes are not effective and neither are they good,' said one of the same students. 'In fact, every month, NTV programmes disappear from Biratnagar for days. This does not happen with the satellite channels.' Another said: 'Before City-cable came to Biratnagar, we had to watch the boring programmes of Nepal TV and I can say no one actually sat completely through any of them.' 'If we had only Nepal TV,' said a third, 'we would have come to know of the nuclear tests of India and Pakistan really late.'[1]

Satellite TV has made a huge difference to the choice of viewing available even in relatively small towns in economically under-developed parts of South Asia. It has opened windows to worlds which were inaccessible before except to the well to do, and it has provoked a lively and often heated debate about the implications for nations, communities and cultures.

It has also offered a major challenge to the national broadcasters of South Asia who had the field to themselves for so long. Satellite TV is no respecter of borders. It has created new electronic communities, which transcend old political boundaries. The same programmes can now be watched in Karachi, Kandy, Kathmandu, Kolhapur and Khulna, even if the language isn't always under-stood. It is a challenge not just to national broadcasters but to nationalism itself.

In *Satellites over South Asia*, we chart the progress of the satellite revolution, which brought these new visions to millions of viewers in the South Asian subcontinent during the 1990s. We study its impact as a South Asian regional phenomenon, looking not just at its influence within individual countries but also its powerful overspill effect. We have tapped public opinion in the metropolitan cities and smaller towns of the five main countries of the region—India, Pakistan, Bangladesh, Nepal and Sri Lanka. We have also spoken to a range of experts from those countries regarding their views on the satellite phenomenon: radio and television producers, film makers, academics, journalists, government servants, media entrepreneurs, advertisers, market researchers, politicians and many others. In making their views more widely known, we hope the book will make a contribution to debates about the future of civil society in the region and the role that broadcasting might play in it.

THE GLOBAL BACKGROUND

Three important developments underpin the media revolution, which has changed the way South Asians see the world—the demise of communism, the increasing integration of world markets and very rapid advances in communications technology. In the aftermath of the collapse of the Soviet bloc, free trade and the free flow of information became the dominant philosophies of the late twentieth century, with the United States the chief protagonist of both. Economic barriers tumbled, state control of the public sector was rolled back and liberalisation opened up world trade on market terms. Most states, in some cases with reluctance, put their signatures to plans to dismantle protectionist barriers as outlined in the negotiations to set up the World Trade Organisation in 1995.

The demise of communism accelerated a process of economic globalisation, which was already well advanced. By the 1980s, world financial markets had become increasingly interdependent and many multinational companies had become global economic forces. The balance of power between nation states and transnational interests had begun to shift.

In this process, improved communications have played a central role. The pace of progress in telecommunications, satellite and computer technology has changed the nature of international communication and opened up new commercial opportunities. The Internet has proved its potential for personal communication; its ramifications for broadcasting are still unfolding. The convergence of these technologies is already taking effect.

For the world media, these advances have brought new opportunities for the projection of a global presence. Television could not go global until the commercial development of satellite communications removed its previous dependence on terrestrial transmissions. Since the late 1980s, however, television has developed into a global industry and a key factor in the integration of world markets. Within a very short period, there has been a consolidation of television interests—both production and distribution—positioning them to take advantage of markets where their services were previously unknown.

Herman and McChesney have charted the growth of media consortia into multi-billion dollar enterprises with global ambitions.[2]

They have also shown how the same process is evident in the growing concentration of ownership of advertising and market research companies. Improved communications have made it possible for the same television programmes to be watched at the same time all over the globe and for the same advertisements to project global brands across a multitude of countries. To this extent, technology, the media and advertising are collaborators in the growing globalisation of commerce.

By the late 1990s, a handful of multi-billion dollar companies, most of them American in origin, had come to dominate the global media. The largest of these was Time Warner, publisher of *Time* magazine, owner of Warner Brothers film studios and Home Box Office, the largest cable network in the world. In 1996, Time Warner purchased Turner broadcasting, owner of CNN, which had nearly 100 million subscribers, and the Cartoon Network. In early 2000, Time Warner joined forces with America On-line in what was described as the world's 'biggest-ever' company merger. It brought together the world's leading Internet company with one of the world's leading content providers in a union aimed at exploiting the rapid convergence of communication technologies. At a combined value of US$ 335 billion, the category of media company acquired a new dimension.[3]

After Time Warner, the next largest conglomerate was Disney, which had earlier transformed its structure and purpose to face similar challenges. Previously primarily a content provider, Disney's purchase in 1995 of the ABC TV and radio network made it a media giant in its own right. That network included two ESPN sports channels, providing 24-hour sports in twenty-one languages to 165 countries. Sony, well known as one of the world's leading hardware companies, acquired formidable television expertise when it bought the American news provider CBS. Its plans to exploit the Sony brand in global television included the launch of new services for India. Viacom, which owns Paramount film studios, MTV, the RCA record label, Macmillan, the publisher, and Blockbuster, the world's largest video chain, was also in the top league with a market capitalisation of US$ 37.2 billion.[4]

Finally, as far as Asia is concerned, there was Rupert Murdoch's News Corporation, which had a controlling interest in Star TV. From his origins in Australia, Murdoch extended his media empire first to the UK, then to the USA, and next to Asia. Over 80 per cent of News Corporation's revenues came from the USA and Europe, but it had invested heavily in the Chinese and Indian markets.[5] Other global companies were also trying to exploit the growing prosperity of Asian markets. Time Warner, Disney and Viacom all hoped that Asia would contribute over 40 per cent of corporate profits by 2000, though the East Asian economic crisis of 1997 made that unrealistic.

SOUTH ASIA: THE CHANGING LANDSCAPE

The end of the Cold War and the collapse of the Soviet bloc involved a diplomatic and economic reorientation for the South Asian region. India's conversion to a programme of economic liberalisation, which accelerated considerably after 1991, was a reflection of these new realities. Economic reforms introduced at that time opened up a very large new market for foreign capital and consumer goods, which quickly attracted multinational interest. As a result, foreign trade and investment increased substantially over the next few years. All this seemed highly improbable in the 1970s and 1980s, when India's close relationship with the Soviet Union set the tone for many of its foreign and economic policies.

Satellite television played a role in alerting international business to the size and potential of the Indian market, which is now seen as one of the most promising in the world. Star TV, the first in the field with a range of different programmes, initially targeted the Pacific-rim economies, but India's enthusiasm for the programmes soon put it at the centre of special media planning and attention. Efforts to attract Indian audiences by broadcasting English-language programming from the United States, Britain and elsewhere initially led to accusations of a 'cultural invasion'. But before long, commercial attention was focussed on the Hindi-speaking middle class, with Zee TV emerging very quickly as the most popular and profitable channel. By the mid-1990s, international channels targeting the Indian market were competing both in the North and the South with flourishing channels run by Indian entrepreneurs.

The nature of the new satellite media makes earlier notions of western cultural domination look very oversimplified. Schiller's view, expressed first in the late 1960s, that the media would spread American lifestyles around the world and that a homogeneous globalised culture would gradually replace other local and regional cultures plainly does not fit the facts.[6] Barriers of language and the political and economic empowerment of a growing middle class over the past thirty years have stood in the way of such a scenario. Even in former British colonies, the English speaking elite, though still influential in the professions, is no longer politically or economically dominant.

At the same time, the fact that international media entrepreneurs are making programmes in Hindi to appeal to the Indian middle class is not proof that all elements of the 'imperialism' thesis have to be jettisoned. The satellite revolution enables the international media to speak to the English-knowing middle class in one language and the greater Indian middle class in others. The programme preferences of these audiences may not overlap very much—though there are some indications that the overlap is increasing—but the fact that these audiences watch programmes in different languages does not prevent them from being targeted with similar products and lifestyles. For the advertiser, whether national or multinational, the language is a means to reach the audience. To this extent, the development of programmes in Hindi by Star TV or of popular soap operas by Zee TV is assisting the integration of India into the global consumer economy.

Advertising agencies have the most demonstrable claim to be the midwives of satellite television. Television advertising has helped to create whole new markets in South Asia, both for new products and for the re-branding of a range of consumer goods. But while advertisers have been targeting the Indian market, they have created audiences across South Asia in general and in the Gulf as well. The westernised middle class in Colombo or Karachi now watch the same English-language programmes on CNN or BBC, Star News or Cartoon Network. Pakistanis watch programmes made for India, particularly the Hindi entertainment channels. Tamils in Sri Lanka have access to satellite channels in their language aimed at South India. Bengali satellite channels have audiences in both Bangladesh and West Bengal. Much of this communication is still one way—from India outwards—but it has already affected the nature of relationships between states and peoples.

At the moment, there is no South Asian economic market, though the countries of the region are committed to creating a free trade area in the longer term. There is plenty of awareness of the natural economic synergies which closer co-operation could offer. But progress towards such a goal has been held up by economic nationalism, political suspicion and, in the case of India and Pakistan, a long history of hostility and war. What satellite television has created, however, is a new cultural market, which transcends national boundaries and has acquired geopolitical significance for this reason.

TAKING A REGIONAL VIEW

Given the history of the region and the nature of the medium, we believe it is valuable to look at these trends from a South Asian perspective. India, Pakistan and Bangladesh were, in colonial times, ruled as one country from the same capital, while Sri Lanka formed part of the same Empire. They inherited much from that period which has influenced their subsequent development: forms of government, the rule of law, the role of English as a link language and common approaches to broadcasting. Even Nepal, which did not come under formal British rule, emerged as a nation state in the shadow of colonial power and has since gradually conformed to the South Asian political model.

What these countries have experienced in common, however, has been overshadowed for the last half century by the differences between them. Each nation state has tended to define itself in contradistinction to its neighbours. India's Congress leadership projected a secular image, contrasting with Pakistan's emergence as a homeland for Muslims. Pakistan projected India as a 'Hindu' state to justify the act of separation. Bangladeshi nationalists put language first when seceding from Pakistan, but later had to square their secular nationalism with their Islamic inheritance. Islam was reasserted to distinguish the new state from India. For similar reasons, the Sri Lankan state emphasised its role as a guardian of Buddhism, though this contributed to the alienation of its own Tamil population. Nepal has promoted the Nepali language as a key marker of difference, rather than the cultural and religious heritage it shares with India. In all these countries, nationalism has emphasised differences with neighbours, which the satellite revolution now threatens to undermine.

In this shaping of national identity, the state-controlled electronic media have played a central role. They have been deployed by central governments as an integrative force, championing in each country the chosen language of nationalism—the persianised Urdu of Radio Pakistan, the sanskritised Hindi of All India Radio, the Bengali of Bangladesh Radio, which differs in important respects from the same language broadcast by All India Radio, Calcutta. National radio and television have assisted in reinterpreting the histories of the colonial and pre-colonial periods, projecting the heroes of their freedom movements, broadcasting 'national' literature and music, and inspiring their populations with the notion of being citizens of new states.

This nationalist project has also involved, to different extents in each state, discouraging the articulation of 'regional' cultures and languages. In effect, it has erred on the side of uniformity while paying lip service to nostrums of 'unity in diversity'. In most South Asian states, governments have recognised the value of broadcasting in many languages, on radio if not on television. But they have not encouraged a genuine pluralism. India—South Asia's most diverse state—goes further than others in acknowledging its own diversity. But even in India, concessions to regional opinion have often been made only in the face of intense political protest. In Sri Lanka, the state media did recognise the country's diversity in the early years, but has done so less effectively since the Tamil insurgency broke out in the 1980s. Pakistan's concessions to regional identity have been much more limited. Nepal made almost no concessions until the 'People's Movement' of 1990.

Because of the centralised character of the nation state, the satellite revolution in South Asia has been more disruptive and far reaching than in many other parts of the world. In most South Asian countries, satellite channels brought the first direct challenge to the state-controlled sector and its bureaucratic broadcasting culture. The new channels have offered better-produced and more wide-ranging international news and current affairs programmes and many new entertainment programmes. They have brought the consumer values of the western world to a middle class accustomed to a diet of more high-minded programmes with a national focus. In the new atmosphere of liberalisation, they caught on like a forest fire in a dry summer. In some South Asian metropolitan centres, middle class audiences for national broadcasters have virtually disappeared. In this influential segment of the community, a key instrument of state cultural control has been made almost redundant.

RETHINKING THE ROLE OF THE STATE

What does all this mean for nationalism and the nation state in South Asia? If the development of print capitalism was central to the emergence of nationalism in the nineteenth century, as Benedict Anderson has argued, what are the implications of transnational media technologies for present-day nationalisms?[7] In the twentieth century, radio and television extended the process of nation-building, drawing much larger audiences than national newspapers and extending the sense of belonging from those who could read to those who could not. The new era of 'television without frontiers', however, creates different possibilities, some exciting and liberating, others threatening to notions of nationally autonomous cultures. Satellite technology has created the means to build communities across frontiers and even to challenge established political demarcations between states.

Collins, Garnham and Locksley in their analysis of trends in Europe have argued that 'the maintenance of national sovereignty and identity is becoming increasingly difficult as the unities of economic and cultural production and consumption are becoming increasingly transnational'.[8] For them, the development of global satellite media is part of the same economic process as the growing integration of world financial markets, and it threatens not just the autonomy of the nation state but the concept of citizenship, which goes with it. In Europe, national politicians have to balance the advantages of economic integration against the growing assertion of regional identities within their own countries. We are witnessing what another commentator has called 'a leaking away of sovereignty from the state, both upwards to supranational institutions and downwards to subnational ones'.[9]

In South Asia, moves towards economic integration are at an early stage and many politicians still exhibit a severely nationalistic mindset. Most South Asian states have their own repressed regional cultures and their own crises of identity thrown up by the flawed politics of nationalism since independence. In recent decades, India, Pakistan and Sri Lanka have all faced major challenges to their central governments from ethnic minority groups. The satellite revolution has posed new questions about these issues of identity and about the capacity of existing state structures to deal with them.

The new circumstances also call for a re-examination of how the public interest is defined. Until recently, the concept of public service broadcasting centred on the nation state and on state-controlled media. National broadcasters have not only acted as custodians of national culture; they have also seen it as their job to provide a universal service. The national radios of India and Pakistan have been broadcasting in all the main languages of their countries and many dialects as well, even if the core message has come from the capital cities. They have been providing pro-grammes for schools and farmers, on health and hygiene, as well as education for citizenship and classes in literacy. Many of these programmes have not been made well, but they have reflected a perceived state responsibility towards all citizens.

National television, a more recent and more expensive medium, has pursued these objectives less comprehensively. It has served the middle classes first and others afterwards. Satellite television has more restricted audiences and strictly commercial objectives. In the new era of liberalisation, the tendency of different govern-ments has been to follow global trends and leave broadcasting increasingly to market forces. One of the questions we examine in this book is whether this makes sense for states in which as many as 40 per cent of the population is defined as poor.

In Europe, as commercial broadcasting has proliferated and audiences have become more fragmented, the erosion of the public service ideal has raised the spectre of national broadcasting cultures being displaced by a new homogenised culture, conceived largely according to American ideals. In their book *Spaces of Identity*, David Morley and Kevin Robins envisage new 'audio-visual geographies...detached from the symbolic space of national culture and realigned on the more universal principles of inter-national consumer culture.'[10] It is a prospect that worries them in Europe, where average standards of living are relatively high. It is more worrying in South Asia, where international consumer culture, despite its attractions to the middle class, is very much less 'universal' than the concepts of citizenship which it threatens to displace.

COMMERCE AND COMMUNITY

In his prophetic look at media trends in *Towards 2000*, Raymond Williams envisaged a world pulled between 'false and frenetic nationalisms' and 'reckless and uncontrollable transnationalisms'.[11] His fear that the development of technology would strengthen the hands of the state and of transnational economic interests has become a much more widely shared anxiety today, though it is counterbalanced by the opportunities for personal and cultural expression, particularly for the middle classes, provided by the growth of the Internet.

The trend towards globalisation has also produced a countervailing public demand, particularly in western countries, for greater devolution of political power and more local democracy. The fact that the discourse on devolution and community has been appropriated by the global conglomerates themselves is perhaps the best evidence of popular resistance to these globalising trends.

South Asia has no shortage of nationalities, ethnic groups and communities who might benefit from new media technologies, nor of development needs which the media might help to meet. But early expectations of the benefits of mass media technologies in these fields now look exaggerated and there is greater appreciation of the complexity of social influences, of which the media are only a part.

The satellite media in South Asia have given access to new and articulate voices. Politicians and public figures have been called to account in programmes which have broken with the deferential tradition of state broadcasters. Audience participation in debates, discussions and interviews has added a new dimension to civil society. But these welcome improvements in programme choice and quality have come within a framework of market economics in which mass entertainment dominates the schedules and the Hindi language reaches the largest audiences. In its initial phase at least, the market has reinforced the dominant position of Hindi as the lingua franca of India and by its very success and attractiveness has raised questions about the future of other cultures.

Only in the southern states of India did the satellite revolution foster an immediate flowering of alternative regional language channels—in Tamil, Telugu, Kannada and Malayalam. Despite the Indian government's long-established dominance of the electronic media, southern entrepreneurs succeeded, as others did not, in throwing off the straitjacket of central control and articulating their regional cultures in the new medium.

Another area in which the satellite media have had remarkable success is in linking up South Asian communities across the globe. The great diasporas of Gujaratis, Punjabis, Kashmiris or Tamils living in the Gulf, Europe or North America can now watch the same programmes as their relatives at home. Some of the private satellite channels have actively developed new market opportunities among the South Asian diaspora, while state broadcasters have seen the importance of registering their presence on the same screens. Part of the motive—for India and Pakistan especially—has been propagandist, to ensure that audiences in neighbouring countries and their citizens abroad have access to their own culture. But there is also an international constituency for South Asian films, popular music and dance, which transcends South Asian borders. The cultural invasion has been turned into an 'outvasion' to exploit the global appeal of South Asian culture.

Arjun Appadurai has argued that satellite television has helped to create what he calls 'diasporic public spheres, phenomena that confound theories that depend on the continued salience of the nation-state as the key arbiter of important social changes'.[12] Satellite television has certainly played a part in the creation of a new kind of hybridity which is characteristic of contemporary metropolitan living; it is a new and powerful influence challenging the nation state's role as a purveyor of culture. But talk of a 'terminal crisis' of the state may be premature. As James Curran and Myung-Jin Park have argued: '...globalisation theory...is often based on an aerial perspective that simplifies. In particular, it tends to understate the continuing importance of the nation.'[13] The nation state remains resilient, certainly in defence of its own prerogatives, and we will argue that it needs to play a greater role as a regulator in order to ensure that the public interest is safeguarded in the new media environment.

Amartya Sen has pointed out that

> the threat to native cultures in the globalising world of today is, to a considerable extent, inescapable. The one solution that is not really within reach is that of stopping globalisation of trade and economics, since the forces of economic exchange and the division of labour are hard to resist in a competitive world.[14]

Some smaller cultures and languages are certainly at risk of extinction, but most are in a constant process of adaptation and are much less discrete and autonomous than their defenders sometimes argue. Cross-cultural influences can be liberating, as can the vision of prosperity and materialism, which the new media market offers. But leaving everything to the market does not ensure the level playing field that even private entrepreneurs require. We argue that there is a need for a regulatory environment, which offers fairness, respects uniqueness, encourages diversity and enables the media to work towards those ends rather than against them.

Whether the state is in a position to play this role is an open question. The state in South Asia has its own dilemmas of centralisation and bureaucracy, which are only partly inherited. It has played an active managerial role in nation-building and has only recently begun to de-nationalise important sectors of the economy. This same legacy of centralisation and bureaucracy stands in the way of more autonomy for state broadcasters or more decentralisation of responsibility and resources. Our research shows that they do still have a constituency, but there is disappointment that they have not risen to the challenge of the satellite era more distinctively.

THE MEDIA AND CIVIL SOCIETY

One important result of the satellite revolution is the development of a lively contemporary public debate about the role the media should play. There is a great deal of media comment, political argument and sociological analysis in all South Asian countries. In India and Sri Lanka particularly, the terms of debate on issues of democratic representation, national sovereignty, civil society and cultural identity are perceived to hinge more than before on the influence of the media, with the print media still paramount but the private electronic media playing a catalytic role in some fields. In other countries, the state retains greater control, though similar influences are working there too.

In discussing the role of the media, we use the concept of 'civil society' as one whose 'institutional core...is constituted by voluntary unions outside the realm of the state and the economy'.[15] We believe the term remains a valuable one, despite the fact that it has sometimes been taken to exclude categories of gender and ethnicity, which are central to contemporary ideas of participatory democracy. Ultimately, we argue, reform of the national media will depend on the development of a more active public opinion on media issues and the creation of a new relationship between the media and civil society.

Government policy towards the media has largely been based on a functionalist approach, in which the media are seen as a causal influence for continuity, integration and normality in society. The approach continues to provide a widely used and widely understood terminology for discussing the relationship of the mass media and society, even if its shortcomings are now well known.[16] Those shortcomings are amply borne out by the responses that we have recorded of those who are exposed to the broadcast media. The active engagement of audiences and their scepticism and capacity to resist as well as to accept media messages underlines the autonomy of individual viewers and listeners. But we share a perception common to broadcasters and policy-makers that television and radio can generate or promote desirable or undesirable social and cultural trends, and that they have an influence in negotiating ideas of modernity in the countries of South Asia, and the place of the individual and the community in them.[17]

The book begins with a brief history of the development of the electronic media in different South Asian countries from the colonial period until 1990. The next chapter tells the story of the opening of the skies, the media companies involved, the means of distribution and the reception given to the programmes. After an examination of development of the new television market in India in Chapter 4, the following three chapters examine the cultural influence of satellite programmes across the whole region. Chapter 5 shows that satellite television has been instrumental in creating a new South Asian popular culture, which has proved both attractive and controversial in each country. Chapter 6 looks at the implications of the popularity of Hindi entertainment channels for other regional cultures in northern India. It draws a contrast between Maharashtra and West Bengal, where satellite services in regional languages did not initially develop, and Tamil Nadu, where a thriving commercial satellite sector emerged very rapidly. Chapter 7 tests opinion among India's neighbours on their exposure to the new Indian satellite channels. The next two chapters look at the role of the state in South Asia: first, at government reactions to the breaking of the state monopoly and efforts to produce a new regulatory framework and, second, at the problems of centralisation which have impeded the development of effective local or community media. The last two chapters examine the role of broadcasting in serving the wider public interest and at practical policy issues which arise for the future.

NOTES AND REFERENCES

1. Focus Group Discussion, College students, Biratnagar, Nepal, June 1998.
2. E. Herman and R. McChesney (1997), *The Global Media: New Missionaries of Global Capitalism*.
3. *Financial Times*, 11 January 2000.
4. *Ibid.* On 7 January 2000, the market capitalisation of Time Warner was US$ 76.4 billion, Disney US$ 65.2 billion and CBS US$ 44.2 billion.
5. In early March 2000, Rupert Murdoch's global media company was estimated to be worth US$ 43.5 billion. See, *Financial Times*, 2 March 2000.
6. H.I. Schiller (1976), *Communication and Cultural Domination*.
7. See Benedict Anderson (1992), *Imagined Communities*.
8. R. Collins, N. Garnham and G. Locksley (1988), *The Economics of Television: UK Case*, p. 55.
9. R. Lipschutz, 'Reconstructing World Politics: The Emergence of Global Civil Society', in *Millennium: Journal of International Studies*, 21(3), 1992.
10. D. Morley and K. Robins (1995), *Spaces of Identity: Global Media, Electronic Landscapes and Cultural Boundaries*, p. 11.
11. Raymond Williams (1983), *Towards 2000*, pp. 198–99.
12. Arjun Appadurai (1997), *Modernity at Large: Cultural Dimensions of Globalisation*, p. 4.
13. James Curran and Myung-Jin Park (eds) (2000), *De-westernising Media Studies*, p. 15.
14. Amartya Sen, 'Culture, Freedom and Independence', in *UNESCO World Culture Report 1998*, p. 319.

15. Jurgen Habermas, 'Further Reflections on the Public Sphere', in Craig Calhoun (ed.) (1992), *Habermas and the Public Sphere*, p. 453.
16. Cf. Denis McQuail (1994), *Mass Communication Theory*, p. 78.
17. For a discussion of the role of television in this process in the Indian context, see, Nilanjana Gupta (1998), *Switching Channels*, Chapter 5.

Two

COLONIAL BEGINNINGS AND NATIONALIST IMPERATIVES

Responses to the satellite revolution in South Asia have been conditioned by the history of broadcasting in that region over the previous seventy years. Over that period, all South Asian governments came to treat radio and television very differently from the press, which they left to the private sector. They could bring pressures to bear on the press through systems of licensing, the distribution of advertising, control of newsprint or through legislation on libel or national security. But they came to manage broadcasting directly and to use it as a tool of national policy. In this chapter we look at how the state came to control broadcasting in colonial times, how national governments continued that system of control to achieve their own objectives and how it was coming under pressure even before the satellite revolution took place.

ORIGINS

In the early days of radio, the South Asian state's eventual dominance of the electronic media could not easily have been predicted. In colonial India, as in the UK and the USA, it was largely the radio manufacturers who made the running, with amateur enthusiasts and private companies taking up the challenge. The government remained an onlooker, principally concerned with regulatory problems.[1]

The Times of India building in Bombay was the site of the first experimental broadcast in 1921, which was heard by Governor George Lloyd 100 miles away in Poona. The Radio Club of Calcutta began the first systematic broadcasts in November 1923. The Bombay Radio Club followed suit in June 1924. Both clubs used transmitters provided by Marconi, which was the prime mover on the manufacturing side.

Indian engineers were involved from the start in developing the new technology. In South India, the moving spirit behind the formation of the Madras Presidency Radio Club was C.V. Krishnaswami Chetty, a Tamil engineer who returned from his studies in England with the components of a small transmitter in his luggage. It was this transmitter, broadcasting within a radius of only 5 miles, that was used for the first Madras broadcasts in the summer of 1924.

There was no certainty that radio would catch on. In fact, by 1927, the Madras experiment had folded and the transmitter had been handed over to the Madras Corporation, which later took up the patronage of broadcasting itself. In the same year, the Bombay and Calcutta Radio Clubs got together to start the Indian Broadcasting Company—the first commercial broadcasting venture in India—in which Marconi was a major shareholder. By this stage, the Government of India was sufficiently interested for the Viceroy, Lord Irwin, to attend the launch in Bombay. As a regulator, the government sanctioned a radio licence fee of Rs. 10 per annum and a 10 per cent surcharge on the sale of radios. The only problem was that retailers levied it and it had to be collected from them, which did not prove easy. By 1930, there were some 8000 licences, but the business was not growing fast enough to warrant further investment, and the company went bankrupt.

Initially, the government seemed prepared to accept the logic of the market, but public pressure ultimately persuaded it to step in. From 1930, it began meeting the deficit from its own funds, though it resisted suggestions that it should become more pro-active. It took the view that broadcasting should pay for itself and that its spread should depend on the growth of public interest. In 1931, during a serious financial crisis, the government actually decided to withdraw its subsidy, though public pressure again persuaded it to reverse its decision.

The government's view that broadcasting should be sustained by the market and that its own role should be a regulatory one has a surprisingly modern ring about it. As the medium developed, however, the potential of radio became more widely appreciated, particularly by government servants working in rural areas. The

Punjab's Rural Reconstruction Commissioner, Frederick Brayne, wrote:

> Properly handled, the wireless can be made to mean for the Indian village such health, wealth and comfort as it has never known. Broadcasting can do more in a few years in the general spread of knowledge than all other methods of education put together can do in a lifetime.[2]

Brayne conducted a radio experiment in 1932 from the YMCA in Lahore. Broadcasting in Punjabi to a dozen surrounding villages, he came to the conclusion that 'each item to be attractive must be extremely brief. The local dialect should be used and the matter must, for the most part, be familiar to the hearer in relation to his daily life.'[3]

Charles Strickland, another Punjab civilian and former registrar of Indian Friendly Societies, gave a lecture on the use of radio for rural development at the East India Society in London in October 1933. Drawing on Brayne's experience, he presented a blueprint for the setting up of district radio stations. These would use small transmitters, broadcasting in local dialects and providing a diet of folk songs and folk theatre, interspersed with news on agricultural prices. He also expected the villagers to operate and pay for this themselves. One month later, the Punjab government asked Brayne to work out the cost of 'a fairly large-scale experiment in village broadcasting'.[4]

Brayne and Strickland were not pursuing these ideas in a vacuum. They were aware of the widespread use of radio in the Soviet Union, where over half a million radio sets were deployed in villages by the late 1920s, and saw similar possibilities in India. For them, radio held out the prospect of an end to the touring of districts and repetition of messages, which was the daily routine of officials working in rural reconstruction. To this extent it was seen as a valuable aid to development. In Strickland's plan, the radio would serve the whole village, be held in the headman's house and be tuned to only one wavelength. But the same scheme also emphasised the role of radio as a vehicle for local culture and entertainment, a creative strand of thinking which later petered out.

There were a number of other experiments in the early years: at Allahabad and Lucknow Universities, by Brayne's counterpart at

Poona, at Delhi (where an experimental station broadcast to the villages around the capital) and at Peshawar (where a very small transmitter of 0.25 kilowatts was used for rural uplift from 1933 onwards). Some of the most ambitious use of radio was in Madras, where the Corporation set up a successful station in the early 1930s, using loudspeakers in public places and providing radios to schools. By 1934, the provincial government was looking into establishing a service for the Presidency as a whole and commissioned an engineer from the BBC to conduct a feasibility study.[5] However, none of these experiments survived. All the viable ones were later absorbed into the national broadcasting service and in the process lost much of the community focus which had inspired the pioneers. It was to take more than sixty years to revive this decentralised vision of radio.

BROADCASTING BETWEEN CENTRE AND PROVINCES

The Government of India's 'hands-off' attitude to broadcasting, intervening only where necessary and committing no substantial funds of its own, changed dramatically in 1934. In a note of January that year, the civil servant responsible for broadcasting had written that the Government of India would not open any more stations 'unless broadcasting pays its way', the likelihood of which he regarded as 'non-existent...for many years to come'.[6] However, by the middle of the year, it was decided to build a new station at Delhi, and not long afterwards a national network of stations. This change of direction seems to have been in part due to persuasion by the BBC and in part to a growing realisation that the changing political situation in India and abroad required a more active policy.

The BBC's founder and first director general, Sir John Reith, felt from the beginning that broadcasting in India was not being developed vigorously enough and in the mid-1920s even contemplated going out there himself. His initial approaches to the India Office had been met with a lukewarm response from the Government of India, whose enquiries in the provinces had elicited little interest, except in the Punjab and Madras. He noted in his diary that there was 'neither vision nor recognition of the immense potentialities of broadcasting; no ethical or moral appreciation, just commercialism.'[7] In those years, the Government of India treated broadcasting as a devolved subject, laying down central guidelines but allowing its development to proceed under the auspices of provincial governments. By the mid-1930s, however, with full provincial autonomy in prospect under the terms of a new constitution, it began to see that broadcasting was too powerful an instrument to be treated in this way.

During a visit to London in 1934, Viceroy Lord Willingdon was convinced by Sir John Reith that the Government of India should do more to develop a national broadcasting service. Their meeting was followed by a note from the BBC setting out Reith's vision for Indian broadcasting, which pointed out that 'in almost every great country, a central system is already in operation; where not, the tendency is towards it'. Regional activities were desirable, particularly where language problems existed, but central control was essential for the greatest efficiency in every sense. The note underlined the importance of a common language in the development of nation states and the role that Hindustani might play in India. It said: 'If two thirds of the native population can understand, even if it cannot speak Hindustani, the problem might not be so difficult....' It also warned that if India's needs were not met by its own broadcasting system, Indians would listen to the short wave broadcasts of other countries, particularly Russia and Germany. Despite the undoubtedly high costs involved, therefore, the BBC submitted that 'a British corporation be established in India with the ultimate aim of providing sufficient transmitters to cover the greater part of the continent....'[8]

These arguments for a centralised system of broadcasting did not go down well with the Indian provinces. Broadcasting—though not the technical control of it—was a provincial responsibility under the new constitution and they were naturally jealous of their powers. But the Government of India now began to put up money for a network of stations and transmitters. Over the next two years, Rs. 4,000,000 was provided for this purpose and Willingdon turned to Reith for the staff to make this happen. In announcing its plans, the Government of India declared that its role would be to provide capital expenditure for radio stations and some central services, leaving the provinces 'complete autonomy in the matter of local programmes'.[9] In reality, however, the central government was beginning to resume powers which had been devolved.

This resumption of powers was the subject of a vigorous debate in London, where Sir John Coatman, a former director of public information in India who had become a BBC news editor, argued the case for a centralised system of broadcasting very strongly. His case, encapsulating the political and bureaucratic arguments for the centralisation of broadcasting, was to hold the field for the rest of the twentieth century. He had no doubt that Indian ministers in provincial ministries had seen in broadcasting 'an incomparable instrument for their political purposes'. But if the provinces were given control, he foresaw dangers that broadcasting would be used as a weapon in inter-provincial rivalry, in disputes with the central governments or even for anti-imperial purposes. Coatman wrote:

> Existing fissiparous tendencies, which arise from historical and racial causes, will be enormously strengthened under the new regime. *Broadcasting could and should be the master unifying element if controlled from the centre.* There is not only the danger, there is the certainty, that in the absence of such unifying forces, systems of education, police, local self-government and other vital departments of the administration, which are all provincial subjects, will diverge widely from province to province, *with disastrous results for the prospect of creating a homogeneous Indian nation* (our emphasis).[10]

Coatman's arguments did not go uncontested.[11] Under Section 129 of the *Government of India Act of 1935*, which introduced provincial autonomy for the first time, broadcasting remained a provincial subject, though the centre retained control of technical development and standards. But by 1935, the Government of India had already decided to construct a broadcasting service which would operate more effectively in the Imperial interest.

FIELDEN'S FOUR YEARS IN INDIA

The person chosen to put Indian broadcasting on a new footing was Lionel Fielden, who was appointed Controller in 1935. A well connected and flamboyant individual who had made his name as a creative producer in the early days of the BBC, Fielden set off for India with Reith's blessings and a caution that he should keep his temperament in check in the wider interests of the project. This did not come easily to Fielden, whose impatience with bureaucracy in India leaps from every page of his autobiography. But he was soon on good terms with the viceroy, Lord Willingdon, who helped him cut through some of the red tape in his early days.[12]

Fielden's brushes with bureaucracy point to the conflict between the artistic and the bureaucratic, which has been a permanent feature of South Asian broadcasting since those days. One of Fielden's earliest recruits, Syed Rashid Ahmed, describes Fielden as 'the opposite of Colonel Blimp: he wanted to make friends; he wanted to learn the culture of the place; he wanted to devise what would be right in India.' Rashid Ahmed attributes the successful transplanting of broadcasting into India to Fielden's 'dynamic and non-conformist personality' and his ability to gather round him 'a band of idealistic and imaginative young Indians, who were attracted by the romance of broadcasting.' [13]

In those days, Fielden's chosen few were given remarkable freedom to develop broadcasting according to his prescriptions. After a spell at Delhi as director of programmes, Syed Rashid Ahmed was sent to Lahore at the age of 26 to set up the new station, to find buildings, recruit staff and train well-known writers and artists in the use of the microphone. In carrying out this responsibility, he had no sense of serving an imperial purpose; rather he felt that Fielden had given him an opportunity to develop broadcasting as a new medium. As he put it in an address to mark the fiftieth anniversary of the Lahore station: 'The broadcasters recognised that radio was not only a chapter in the development of art and technology but also in that of power. But they tended to leave this latter aspect to the government and among themselves debated endlessly about the affinity of radio with the theatre, the music hall, the pulpit or the classroom.'[14]

Fielden's most famous Indian recruits were the talented Bokhari brothers: Zulfiqar, whom he poached from the army training school in Simla, and his elder brother Ahmed Shah, a teacher at Government College, Lahore, whom Fielden later recruited, against Zulfiqar's advice, to be his deputy. Their prominence in All India Radio gave rise to the well-known jibe that Fielden had established an Indian BBC or Bokhari Brothers Corporation. Zulfiqar, an Urdu teacher and poet and a fine broadcaster, went on to be the first director general of Radio Pakistan. Ahmed Shah, a very capable administrator who later became the first director general of All India Radio, was held by Fielden to be 'one of the wittiest men I have ever known, a brilliant conversationalist with a wide culture'.[15] However, Fielden's homosexuality and his choice of subordinates did attract criticism. The fact that many recruits came from the Muslim North West also gave rise to accusations that All India Radio was favouring the Urdu language and Muslim artists. Fielden's defenders maintain that he was completely free of ethnic bias. But others accuse him of being misled by what K.S. Mullick, another of Fielden's recruits, called his 'elite set of favourites.'[16]

The role of language in the construction of national identity—a theme of equal significance in post-colonial India and Pakistan—was at the heart of controversies over Fielding's choice of broadcasters. Advocates of Hindu nationalism and Muslim separatism were campaigning for pure forms of Hindi and Urdu, and every broadcast was being analysed for bias of one sort or another. Such accusations were part of the politics of the Partition period and were by no means universally shared by Indians who worked with the Bokharis. In those days, Mahatma Gandhi himself was the most ardent campaigner for Hindustani and Ahmed Shah Bokhari would have claimed that he was fighting for the same cause. On this vexed question of language, he seems to have stood his ground against purists on both sides in the interests of intelligibility. During the war years, he endeavoured to develop a consensus around a commonly understood Hindustani vocabulary for news and other purposes. But after the war, Partition put paid to these efforts.

Fielden acted with extraordinary decisiveness, even arrogance, in the early days. He created posts and raised salaries at will and cut through a huge amount of red tape to get things going. But in the process, he also made enemies. Fielden had his own way in handpicking the first group of broadcasters and producers, but powers to appoint station directors and programme directors and even programme assistants and probationers, were subsequently taken from him by the Public Services Commission. This was the beginning of bureaucratic interference in broadcasting, which after independence became much more detailed, intrusive and debilitating. As early as 1937, Fielden pointed out that treating broadcasting like any other government activity would not serve the organisation well. 'As a result,' he wrote, 'we are going to have a completely bad organisation. It is quite impossible for the Public Services Commission—they are charming and quite admit it—to judge men for broadcasting, and what it comes to is that the worst kind of influences get to work and utterly unsuitable men get appointed.'[17]

If Fielden was generally impatient with bureaucracy, he was at one with many bureaucrats in thinking that the new constitution had surrendered too many powers to the provinces. So he took it upon himself to build up what he called 'an all India personality' for radio before the Reforms took effect. Later, he persuaded the new viceroy, Lord Linlithgow, to change the name of the organisation from the Indian States Broadcasting Service to All India Radio.[18]

In this endeavour, the India Office in London backed Fielden. In a letter to him at the beginning of his work, an official wrote: 'To my mind we were quite wrong in setting up a system whereby only the technical side of broadcasting is central and the rest is left to the provinces, and it seems to me that the only way of counteracting this is by you getting on with an organisation more or less on the BBC lines with central control and regional organisation before the new act is fully in force.' The official, Hugh Macgregor, told Fielden that he had 'the most important job in India'. In his view, broadcasting was vital to the Imperial connection because '...but for broadcasting and a small section of the press' the Governor General would be 'isolated from Indian opinion, the support of which is vital if that connection is to be maintained.'[19]

By the time Fielden left India in 1940, this rearguard action against the decentralisation of broadcasting in India had largely been won. A national network of radio stations had been set up in eight major cities. This network absorbed the earlier stations established in Calcutta, Bombay and Madras, and added new ones at Peshawar, Delhi, Lahore, Lucknow, Trichinopoly and Dhaka. Short wave transmitters were established to link up the different stations—a strategy Fielden had picked up in Italy during a visit there in the mid-1930s. In another important move, Fielden also set up a central news organisation, providing midday and evening bulletins by teleprinter to the different regional stations. But despite his commitment and enthusiasm, the spread of radio proved disappointingly slow. By the time Fielden left India, there were only 85,000 licence holders. As he put it himself: 'It was enough to make a cat laugh. It was the biggest flop of all time.'[20]

One reason for this slow progress was the cost. Though community listening became popular in the cities, only wealthy individuals could afford to pay Rs. 500 for a receiver. Another reason may have been the suspicion with which the service was viewed by nationalists, despite Fielden's efforts to bridge the divide. In his early years in India, he defied a government order preventing him from meeting Gandhi and attempted to induce the Mahatma to broadcast. But Gandhi saw beyond personalities. He wrote:

> My dear Fielden, you know and I know that if I do so, I shall increase the number of your listeners overnight by four or five millions. If I knew you were going to stay in India, I might do it. If you don't I shall merely increase the strength of my enemies.[21]

Fielden was also on good terms with Nehru, whose reactions were very similar. Nationalist leaders refused to broadcast on All India Radio until independence had been promised and an interim government had been set up.

THE IMPACT OF WAR

The next important stage in the development of All India Radio came with the outbreak of the Second World War. Because of the war, broadcasting assumed a central role in the government's propaganda—both in India, where it had to contend with nationalist opposition to the war effort, and abroad, where the propaganda of Germany, Italy and Japan had to be countered. As a result of the war, in India as in Britain, the government assumed more direct control of broadcasting and transmission facilities were substantially upgraded. In Ceylon, the War Office paid for the installation of a 100-kilowatt transmitter capable of serving imperial purposes in the South East Asia Command. This station in Ceylon, which was known as Radio SEAC, eventually had a staff of over forty broadcasters and was on the air for 16 hours a day.[22]

The war brought a huge increase in broadcasting from India to foreign countries. By the end of the war, All India Radio was broadcasting in twenty-two languages to the Far East, the Middle East and Europe. As part of this propaganda effort, a Far Eastern Bureau was set up in Delhi, which operated as part of All India Radio but came under direct British control. This bureau was also responsible for monitoring foreign broadcasts in the Asian region.

During the war, news increased in importance and became a more centralised function under a Director of News and External Services. Centralisation was also a means of ensuring that the organisation spoke with one voice in all these languages. As a result of the investment in broadcasting during the war, official perceptions of its influence changed dramatically. A relatively new toy was transformed into a very powerful instrument of persuasion. A Cabinet committee on broadcasting came to the conclusion in 1945 that broadcasting should be seen as a priority for India and for the colonies in the post-war period. The ultimate aim should be 'that no part of their territory should be out of reach of wireless programmes...designed for the local population and capable of being picked up by comparatively cheap sets.'[23] However, that objective remained elusive. Cheaper sets, the key to radio becoming a mass medium, only became a reality with the transistor revolution of the 1960s.

THE COMING OF INDEPENDENCE

One consequence of Partition in both countries was more detailed government control of broadcasting. In British times, matters of policy were debated in government and the Public Services Commission recruited senior staff, but there was little day-to-day intervention in broadcasting. That all changed in India after 1947. As K.S. Mullick puts it: 'Henceforward , even day to day matters came under the Minister's scrutiny'.[24] After independence, the new Indian government opened the way for more political access to the airwaves and a more vigorous use of radio as a tool of public policy. From then onwards, with the Indian National Congress comprehensively dominant across India until the 1960s, a certain one-sidedness almost seemed politically justifiable; there was no need for the kind of balance which becomes more necessary in multi-party democracies.

At Partition, Pakistan inherited three stations—at Lahore, Peshawar and Dhaka—while India inherited five—at Delhi, Bombay, Calcutta, Lucknow and Trichinopoly, not including those in the Indian states. The assets of Broadcasting House in Delhi were divided in the proportions two for India and one for Pakistan, with the Pakistani share being shipped off to Lahore. Those broadcasters who were government servants had to opt for one state or the other and for the most part religion was the deciding factor.

In north India, Partition put paid to the common culture and language which All India Radio had been trying to develop. Bokhari's efforts to develop an accepted Hindustani vocabulary for communication to the common man gave way to the broadcasting of more purist Hindi and Urdu on either side of the border. Vallabhai Patel, the first and undoubtedly the most powerful of India's ministers of information and broadcasting, was pleased to see Bokhari return to Lahore to become principal of his old college. According to his secretary, he saw the ending of 'Bokhari's empire' as an essential prerequisite for the reshaping of All India Radio in a new nationalist image.[25] In Bokhari's place, Patel appointed the first civil servant to be director general and began a campaign to clean up radio. No engagements were to be offered to musicians 'whose private lives were a public scandal'. Many singers and musicians—particularly Muslim women artists—were banned from the studios and broadcasts took on a new moral tone. Hindi was given pride of place, particularly after it was adopted as the national language in the constitution, and there were competitions to select the best national songs.

A primary objective in those early days was to extend the network of radio stations and transmitters to cover the whole country. Between 1947 and 1950, the network rose from five to twenty-one stations, including those in the Indian states which were integrated into the Union. Not surprisingly, in the aftermath of Partition, with thousands killed in communal violence and war taking place over Kashmir, propaganda and counter-propaganda became a broadcasting imperative. But India did not in those early days have the technical capacity to project a national service, nor it seems did the nationalists give it priority.[26]

The pattern in Pakistan was very similar. Zulfiqar Bokhari assumed charge as the first director general and began the task of building up a broadcasting service for the new state. His first priority was to set up a station in Karachi, the new capital, and to establish links—first by landline and then by short wave transmitters—with the provincial stations at Peshawar, Lahore and Dhaka. At the same time, a central news department was set up in Karachi on the Indian model to feed the stations with national bulletins.

In both countries, tighter government control slowly turned what had been a relatively self-contained broadcasting service with its own ethos into an arm of government whose staff were interchangeable with those of other departments. In India, the new government began by vetting all senior broadcasting staff. During the 1950s, most DGs were from the Indian Administrative Service and the professionals came to feel—wrongly as it turned out—that they could not aspire to the top position. This process of bureaucratisation was carried a stage further in 1960, when staff of the news division were made part of a Central Information Service. This service included the Press and Information Department and the Publications Division, whose role was to publicise the government's work. This inevitably diminished the credibility and effectiveness of the news operation.

Pakistan witnessed very similar trends. According to Syed Rashid Ahmed, the government provided very good support for the technical development of broadcasting but not a sensible administrative structure. As a result there was 'a rapid exodus of talent from the organisation and a depressing fall of morale'. The culmination of this process was the decision in 1963, very much along Indian lines, to create an Information Service, which 'broke up what remained of the structural unity of Radio Pakistan'. This brought officers of Radio Pakistan, the Pakistan Film Corporation, the Publications Division and the Information Division into the same service and made it virtually impossible to maintain a broadcasting ethos. As Rashid Ahmed put it: 'I fought for the developing of broadcasting as a composite and self-contained service...not for a service in which you suddenly shot out from broadcasting to film, from films to publications and back to broadcasting.... You can't do that and retain your broadcasting camaraderie....'[27]

In India, the embodiment of this new world of serious purpose and ministerial interference was Dr. B.V. Keskar, the country's longest serving minister of information and broadcasting, who held the post for ten years from 1952. Keskar was a man with a deep love of Indian classical and folk music, who presided over a remarkable expansion of All India Radio's patronage in this field, even to the extent of selecting many of the musicians himself. But he is best known for his aversion to film music, which he described as 'cheap and vulgar', and for his orders that lyrics were to be studied and only those tunes broadcast which conformed to good taste. As a result, film music was reduced to about 10 per cent of AIR's music output, while classical music rose to nearly 50 per cent. The next few years proved to be a testing time for high culture, as more and more Indians switched off All India Radio and tuned to Radio Ceylon.[28]

RADIO CEYLON AND THE CHALLENGE OF COMMERCIALISM

The role of Radio Ceylon in challenging state monopolies of radio in the 1950s has remarkable parallels with the challenge of satellite broadcasters to state television in the 1990s. In both cases, commercial competition shook the complacency of the government sector and forced it to modify its agenda to take account of the very evident audience demand for entertainment.

Broadcasting in Britain had begun on a commercial basis but by the 1930s governments were solidly committed to the BBC model and opposed to commercial broadcasting in principle. Even as late as 1945, a Cabinet committee on broadcasting expressed the hope that post-war Europe would stop commercial broadcasting across frontiers.[29] It was, as it turned out, a forlorn hope, though it illustrates the extent to which broadcasting was seen as the prerogative of the nation state, despite the huge increase in the use of broadcasting for propaganda across frontiers during the war.

When the newly independent Sri Lankan government announced that it was interested in using the 100-kilowatt short wave transmitter it had inherited from Britain for commercial broadcasting, it raised some awkward questions in Whitehall. Britain had an interest in the continuing use of the transmitter to relay BBC broadcasts to the Far East and initially suggested that it should remain in British hands and the BBC should run it. But the Sri Lankan government was rightly jealous of its new independence and refused. It was prepared to allow the BBC use of the transmitter but it insisted on sovereign control. It was also resistant to Whitehall pleas that the transmitter should not be used for commercial purposes: all it would concede was that it would consult Britain first and would give preference to clients from Britain and other Dominions. In the end, Whitehall had to accept a surrender of control.[30]

What happened subsequently is part of South Asian folklore. There are few older people in India and Pakistan who don't remember tuning into Radio Ceylon in the 1950s and 1960s when it developed a huge audience throughout the region for its popular music. It played all the film tunes which Dr. Keskar had banned on All India Radio and soon stole a march on its more serious rival. The technical basis of Radio Ceylon's success was its 100-kilowatt transmitter, which in those days was heard clearly as far afield as East Africa, the Middle East and Japan. There were even reports of listeners in Sweden. This made Radio Ceylon the most effective means for advertisers to reach an all India or wider Asian audience because at that time there was no other commercial broadcaster in the region.

The person recruited to start Radio Ceylon's commercial service was Clifford Dodd, an Australian with experience in this field at home. But the financial success of the project owed much to the efforts of the Radio Advertisers Society, an American organisation based in Bombay. Studios were set up first in Bombay and later in Madras, which made programmes in different Indian languages for broadcasting on the Radio Ceylon commercial beam. The operation began with English and Hindi but later expanded to include the main South Indian languages. In due course, the Radio Advertisers Society was providing Radio Ceylon with six or seven hours of programmes per day, and advertising revenues were running into crores of rupees a year.[31]

Two broadcasters who became household names at that time were the Sayani brothers, Hamid and Ameen, who worked in Bombay for Radio Enterprises, which was the production arm of the Advertisers Society. Hamid, the elder brother, was the programme manager and also compered regular English language quiz programmes. Ameen made his name fronting a very popular music programme—*Binaca Geet Mala*—which was a Hindi pop music hit parade sponsored by a leading toothpaste manufacturer. Radio Ceylon laid down the guidelines—on advertising and sponsorship rates and on the quantum of advertising—and left its contractors to negotiate with Indian advertisers and to produce the programmes.[32]

The commercial broadcasters in Bombay saw themselves as an antidote to Dr. Keskar's All India Radio. According to Ameen Sayani: 'Dr Keskar...had created a kind of sombre, highly "holier than thou" kind of dignity in AIR presentation styles which verged on boredom...so to act as an antidote to that...we were going all out painting the town red.... We would be exuberant, we would be enthusiastic, we would be punchy...we would be slightly larger than life...and somehow with a nation waiting to enjoy itself...the style took off.'[33] Sayani points out that in many ways AIR could not have chosen a worse time to ban film music because the 1950s and 1960s were its golden age. AIR's loss was Radio Ceylon's gain as famous singers like Talat Mahmud and Geeta Dutt began making sponsored programmes for Radio Ceylon, which attracted very large audiences. Sayani believes that in the late 1950s as many as a hundred million people may have been listening to *Binaca Geet Mala* in East Africa, the Middle East and Asia. There is no quantitative research to back his hunch, but anecdotal evidence supports a high figure.

Radio Ceylon's commercial beam was not intended for Ceylon, but there is plenty of evidence to show that its English, Hindi and Tamil programmes did have an audience in the island. So much so that many Sinhalese were up in arms against it in ways that mirror reactions four decades later to the satellite revolution. The submissions to the Weerasooriya Commission on Broadcasting in 1953 make remarkable reading. The Sinhala Programme Organiser of Ceylon Radio said that the commercial service had done more damage to Sinhalese culture in two years than 400 years of colonialism; the Buddhist clergy complained about the decline in morals and the increased interest in gambling and racing; university professors claimed that Sinhala was being diluted with too many English words. The Commission was alarmed enough to recommend that commercial broadcasting should be closed down. But the government ignored the recommendation.[34]

Ceylon's early success in commercial broadcasting illustrates the importance of superior technology in creating new markets. But by the mid-1950s India was catching up. The prime broadcasting objective of the Indian government's Second Five Year Plan was to meet the growing demand for national programmes and to ensure countrywide listening to national broadcasts.[35] Two 100-kilowatt short wave transmitters were opened at Bombay and Madras in 1957 to provide national coverage for a new all-India variety and light music programme—Vividh Bharati—which had been set up 'to beat Radio Ceylon at its own game'.[36] By this stage Dr. Keskar had to accept that the Indian masses needed to be entertained as well as educated.

Radio Ceylon still had another ten or fifteen years of success. But the spread of medium wave broadcasts and the building of more powerful transmitters did gradually undermine its popularity. By the mid-1960s, as a result of an intensive building programme, medium wave coverage had been extended to 70 per cent of the Indian population, which improved reception for Vividh Bharati in the towns where Radio Ceylon was most popular.

THE TRANSISTOR AGE

India's investment in medium wave transmitters, which helped it to rival Radio Ceylon's popular commercial beam, also heralded the arrival of the transistor revolution, which made radio affordable for a whole new range of people. By the late 1960s, cheap transistor sets were becoming increasingly popular and by the 1970s they had become status symbols in rural areas. The Indian government's offer of transistor radios as inducements to men to undergo vasectomies during the Emergency became a politically explosive issue.

One of the early problems of popularising radio in South Asia had been the cost and size of the standard four-valve radio set which held the field from the 1920s to the 1960s. A substantial piece of equipment, dependent on electricity supply, it was a physical focus for family or community entertainment, as the television is today. But it did not have the mobility, which was to make the transistor so popular.

Statistics on the spread of radio in India show a relatively slow start, with less than 100,000 licences on the eve of the Second World War, almost two decades after its inception. This rose to a quarter of a million at independence, a million in 1955 and two million in 1960. But the most rapid expansion came in the 1960s and 1970s, with a million licences a year being taken out during much of that period. From five million licences in 1965, the number rose to twenty million in 1977, the year the Congress lost power for the first time after Mrs Gandhi's Emergency rule.[37]

It is no accident that the heyday of political populism in South Asia—whether in India or Pakistan—coincided with this expansion of radio ownership. Radio had become an important means for the integration of new classes into politics. It gave opportunities for political leaders to speak to the masses directly and it opened the way for a new kind of politics which bypassed traditional mediators and encouraged the transistor owner to believe that he (and at that time it was largely men who owned the radios) mattered nationally in his own right.

The use of radio during the Emergency in India provides a graphic illustration of V.C. Shukla's remark that it was 'the most potent medium that the government has at its command....'[38] As Mrs Gandhi's minister of information and broadcasting, Shukla instituted a system of personal control over All India Radio's activity, which involved the detailed supervision of all news and propaganda activities. As a result, news ceased to reflect, even in a limited way, opposition viewpoints. The arrests of opposition leaders like Jaya Prakash Narayan, Charan Singh and Atal Bihari Vajpayee were blacked out, as were many other inconvenient stories. Even during the general election called in 1977, instructions were issued that the ratio of government to opposition news should be 8 to 1.[39]

During the Emergency, the main purpose of radio and television was to project the personality of Mrs. Gandhi and her son Sanjay. In that two year period, AIR broadcast nearly 50,000 items about Mrs. Gandhi's 'Decade of Achievements' and about her Twenty Point Programme. Station directors were left in no doubt that their role was to serve the government of the day. If they found that difficult, Mrs. Gandhi told them at a meeting in 1975, nobody was stopping them from resigning. Shukla told the same meeting: 'This forum is not run by the government to have a debate on various kinds of ideologies or various kinds of differences of opinion. This media is conducted by the government to see that the government's policies are properly understood by the people'.[40]

Such total control of the media, however, did not bring the expected rewards. Despite censorship of the press and the tightest possible regulation of All India Radio and Doordarshan, the electorate voted the Congress party out of office and Mrs. Gandhi herself out of parliament. It was one of the most ringing public rejections of politics by brainwashing that India had ever witnessed.

The transistor radio facilitated the beginning of a genuine mass media in South Asia and set the pattern for the introduction of future media technologies. Television spread in the same way from urban areas to rural areas and in the process the media market became more segmented, particularly with the arrival of satellite television and of digitisation.

TELEVISION IN PAKISTAN AND INDIA

Television was first launched in India and Pakistan in the late 1950s and early 1960s, though it did not become a mass medium until the 1980s. India, the first to introduce the new medium, approached it from a more puritanical standpoint than Pakistan, putting development first and entertainment last. Prime Minister Nehru was against the introduction of television because he felt that it was a luxury, which would only be enjoyed by the middle class. In Nehru's view, radio was more appropriate for India's stage of development.

When Indian television began in 1959, on an experimental basis in the Delhi region, the programmes reflected India's development priorities. The first systematic television service, funded by UNESCO, was principally aimed at the rural areas around Delhi and was designed to increase understanding of the responsibilities of citizenship. Later, there were experiments in educational TV, with sets being provided for secondary schools in the Delhi area. These early ventures were the subject of much analysis, but the broadcasts did not catch on and the government did not increase its investment. It was not until 1972—thirteen years after the opening of the Delhi station—that India acquired a second TV station in Bombay.[41]

Indian television in its infancy was managed by All India Radio, which may have been an impediment to its natural development. In Pakistan, on the other hand, a conscious decision was taken not to make Pakistan radio the midwife on the grounds that it 'did not have either the expertise or the potential to manage it'.[42] Instead, a tender was floated and the Nippon Electric Company of Japan was asked to set up two experimental stations at Lahore and Dhaka and was given three months to show that the experiment would work. Through their local associates, they gave the programme responsibility at Lahore to Aslam Azhar, who later became the director general of Pakistan TV. He was completely new to television himself; he had made his name in amateur theatre in Karachi. But under his leadership, the early days of TV in Pakistan acquired some of the same excitement and creativity as the early days of radio. He recognised that it was no good looking to radio as a model; he took some talented radio people but he recruited others from the performing arts and photography. In those early days, live TV performances alternated with imported BBC documentaries and comedies and it was the spirit of the theatre which dominated, as different acts prepared to go live while the film sequences ran. It was this early experience which led to Pakistan TV's excellence in the field of drama. Aslam Azhar says he 'resisted consciously from day one...getting in anyone from the film industry...because...the state of the film industry...was deplorable to put it very politely...and the result was that our cultural level was far higher than the film industry had ever achieved or has achieved.....' In India, where the film industry was much more commercially successful, such a deliberate act of policy would have been more difficult to pursue, though in Aslam Azhar's opinion 'Indian cinema has set a very bad example for Indian television'.[43]

As Pakistan television grew, with new stations established at Islamabad and Karachi and microwave links to provide co-ordinated national coverage, Pakistan's military ruler, Field Marshal Ayub Khan, was excited over its potential as 'a major instrument of national integration'.[44] Aslam Azhar had not been aware of any government objectives in setting up television; he had a free hand to develop it according to his own inspiration.

But it seems from the government's subsequent use of the medium that there was a clear political purpose. In 1968, Aslam Azhar was asked to develop programmes to celebrate Ayub's 'decade of development'. It was the first instance of television being used in South Asia for propaganda purposes and it backfired badly. According to Aslam Azhar, it filled people with disgust at government control of the medium and contributed to Ayub's growing unpopularity.[45]

Pakistan Television also provided the first TV election coverage in South Asia during the interregnum after Ayub's demise, when General Yahya Khan held Pakistan's first and probably fairest national elections. Aslam Azhar describes that period as 'our finest hour in current affairs'.[46] But the ensuing crisis in East Pakistan, which led to the emergence of Bangladesh, brought a re-imposition of the old controls. These also continued under the new prime minister, Zulfiqar Ali Bhutto, who maintained emergency rule for several years.

India went through the 1971 war with the sensitive border areas of Punjab and Kashmir within range of Pakistan's stations at Rawalpindi and Lahore and with no means of counter-attack. As a result, Mrs. Gandhi began to take television more seriously. The Bombay station opened in 1972, followed the next year by stations at Amritsar and Srinagar, to counter Pakistani propaganda in those strategically important regions. In Kashmir, community sets were provided by the government to hundreds of villages to support this project.[47]

By this stage, both Mr. Bhutto and Mrs. Gandhi were embarking on new and more populist policies. Both saw television as an important new means of communication with the masses and set in train significant television building programmes. In Pakistan, shortly after Bhutto assumed charge as president, he made Aslam Azhar managing director of television and asked him to put up two new television stations—in Peshawar and Quetta. Told that this would probably take twelve to fourteen months, Bhutto apparently replied: 'I am not asking you to build me a couple of nuclear reactors; all I want is two television stations. I'm giving you three months!'[48] In India, after the expansion provoked by the war, the next spurt came with Mrs. Gandhi's declaration of the Emergency. The Calcutta, Madras and Lucknow stations all opened within six months in 1975 and the following year television was finally separated from All India Radio and given its own director general. In 1976, to make TV more popular, the government reduced excise duties on cheaper sets, and local manufacture began to take off. In 1969, when the first Indian television factory opened at Kanpur, only 1250 sets were manufactured, but by 1977, forty manufacturers were producing nearly a quarter of a million sets a year.[49]

Despite this rapid development under Mrs. Gandhi, Indian TV remained an urban phenomenon confined to the well to do. It did not become a mass medium until the 1980s, when Rajiv Gandhi's interest in technology provoked a quantum leap in all communications, whether TV, telephones or computers. In the case of TV, the fillip came with the Asian Games held in Delhi in 1982, which Indira Gandhi saw as an opportunity for India to showcase its achievements to the wider world. A decision was made to go for colour TV, new equipment was imported, and an early phase of economic liberalisation saw duties reduced on a wide range of electronic imports. Changes were also made in the manufacturing regime. From the 1960s, as a matter of policy, many Indian TV sets had been made by small factories, but from the early 1980s, in the run up to the Asian Games, multinationals and large Indian consortia were allowed into the field and import restrictions on colour TV components were relaxed. By 1986, India was producing over 3 million sets a year, including 700,000 colour sets.

This change in manufacturing practice was accompanied by a massive transmitter building programme. From eighteen television transmitters in 1979, the number rose to forty in 1982 and 176 in 1985, by which stage 81 per cent of the urban population and 50 per cent of the rural population were covered.[50] By the mid-1980s, India had become a television society and thanks to the development of indigenous satellite technology, Doordarshan became capable of broadcasting national programmes for the first time. This paved the way for the creation of a national market for television advertising, which brought powerful new commercial influences to bear on the production of programmes. As the Congress and its Hindu nationalist rival, the Bharatiya Janata Party, battled it out for the votes of the burgeoning middle class in north India, television became a vehicle not just for a new consumerism but also for a broader political appeal to Hindu values. The broadcasting on Doordarshan of major television serials based on the great Hindu epics—the *Ramayana* and the *Mahabharata*—drew millions of Indians to television for the first time and signalled its appropriation for a new kind of popular culture. Before the arrival of satellite competition, Doordarshan had already staked out the ground for future commercial competition.

THE ELECTRONIC MEDIA IN BANGLADESH

In the creation of Bangladesh, radio played a more influential role than television. Before the crackdown by Pakistan troops in March 1971, there was a period of more than two weeks when both television and radio were virtually free and the staff was making programmes in support of the Awami League. But on 25 March, the army took over Dhaka TV and radio stations and it was then left to radio outside Dhaka to support the cause of the Awami League. The Chittagong radio station continued to broadcast a message of resistance until it came under attack from jets of the Pakistan airforce. Afterwards, the transmitter was moved around on a lorry to avoid detection by Pakistani forces. This radio station, known as *Swadin Bangla Betar Kendro* (Independent Bangla Radio Station), became a symbol of the struggle for freedom. It later moved its operations to Calcutta, where it was run by former staff from the Chittagong and Rajshahi stations, with support from guerrillas and students. The station played an important part in keeping up morale during Bengali resistance to Pakistani rule.

Once the state had been won, however, media management reverted to the practices of earlier times. One of the first acts of Sheikh Mujibur Rahman's government was to end television's status as a public corporation, notional though it had been, and to bring it under direct political control. When Sheikh Mujib responded to growing economic and political opposition in 1974 by declaring the country a one party state, radio and television became mouthpieces of his new authoritarianism.

During the military regimes of General Zia ur Rahman and General Ershad, the two leaders skilfully used the media, particularly television, to project their own personalities and the role of the army in national life, whether in digging canals or rescuing the victims of perennial floods. This reinforced the process of centralisation and politicisation of the media, which had begun earlier. In fact, for much of the 1980s, Bangladesh seemed very much a mirror image of Pakistan, the state from which it had broken away. These were not the circumstances for establishing new media conventions and it was only after 1991, when the country returned to democracy, that the future of the electronic media became a subject for political debate.

What the emergence of Bangladesh did bring, however, was important new cultural policies. During the Pakistan period, the Dhaka station of Radio Pakistan was perceived as 'His Master's Voice'. It projected Urdu as the national language and the Bengali language it used was laced with Urdu words. Mr. Jinnah's efforts to enforce Urdu in East Pakistan, in which Radio Pakistan played its part, illustrated at an early stage for the Bengalis the problem of unequal access which was a feature of rule from West Pakistan. As one commentator puts it: 'There was a sense that they were imposing their culture on us'.[51] This was particularly the case after the 1965 war when the poetry and music of Rabindranath Tagore were banned on Radio Pakistan. This provoked an outcry and helped to fuel the development of Bengali linguistic nationalism.

After 1971, the Urdu-speaking elite within Bangladesh, which had been influential in cementing ties with West Pakistan, was finally eclipsed. The Bengali-speaking middle class assumed a dominant role and the electronic media became vehicles for a renaissance of Bengali language and literature. Tagore's poetry and songs were once more heard on the airwaves. Though qualified on both sides by political differences, there was a new sense of political and cultural affinity with India and with West Bengal.

TELEVISION IN SRI LANKA

Sri Lanka was not the market leader in television it had been in commercial radio. In the 1960s, Prime Minister Dudley Senanayake thought it would do more harm than good. His successor, Mrs. Sirimavo Bandaranaike, who headed a left wing coalition for much of the 1970s, attempted to find refuge from Sri Lanka's growing economic problems in a siege economy. In her days, the atmosphere was hostile to international business and to technical innovation. With the election of J.R. Jayawardene in 1977, Sri Lanka reversed these policies, attempting to model itself on Singapore's successful open economy. Under Jayawardene, Sri Lanka became the first South Asian country to introduce economic liberalisation, which involved rolling back state control, promoting competition as the engine of growth and encouraging foreign investment. This new approach also resulted in increased competition in the media. In 1979, Jayawardene, who had long been an advocate of television, sanctioned an experiment by the private sector and in 1982, with Japanese aid and technical assistance, established a public broadcasting system. The man chosen to set up Rupavahini was M.J. Perera, who had also been the first Sri Lankan director general of radio. Perera appointed a number of radio professionals to key posts and followed many radio precedents. As on radio, there were news bulletins in English, Sinhala and Tamil, all based on a central text, televised at different times during the evening. Maintaining a strict balance of other programmes was more difficult. The cost of television and the existence of only one channel meant that there were fewer Tamil programmes on television than on radio. Sinhala programmes tended to dominate the schedules, with Sinhala drama a particular favourite. The other problem was that the television signal was not received well in the north of the island, which may have increased the sense of alienation among the Jaffna Tamils.

The coincidence of the launching of TV and the outbreak of Sri Lanka's prolonged Tamil insurgency in Jaffna makes the country a test case for the role of the media in conflict situations. In 1983, the killing of seventeen soldiers in a landmine explosion was followed by a politically directed pogrom against Tamils in Colombo. Prime Minister Premadasa's television broadcast after these events came so close to defending communal victimisation that M.J. Perera refused to repeat it and was ultimately supported by President Jayawardene in that action. The incident illustrated the rapid politicisation of the media under the pressure of war and insurgency. In 1988 and 1989, during the JVP insurgency in the south, radio and television were taken over by officers of the armed forces and the stations run like barracks under siege to maintain an essential service.

The retirement of Jayawardene and the election of President Premadasa brought what M.J. Perera calls 'the worst period of politicisation'.[52] Jayawardene monitored TV and radio closely but he very rarely intervened. Premadasa, on the other hand, saw television as a vehicle for his own glorification. According to

M.J. Perera: 'He used to go round the country making speeches and all that had to be broadcast on the radio and TV...so much so that I gave up listening to the news....' One measure of this greater control was the opening of an office for the minister of information, A.J. Ranasinghe, in the Rupavahini building. The minister made regular visits, '...giving orders to the chairman and others...and appointed his own people to various jobs.... It was a very sad period.'

Despite the political crisis in the country, economic liberalisation continued and within strict limits brought growing competition in the media field. The first private television company, ITN, which was set up in 1979 by the president's nephew Shan Wickremesinghe, folded after only a few months and was taken over by the government and run as a second channel. But by 1992, television had attracted sufficient advertising for another channel to be set up. A licence was given to the Maharaja group, which was run by Colombo Tamil businessmen close to President Premadasa. The Maharajas had no previous media experience, but with technical assistance from Singapore and elsewhere, Maharaja TV soon became commercially viable. This encouragement of private sector television, though slow and halting at first, marked Sri Lanka out from other South Asian countries, which had retained control in government hands. By the mid-1990s, the country had proved that television could be pluralised successfully even in a small country with a limited advertising market.

THE MEDIA IN NEPAL

Nepal was slow to introduce both radio and television. The successful diplomacy of the Ranas had protected Nepal from the direct impact of British colonialism but left it with a lot of catching up to do once its leaders chose to tread the same path of development as its neighbours. Under the Ranas, it was not permitted to own a radio until 1945 and Radio Nepal was only set up in 1951 once Rana rule had been brought to an end.[53] Modern communications were introduced at the same time as a fledgling democracy, but as democracy faltered and King Mahendra reasserted the powers of a restored monarchy, radio became the voice of his government.

Radio offered a chance to link up different communities and to spread the message of development. But the Nepalese monarchy proved wary of technical innovation; even as late as the 1980s large areas of the country, particularly in the west, were outside the range of radio transmitters. Radio did play a part in promoting Nepali as the country's national language. King Mahendra believed that the Nepali language was the key to national integration; so much so that for nearly forty years Radio Nepal did not broadcast in any other language, despite the extraordinary linguistic plurality of the country. As a result, many Nepalis spent much of their time listening to All India Radio in Hindi and other languages. In the terai region on the border with India, Nepalis speaking Bhojpuri and Maithili were able to hear broadcasts in those languages on All India Radio but not from Radio Nepal.

Nepalese TV started in 1985, much later than in India or Pakistan. According to Neer Shah, the first general manager, the project was viewed with hostility in official circles and was not properly planned or funded.[54] It was only after the first experimental broadcast during King Birendra's visit to Australia that the palace began to realise that television could be a powerful means of projecting the government and the monarchy. The objective was 'to promote national integrity, Nepali arts, culture and education', which had become more urgent because of the rapid development of Indian TV. By the mid-1980s, Doordarshan had begun to attract Nepali audiences even in Kathmandu and there was talk of a 'cultural invasion from India'.[55] Despite the huge costs involved for a small and relatively poor country, the new medium had become a necessary tool in the battle for cultural influence within Nepal itself. In this sense, Nepal had already experienced something very similar to the satellite revolution before it started.

In the media, as in much else in Nepal, it was the 'People's Movement' of 1990 which ushered in the most radical change. After many years in the wilderness, the Nepali Congress and its communist allies forced the king to surrender his absolute powers and to introduce a form of parliamentary democracy. One plank of their joint programme was the liberalisation of the media. After these changes, Radio Nepal became, for a time, more critical of government, more open to different viewpoints and to public access, more investigative, more satirical and more entertaining. Within a few years, it reverted to the prevalent South Asian model of 'party in power' control. But the liberalisation of politics and economics did have important repercussions. The state monopoly ended and state radio and television were step by step forced to compete with the private sector.

BROADCASTING AND THE CRISIS OF THE NATION STATE IN SOUTH ASIA

By the 1980s, broadcasting, as a tool of central government, had become part of an acute crisis of centre-state relations in India, Pakistan and Sri Lanka. The breakaway of Pakistan's eastern wing to form Bangladesh was only the most dramatic example of a trend which affected almost all countries of the region. Pakistan governments were faced, over the next two decades, with insurgency in Baluchistan, an uprising in Sind and a growing sense of alienation among the Muhajirs, who had migrated from India to become citizens of the new state after 1947. Indian governments faced insurgencies in Assam, Punjab and Kashmir and resorted to military action in all three states to suppress separatist movements. The sight of Indian tanks inside the Golden Temple at Amritsar provided a graphic illustration of a crisis between the central government and the Sikh community. In Sri Lanka, the collapse of government authority in the north and east of the island and the failure to resolve the long running Tamil insurgency, either by diplomacy or war, illustrated the same factors.

National broadcasters helped to increase the sense of alienation by acting as propagandists for ruling parties, by denying space to opposition politicians or critics of government policy and by neglecting regional cultures and concerns. Centralised control of broadcasting enabled the Indian or Pakistan governments to supervise the detail of hundreds of daily radio news bulletins in scores of languages and dialects. But most of these bulletins were translations of a central script giving the ruling party's view. Control of output was tight and there was very little interactive broadcasting.

In linguistically diverse countries, central control tended to involve the reinforcement of a dominant language—in India, Hindi; in Pakistan, Urdu; in Nepal, Nepali. In India, only the linguistically assertive Tamils succeeded in resisting these pressures.

Efforts to use broadcasting to reinforce national identity made broadcasting a focus of attention in the tussle of wills between the centre and its regional opponents. In India, the centre dragged its feet on broadcasting initiatives suggested by the states, even when the Congress controlled most states as well as the central government. But public differences increased once other parties began to capture state power. 'The authorities seem to forget that India is a federal polity, with its multi-racial, multi-lingual and multi-cultural components...', wrote Jyoti Basu, the long-serving chief minister of West Bengal. In his view, the refusal to decentralise power and resources gave rise to glaring distortions in centre-state relations and 'encouraged separatist forces to rear their heads'.[56] The communist government in West Bengal argued for many years that states should have a channel of their own, but the appeal fell on deaf ears.

The centralisation of Indian broadcasting was highlighted by a number of different reports commissioned by the government itself. The Chanda Report of 1966 pointed out how little authority had been delegated to the director general, leave alone the station directors. It recommended that broadcasting be delinked from government and given autonomy. That recommendation was turned down by Mrs. Gandhi as 'untimely' and most of its other suggestions for reform were ignored. Only its recommendation that radio should accept commercials was promptly implemented.[57]

A decade later, after the experience of censorship and media control during the Emergency, the Janata government set up the Verghese Committee to decide what form autonomy should take. That committee also very strongly underlined the need for decentralisation. 'After fifty years of official tutelage, central government management of what are simultaneously national, regional and local media is becoming less and less tenable'. It concluded what was required was not just autonomy vis-à-vis the government but more responsibility for the regions and a new 'culture of independence' within the organisation.[58] But by the time a bill had been drafted, Mrs. Gandhi was back in power and the whole issue was shelved again. It was only with the election of another non-Congress government in 1988 that the project was revived and the Prasar Bharati Act passed. But even then, it lay on the statute books unimplemented for a further decade until India's third non-Congress government scrambled it into place just days before leaving office.

The experience of other South Asian countries shows that changes of form are not necessarily significant. In Sri Lanka, a parliamentary commission recommended in 1967 that Radio Ceylon become a corporation with a board of governors on the BBC model. But the first act of the board was to appoint its own chairman, Neville Jayaweera, a high ranking civil servant, as director general, so eliminating the supposed separation of powers. The Pakistan Broadcasting Corporation, established in 1972, was run on similar lines. The new status was supposed to give more freedom to the broadcasters, but government remained very powerful, the organisation became more bureaucratic and the tradition of drafting senior civil servants into top jobs carried over into the new corporate existence.[59]

In the 1980s and early 1990s, when the crisis of centre-state relations worsened and several South Asian governments faced uprisings against their authority, their militant opponents singled out broadcasters as instruments of central rule and in some cases assassinated them. In the Indian state of Punjab, the station director of All India Radio Amritsar was assassinated and the station stopped broadcasting in Hindi for a period.[60] In 1990, the station director in Srinagar was assassinated by Kashmiri militants. In both cities, stations had to be fortified and defended by troops. In Sri Lanka, radio and TV were targeted by the JVP militants in their uprising against the government of Ranasinghe Premadasa. In 1989, the chairman of the SLBC, one of the country's most distinguished broadcasters, D.T.L. Guruge, was shot down by militants near his home in Colombo.[61] Death threats also prevented the director general designate of Rupavahini from taking up his job; instead, a former air force officer was drafted in to put the station on a war footing.[62]

INDIA ENTERS THE SATELLITE AGE

The early development of satellite communications in India is an exception to the rule that the state generally sees technology as an aid to central control. In the 1960s, when India had only one television transmitter in Delhi, Indian scientists became convinced that the country could speed up its development by leapfrogging existing technologies. The prime mover in this leap of imagination was the chairman of India's Atomic Energy Commission, Dr. Vikram Sarabhai, a trusted scientific adviser to Prime Minister Indira Gandhi. Sarabhai conceived the idea of combining terrestrial microwave relay transmitters with communication satellites to bring television to the vast areas of rural India which were otherwise inaccessible. For a trial year, the Satellite Instructional Television Education project (SITE) brought TV to 2,400 villages in some of the least developed areas of rural India.

Much has been written about SITE—the vision, the practical achievement, the ultimate abandonment of the concept and technology on which it was based. One of its most noteworthy features was the cultural and political context in which it was realised. The technology was developed with the use of an American satellite ATS-6 and in close association with the United States. It was not so much an exercise in technological transfer as one of transglobal communications co-operation. Its boldness was more remarkable in the light of India's commitment to a policy of nonalignment in international affairs.

The project held strategic attractions for the Indian government. Under Nehru's influence, Indian governments had always stressed the importance of the country developing its own national expertise in modern technologies. The SITE programme offered a context in which to devise and implement new communication strategies for education and development, especially in rural areas. It also presented opportunities for the transfer of skills in the latest communications technology, with a wide range of potential applications. Subsequently, the Kheda and Jhabua communications projects promoted further practical applications of space technology in the Indian context. [63]

India's size, its state of economic development and the human and professional skills of its people set the stage for the bid to reach a new TV audience without the need for an existing terrestrial infrastructure. There were no commercial imperatives, or even obvious commercial advantages. Problems of hardware, access, maintenance, extension and ultimately competition from Doordarshan itself led to the programme being abandoned after an experimental period.

However, India's satellite programme derived long-term benefits from collaboration with the United States. India designed and launched two satellites in the 1980s with American co-operation.

The short-lived INSAT-1A was operative only for four months from April to August 1982 before technical problems closed it down; its successor, INSAT-1B, built in California by Ford Aerospace, was launched on the Challenger space shuttle in October 1983.

This second INSAT satellite became the means for a major expansion of television across India. Through satellite-fed, low-powered relay stations, Doordarshan was able to introduce a national network for the first time. In 1982—the year that colour TV was introduced—a regular satellite link between the Delhi Doordarshan station and other Doordarshan centres was established. Two years later, a second channel called DD-2 was launched in Delhi and later extended to Mumbai, Calcutta and Chennai.

By this stage, satellite technology had made possible national programming and the centralising instinct re-asserted itself. In Mumbai, Calcutta and Chennai, Doordarshan centres which had enjoyed a degree of autonomy for a decade found their room for regional expression and appeal restricted. It was the beginning of a decline in Doordarshan's service to the regions which commercial satellite channels were later to exploit for their own benefit.

AUDIENCES IN WAITING

By the early 1990s, a number of factors had come together to challenge the viability of governments' control of the electronic media. Among these were the emergence of a democratic consensus across the region, the growth of a more independent press, the popularity of video, the beginnings of economic liberalisation and the development of a new, extended, urban middle class in India and other countries.

For the first time in the history of modern South Asia, all the main countries of the region were being run as parliamentary democracies. The military regimes of Pakistan and Bangladesh gave way to elected governments in 1988 and 1991, while in Nepal, King Birendra bowed before the popular movement of 1990 and agreed to become a constitutional monarch.

In these countries, greater democracy brought greater freedom of the press, which was underpinned by the growth of newspaper readership and a reduced reliance on government advertising. In Pakistan and Bangladesh, some of the more commercially successful newspapers began to play a more independent role. In Nepal, the commercial newspaper sector began to develop more vigorously.

In India and Sri Lanka, where democratic systems had functioned since independence except for short periods of emergency rule, the press was already a powerful influence on civil society. This was particularly so in India, where the 1980s saw a quantum leap in the development of the regional press. Robin Jeffrey has shown how this phenomenon both reflected the emergence of new regional middle classes in India, particularly in the south and the west, and contributed to the growth of new regional political parties. In this sense, the development of the regional press in southern India anticipated where satellite television in regional languages would bring the easiest rewards.[64]

The Sri Lankan press had a less impressive record in the 1980s. Its English language newspapers declined, while the Sinhala press extended its circulation and became more commercially dominant. Tamil newspapers struggled to remain viable, except where they existed as arms of larger concerns. The war in the north and east of the island had a very distorting effect on the development of civil society.

In much of the region, however, government control of the electronic media made less sense. There was an obvious mismatch between the practice of democracy and the continued suppression of important political news on government-controlled radio and TV. A Pakistani commentator wrote: 'Our democratic system is based on an interplay of many parties and points of view. However, our electronic media is working largely on the pattern of one-party dictatorship, for the benefit of the shortsighted and unprincipled men in power.'[65]

In the heyday of radio, governments' tight control of news created a considerable constituency in South Asia for foreign radio broadcasts, of which those from the BBC in London were the most popular. The United States, the Soviet Union, China, the UK, Germany and other countries broadcast to South Asia in English and in some other regional languages. But the BBC's coverage of regional news and current affairs in English, Hindi, Urdu and

Bengali came to be seen as a necessary additional source of information, particularly in times of political crisis.

By the 1980s, the emergence of television as a mass medium was attracting audiences away from radio, whether domestic or international, and setting new standards of quality for international broadcasters to match. Listening to programmes on short wave became more difficult once colour television was available. International broadcasters responded where possible by using medium wave transmitters or by hiring transmitters closer to their audiences. By the 1990s, in a more liberal atmosphere in South Asia, they attempted to secure re-broadcasting agreements on government or commercial channels. The aim was to add value to local broadcasters rather than relying on a direct radio signal. But the strategy was not universally successful.

The development of video breached government's monopoly of the electronic media in a different way. Though more a threat to cinema than to TV, it gave the middle class a greater choice of entertainment, whether imported western films or the latest products of Bollywood. Video supplemented the more restricted diet on offer from the national broadcasters and invited comparisons with it. It was the beginning of more varied home viewing and created a market, which the satellite channels could exploit. It also led, for an interim period, to the creation of a market for weekly current affairs videos. These were pioneered in India by leading English-language newspapers and journals and acted as test-beds for the first generation of television journalists operating free of government control.

For almost fifty years after Independence, South Asian governments maintained a monopoly of the air waves, whether radio or television, and for the most part used them for party political purposes. They did so, despite overwhelming evidence that their news services were not credible and their audiences demanded more choice. By the 1990s, however, the Indian middle class in particular had become a massive market, both for consumer goods and for alternative media services. South Asian governments were locked in a centralising mind-set, which apparently prevented them from responding creatively to these new challenges. But they were about to face a challenge from the skies, which would threaten the mind-set, the monopoly and the projection of national cultures which went with them.

NOTES AND REFERENCES

1. This brief history of early Indian broadcasting draws on reports and correspondence in the India Office Records (IOR) in the British Library. Of published material, H.R. Luthra's, *Indian Broadcasting* (1986) gives a detailed historical account from an insider's perspective. See also Appendix A ('Indian Broadcasting in Retrospect') of the *Report of the Working Group on Autonomy for Akashwani and Doordarshan* (The Verghese Report), Vol. II, pp. A2–17.
2. IOR/L/1/445, File 223/1, *World Radio*, 25 November 1932, pp 1177–79. As quoted by Lt. Colonel Hardinge in his article 'Broadcasting and India's Future'.
3. *Ibid.* C.F. Strickland, 'Broadcasting to the Indian Village', a lecture given to the East India Association, 10 October 1933. This is Strickland's summary of Brayne's results.
4. *Ibid.* Punjab government press note, 16 November 1933.
5. *Ibid.* A.H. Joyce, 'Note on Rural Broadcasting', 3 January 1934.
6. *Ibid.*
7. As quoted in Luthra, *Indian Broadcasting* (1986), p. 3.
8. IOR/L/1/445, File 223/1, BBC Memorandum, 28 February 1934.
9. *Ibid.* Note on 'Broadcasting in India', 12 July 1934.
10. *Ibid.* Note on 'Broadcasting in India' by Professor J. Coatman, 28 July 1934.
11. Partha Sarathi Gupta (1995), *Radio and the Raj 1921–1947*. In these two lectures, given in 1988, Professor Gupta shows the Government of India's caution over the development of broadcasting and the role Lord Reith and the BBC played in pressing for a centralised system. Some of the opposition to Coatman's view came from retired civil servants who favoured 'the provincialisation of the Indian polity'.
12. Lionel Fielden's autobiography, *The Natural Bent* (1960) gives a lively account of his early years in the BBC and his time in India.
13. Syed Rashid Ahmed, Karachi, March 1998.
14. Syed Rashid Ahmed, *Speech on the 50th anniversary of the Lahore Station*.
15. Fielden, *The Natural Bent* (1960), p. 195.
16. K.S. Mullick (1974), *Tangled Tapes*, pp. 105–10.
17. IOR/L/I/445, File 223/1, Fielden to Macgregor, 6 October 1937.
18. Fielden, *The Natural Bent* (1960), pp. 144–45 and p. 193.
19. IOR/L/I/445, File 223/1, Macgregor to Fielden, 17 February 1936.
20. Fielden, *The Natural Bent* (1996), p. 204.
21. *Ibid.*, p. 196.
22. IOR/L/I/1, File 462/57R. Government of India reports on broadcasting development 1942-IOR/L/I/1/440, File 217/8, Radio SEAC, Ceylon.
23. IOR/L/I/958, File 462/57 GG. See Lord Wootton's first draft of the War Cabinet Broadcasting Committee Report, 19 February 1945. See also, War Cabinet Committee Meeting, 20 September 1944.
24. Mullick, *Tangled Tapes* (1974), p. 116.
25. V. Shankar (1974), *My Reminiscences of Sardar Patel*, Vol. I, pp 22–26. See also, Luthra, *Indian Broadcasting* (1986), p. 162, for a different view of Bokhari.
26. See Luthra, *Indian Broadcasting* (1986), pp. 191–97.
27. *Ibid.*

28. See Luthra, *Indian Broadcasting* (1986), pp. 305–13; see also, Mullick, *Tangled Tapes* (1974), p. 122.
29. IOR/L/I/1/958, File 462/57GG. See section on 'Commercial Broadcasting from overseas' in Lord Wootton's draft report of the War Cabinet Broadcasting Committee 1945.
30. See, IOR/L/I/1/44, File 218/8. The India Office Records provide details of the negotiations in which the War Office was also involved. Livy Wijemanne, in his autobiography, *A Broadcaster Looks Back*, gives his own account of how Radio SEAC was acquired by Radio Ceylon. Sir Oliver Goonetilleke, Ceylon's home minister, apparently refused to pay rent for it, then demanded it be dismantled and finally shamed the British into giving it to Ceylon without payment.
31. Nandana Karunanayake (1990), *Broadcasting in Sri Lanka*, pp. 132–34.
32. S.V. Venkataraman, Chennai, February 1998.
33. Ameen Sayani, Mumbai, February 1998.
34. See, Karunanayake, *Broadcasting in Sri Lanka* (1990), pp. 135–36.
35. See, Luthra, *Indian Broadcasting* (1986), p. 202.
36. Mullick, *Tangled Tapes* (1974), p. 45.
37. *The Verghese Report* points out that licences were not necessarily a very accurate guide to numbers of listeners. In the late 1970s, 3 million radio sets were being produced annually, but licences were only increasing at about 1 million per year. (See, *Verghese Report*, Vol. I, p. 91.)
38. Government of India (1977), White Paper on Misuse of Mass Media during the Internal Emergency, extract from the speech of Shri V.C. Shukla at Station Directors' Conference on 9.9.1975, New Delhi, Appendix 7, p. 15.
39. *Ibid.*, Appendix 7, p. 70.
40. *Ibid.*, Appendix 7, p. 15. For a broadcaster's view of the Emergency, see P.C. Chatterji (1998), *The Adventure of Indian Broadcasting*, pp. 251–68.
41. See, Luthra, *Indian Broadcasting* (1986), pp. 407–34.
42. Aslam Azhar, Islamabad, March 1998.
43. Aslam Azhar, Islamabad, March 1998.
44. Altaf Gauhar (1994), *Ayub Khan: Pakistan's First Military Ruler*, p. 410.
45. Altar Gauhar, Ayub Khan's information secretary, claims that what had been intended as a modest celebration was hijacked by different departments of government and got completely out of hand. Interview, Islamabad, January 1999.
46. Aslam Azhar, Islamabad, March 1998.
47. Luthra, *Indian Broadcasting* (1986), pp. 412–14.
48. Aslam Azhar, Islamabad, March 1998.
49. Prem Kumar (1988), *The Television Industry in India: Market Structure, Conduct and Performance*, Table 2.3, p. 42.
50. *Ibid.*, pp. 113–17.
51. Afsan Chowdhury, Chennai, January 1999.
52. M.J. Perera, Colombo, March 1998.
53. Thapa and Sharma (eds) (1996), *Mass Media and Democratisation: A Country Study on Nepal*, pp. 37–38.
54. Neer Shah, Kathmandu, March 1998.
55. Durga Nath Sharma, General Manager, Nepal TV, March 1998.

56. Jyoti Basu (1986), 'Indian Television: The Deficiencies of Over-centralisation', in *A Vision for Indian Television*, a feedback project organised by NAMEDIA (Media Foundation of the Non-aligned), pp. 146–48.
57. *Radio and Television*, Report of the Committee on Broadcasting and Information Media, (1966), pp. 53–55. See also, P.C. Chatterji (1991), *Broadcasting in India*, pp. 165–66.
58. *Verghese Report*, Vol. I, pp. 20–25.
59. Sabih Mohsin, former director of programmes, Karachi, March 1998.
60. Ramesh Thakur (1996), *The Government and Politics of India*, p. 26.
61. Karunanayake, *Broadcasting in Sri Lanka* (1990), p. 131.
62. Shirley Perera, Colombo, March 1998.
63. For an account of the SITE experiment see, Arvind Singhal and Everett M. Rogers (1989), *India's Information Revolution*, pp. 62–64. See also Chapter 9, pp. 303–05.
64. Robin Jeffrey (2000), *India's Newspaper Revolution: Capitalism, Politics and the Indian Language Press 1977–1999*.
65. Khalid Ali, 'Freedom for TV and Radio', *Dawn*, Karachi, 9 April 1994.

Three

SOUTH ASIA GOES GLOBAL

The decade of the 1990s saw a massive change, both conceptual and practical, in the application of satellite communications to broadcasting. Satellite communications transformed the immediacy of news and changed the nature and style of broadcast journalism. A global audience was first made vividly conscious of this new medium through the Gulf War in 1991. The monopoly of national broadcasters was brought to an end, without negotiation or discussion of the international implications.

The audiences created by the new media were an irresistible market for global advertisers and their multinational corporate clients. As the diversity of channels increased, competition accelerated the consolidation of global media corporations. They brought foreign and culturally unfamiliar programmes into people's homes. These often challenged traditional values. But they offered a welcome contrast of styles with national TV services.

The new channels also created opportunities for promoting regional cultures and languages. Cable and satellite audiences were matched against the reach of the national broadcasters, giving advertisers a choice where to spend their budgets. Programming was measured by its revenue potential. State broadcasters had to square public service objectives with commercial priorities. Broadcasting was put into the market place.

THE SATELLITE ERA

These changes have had radical implications for all countries of the region. But India's earlier satellite programme makes it misleading to date the 'satellite revolution' in South Asia to the beginning of the 1990s. Arthur C. Clarke's vision of the communications potential of satellite technology dates back more than fifty years. The then British RAF pilot later settled in Sri Lanka and became the country's most eminent foreign citizen, author of many highly successful novels, inspiration of the 'Space Odyssey' films and architect of a whole futuristic mythology. But nothing he wrote has proved more visionary than the technical article which he wrote in 1945, describing the theory of a satellite in geostationary orbit above the equator. The prophecy was first realised in practice eighteen years later, with the launch of NASA's Syncom satellite in 1963. Clarke's article foreshadowed in an uncannily accurate way what was to become the basis of the telecommunications world of the late 20th century.[1]

The basis of a mass television audience was laid in Asia, as in the United States and Europe, by national television services. By 1991, the audience for television across the world had grown by three times compared to 1979. The media companies that had established satellite and cable services in the United States from the middle of the 1980s were becoming global media enterprises. The concept was familiar in the print media and in radio. The dominance of international news agencies and major international broadcasters in mediating the international flow of news and infor-mation was a key element in the critique by developing countries in the 1980s, which led to the demand for a New World Information Order. But new global institutions were establishing the concept of global television for the first time.

This was a period not only of unprecedented media expansion but of global consolidation in the advertising industry. By 1990, mergers and takeovers in the advertising industry meant that the world's seven leading advertising agencies accounted for busi-ness worth US$ 73 billion. Five of them were American or joint American-British, one was Japanese and the other French.[2] Europe and Japan lagged behind the United States. While big US organ-isations dominated the global media markets, the ownership of these corporations was becoming more diffused among share-holders and companies in the advanced developed world.

Throughout South Asia, television services were government-controlled monopolies. Audiences could have a taste of the pro-gramming carried on the new channels if some of the satellite output was re-broadcast on the national TV networks, or by installing a satellite receiver dish of their own, or by subscribing to a cable service where it was available.

The direct reception of foreign satellite channels through domestically owned satellite dishes was limited in some parts of South Asia by the size of the dish required. Sri Lanka, which was right on the edge of the AsiaSat-1 footprint, needed a massive 25ft dish to pick up the signals, making these services effectively beyond the range of all but the wealthiest consumer. In north India and Pakistan, the same satellite channels could be picked up by a dish one quarter the size. Privately-owned satellite dishes created the initial awareness of the new channels. Their well-to-do owners were, for the most part, exercising the option for more exciting home entertainment than their single channel national TV services offered. The availability of this choice proved the trigger for a media revolution throughout South Asia.

INDIA'S SATELLITE PROGRAMME

Of all the countries of the region, India's longstanding international co-operation in satellite telecommunications apparently placed it in an advantageous position to meet the challenge of this 'invasion'. For more than twenty years Indian policy and Indian scientists had been directly involved with satellite communication and the use of satellites in broadcasting. India was already known as an important laboratory for experimentation in the potential and effectiveness of the new technology. The Indian experience was of global relevance in assessing the application of the new media to the communications needs of a large and culturally complex nation and society.

The technology and the use of it for broadcasting were not novel. But the intrusion of private international television broadcasters into a field which was always assumed to be a national prerogative was highly unwelcome. Broadcasting institutions were entrenched as a national monopoly. The frequency spectrum, transmission hardware and programming policies were controlled by government or regulated by international agreements. In this perspective, the intrusion seemed almost equivalent to piracy and of questionable legitimacy under both domestic and international law.

In the early phase of the satellite era, programming on the general entertainment channels, whether in English or Asian languages, was commercially focussed and politically neutral. Culturally, much of it was of dubious relevance and uncertain appeal. But the satellite output raised fears of exposure to a flow of externally mediated information and alien cultural influences. It was not so much the volume of exposure to external programmes which was a cause of concern. This was not high. But there was a sharp contrast between these programme schedules and domestic television output, and foreign programming was no longer chosen or controlled by national broadcasting authorities.

In earlier years, an Indian government would perhaps have followed through the instinctive wish of its officials to preserve the national monopoly by any means. But the context was set by a commitment to liberalisation and opening of international trade. India, in particular, with its own substantial industrial capacity and a growing consumer class, had long been considered a tantalising prize. Small in relation to the size of the population, the middle class consumers were nevertheless in absolute terms a big potential market.

With the development of India's own satellite launching capacity, the INSAT programme grew into a major project involving Indian design and technology. Before the international satellite invasion hit India, over 90 per cent of the country was covered by satellite-fed terrestrial signals. This was a formidable infrastructure. It had been designed to extend the range of the national broadcaster's public service remit. But when external realities and government policy changes in the 1990s pushed Doordarshan into a commercially competitive television environment, it served the state broadcaster well.

India's record of technical achievement and experimentation in satellite television should have put it in a commanding position to set the agenda of the new communications technology. It had created a new national audience that was to make television a successful marketing instrument. But conditions had changed. Others moved in to take advantage of the telecommunications infrastructure already built at state initiative.

The new market was primarily one of a growing middle class. The new distribution systems enabled this audience to be distinguished from the national audience created by the expansion of the 1980s. Separate markets were defined by satellite channels in regional languages.

THE GLOBAL WINDOW

CNN International's global coverage of the Gulf War in 1991 heralded a new era of international television. It established the Atlanta-based company, which had been launched in 1985, in a position of leadership both as a broadcaster and as a pioneer in a new style of news broadcasting—lively and informal, though to its critics, rough hewn and crudely edited. The telecasting of live events set a new standard of immediacy for television journalism. The television event would become internationally—as it already was domestically in the United States—a substitute for more traditional channels of diplomatic communication and political opinion forming. The role of the electronic media was reinforced, both as a vehicle of information and publicity and as a negotiating tool.

CNN created an awareness of television as a new medium in international broadcasting, but it took other agents to transform the broadcasting environment in South Asia. The first was the AsiaSat-1 satellite—the first Asia-specific satellite available for television broadcasting in the region. Second, the entertainment-oriented schedules proved to be a highly attractive contrast to programming on the national TV networks. The third key element was the cable system created to meet local demand for the new satellite service.

AsiaSat-1, launched in 1990, was the first broadcasting satellite to cover the Asia Pacific region. It was the product of a highly successful Asian institutional tradition—that of Chinese private capitalist enterprise operating out of Hong Kong. Owned and operated by the entrepreneur Li Ka-Shing, it was available to national and private broadcasters alike across a region stretching from Turkey to Japan. But it was Li Ka-Shing's own Hong Kong-based broadcasting company Hutchison Whampoa that provided the broadcasting catalyst for the South Asian region in the form of Star TV (Satellite Television Asia Region).

Star TV combined entertainment, movies, sports and news in the English language for a television audience across East, South and South East Asia. It offered a programme mix of chat shows, quizzes, soap operas and serials. Though made originally largely for a western audience, these began to capture the imagination of the urban English-speaking TV audience, particularly in South Asia. The phenomenal success of Star in winning an audience in

India was a surprise to Star's own managers. India had not been a central target. But within six months, it was their largest market.[3] As cable connections multiplied, the monied and glamorous lifestyle, business intrigues and tangled personal relationships of the fictional characters of series such as *The Bold and the Beautiful* and *Santa Barbara* acquired an avid new following.

An assessment of the real impact of Star TV in India has to take account of the limitations imposed by the English language, in which all its output was screened until 1996. For middle class homes that were the first to acquire satellite dishes or cable connections in India, language was only a minor barrier. It is argued that although only 5 per cent of the Indian population may speak or understand English, even viewers who do not understand the language are attracted to American programming for its visual entertainment value. The same would be true of Pakistan or Bangladesh. Moreover, the political and social influence and economic weight of English speakers to some extent offsets their proportionally small numbers in India's total population, even within the middle class. The growing strength of other Hindi language channels, the relative success of Star's own Hindi output, and the impact of South Indian regional language channels suggest that English language programming for India has since become relatively marginalised. But the importance of the English-speaking audience in India for the profile of Star TV's English language programmes in Asia as a whole is indisputable.[4]

Of the AsiaSat channels beamed from Hong Kong, the Hindi language entertainment channel, Zee TV, can claim more than Star TV to have reinvented the medium for a mass Indian market. Zee's founder, Subhash Chandra, had run a family grain business in Haryana, and made a success of exporting rice to the Soviet Union in the early 1980s; he also ran a toothpaste packaging business and launched India's first amusement park. When, in 1992, he paid US$ 5 million to the owners of Star TV for a satellite channel, he had no previous media experience. But he had demonstrated a flair for 'dabbling in innovations before the market was quite ready for them'.[5] His achievement in making a profit within less than a year of its launch was highly unusual in the satellite TV business. In the partnership he entered into with Rupert Murdoch's News Corp in 1993, he retained a majority share. Within two years of entering the business, Subhash Chandra had himself become a major international player, and in 1999 he bought back the bulk of News Corp's share in Zee TV.

In India, the popularity of Zee TV helped the cable TV networks to expand from a cottage industry to a national media presence, opening India to plurality and competition in its own domestic TV environment and giving access to a showcase of international voices and images. The key selling point for this new channel was the one that made it specific to India and within India to the 400 million or more Hindi speakers. It was not just the appeal of the national language. The popular culture of the Mumbai-based Hindi cinema provided a readymade point of access to a mass audience beyond the Hindi-speaking heartland. Before the satellite era, Doordarshan had shown Hindi films sparingly to sweeten a more serious agenda. Zee TV made the Saturday night treat into a daily diet. TV was repackaged unashamedly as a medium of popular entertainment in which films and film-based programmes became the staple fare.

The key to Zee's success has been 'hindigenisation'—the adaptation of a general entertainment formula to the Hindi language, unlocking the north Indian market. It boosted the demand for cable connections in the metropolitan cities of the north and became a magnet for advertisers. Within nine months of coming on air, Zee was breaking even. In 1994, Zee had a 65 per cent share of the cable and satellite market to Star's 15 per cent; Zee's share peaked in 1995 at 72 per cent to Star's 11 per cent. The following year, Zee's share dropped to 60 per cent, losing to competition from Star, Sony Entertainment Television and, in South India, Sun TV. Zee appeared to have discovered a magic formula for a new and lucrative media industry. But as competition intensified, the magic was not easy for Zee to sustain or for others to imitate. The advertising market was growing fast, but not fast enough to sustain the number of channels dependent on it. Many of Zee's imitators struggled with their losses or fell by the wayside.[6] Sony was an exception. Despite a shaky start, it established a growing share of the market at the expense of Zee as well as Doordarshan.

REGIONAL VARIANTS

The Indian market has proved a spectacular success for the international channels. But a special feature of India's induction into the global television broadcasting market has been the richness of the regional programme variants within India itself.

In southern India, satellite channels have discovered their own niche independently of the national Indian market or the global English language channels. The Hindi language and Bombay film culture, which in northern India, Nepal, Pakistan and even in Bangladesh had opened the door to a mass audience, did not have the same mass appeal here. The southern Indian commercial channels broadcast on different satellites—Intelsat 703 and Intelsat 704. But the underlying story of commercial development is very similar, with the Tamil language entertainment channel Sun TV replicating the success of Zee TV in winning a mass satellite TV audience.

The Sun TV group is controlled by Kalanidhi Maran, son of Murasoli Maran, a politician and businessman with close links to the DMK, who was appointed commerce minister in the BJP-led government following the 1999 elections. Murasoli Maran is a nephew of DMK president and chief minister of Tamil Nadu, M. Karunanidhi, a moving force behind the channel. These political links foreshadowed a development new to television in India and one that would spread. The pull towards politicising the satellite media business was from two directions. On the one hand, regional and opposition politicians who did not have access to national TV were quick to grasp the reach and power of the new satellite medium. On the other, the channels themselves had an interest in the national regulatory decisions affecting their operations.

The DMK has relied heavily on mass communication to promote the party and Sun TV was initially seen as a DMK propaganda vehicle. Its name and logo reinforced this belief, as the DMK party symbol is the rising sun. Since the days of the party's founder, C.N. Annadurai, feature films have been used as a vehicle to convey the DMK ideology and Karunanidhi has himself written a number of film scripts. It was widely expected that Sun TV would try to support the DMK's sagging image in opposition. But the American-educated Kalanidhi Maran rejects the idea that a TV channel can or should play an overt political role.[7] With the introduction first of news programmes and then of a full news channel, Sun TV has contributed to raising political awareness in the state. It is sometimes partisan, but it does not unequivocally reflect the policies and ideologies of the DMK.

The channel started with a 3-hour transmission in April 1993; it was gradually increased to 12 hours and is today a 24-hour channel. From an initial investment of Rs. 2.5 million, Sun TV's success, like that of Zee TV, was rapid; the channel achieved a turnover of Rs. 200 million in 1994. In 1997, Sun TV netted an estimated Rs. 97 million in advertising revenue, making it the largest channel in the South and the most popular channel in Tamil Nadu. In the first year of its operations, 95 per cent of Sun TV's programmes were film based, a tactic that made good business sense in exploiting the high public interest in the cinema in Tamil Nadu. Maran acquired the rights for 800 movies. The initial heavy dependence on film programming was modified in subsequent years. By the time the Sun News channel was set up in 1999, film and film-based programmes accounted for just half the schedule.

The urge to add more channels has been a feature of Sun's business strategy, partly explained by its inability to replicate the success of its flagship channel. Sun's earlier experimentation with spinning off two special channels in the Tamil language, Sun Movies and Sun Music, did not prove very successful. Sun therefore started setting up channels in other southern languages. The group acquired controlling stakes in Gemini TV, a Telugu channel, and set up the Kannada-language Udaya TV. In March 1999, it also started a new Malayalam channel, Surya TV.

In early 2000, Sun remained the most commercially successful of Tamil channels, with a track record to match that of Zee in the north. Among its competitors, Vijay TV, which was bought by the Bombay software house UTV in 1999 and revamped to cater to the youth market, was never in the same commercial league, though it did attract attention for its support of the AIADMK and its leader Jayalalitha. It had been started by a drinks manufacturer, N.P.V. Ramaswamy Udayar, the owner of Golden Eagle brewery, and was later sold to Vijay Mallya, the flamboyant owner of the United Breweries Group, but neither was able to make money out of it. The only other private channel with a substantial following was Raj TV, which grew out of a video business owned by three Sri Lankan Tamil brothers. Founded in 1994, Raj TV was Sun's first serious competitor, with a largely film-based schedule in the early years. In March 1999, it systematically rescheduled its programmes to pit its most popular serials against Sun's prime time successes. It also started a second channel—Raj Plus—with a menu of films

and music aimed at the youth market. In this more intense competition, Raj succeeded in increasing its audience share, though
Sun remained the market leader.[8]

In Andhra Pradesh, the initiative for regional language TV
serving the Telugu-speaking population grew exceptionally out
of an existing and successful media enterprise—Ramoji Rao's
Eenadu group, of which Eenadu TV (launched in 1995) is a part.
Rao, like Murasoli Maran, has close political connections and
wields real influence in Andhra Pradesh. Besides running the
Eenadu newspaper, Rao's businesses include hospitality, entertainment, shipping, foods, the traditional insurance schemes known
as chit funds, and other financial services. It was Rao's *Eenadu*
newspaper that came to the rescue of former Andhra Pradesh chief
minister, N.T. Rama Rao, in the 1980s when the Telugu Desam
party chief was attempting to take on the Congress. Similarly,
Eenadu TV supported Chief Minister Chandrababu Naidu when
he raised the flag of revolt in 1995 against N.T. Rama Rao, his political mentor and father-in-law. By 1997, the channel's audience
was equivalent to more than half the television audience in Andhra
Pradesh.

The other Telugu language channel competing in Andhra
Pradesh is Gemini TV. The channel was the offshoot of a prosperous company providing facilities to the film and entertainment
industries in Mumbai. Its founder, Manohar Prasad, launched the
channel in association with Kalanidhi Maran of Sun TV. Like other
entertainment channels, it relies heavily on film-based programmes, with a focus in prime time on original Telugu serials
and serials drawn from Sun TV's Tamil output and dubbed into
Telugu. The formula brought substantial audience gains for the
channel between 1995 and 1997, especially among more prosperous households. Its audience figures, among all social groups,
are comparable to those of Eenadu TV.[9]

The Kannada language Udaya TV was started in the same year
as part of the Sun group and is managed by Dayanithi Maran,
another member of the same family. Udaya TV has filled a gap in
regional programmes in Kannada, but its reach is poor and it has
not fared well in competition with Doordarshan's Kannada channel. With lower advertising rates, Doordarshan in Bangalore earns
more than twice Udaya's advertising revenue. Industry sources
say that Udaya TV is making losses, although Maran denies this.

Run on the same lines as Sun TV, with many programmes remakes of popular Sun TV fare, Udaya also offers a staple diet of movies and movie-based entertainment programmes. There is a ban on dubbed serials in Karnataka, which has added greatly to the channel's programme costs. Ramanand Sagar's enormously successful epic *Ramayana*, originally shown on Doordarshan, was aired by other private channels in Hindi and dubbed in regional languages, but for the Karnataka audience, Udaya TV was obliged to re-film the whole drama in the Kannada language.

Highly literate Kerala gave birth to Asianet, a channel which relied less on films and film-based programmes and paid more attention to news, current affairs and documentaries. It was a difference of emphasis rather than a totally different format, but it displayed a seriousness about the business of broadcasting which its founder director Sashi Kumar attributed to the special character of the Keralite audience, its political consciousness and its interest in news.[10] Until 1999, Asianet competed in the Kerala market only against Doordarshan's Malayalam channel and its success in pioneering a blend of entertainment and public interest programmes was taken as an exemplar for others. When Sun TV entered the market with its own Malayalam channel, however, competitive pressures increased. In November 1999, Asianet sold its cable interests in Kerala to the Mumbai-based Sindhi business group Hathway Investments. Five months later, it signed a memorandum of understanding with Zee TV, which transferred a 51 per cent controlling interest in the company to the north Indian entrepreneur.[11] This left Tamil Nadu and Andhra Pradesh as the only southern states with locally-controlled satellite TV channels and illustrated the growing pace of media consolidation across India.

The southern regional channels, as majority Indian owned enterprises, have been quick to take advantage of the 1998 legislation allowing uplinking from Indian soil. The perception that this was a growth area was enhanced when new regional language channels were started in Marathi, Gujarati, Punjabi and Bengali by Zee TV and others. But until 2000, no north Indian entrepreneur had attempted to confront Sun TV in its own strong Tamil market, nor had Sun, despite its commercial success, ventured into the highly competitive Hindi market. With Zee's decision, as part of its new deal with Asianet, to launch new channels in Kannada, Telugu and Tamil, the scene was set for a much more competitive phase in the South.

GLOBAL NEWS IN SOUTH ASIA

Initially, few concessions were made by the international channels to the varied cultural traditions of the countries within AsiaSat's massive footprint. CNN was the first in the field as an international news channel. The BBC's 24-hour news and information channel on the Star network gave an alternative perspective and made a start in incorporating programmes designed for the Asian region. It was some years before CNN began to focus on Asia as a market and as a theatre for news reporting. Its Asian production centre in Hong Kong was opened in 1995—ten years after the channel's launch. By 1998, seven of its thirty-six news bureaus worldwide were in the Asia Pacific region—two in South East Asia (Bangkok and Jakarta) and one in South Asia (New Delhi). Despite its reputation as a global news channel, CNN was slower than other international stations in Asia in extricating itself from the North America-centred agenda of its news programmes. Four programmes on the CNN schedule were specifically tailored for Asian audiences—all of them launched after the opening of the Hong Kong production centre in 1995. None of these were specifically targeted to South Asia or to the Indian audience.

In the field of regional programming for South Asia, other broadcasters were taking the lead. The rapid growth of the East and South East Asian 'tiger' economies before the collapse of 1997 put Asian regional television in the forefront of media and marketing expansion. Asian regional TV was seen as the fastest growing market place. In an area of high investment, television could be the most effective means of reaching key decision-makers. Deregulation was set to provide new opportunities for broadcasters in a previously government-dominated information environment.[12] International cross border broadcasting would encourage trade between Asian countries and provide a flexible reaction to the accelerating process of change.

A new genre of business television programming, as developed by the Singapore-based Asian Business News International (ABNI), was a form of niche broadcasting or 'narrow casting' which took advantage of the global reach of satellite channels and their ability to address themselves to specific audiences within the Asian region. Within that niche there was a dual target: viewers and opinion-formers as well as potential investors. Programming specific to the region was identified as the best means to reach them both.

In the boom of the early 1990s, ABNI conceived and implemented ambitious and expensive regional news gathering aims with the help of local partners. These were scaled down in 1996–97 and the channel was merged with CNBC in February 1998. ABNI developed a policy of commissioning business programmes from independent production companies such as India's TV18. It carried items from 'Pakistan Business Update', a product of the largest independent film and TV production company in Pakistan—the Karachi-based EverReady Company. This gave the channel a distinctive South Asian flavour and was an important influence in developing international links among India's new and expanding independent software production houses. TV18, founded by Raghav Bahl, was also the first independent Indian programme supplier to the BBC World Service.

The nature of globalisation in the 1990s underlined the importance of strategic alliances between broadcasters, or between broadcaster and distributor, and the short-lived nature of some of those agreements. CNN has been through several stages of experimentation in the South Asian region: it has operated independently and in collaboration with private and public broadcasters in the region. It opened its New Delhi bureau in 1992 with small-scale collaboration agreements. One of them, in January 1993, was an agreement with the private company New Delhi Television (NDTV) for selected news coverage to be shown on Doordarshan's national network. From this small beginning, NDTV, headed by Prannoy Roy, has now become one of the most prominent and successful private TV news organisations.

Turner International, the CNN parent company, negotiated successfully in 1995, in competition with the BBC, for a partnership with Doordarshan, making CNN the first private broadcaster to be allowed on an Indian satellite—INSAT 2B. The agreement was revoked within two years, leaving CNN where it was before. In 1995, CNN initiated a 24-hour broadcast with the private company Dynavision in Sri Lanka. It also had a terrestrial re-broadcast agreement with Shalimar Television Network—a majority owned government subsidiary of the national TV broadcaster in Pakistan—and a re-broadcasting agreement with Bangladesh TV, which was suspended in 1998.

Unlike other international broadcasters, CNN has been wary of subcontracting programmes to private production companies. Similarly, TNT (now TCM) and Cartoon Network has relied on its extensive library of Hollywood movies and cartoons to fill its schedules without any significant local input from any part of Asia. While CNN has remained a small niche broadcaster in South Asia, TNT and Cartoon Network have been able to disregard the maxim 'act locally' in reaching a children's audience across the subcontinent. This success was a significant social and cultural development from which advertisers and marketing consultants drew practical conclusions for media planning.

The BBC's international television service has been heavily constrained financially by the terms of the BBC's charter and its financial obligations as the British domestic public service broadcaster. Launched in Asia under a contract to Star, the BBC lost both the contract and its place on the AsiaSat carrier satellite when Rupert Murdoch's News Corp bought a controlling share of the network in 1993 and the BBC ceased to fit with the strategy for Asia of Star's new owners. It was a demonstration of the regional and local exigencies of the new globalism that although in Europe the BBC and Murdoch had been able to reach a collaboration agreement, in Asia their plans did not match.

Like CNN, the BBC negotiated its own agreement for terrestrial links with national and private broadcasters. It lost to CNN on the elusive and short-lived prize of a re-broadcasting agreement with Doordarshan. Other South Asian countries such as Bangladesh were happy to balance their co-operation with CNN with the BBC, to some extent playing one off against the other and keeping windows open to both.

The loss of its place on the AsiaSat satellite was an inconvenience for the BBC, but by the time it took effect in March 1996 satellite transponder capacity was no longer at a premium. An important factor for an international broadcaster to India and South Asia was that cable operators should have comparable access to the satellite signal. The American PanAmSat satellite PAS-4 provided this. It put the BBC in good company, sharing a satellite with other international broadcasters interested in the South Asian audience, including CNN and the soon-to-be-merged ABNI/CNBC. But going it alone and securing advertisements on its own was not an easy option for the BBC. It could provide news services to other broadcasters but it was never in the driving seat itself. There were also problems of accountability. Though the BBC's commercial arm, BBC Worldwide, created in 1996, was separated from the publicly financed domestic television services and World Service radio, the news operations were closely integrated.

The BBC's partnership with the Hong Kong-based Hutchison Whampoa Group in providing a news and information channel for the Star TV Network was a radical departure for the British public service broadcaster. At the time, for both Star and the BBC, the alliance was one of mutual advantage. The BBC gained the opportunity to launch a rival 24-hour TV news network to CNN without government funding. For Star, the BBC gave a serious news profile to the network in bringing an established broadcaster with a high international reputation to what was primarily an entertainment network.

But once Rupert Murdoch gained control, the Star-BBC alliance was short-lived. The BBC was dropped first from the northern beam of the AsiaSat satellite (which delivered the Star signal to China and East Asia) and later from the southern beam serving India and South Asia. In the first case, Chinese government objections to BBC news coverage threatened the distribution of the Star network in China, where cable distribution—and the government control that allowed it—was actively promoted by the Chinese government. In the second case, the BBC was not so much a commercial or political embarrassment (though it always had that potential as the coverage of the destruction of the Babri Masjid at Ayodhya by Hindu activists in December 1992 had shown), but was superfluous to Star's own development strategy, which was to emphasise regional rather than international news.

The BBC had long realised in radio broadcasting that the attraction of an international broadcaster lay in its ability to provide not only global news but regionally focussed programming. It was a lesson which Star took to heart in launching its 24-hour news channel aimed primarily at the Indian market. The very large cable and satellite audiences for Star's comprehensive coverage of the national elections in 1996 and 1998 gave a sharp edge of topicality and interest to its regional profile, though the heavy investment involved was part of a long-term strategy and not geared to short-term profitability.

In another collaboration, the BBC signed a deal to supply Hindi news programmes to Home TV, one of the less successful Indian entertainment channels, which was cancelled in early 1998 leading to the disbandment of the BBC Hindi news team which had been based in Delhi. This setback put paid for the time being to the BBC's hopes of establishing itself in the growth area of Indian television in South Asia—regional language channels.

A plan for strategic co-operation announced in 1997 between the BBC and Discovery channel, seemed a more promising partnership. These were two channels with established reputations as public service broadcasters in the widest sense. There was much common ground between a publicly funded organisation such as the BBC with a growing commercial arm and a commercial organisation such as Discovery with a programming strategy comfortably in step with public service broadcasting objectives.

As news and information acquired more prominence in the programme strategy of Star and other major channels, it also became more central to their perceived impact on South Asian societies and to government attitudes to their regulation. Much of the dynamism and effectiveness of these channels was derived from their employment of Indian production companies like NDTV. After its initial collaboration with CNN, NDTV had been contracted to provide current affairs programmes for Doordarshan as a means of upgrading the national broadcaster's news profile, and it was after proving itself in that arena that it was subsequently commissioned to provide Star TV's new 24-hour news service in English and Hindi. Doordarshan's own role in outsourcing programmes and in encouraging private production companies played an important part in creating the expertise which was later to enable Star TV to make its powerful debut as an independent regional news provider.

Among India's northern neighbours, Pakistan was quick to realise and exploit the possibilities offered by direct satellite broadcasting. It did not have its own technology, but in 1992 it hired a transponder for PTV on the AsiaSat-1 satellite. This gave Pakistan the opportunity to broadcast information, propaganda and entertainment to India, to other parts of South Asia and to the Gulf, where hundreds of thousands of Pakistanis were employed. At home, both Pakistan and Bangladesh were receptive to agreements with foreign channels allowing state TV to re-broadcast parts of their output. But there was no government encouragement for private entrepreneurs interested in investing in satellite channels and in Pakistan none of these plans came to anything. Not until 1998 did the Pakistan government respond to the popularity of the Hindi channels with the launch of PTV World with a brief to meet Pakistani entertainment and cultural needs among the South Asian diaspora.

In Bangladesh, the viability of an audience for a Bengali channel reaching over the political boundaries to Bengali speakers in India and Bangladesh was openly debated. In 1997, plans by a Bangladeshi businessman to set up a Bengali channel uplinked from Singapore collapsed in the wake of a financial scandal over one of his other business ventures.[13] In 1998, ATN launched a channel under Bangladeshi management aimed at the all-Bengali market with some success despite the poor quality of the programming. In the same year, the Bangladesh government invited tenders and awarded an exclusive license to a private company—both for a second terrestrial channel and eventually a satellite channel.

Elsewhere in the region, Sri Lanka and Nepal did nothing to move into satellite broadcasting. The Sri Lankan strategy was to licence new terrestrial channels and to leave the selection of satellite programmes to them. While India banned uplinking from its own territory, there was a temporary window of opportunity for Nepal in providing facilities for TV channels broadcasting to the Indian market. Some entrepreneurs recognised the possibilities. BITV, the TV venture of Ashok Advani's Business India group, was actively planning a bouquet of channels centred on a news and information service to be uplinked from Nepal. But there were problems with the Russian satellite and after long delays the deal fell through; eventually a single channel was launched as TVi, up-linked from Singapore.[14]

So the South Asian countries outside India were not prime movers in the satellite revolution. They were on the receiving end of programming devised primarily either for an Indian or an international audience. It was a largely passive role as Indian cultural products secured unchallenged dominance in the market. This dominance was not acquired because India was more permissive in its regulatory framework than the other countries. The main reason was the size of the potential market, indicated by the number who spoke different Indian languages and the spending power of consumers within those language communities. But the key to tapping the market and to the influence of the satellite media was the means and cost of distribution.

THE DISTRIBUTION CHAIN IN INDIA

It may have been CNN that alerted the world and the countries of South Asia to the global phenomenon of direct satellite TV broadcasting, but in South Asia the number of those who could watch it was small. The potential audience for an international news channel in English was significant for those who formed opinion in all the countries of the subcontinent. But the satellite revolution of the 1990s in India took a different course to its immediate neighbours. This was not because of a more advanced technology, but an unforeseen combination of local enterprise and regionally-focussed entertainment programming. Local entrepreneurs set up local cable networks as a cottage industry for the electronic age. It started in Mumbai and spread rapidly to the other major metropolitan cities and large towns of India. The entertainment provided by this new distribution system was the popular culture of the Bombay film industry. The first channel to provide this—Zee TV—provided the momentum to the penetration of cable. It was the cable network in turn that transformed satellite television from a private facility for wealthy homes to a mass entertainment and communication phenomenon.[15]

The first cable operations in Mumbai were started in 1981 by Ronnie Screwala, head of what was to become one of the two largest independent software production houses in India. But the retail cable enterprises which spawned today's multi-million rupee business started in 1987 distributing films on video. These pioneering enterprises are dubbed affectionately by corporate executives as 'mom and pop operations'.[16] It could not at that time be properly described as a network. Individual entrepreneurs were using makeshift technology; there was neither infrastructure nor the most rudimentary common technical standards. There was no licence, legal framework or institutional protection. Cable operators served purely local needs and they had to provide their own protection. The boundaries of their operations were defined by local competition or physical boundaries such as roads which could not have a wire strung across them. They were dependent on ingenuity and initiative, and indigenous manufacturing capacity. Their managerial tasks included providing protection for their facilities and enforcing the collection of subscription fees from reluctant customers. Within these limited boundaries, the operator provided a very profitable service to 200-300 subscribers, initially with a single channel.

The service spread quickly in the metropolitan cities. In Calcutta, for example, by the end of 1994 there were some 300,000 households with cable connections. The registered association of cable operators in the city had 3000 members. From the start the cable operators were locked in competition with each other. The cable operators' association aimed to promote co-operation between its members, and organised exhibitions and technical conferences. They aimed to improve the cable operators' technical capacity and negotiating position. Smaller companies saw advantages in mergers, which enabled them to increase the number of channels on offer. But the process of consolidation was not rapid everywhere. Even in 1998 there were more than 1800 members of the cable operators' associations in Pune.[17]

The early stages of the cable enterprise had shown that cable was the gateway to a mass market. When Zee set up Siti Cable in 1995 to provide support for the Zee channel, cable was still an unorganised and non-formal business. In investing in the company, Zee's motivation as a broadcaster was to seek control over the channels of distribution, both of its own and rival channels. Siti had the initiative and the resources to meet the growing demand for the rapidly increasing numbers of TV channels. But Siti recognised that the existing cable operators had shown aggressive entrepreneurship in setting up their businesses and it wooed them with assurances that its aim was not to get rid of them but to organise them on a professional basis. In adopting the concept of franchising, Siti saw itself as the wholesaler, while the cable operator worked like a retailer.[18]

In the initial stages of satellite television, with most of the channels available free to air, only the cable entrepreneurs were sure of making money. The long-term objective of Siti and of its rival

cable company, the Hinduja-owned Indus Group InCable Net, was
to develop an infrastructure for a market for subscription TV.
The attempt by Siti and other big cable operators to reconcile
these objectives with the interests of small cable operators was
only partially successful. Forming themselves into associations,
small operators put up stiff resistance to the takeover of the business they had established. They protested vigorously at what they
regarded as underhand tactics adopted by Siti and other big companies to persuade them to give up their independence and become franchisees.

In September 1995, cable operators blacked out advertisements
on the Zee channels in protest against the entry of Siti Cable into
Calcutta. Local cable TV operators united to form their own powerful master control rooms across the city, with a network by then
of 500,000 viewers.[19] The Delhi Cable Operators Association criticised Siti for not keeping its undertakings either to the small
operators or the government; they rejected the claim that the bigger
companies invest more in better equipment; they also made alle-
gations of sabotage which the bigger companies dismissed.

The cable operators argued that their customers would not pay
for extra channels on a continuing basis, though by 1999 this reluctance was beginning to dissolve.[20] More channel operators such
as Star, ESPN and Zee were encrypting their specialist sports and
entertainment channels. As Table 3.1 shows, throughout the 1990s,
subscription and access fees formed about half of the commercial
revenues from television and the bulk of that went to the cable
operators. But pay-TV was giving some of the control over distribution back to the broadcasters.

Table 3.1   TV Commercial Revenues (Actual and Forecast)

						(Rs. million)
	1995	*1997*	*1999*	*2001*	*2003*	*2005*
Ad revenue	6,008	10,531	18,381	30,108	45,831	64,457
Subscription & access fees	7,346	11,766	19,251	30,513	45,026	63,981
Total commercial revenue	13,354	22,296	37,922	61,043	91,444	129,236
TV households (million)	49	55	65	80	98	120

Source: Extracted from Salomon Smith Barney's report on Indian Television.
Published in *Financial Express*, Mumbai, 12 February 1998.

Elsewhere in the world, cable channels co-exist with broadcasters to their mutual advantage. On the whole, cable operators neither charge broadcasters for carrying channels on prime band nor do they pay the broadcasters for channels which are free to air. But with some exceptions, the channels broadcasting to India have been losing money. Until pay-TV is well established, it is only the distributors who are confident of making a good profit. This is a source of conflict and resentment among the broadcasters. The film industry also strongly resents the cable industry making a substantial part of its profits from pirated films.[21]

The cable distribution system in Tamil Nadu, a network of local small time operators, was similar to the north Indian cities but was slower to develop. Sun TV's initiative in offering cable operators instalment schemes on behalf of the makers of dish antennae was in large part responsible for the high cable and satellite penetration in Tamil Nadu—53 per cent of TV-owning households by 1997.

Siti Cable has had considerable success in Andhra. Its service in Hyderabad, where it installed India's first pilot addressable system, was judged by one advertising professional the best cable network in the country.[22] But in general there has been less consolidation and franchising by big cable operators in south Indian cities and towns than in north and west India. In the south, small cable operators are trying to expand their reach by forming networks and localising their coverage through their own cable services. Chennai, Coimbatore and Thiruvananthapuram already have entrepreneurs successfully running such community channels.

In Kerala, the Malayalam channel and cable network, Asianet, developed in a more organised way. It was the first TV cable company to negotiate a ten-year co-operation agreement with a government agency—in this case the Kerala State Electricity Board. It allowed the company to use the same poles which carry the state electric power supply for the distribution of cable TV. It was an early indication of the possible synergies and common purpose between separate institutions responsible for now converging communications technologies. Though Kerala is less extensively cabled than either Tamil Nadu or Andhra Pradesh (only 32 cent per of the rural and urban population is able to receive cable at home), Asianet claims 40 per cent of the subscriptions in the state.[23]

Cable operation was the first part of the new media that the Indian government attempted to regulate. In an attempt to give some guidelines to an unregulated industry, in 1993 the government reached an understanding at an all-India level with the Cable Operators Federation of India (COFI), which was formalised in the 1995 *Cable Regulation Act*. Since cable operators were the only part of the broadcasting chain subject to regulation, the act placed a disproportionate burden of responsibility on them for controlling the content of the channels. This is seen as deflecting the responsibility for the content of programmes from the broadcaster to the cable operator.[24] In the advertising industry, it is acknowledged that the cable operators are an influential lobby, and given their legal obligations to transmit signals as they receive them, it is not realistic to hold them responsible. They are, however, responsive to temporary administrative pressures.[25]

CABLE IN BANGLADESH

TV satellite channels had arrived in Bangladesh in the early 1990s as wealthy homes, attracted by the entertainment on offer, installed a dish antenna to receive them. The legality of this satellite reception was uncertain from the start. Most of the dishes had been smuggled in through customs loopholes. Existing laws did not cover the technological needs and no legislative changes were introduced to fill the gap.

The initial response of the public to satellite TV was negative. Popular perception saw satellite TV as a vehicle for numerous alien cultures; there was a danger of being swamped. The middle class, who could not afford the dishes, led the protest, but this had no effect in excluding the new sources of information and entertainment. The foreign channels highlighted the culturally one-sided nature of satellite TV. 'We don't seem to exist there', a Bangladeshi editor complained.[26]

In some respects, there are close parallels between the cable industry in Bangladesh and that in India. The status of cable operators is not formalised; as was the case in India until 1995, they are neither legal nor illegal. Negotiations between the Bangladesh government and the cable operators for a licensing system, which began in 1994, had by the end of the 1990s still not resolved their legal status. The bigger entrepreneurs in the business remain powerful. The operators want legitimacy; they see themselves as especially vulnerable to the representatives of the transnational broadcasters. The most significant relationship they have is with the viewers, but the government does not appear to consider them an influential sector.[27]

The cable industry in Bangladesh started in 1992 with a few small networks working for a single company. This company—Translinks—began as a franchisee of the Star group. After actively marketing them for some time, the company's owner, Humayun Akhtar, gave up his rights to most of the Star channels except for ESPN/Star Sports. Akhtar claimed that the programmes were 'anti-national culturally and anti-Islamic'.[28] However, he continued to maintain active business relations with the Star group and continued to sell decoders to cable operators for the sports channels.

The company developed as a small conglomerate, establishing a stake in every aspect of the satellite TV industry from programme franchises to manufacturing satellite dishes. It had the market monopoly of satellite reception equipment and claimed to have produced 30,000 dishes in the six years till 1998. Importing 90 per cent of the basic equipment, the company manufactured the dishes required for establishing a cable operation and acquired the rights to the most important programmes. It had a dominant position until the late 1990s, when other players with international connections entered the market.

Most of the cable operators have little education. Their capacity to survive in a volatile and insecure business depends to some extent on their muscle power. As one put it '…when a rival supplier is hooking another line, he may chop mine and then offer better services. If he knows that I have muscle, he will not do it.'[29] Competition means customers can afford to choose and are quick to complain; expectations are high and operators run on low profit margins.[30] At the same time, in the wealthier parts of Dhaka there is a growing demand for improved quality of reception and service.

In Bangladesh, as in India, there is a strong mutual dependence between broadcasters and cable operators. To reach a mass audience, broadcasters are dependent on the cable operators making their channel available. The cable operators, in turn, are answerable to their clientele for the channels they provide and if they fail to provide a popular channel, the customer goes elsewhere.

The Bangladesh experience reflects the much larger battle for consolidation and control of the cable business that has been conducted in India since the 1995 *Cable Regulation Act* was passed. When cable operators in Bangladesh attempted to set up a united front to improve their negotiating position, Translinks set up a rival association.[31]

This was a battle in whose outcome the government had little direct interest. Cable companies were seen to be providing mainly entertainment; they were not broadcasting news or views critical of the government. Bangladesh state television was at that time re-broadcasting BBC and CNN. Clearly there was no perceived cultural or political threat in what was broadcast .

There is no doubt that the influence of cable in urban areas is growing. But the most obvious gap in the cable business in Bangladesh has been the lack of expertise and professionalism; there are few trained technicians. Their potential as community level broadcasters has been limited by their equipment, capacity and mentality. But media observers believe that they could, in time, play that role.[32]

CABLE IN NEPAL

In Nepal, both the national public broadcasting service—Nepal TV—and private television distribution services owe much to the enterprise of one man, Neer Shah, the first head of Nepal TV and later chairman of Shangri-La, a film production and microwave TV distribution company. His career and interests brought together private and public involvement in the field of television broadcasting in a way that became almost a pattern for the 1990s.

In using microwave technology to create a TV home distribution service, Shangri-La was the pioneer in South Asia; similar systems subsequently operated in Pakistan and Sri Lanka. The technology is well suited to providing a service when subscribers are thin on the ground. Unlike with cable, a connection can be made immediately, but the system requires an expensive decoder and this proves a major drawback in two ways. It limits customers to those who can afford to buy the decoder. It also exposes the service to pirated decoders. For every official subscriber, Shah estimates there are four to five unofficial users, fatally undermining the profitability of the business.

As a result, despite the advantages of microwave technology and of being first in the field, Shah's company has lost ground to a more recent competitor. He is Jamim Shah, a young entrepreneur who set up a cable distribution system in Kathmandu with American equipment capable of being adapted to fibre optics and to digital TV. By mid-1998 he was providing access to twenty-two channels to a claimed 65,000 subscribers in Kathmandu, and had formed ambitious plans to cable the main urban centres in Nepal. Though his operation was set up before the Broadcasting Act was passed, he appears to have been given an extraordinary licence allowing him to establish a cable system, to re-broadcast any international channel, to broadcast his own channel in Nepal and to uplink his own programmes.

The smaller extent of cable operation networks in Nepal makes comparisons with India unrealistic. There are small neighbourhood cable services characterised by low capital investment and primitive technology. But by the time cable started, the potential of the market had been demonstrated in India. The Nepalese government had put a regulatory system in place and large-scale cable plans had won government support. Jamim Shah's enterprise, like Translinks in Bangladesh, has taken advantage of the confidence that the package of mutually reinforcing services that he offers will not be inhibited by government anti-monopoly regulations. While in India, for want of clear broadcasting legislation, even big companies hesitated to invest in addressability because competition was poorly regulated, in Nepal, licensing restrictions did not present an obstacle to a cable company moving into the newest areas of telecommunications and media development. Jamim Shah later started his own cable channel, which relied largely on local films and offered little original programming.

DISTRIBUTION IN PAKISTAN

Estimates of the number of people watching television in Pakistan have until recently been largely informed guesswork. Although

Pakistan, unlike India, retains a system of licensing for television sets, the number of licenses is not even an approximate guide to the number of households with sets or the number of viewers who have access to them, so official statistics are little help. The number of television licences is only 2.5 million, whereas on the basis of surveys up to 1999 the Pakistani affiliate of Gallup International estimates between 8 and 10 million sets.

With 20 per cent of the population having no access to electricity, the overall reach of television is considerably lower than in India. But access to satellite TV, which Gallup estimates at 13 per cent of the adult population or 8.5 million adults, is on par with the Indian experience. Because of Pakistan's geographical location, dishes are smaller and cheaper than further south—in India and Sri Lanka—and affordable by a wider section of the population.

According to Ijaz Gilani of Gallup, in terms of actual numbers, viewing is 'about the same in rural and urban Pakistan'. A greater proportion of urban Pakistanis watch satellite TV, but viewing in community centres in the rural areas brings up the total numbers there. Moreover, by early 1999, the growth rate in urban areas appeared to be slowing down, while in rural areas the novelty of satellite had not yet worn off and the number of dishes was still increasing.[33]

It is in Pakistan's largest metropolitan city, Karachi, that satellite television is viewed most intensively. Karachi is home to the largest concentration of Urdu-speaking Muhajirs, who migrated from India at independence and who relish the new links with India which satellite makes possible. Karachi is also the only Pakistani city with developed cable systems which can compare with those in India. Some of these were set up in the 1970s, when videos gave Pakistanis a chance to access Indian films easily at home. Since the arrival of satellite, however, cable systems have spread to most of the lower middle class and working class areas. The cabling of more prosperous suburbs has lagged behind poorer localities and has been developed by larger commercial concerns. Apartment buildings in Karachi's Clifton, Defence, Gulshan and other areas are now receiving cable television. But most of these services are operated without official sanction and no figures are forthcoming.[34]

Cable television in Pakistan is notionally subject to strict controls. But until early 2000, when the military government began to address the issue of licensing cable operators, there was no separate cable law or regulatory authority; cable operators lived in the same kind of legal limbo that existed in India before 1995. By 2000, cable systems had begun to spread to Lahore and Islamabad but not on a scale to rival the appeal of direct transmissions. Until that time, the only legal satellite TV distribution system in Pakistan was a pay-TV system run by Javaid Pasha's Shaheen Pay TV Company, which is an affiliate of the Shaheen Board, a charity run by retired air force personnel. The pay-TV system uses a microwave system similar to that installed in Kathmandu. It gives excellent quality, but the decoder costs almost as much as a satellite dish and fewer channels are available. There is also a charge for the service, while few pay the license fee for a satellite dish, and government censorship regulations apply. This can result in the unpredictable obliteration of parts of programmes.

In India, the market which the new satellite channels aim for is loosely described as middle class. Detailed studies have demonstrated that this definition embraces a very wide range of income and patterns of consumption. The higher end of the market for luxury consumer goods is a small proportion of this 'middle class'. We look at these definitions for India in more detail in the next chapter. In Pakistan, just 16 per cent of households had an income of above Rs. 7,000 in 1998 and only about 8 per cent had an income of over Rs. 15,000 a month. One and a half million owned telephones and fewer than 20 per cent of this figure had an income of more than Rs. 20,000 per month–the business and executive elite. Of this elite, about 100,000 owned a satellite dish, slightly fewer than those owning computers.[35] The actual numbers of wealthy people are very much smaller than in India and very few of the advertised goods are available. But the satellite channels have achieved a very high level of penetration and put the state broadcaster, Pakistan TV, under considerable pressure.

CABLE IN SRI LANKA

Sri Lanka, as we have seen, has absorbed the impact of the satellite revolution in ways different to its neighbours. The rapid extension of media competition in Sri Lanka dates from 1992, when the Maharaja group, a Tamil business house close to President

Premadasa, launched an entertainment channel called Maharaja TV (MTV). This was followed in 1993 by TNL, whose proprietor, Shan Wickremesinghe, had been involved in the first TV transmissions more than a decade earlier. MTV, which collaborated initially with Singapore Telecom, soon became the slicker of the two channels, though politically it remained very cautious. Much of MTV's programming was imported from Europe and America, supplemented by relays of BBC World Service international news bulletins. TNL's programmes were more innovative, though less well endowed and well presented.

Neither cable nor satellite dishes have played a big part in the distribution of local and international television programming. Small time cable operators who have played a major role in India and Bangladesh have not been in evidence in Sri Lanka. But that is not to say that the technology is irrelevant, and recently the business possibilities of cable and microwave for TV distribution have begun to attract investment and foreign collaboration.

Sri Lanka's first pay-TV channel, Channel Nine, set up in 1998 with Australian collaboration, is not, strictly speaking, a cable network. Its nine different services are based on the same MMDS microwave technology used in Pakistan and Nepal. A second channel inaugurated towards the end of 1998 is a business investment promoted by a public company based in Canada in partnership with a Sri Lankan government agency.[36] Another venture—Cable TV Network (Pvt) Ltd—planned to present an information and entertainment package initially of thirty channels, including Star TV, ESPN and Star Sports, with provision to add other speciality or niche channels later.[37] The lead entrepreneur, Chandran Ratnam, advertised his intention 'to pay special attention to education and children's programmes, in addition to the greatest movies that Hollywood can offer.'[38]

The cost of dishes and the nature of urban living may have been partly responsible for Sri Lanka's failure to develop cable systems, but the government's diversification policy has also played a part. By the time satellite services in Tamil and Hindi had acquired popularity in India, Sri Lanka already had four or five terrestrial stations competing against each other, picking and choosing from satellite menus and re-broadcasting some of the programmes to Sri Lankan audiences. This made the development of cable systems less of a commercial attraction than elsewhere in South Asia.

Most Sri Lankans watch satellite television on the island's terrestrial TV networks, particularly the commercial channels; they watch foreign programmes, not foreign channels. This does not eliminate sensationalism or controversy, nor quite widespread soul-searching about some of the programmes being scheduled, but the controversies have been more to do with bold treatment of Sri Lankan subjects than about *Baywatch* or the violence of Hindi movies. There has been less talk of cultural invasion and a greater welcome of the extension of choice.

THE SOUTH ASIAN TELEVISION MARKET

The choice of satellites and the availability of transponders was increasing throughout the 1990s; and with digitisation costs were falling. At the end of the decade, the principal satellites servicing South Asia for the international networks were PanAmSat4 (PAS-4), which carried among others the merged ABNI/CNBC business news transmission from Singapore, Sony Entertainment Television, BBC World and CNN International. The two AsiaSat satellites, AsiaSat-1 and AsiaSat-2, continued to carry Star TV out of Hong Kong, as well CNBC/NBC (on AsiaSat-2), the Zee group of channels and Pakistan's second government channel, PTV 2. Intelsat 703 and 704 carried the main commercial channels for South India. APSTAR 1, launched in 1994 leased transponders to a consortium including CNN International, the leading international sports channel ESPN Asia, TNT and Cartoon Network, as well as the Discovery Channel. The same satellite carried American channels adapted for the Asian market such as Disney (Asia Pacific), the US movie channel Home Box Office (HBO Asia), and the youth music channel, MTV Asia, with its offshoots customised for Chinese and Indian youth, MTV Mandarin and MTV India.

In 1990, the state broadcasters had been broadcasting almost exclusively to national audiences. By the end of the decade, a growing proportion of television audiences had access to a wide choice of channels. But the spread, both of TV ownership and satellite access, was uneven within the region and within India itself.

Table 3.2 shows that the proportion of TV sets available to viewers in India and Pakistan is very similar; it may even be slightly higher in Pakistan. In Sri Lanka, the proportion is almost twice either of them. But the overwhelming majority, both of homes with TV and of those with cable and satellite, across South Asia is in India. The dominance of the Indian market for TV advertisers in the region is based on this numerical superiority. Table 3.3 demonstrates, however, that in India the print media still attract over 60 per cent of advertising funds—nearly twice that of Pakistan or Sri Lanka—whereas in both Pakistan and Sri Lanka the proportion of advertising expenditure on television compared to other media is much higher than in India. Radio remains an important advertising medium in Sri Lanka, and in Nepal it exceeds the television share. In Bangladesh, the press share of advertising is significantly higher than in Pakistan and Sri Lanka, but lower than in India. Despite its dominance in the South Asian television market, television in India has the lowest share of advertising.

Table 3. 2   Urban Penetration of TV/CableTV in South Asia

Country	TV Homes (in millions)	TV Sets per 1000	Radio Sets (in millions)	Radio Sets per 1000	C&S Homes (in millions)
India	63.20	67.00	111.00	120.00	18.40
Pakistan	9.00	68.00	6.00	50.00	0.80
Bangladesh	1.50	13.46	4.30	38.67	0.38
Sri Lanka	2.25	125.00	0.5+	NA	–
Nepal	0.10	5.42	2.2+	110.00	0.07
Total	76.05	–	124.00	–	19.65

+ Licensed sets only.
Sources: India: Doordarshan Audience Research Unit (1998).
       Pakistan: Gallup Pakistan (PAS97).
       Bangladesh: National Media Survey OMQ (1998).
       Sri Lanka: SRL FactFile (1998).
       Nepal: ORG-MARG MSA Project Estimates; Asian Communication Handbook (1998). (Also for India, Pakistan, Bangladesh and Sri Lanka.)

Table 3.3   Percentage Share of Advertising Expenditure by Media in South Asia (1997)

Media	Bangladesh	India	Nepal	Pakistan	Sri Lanka
TV	37	26	19	49.0	47
Press	45	61	60	35.0	31
Radio	6	2	21	2.5	22
Other	12	11	–	13.5	–

(Table 3.3 contd.)

(Table 3.3 contd.)

Sources: Bangladesh: ADCOMM and other advertising agencies.
Carat India.
Nepal: S.P. Singh Research.
Pakistan: Pakistan Advertising Scene (PAS).
Sri Lanka: SRL FactFile.

The huge Indian market also has to be differentiated according to the penetration of television, the available of cable and satellite services, and according to language. Distinct language markets have developed in different parts of the country, particularly in the South, and some of them are as large as the markets in smaller South Asian countries. Tables 3.4 and 3.5 show estimates of the TV audience and the audience for cable and satellite, by region and by state respectively.

Table 3.4   Indian TV: Regional Distribution

Region	Audience for all TV (in millions)			No. of TV Homes/Sets		C&S Homes (in millions)	
	Urban	Rural	Total	Urban	Rural	Urban only (NRS-97)	Urban + Rural (IRS-99)
India (North)	39.5	42.3	81.8	–	–	2.70	3.80
India (West)	50.8	33.2	84.0	–	–	5.54	7.20
India (South)	58.5	39.0	97.5	–	–	4.93	9.40
India (East and North East)	36.0	31.9	67.9	–	–	1.27	2.36
India (Total)	184.8	146.4	331.2	35.8	27.4	14.45	22.80
India (Total)	–	–	–	63.2 mn			22.80

Sources: NRS-97, IRS-99 (Round 1) (Courtesy APL Lintas); Doordarshan Audience Research Unit (1998); *Asian Communication Handbook* (AMIC) (1998).

In 1999, the overall penetration of cable and satellite television was 40 per cent of homes with television, lowest in the northern states (25 per cent) and highest in the South (56 per cent).[39] Table 3.5 shows the variation of TV and cable penetration in various Indian states in 1997. The proportion of households with access to cable and satellite TV in urban India ranged from 23 per cent of households with TV in Uttar Pradesh to over 60 per cent of TV households in Andhra Pradesh and Gujarat. Even poor states such as Bihar and Rajasthan had a rate of cable penetration of nearly a

Table 3.5   Urban India: TV/Cable TV Penetration by State

State	TV Penetration (% of Households)	Cable TV Penetration (% of TV Households)
Delhi	85.5	33.1
Haryana/Punjab Himachal Pradesh	82.3	37.2
Rajasthan	72.3	30.1
Uttar Pradesh	61.2	23.2
Gujarat	71.0	64.7
Madhya Pradesh	74.8	44.9
Maharashtra /Goa	76.4	47.1
Assam /North East	78.3	24.1
Bihar	54.8	31.4
Orissa	59.4	40.7
West Bengal	60.1	25.9
Andhra Pradesh	68.3	60.8
Karnataka	72.0	54.1
Kerala	54.0	24.0
Tamil Nadu	64.0	53.0

Source: NRS-97, Table 30.

third of homes with televisions in towns and cities. It was apparent that the number of prosperous rural households with cable connections was also growing rapidly, though accurate figures were not available.[40] But the statistics do broadly indicate a difference between the northern and eastern states and those in the south and west. Except for Punjab, most of the Hindi-speaking areas of north India enjoyed far lower access to satellite services than the southern states. West Bengal and the North East also recorded low figures. On the other hand, all the southern states, except Kerala, had rates of over 50 per cent. The figures are a reflection of the relative prosperity of the different Indian states, though the availability of regional language satellite services also played a part in the spread of cable in the South.

The same figures show the vast extent of cable networks throughout the regions of India despite the differing levels of cable penetration.[41] The returns for large cable operators who have put in a substantial investment have been slower than for the small businesses which they have to some extent displaced. But the direct payments that cable operators receive from customers made it a profitable business from the start. At the end of 1997, most of the broadcasters who supplied the cable operators were losing money.

The exceptions were Zee TV, Channel V and Sun TV, with Zee Cinema, Star Movies and Eenadu TV probably breaking even.[42] Since then, both Zee TV and Sun TV have maintained their lead. But Sony Entertainment TV and Star Plus have made gains, as advertisers spend more of their budgets on satellite channels at the expense of Doordarshan. Zee TV's advertising revenues for 1999 were estimated at Rs. 5000 million; Sony's, with lower rates but more advertising time on the air, were forecast at Rs. 3000 million.[43]

THE CHALLENGE TO THE STATE SECTOR

Table 3.6 below shows that by 1998, despite the attraction of Doordarshan's superior reach, India's ten leading advertisers were spending, on average, over three quarters of their budgets on the satellite channels. Cable and satellite channels overtook Doordarshan in the volume of their direct advertising revenues in 1997–98. Though Doordarshan's revenue figures do not include the producers' revenues, Doordarshan's share has been declining since then in absolute as well as relative terms, throwing the state broadcaster's whole commercial strategy into question.

Table 3.6   Share of Advertising Expenditure on Doordarshan, and Cable and Satellite

Company	Doordarshan		Satellite	
	1997	1998	1997	1998
Britannia India	38	27	62	73
Brooke Bond Lipton	18	24	82	76
Cadbury India	24	26	76	74
Coca Cola India	45	33	55	67
Colgate Palmolive	26	28	74	72
Godrej	34	26	66	72
Hindustan Lever	29	21	71	79
Nestle India	18	14	82	86
Pepsi Foods	56	43	44	57
Procter and Gamble	28	19	72	81
Average	28	23	72	77

Source: 'Current Opinion and Future Trends', Business World, 22 January–6 February 1999.

In all the countries of South Asia, transnational satellite broadcasting was initially seen as an external challenge rather than one that demanded the rethinking of their own domestic broadcasting structures. But the assumption that broadcasting had to be mediated or controlled by governments was no longer valid, despite their reluctance to adjust to change. International television broadcasting had become a new reality. Moreover, the competition was not from other state-controlled broadcasting systems, as was the case for the most part with international radio, but a product of private ventures with different and unfamiliar lines of accountability. Neither India, for all its experience of satellite technology, nor the other South Asian states had prepared strategies for dealing with it.

In this competition between state and private channels, the programmes themselves have been of overriding importance in winning audiences. The state broadcasters' statutory public service objectives demanded one kind of programming schedule; the demands of advertisers another. For more than half of South Asia's population the idea of becoming part of a global market for consumer goods seemed irrelevant. But the middle class audience was important to the state broadcasters both for their own commercial interests and for the maintenance of their pivotal national role.

Already by 1990, Doordarshan was well advanced on the road to commercialisation, reaching the prosperous middle classes and incorporating them directly or indirectly into a global market. It was responding to the interests of its own entrepreneurs and industrialists, as well as the national subsidiaries of transnational corporations. At that stage, the goods which Doordarshan promoted were overwhelmingly produced in India and the programmes which proved effective in attracting a mass audience were Indian products. They were serials based on Indian social or religious themes or products of the Bombay Hindi film industry. But the state broadcaster itself was becoming part of a process in which as Herman and McChesney put it '...the media are being integrated into a global system that caters to those with effective demand and encourages them to want and to spend more.'[44]

This commercial orientation has created new priorities over the public service objectives that dominated the state broadcasting ethos in the past. All state broadcasters had accepted a commercial dimension in television before the satellite era. As monopolies, they were able to keep this within the priority objectives determined by the state and had been secure in the knowledge that advertisers had only one place to go. The end of monopoly undermined that rationale and threatened the viability of the state-subsidised broadcasting system. It created dilemmas that have not yet been resolved. For the smaller countries of South Asia it was a question of maintaining their audiences in the face of satellite channels originating beyond their borders, whether western or Indian in style. For India itself, the main market for satellite channels was within its borders and the programme suppliers who could reach that market were also Indian. In the following chapter we examine the Indian market and the ways in which the satellite media have set out to exploit it.

NOTES AND REFERENCES

1. C.J. Hamelink (1994), *The Politics of World Communication*, p. 86.
2. E. Herman and R. McChesney (1997), *The Global Media: New Missionaries of Global Capitalism*, p. 39.
3. Arnold Tucker, Star TV Vice president, in *Los Angeles Times*, 20 October 1992. By 1993, Star claimed access to more than 7 million homes through the cable network (Star TV Homes Penetration Study 1993 cited in *Asian Communication Handbook* 1998, p. 245).
4. S.R. Melkote, B.P. Sanjay, Syed Amjed Ahmed (1998), 'Use of Star TV and Doordarshan in India: An Audience-centered Case Study in Chennai City', in Melkote Shields and Agrawal (eds) (1998), pp. 157–77.
5. For a profile of Subhash Chandra, see, Sevanti Ninan, op. cit., pp. 160–62. A projection of the family man, practising yoga and meditation and 'a genuine chai-bidi connoisseur equally at home in Hindi and English' could be found in 'The Week', 12 December 1999, in www.zeetelevision.com.
6. Among the early competitors that could not sustain the pace were NEPC, ATN and Jain TV.
7. Kalanidhi Maran, Chennai, November 1999. He has an MBA from Pennsylvania University.
8. See, 'Southern War Cries', an analysis of competition between the channels by Carat Media Services India Ltd. in 'Brand Equity', *Economic Times*, 23–28 June 1999.
9. Figures from NRS-95 and NRS-97. 'South India Private TV Channels Viewership by SEC (Average 1 week) (All Adults)', NRS-97, Table 61.
10. Sashi Kumar, Chennai, February 1998.
11. *Times of India* On-line, Indiantelevision.com, 13 April 2000.
12. Cf. ABNI Regional TV in Asia, 1998.

13. Abul Khair's venture known as SAARC Media Services was due to go on air in October 1997.
14. TVi struggled with severe financial problems and went off the air in 1999.
15. Atul Das, Lloyds Securities, Mumbai, May 1998.
16. J.S. Kohli, Managing Director, InCable Network, Mumbai, April 1998.
17. Maharashtra Dish Antenna Owners Association, Pune. Up to 1998, there was still no franchise system in Pune.
18. Sunil Khanna, Siti Cable, Delhi, April 1998.
19. *The Statesman*, Calcutta, 17 September 1995.
20. Mrs. Roop Sharma, Delhi Cable Operators Association, Delhi, April 1998.
21. K.D. Shorey, General Secretary, Film Federation of India, Mumbai, June 1998.
22. Meenakshi Madhvani, CEO, Carat India, Mumbai, March 1998.
23. Based on figures published by Cable Waves from IRS-98, cited in *Doordarshan 1998* (Audience Research Unit), p. 29. The comparable urban-only figure for Kerala (based on NRS-97) was 24 per cent (cf. Table 3.5).
24. M. Madhvani, Mumbai, March 1998.
25. *Ibid.* Cf. J.S. Kohli, 'The national interest/security argument is of great importance to the government; it was discussed at great lengths during the discussions with the standing committee on the broadcasting bill' (Mumbai, May 1998). The cable operators have complied with informal instructions from the Bombay police not to relay Pakistan TV during times of communal tension.
26. Chinmoy Mutsuddi, Dhaka, March 1998.
27. The fee originally demanded was Tk 100,000. Intermittent negotiations brought this amount down to Tk 25,000.
28. Humayun Akhtar, Dhaka, May 1998.
29. A. Chowdhury Polash, Red Seal Cable Shop and General Secretary, Bangladesh Cable Operators Association, Dhaka, March1998.
30. Rupak Hussain, Super Video, Dhaka, March 1998.
31. A. Chowdhury Polash, Dhaka, March 1998.
32. Chinmoy Mutsuddi, Dhaka, March 1998.
33. Information supplied by Dr. Ijaz Gilani, Chairman, Gallup Business Research Bureau, Pakistan, Islamabad, January 1999 (updated February 2000). See also, I. Gilani, 'The Satellite Revolution: Implications for Marketing and Media Research'; Conference presentation, Karachi, April 1995.
34. *The Nation*, Lahore, 30 November 1997.
35. I. Gilani, Islamabad, January 1999.
36. Ruhunu 2001 Multivision Pvt. Ltd. is promoted by the Canada-based company Rystar Communications Ltd. which has 90 per cent of the shares in partnership with the Southern Development Authority of Sri Lanka.
37. This 100 per cent local collaboration is between Chandran Ratnam of Film Location Services (Pvt.) Ltd. and Grant Communications.
38. *The Sunday Times*, Colombo, 25 October 1998.
39. IRS-99 (Round 1). Information supplied by APL (Lintas) Chennai.
40. Cf. 'Doordarshan Fading Out of its Rural Bastion', *Business World*, 22 January–6 February 1999, p. 27.
41. The size of the market for national cable operations in India was estimated in 1995 at Rs. 15,000 million.(US$ 357 million) and to be growing at 15 per cent

a year. 'Sector Study: Media', Lloyds Securities India Research, June 1995, p. 10.

41. *Cable Waves*, Vol. 3, No. 24, 16–31 December 1997.
42. Ambez Media & Market Research in www.indiantelevision.com, April 2000 (August 1999 update).
43. Herman and McChesney, *The Global Media* (1997), p. 188.

Four

THE LURE OF THE INDIAN MARKET

LIBERALISATION AND THE ECONOMIC CLIMATE

For more than forty years after independence successive Indian governments maintained tight controls over the economy. The spending power and consumer needs of the growing Indian middle class had for long presented a tempting market, untested but potentially profitable. But until the end of the 1980s, access was strictly controlled both for foreign companies and Indian businesses. Competition and entrepreneurial activity were regulated within the framework of planning priorities set centrally by the government. The 'licence raj' was intended to ensure that resources were applied both to meeting priority needs and to extending India's capacity in manufacturing and services.

The policy had notable achievements to its credit, more clearly perhaps in the private sector than in the state industrial monopolies. There is no questioning the entrepreneurial skills of Indian business enterprises. It was the achievement of building an indigenous manufacturing capacity which was the envy of India's smaller South Asian neighbours. But the 'licence raj' became a by-word for industrial inefficiency and bureaucratic corruption. It was increasingly an anomaly, not just in a global environment but in relation to China and to southern and eastern Asia. India's size and resources—particularly human resources—should have made it a formidable player in international trade, manufacturing and services. But little advantage was taken of the natural strengths of the Indian economy. It was nowhere near fulfilling its potential.

It was in this context that economic compulsions forced the Indian political establishment to choose a new economic course. The exchange crisis of 1991 and the subsequent bail out by the IMF, the World Bank and other international aid agencies is part of Indian economic folklore. The newly-elected government of P.V. Narasimha Rao (with Finance Minister Manmohan Singh as the chief architect) ushered in a new era by introducing sweeping measures of economic reform and liberalisation. In July 1991, the industrial licensing regime as practiced for three decades was virtually dismantled. The number of industries reserved for the public sector was reduced from seventeen to eight, and then to six. Foreign exchange regulations were revised to promote investment. Tariffs replaced almost all qualitative restrictions on imports. Customs duties fell from a peak tariff rate of over 300 to 50 per cent in 1994–95, and the average import weighted tariff rate came down from 47 per cent to under 25 per cent. The rupee was made convertible in current account transactions. As one editor wrote: 'It was freedom at last'.[1]

But if the freedom was real, its limitations were obvious. India's middle classes had greater choice than ever of goods and services and a much greater choice in how they could spend or save their enhanced incomes. But could they be made the yardstick of the prosperity of the nation? The sheer weight of numbers had in the past assigned that role to India's rural rather than urban population. The importance of the middle class depended on it being a large enough segment of Indian society to sustain the claim to be the key measure of its prosperity.

The collapse of the Soviet Union had the effect in India of marginalising the old assumptions of the central importance of the state in economic activity, even if it did not erase a traditional socialist commitment to equality. The central perceptions of class politics and class conflict went out of fashion as the commitment to secularism waned. But the middle class gained ground, not just as the focus of a new consumerism but as an articulate agent of these new political priorities.

THE INDIAN MIDDLE CLASS

A nation-wide survey of the size and depth of the Indian market conducted in 1996 provided a fuller and more detailed analysis of the new consumerism and its practitioners than anything done before. 'Indian Marketing Demographics': a survey by the

National Council of Applied Economic Research (NCAER) revealed some startling new facts about the Indian consumer.[2] The study showed that the Indian 'middle class' was no social monolith. It embraced three distinct classes identified by their patterns of consumption rather than their income. In the 'very rich' category were 1 million households—6 million people—with an annual income of Rs. 215,000 or more at 1993–94 prices. The top range of this middle class included a few hundred thousand who were wealthy even by international standards.[3] But it was overwhelmingly the 'middle class of a poor country.'[4] Its buying capacity was much less than that of the South Asian elite of a decade before. It was clear that on its own it could not generate the kind of demand capable of sustaining rapid growth.[5]

But these were not the true bounds of the 'middle class' as defined in the vocabulary of social analysts and market planners. A further 'consuming class' of 150 million people—30 million households—had an income level of Rs. 45,000 to Rs. 215,000 per annum (above US$ 90 per month).[6] With carefully worked out priorities, this class was in the market for an economical range of consumer durables, as well as packaged and branded foods, cosmetics and toiletries. Third, in the 'social climbers' category, were 50 million households—275 million people—with an income level of Rs. 22,000 to Rs. 45,000 per annum (above US$ 44 per month). Their smaller budgets restricted the range of their purchases but they were large in numbers and they provided a surplus which could be used to acquire a predictable range of goods. They became part of the marketing strategy and a key to its success or failure.

Below these and outside the range of the most optimistic definition of the middle class was a category of aspirants—another 50 million households or 275 million people—with an income level of Rs. 16,000 to Rs. 22,000 per annum (above US$ 32 per month). These too were consumers, responsive to the marketing of a range of basic consumer goods which in small ways affected their aspirations and lifestyle. Finally, there were the destitutes—35 million households comprising 210 million people—with an income level of less than Rs. 16,000 per annum.

This approach by the NCAER strikingly included in the 'middle class' a much larger range of income levels than other definitions have allowed, but placed fewer people at the top end of the range.[7] The survey showed that consumer patterns and aspirations were shared over a range of income much wider than the 'middle class'. Low income households were acquiring a higher proportion of consumer goods. Marketing experts advised businesses to concentrate on expanding the lower end of the market on the grounds that the big rewards would come from there.[8] The shopping list might include products new to the lifestyle and spending habits of those who aspire to them, for example, cosmetics or toiletries.

In terms of consumer behaviour, at least 80 per cent of India's population bought washing cakes and cooking oil at least once a year. There were estimated to be 504 million consumers of Fast Moving Consumer Goods (FMCGs)—non-durables—in 90 million households. Up to 30 million households or 168 million people were in the market for consumer durables of all kinds. Between 61 and 90 million households owned bicycles and transistor radios and regularly bought electric bulbs, casual footwear, washing powder and body talcum powder. Between 21 and 60 million households regularly bought packaged biscuits, PVC footwear and cooking oil. Between 11 and 30 million households owned sewing machines, black and white television sets, mixers/grinders and electric irons; they also regularly bought shampoos and face creams. Up to 10 million households owned refrigerators, mopeds, scooters, motorcycles; these also regularly bought nail polish and lipstick.[9]

The NCAER study has been criticised for several reasons, but its findings continue to excite market analysts and influence their strategies. The number of car owners is 2.25 million, proportionately less than Pakistan where a population one-fifth the size owns 1.3 million cars.[10] The affluent middle class in India may number no more than 6 million. But the market is much wider. For the 63 million households with televisions, 16 million with colour TVs and 20 million with cable connections, television is the principal gateway to this market.

GLOBAL ADVERTISING AND ITS LIMITS

The policies of liberalisation implemented by the Indian government from the beginning of the 1990s created the conditions for the opening of a vast new market and a hitherto untapped demand for consumer products. The emergence of the opportunity coincided with a heightened pace to what is described by one expert as 'an era of global marketing warfare'. In this 'the number one tactical weapon of the age is advertising'.[11] In the words of S.L. Rao, former director of the research agency whose redefinition of the Indian middle class we have quoted, 'advertising has made the major difference to demand growth, especially consumer products, in the 1990s. This was because of the enhanced reach of advertising messages through television'.[12]

The prospect of the opening of the Indian market stimulated the formation of links between the advertising industry in India and major international agencies. In an increasingly integrated global media industry there are many advantages for national firms to operate in an international network. But it is not a one-sided advantage. Leading Indian advertising executives argue that without local knowledge, contacts and cultural awareness, a multinational firm attempting to operate in India would be wasting its money. 'The Indian market place has no parallel in the world. There is nothing that can be predicted', says M. Suku, senior manager of one of India's biggest advertisers, Colgate Palmolive.[13] Advertising is not a manufacturing process, producing a machine that will work equally effectively for whoever uses it. It is culturally highly sensitive and the advertiser who does not know the sensitivities or ignores them is not likely to be effective. Alyque Padamsee, the doyen of Indian creative advertising, argues that despite its corporate links with multinationals, Indian advertising does not submit to global direction, just as he says that India as a country will not submit to global cultural imperialism. Cricket, for example, though originally a cultural import, 'in India is a great Indian game'. Coca-Cola now centres its advertising in India around cricket. Previously, according to Padamsee, the company had wanted to bring its global advertising to India, and that did not feature cricket. The company had said 'We invented the world, and we will invent it in India'. But it did not work. Subsequently, Coca-Cola changed tack and adopted the slogan 'Eat cricket, sleep cricket, drink only Coca-Cola'.[14]

Multinational corporations operating in India characterise their relationship with their Indian offshoots or partners as one of mutual benefit. By 'thinking globally and acting locally' the strategic advantage of a global presence can work to the benefit of local entrepreneurial ambitions and tactics. Their critics describe the relationship in terms of dominance, in which the weight of strategic and tactical advantage lies with the multinational companies and with the World Trade Organisation as the agency of global liberalisation. But it is also the case that Indian firms are themselves globalising. Indian companies have realised that the only way to fight multinationals in India is not by being defensive at home but by being aggressive abroad. Indian advertisers have been adapting themselves both internally and externally to the demands of the global market place.[15]

On the eve of globalisation, India's internal market and its media support in the form of television advertising had already shown its capacity for growth. India was prepared for the satellite revolution on two fronts: its own satellite and telecommunications technology was already in place and so were the foundations of a new advertising infrastructure. A new national television network had helped to create a national market and give access to a consuming middle class that crossed the boundaries of regional, cultural and economic diversity. By the end of the 1980s, the stage was set for large-scale changes in Indian society. The driver of these changes, according to a widely held view, was satellite television. But the ground had been laid before.

The real stimulus for advertisers came in 1982 when the medium went into colour. Satellite-fed transmissions created a national network for the first time. At the same time, the Asian Games promoted a sense of a shared national agenda on television. The popularity of television as a medium began to change the choices that advertisers made. Before 1982, Indian television was barely considered an advertising medium; it was primarily an education and information medium. Media advertising was carried by newspapers. It was targeted at the main earner in the family and to a lesser extent the housewife. 'Business had begun to try and begin to use and understand the potential of the medium, but advertising mostly consisted of slide and sound, and a combination of video jingles and filmed messages'.[16] After 1982, advertisers could address a national market which did not exist before. They began to realise that through television, the manufacturer had direct access to new consumers. Until then, the dealer had been of supreme importance in the chain. Now the manufacturer could speak to the housewife in her home. The power of the medium was beginning to be felt. The relationship of the advertiser to the consumer had changed; sales multiplied.

Roda Mehta of O&M Advertising argues that the middle class market existed before its significance was fully noticed or appreciated. The television revolution preceded the boom in consumerism and the demand for products. 'Television came and woke it up'. But she argues that the hardware was not as important as the programmes themselves. 'Technology was only providing the means. Through programmes on television people were being sensitised to newer product categories, about materialistic possibilities that life could offer.' She sees this as the precursor to the 'final stage' of liberalisation, the opening of India to foreign manufactured products. 'Manufacturers abroad saw this huge amount of buying of goods and services in India and realised that the Indian market had matured enough for them to make an entry into it. Television has played the single largest role in creating this market'.[17]

A contrasting view from M. Suku of Colgate Palmolive is that it would be wrong to single out satellite or television as the sole driver for the consumer boom. The satellite revolution happened in parallel with the economic policies introduced from 1986 onwards. 'Satellite has been the subset of that liberalisation'.[18] Suku attributes a growing maturity in the markets to the process of liberalisation itself, not the influence of television marketing. He argues that television is increasing awareness, but that by itself cannot create a consumer boom.

The wide reach that the state broadcaster Doordarshan achieved in the 1980s also determined the distribution of consumer goods. Roda Mehta explains: 'Even when a manufacturer was not reaching all of his potential markets, the 145 transmitters were pulling his brands into the market. As a result of this, it became a flood. Every advertiser wanted to be on television.' Even if advertising budgets were small, the medium was relevant. The consumer began to accept that the TV set itself and the products advertised through it were not just luxury items. Mehta believes that women were the main agent in this change of attitude. 'The category was being driven by women and the brand by the household. All factors were moving in synergy at that time. From a few drops, it became a river and then an ocean. It flooded up everything. All of

us were just caught in it and swept away. That was really the
genesis of television advertising.'[19]

SATELLITE AND SEGMENTATION

Before satellite and cable, advertisers saw television as a monolithic
medium. They had the same set of options, whether they wanted
to reach a 1,000 people or 100,000 people. Up to the end of the
1980s, most marketing specialists essentially used it for single,
mass brand advertising. Different brands of toothpaste produced
by the same company—Colgate Toothpaste and Colgate Gel—
were both advertised on Doordarshan because there was no choice.
This worked for Colgate Toothpaste because it was a mass brand.
But the other product was a significantly smaller brand, for which
it was wasteful to advertise to a mass market.[20]

The satellite channels changed this picture. For the first time,
viewership began to get fragmented, giving the chance to reach
both demographically- and geographically-specific audiences.
Previously there had been a choice between Doordarshan's national and regional networks. Zee TV gave a channel in Hindi covering
the north and the west, while much of the South was covered by
regional channels in the four southern languages. Between them
they reached the top 30 to 40 per cent of the viewership. India
could now move from mass marketing to more segmented marketing. So, media planners no longer tried to buy the biggest audience as cheaply as possible as they had done in the past.

The satellite channels gave an opportunity to launch more
sophisticated products for specific markets. The process of media
decision making was radically altered by the existence of this new
choice. So was the demand for information about markets and
awareness of what was missing from market research. The emerging new advertising market changed the relationship between
manufacturers and consumers. The changing pattern of media
consumption was part of this process.

Meenakshi Madhvani of Carat India explains: 'From being a
backroom function in which the client was not interested, media
planning for marketing products became a central part of marketing strategies.... The industry in India grew phenomenally
between 1994 and 1996, until an overall economic slowdown

brought the rate of growth down, to a comparatively sluggish 9 per cent. In absolute amounts the industry in India is still very small. But this rate of growth has outpaced industrial growth or that of the economy as a whole'.[21]

To their audience, satellite channels arrived in India without a price attached. But their arrival in the market created a vigorous new competitor for a share of advertising. The print media had historically claimed the greatest share. In 1982, the print media had 78 per cent, according to Doordarshan estimates, while the remaining 20 per cent was divided almost evenly between television, radio, cinema and other outlets.[22] Despite the growth of both terrestrial and satellite television outlets, this dominant position of the press remained. The press had a continuing advantage for certain kinds of advertising which the electronic media had not challenged. This included government advertising, tenders for contracts and goods for which the market was almost exclusively among newspaper readers.

But the share of the print media overall was being substantially eroded. By 1992, in a space of ten years, the print media share was reduced to around 66 per cent. The biggest growth in the television share of advertising took place in these ten years, before either cable or the new direct satellite media had begun to make an impact. Television's gain was at the expense of the print media, radio and cinema, while outdoor media, like hoardings, increased. Mobile audio—the loudspeaker on the back of a rickshaw— continued to prove itself a cheap and effective publicity medium in the densely populated towns and cities. By 1998, according to advertising industry estimates, the print media had declined to 56 per cent and television as a whole had risen to 36 per cent.[23] Radio stabilised at a share of around 2 per cent and cinema at 0.2 per cent, while other outdoor advertising continued to grow, perhaps because of the popularity of televised sport and other public events.[24]

Estimates of the time spent every day in consuming different types of media underline the growing importance of television. According to the authoritative National Readership Survey (NRS) of 1997, 56 per cent of adults watched TV every day; the share of media time taken by television was 69 per cent compared with 15 per cent for radio and 16 per cent for the press.[25] The other important message for advertisers was that young people were spending an increasing amount of time watching TV—118 minutes per day, 161 minutes on Sundays. There were also big differences between rival channels in their ability to find a young audience and hold its attention.[26]

MARKET RESEARCH

As long as television and radio broadcasting was a monopoly, there was interest but little commercial value in information about who was watching or listening. Commercialisation and diversification of the media boosted awareness of the importance of market and media research. With television advertising expenditure in India reaching an annual figure of Rs. 25 billion (approx. US$ 600 million) in 1998, advertisers could not afford to base their spending decisions on guesswork alone.[27]

Doordarshan produces audience data for its own broadcasting activities at regional and national levels. But the information this provides is inadequate for the needs of private broadcasters. Doordarshan maintains its own DART audience measurement system, which is based on a larger sample than the private agencies can afford. But it is focussed primarily on audiences for its own services, not those of its competitors. More fundamentally, because the DART system is administered by Doordarshan itself, it lacks credibility for the advertisers as a basis on which to make spending decisions. Advertising agencies and their customers demand an independent source of research and information on the media which can be relied on by the industry as a whole.

Several professional market research agencies undertake work to the highest global standards of accuracy. But the size and complexity of the Indian market make an agreed system of measurement of reach and audience share highly desirable. In the spirit of competition, which some in the industry find excessive and exasperating, India has two systems–the National Readership Survey (NRS) and the Indian Readership Survey (IRS).

The amount of work involved in carrying out these surveys makes them some of the most ambitious research projects in the world. With sample sizes of over 100,000 across all the states of India, they provide a wealth of information for all media users and analysts. But the fact that two national surveys are carried out is symptomatic of a lack of common standards across the industry, which can sometimes result in widely differing estimates of audiences. In this situation, media organisations themselves have found it easier to make the running. As one market researcher put it: 'These are the real issues we face in data bases in the country...but nobody is interested in revealing anything to you because there are millions of rupees riding on each one of these figures.'

The first readership survey in India was carried out in 1971 by ORG, a company started by Dr. Vikram Sarabhai, the scientist responsible for the SITE experiment. Others followed at five or six year intervals, in 1978, 1983 and 1989. All of these were single agency surveys carried out either by ORG or IMRB. By the 1990s, however, media owners and advertisers had become more vocal about their needs and had begun to put pressure on the agencies to make their research more market-led and user-friendly. At that stage, representatives from advertisers, publishers, advertising agencies and broadcast and other media set up a non-profit making organisation called the Media Research Users Council (MRUC) to lobby, among other things, for a common basis of evaluation and more consistent and compatible research information.

In 1995, two major surveys were conducted—a National Readership Survey and an Indian Readership Survey.[28] By that stage, pressure from users led them to be managed more independently. The advertisers and newspaper owners' associations which commissioned NRS-95 decided it should not be conducted by a single agency and set up a special unit in the Audit Bureau of Circulation to manage it. The commissioning agency for IRS-95 was the newly formed MRUC.

Until the late 1990s, the Indian Readership Survey was the only survey of its kind to cover both urban and rural areas with essentially the same sampling procedure.[29] The National Readership Survey, previously confined to urban areas, followed suit with NRS-99. Despite their names, the readership surveys are not confined to the print media, and cover TV, radio, cinema and the Internet. They are more properly Indian media and market studies, which aim to facilitate multi-media planning. They give information on viewership of channels within a household but do not set out to provide a measurement of the audience. The information on individual programmes generated by both surveys is indicative rather than quantitative.

From week to week, broadcasters and advertisers rely on pro-gramme ratings which are produced by several leading agencies. These go under the name of Television Audience Measurement (TAM). IMRB, a research company owned by its employees but linked to Hindustan Thompson Associates, the advertising agency, has been at the forefront of this kind of measurement.[30] It started its diary-based system of measuring TV audiences in 1986, using panels of representative individuals in nine key cities across India. In 1995, in response to the demand for more accurate information, it introduced—in collaboration with AC Nielsen—the more accur-ate 'People Meter' system. This replaced the individual diary with a device attached to the television set which recognised which channel was being watched. In a family viewing situation, all viewers have their own buttons to press when they start and stop viewing. The device keeps a record of their preferences, which is converted into more accurate TAM ratings. Though this system also has its critics, IMRB claims the accuracy of its television ratings to be 'of a reasonably high order'. The panels they use are selected from bigger sample surveys as a means of reducing sampling errors, and the fact that information is generated week after week from the same source gives continuity and uniformity. ORG-MARG has also introduced People Meters, though in both cases the information is drawn from a limited number of cities.

The advent of satellite channels and fragmentation of audiences have increased the demand for information. The need for larger sample sizes is not so much a function of the vastness of the popu-lation but of the heterogeneity of the Indian television universe, compared to the United States or to China and other Asian markets. In marketing terms, the national terrestrial broadcaster Door-darshan forms a universe of its own, distinct from the cable and satellite universe, though overlapping it. But with the growth in the number and distinctiveness of cable and satellite channels broadcasting in regional languages, the demand for more precise research continues to grow.

STRATEGIES FOR SURVIVAL

In the competition for audiences, the segmentation of the TV mar-ket should present good opportunities for smaller broadcasters and production companies. But despite this apparent advantage, many professionals in the industry believe that only companies with the deepest pockets can survive. Meenakshi Madhvani of Carat India shares this view. 'Channels haven't managed to sustain themselves in a situation where advertising revenues are not large enough to be spread slightly more evenly. You need to have really deep pockets.' Madhvani predicts that only two genuine Indian/ Hindi platforms, probably Zee and Sony, will survive.[31]

From offering general entertainment in the English language, Star changed its strategy in 1996 in favour of broadcasting in both Hindi and English. In the run up to the 1998 election, Star launched a 24-hour news channel in partnership with Prannoy Roy's New Delhi Television. Star's venture into Hindi language programming put it in conflict with Zee TV, in which Murdoch's Newscorp retained a majority share-holding. In an important strategic change of direction, in 1999, Subhash Chandra bought back Murdoch's 50 per cent shares both in Asia Today, the Hong Kong-based broadcasting company which broadcasts the three Zee TV channels, and in Siti Cable, which Chandra also owns. The transaction established Zee TV as the first predominantly Indian media enterprise integrating production, broadcasting and distribution, with plans to expand into publishing, education and radio. It also cleared the way for Star to develop its position in the Hindi language market in full competition with its former partner.[32] In an environment where 'the strong guy gets stronger', the lines were being drawn for a battle in which Zee, the strongest Indian group of channels currently dominating the north Indian market, was pitted against the global resources of the Murdoch empire.

For rival channels, the key to success in reaching the Indian market lies in their programme schedules. The perception in the early 1990s of the Indian market as a potential money spinner appeared to leave little room for considerations of quality programming. But Meenakshi Madhvani (who was earlier with Zee TV) believes that channels will have to market themselves hard, and that in this field Zee's strategy is the best example. Madhvani claims that the driving force for Zee TV was not just to earn revenues but to establish a genuinely good channel. The idea was to make the channel appeal to all segments of society. Not all types of programmes are revenue earners. But over a period of time, programmes for different segments of the audience begin to recover costs.

Sony Entertainment TV has a very similar explanation of the programme element in its business strategy. The first objective was to establish itself on the cable networks as a movie channel. Hindi films were seen as the most popular product on air and access to them all-important. Sony's chief executive in India, Kunal Das Gupta, explains: 'We did research into the past 50 years of the Hindi film industry and isolated from each the top box office earners, and from that list we drew out a list of about 500 movies; from that we acquired satellite rights for 400 of them'. Sony's Indian operation now claims to have the richest library in the country.

With this resource, the channel initially scheduled films five out of seven nights a week. Once a threshold had been reached in which Sony was available in about 10 million homes, it began to reduce the number of films on air and replace them with original programming. The channel also promoted the Sony brand by advertising heavily in other media. This strategy lies behind Sony's acknowledged success in establishing itself as the main rival to Zee TV in the field of Hindi entertainment programming.[33]

One important constraint in the development of segmented markets is the pattern of TV ownership. Though in affluent homes the trend may be towards owning two or more TV sets, the overwhelming majority of the television-owning population in 1998 were single-set households.[34] At prime time, the family's preferences tend to be for entertainment and not news. Television channels operate on the 80:20 principle, where 80 per cent of the programmes earn 20 per cent of the revenue and the top 20 per cent of the programmes earn 80 per cent of the revenue. Even in the cable and satellite market, the advertiser is basically interested in programming that attracts large audiences, and these are entertainment programmes. The spread of cable TV has enabled advertisers to concentrate on the middle class market, but the development of real niche channels will have to wait until multi-television households grow in numbers.[35]

The appeal of cable as an advertising option has also grown as cable channels consolidate.[36] The localised appeal and rising share of viewership of local cable channels has attracted advertisers and marketing managers.[37] In 1998, for example, InCable Net charged

Rs. 4,000 for a 10-second spot and smaller cable operators even less, compared to Hindi satellite channels such as Zee and Sony which charged anything between Rs. 12,000 and Rs. 90,000, depending on the time-slot. According to a senior media planner, the cable option is always considered with clients as an important and cost-effective medium.[38] But the total revenue is not high and it does not pose a threat to the big channels.[39]

IDENTIFYING THE AUDIENCE

A demographic profile of the audience for the main channels beaming programmes into India gives an indication of how the urban audience was divided between the different television channels in 1997 (Table 4.1).

Table 4:1   TV Viewership by Age and Educational Attainment (India)

Channel	Age Group(%)				Educational Qualifications		
	15–19	25–34	35–44	45+	Illiterates	SSC/ HSC graduates	Post- graduates
DD1	72.9	65.0	66.0	58.0	41.2	77.0	79.4
DD2	26.8	25.0	24.0	21.0	11.6	30.8	36.1
Star Plus	9.1	8.2	5.8	5.2	0.4	11.3	20.5
Star Sports	10.8	8.6	6.4	4.9	0.5	13.6	19.2
ESPN	4.8	3.7	2.5	1.8	0.2	5.5	8.8
CNN	0.5	0.6	0.6	0.5	0.1	0.7	1.9
BBC	2.3	3.0	2.5	2.8	0.1	4.1	10.5
Discovery	5.3	4.6	3.9	3.6	0.2	7.4	12.3
Cartoon Network	3.9	2.4	1.7	1.1	0.1	3.7	5.1
Zee	23.9	21.0	18.0	15.0	5.3	28.7	39.4
Sony	18.3	15	12.0	9.9	3.9	20.3	27.3
MTV	1.6	1.2	0.6	0.5	0.1	1.8	2.9
Channel V	2.3	1.5	0.8	0.6	0.1	2.4	4.1

Note: In the full NRS table, 61 channels are listed. In the age group category there are five subgroups: 15–19, 20–24, 25–34, 35–44 and 45+. Among the educational qualification category there are four categories: Illiterate, SSC/ HSC (which in India is the secondary school level and junior college level), Graduate and Postgraduate.

Source: NRS-97, Table 63.

The Doordarshan national channel DD1 commanded the highest audience, more than twice that of DD2 in every age and educational category. In the younger age categories, Zee TV was running close; significantly in the highest educational category Zee TV exceeded the audience for DD2.

In the nation-wide urban picture given by the National Readership Surveys, the audience figures for the DD regional channels underestimate their wider local impact. But across urban India the most successful southern regional private channels were reaching a substantial audience in national terms. For example, Sun TV had between 5.5 per cent and 7.5 per cent of the national urban audience and Eenadu TV between 3.8 per cent and 6.6 per cent.

An analysis in 1998 by a private Mumbai-based media research and planning organisation indicated that some of the Doordarshan satellite channels in regional languages had a larger proportion of viewers in the higher educational categories. They include Bengali, Oriya, Malayalam (with over 30 per cent), and Gujarati, Punjabi and Assamese (around 28–29 per cent). Other DD satellite channels in southern languages and in Marathi had a smaller audience in this category, perhaps because in the case of Telugu and Tamil they had a choice of private channels in the regional language not available to Bengali or Oriya viewers.[40]

In the NRS-97 survey, both BBC and CNN had a consistent proportion of the audience across all age groups. CNN varied between 0.5 and 0.7 per cent, peaking in the age group 20–24 (omitted in Table 4.1) at 0.7 per cent. BBC's audience ranged from 2.3 per cent to 3 per cent, peaking in the 25-34 age group. Discovery, the third serious information channel, with the advantage of a Hindi language transmission, reached between 3.6 and 5.1 per cent of the audience, with the peak in the youngest age range. All these channels had their largest audiences in the same educational groups: secondary school leavers, undergraduates or graduates; in economic terms a niche market, in social and cultural terms potential opinion-formers.

The occupational profile of television audiences for different channels shows, perhaps not surprisingly, that the highest urban audiences are among those who are unemployed or in the 'no work outside the home' category (Table 4.2).[41]

Table 4.2 TV Channel Viewership by Occupational Categories (India)

Channel	Officer/ Executive	Petty Traders	Shop Owners	Clerical/ Salaried	Skilled	Unskilled	Student	No Work
DD1	74.8	53.8	70.5	79.0	64.1	48.9	80.8	63.2
DD2	34.8	17.0	24.2	32.8	23.7	15.8	33.2	23.0
Star Plus	22.3	3.9	9.7	13.3	5.4	2.1	14.1	5.2
Star Sports	21.4	4.9	13.3	14.7	8.1	2.9	12.4	4.8
ESPN	9.9	2.2	5.7	6.3	3.0	1.0	7.7	1.7
CNN	2.4	0.3	0.5	0.8	0.4	0.2	1.0	5.0
BBC	12.9	1.2	4.0	5.7	1.6	0.5	4.7	1.8
Discovery	14.1	1.9	5.2	7.9	3.5	1.1	8.4	3.3
TNT	3.0	0.4	1.8	1.9	0.6	0.2	1.9	0.6
Cartoon Network	5.2	1.1	2.5	3.3	1.4	0.4	5.4	1.8
Sony	25.3	8.7	18.7	19.0	9.7	5.8	24.2	12.8
Zee	40.2	13.7	28.2	28.1	15.0	8.0	31.2	17.7
MTV	3.4	0.4	1.6	1.7	0.9	0.3	7.7	0.6
Channel V	4.4	0.6	2.1	2.1	0.8	0.4	4.0	0.8

Source: NRS-97, Table 64.

Seven occupational categories are enumerated : Officer/Executive, Petty Trader, Shop Owner, Clerks/Salaried, Skilled, Unskilled, Student, No Work.[42] The last category, which includes not only the unemployed but housewives or women working at home, represents the largest number of people watching any channel. Otherwise, the viewership is fairly evenly distributed among the others. Students take a good share of the viewing of all channels; after them the officer/executive and clerical categories provide a higher proportion of viewers than shop owners or unskilled workers. Self-employed petty traders provide the lowest proportion of viewers for most channels.

For all satellite channels, the maximum viewership and income categories are B1/B2 and Rs. 2,000–Rs. 4,000 respectively (Table 4.3). The other high socio-economic categories (SEC), especially A1/A2 and income groups Rs. 4,000–Rs. 6,000, also give more than 20 per cent viewership. This is not the case with Doordarshan's terrestrial channels DD1 or DD2, which are less well represented in the higher income brackets. These statistics also point to variations in the income levels of audiences for different DD regional channels, which are very similar to those noted in the educational category. The Bengali, Oriya, Gujarati, Punjabi and Assamese channels reached a high proportion in the upper income ranges; Telugu, Kannada, Tamil and Marathi less so.

DOORDARSHAN AND ITS COMPETITORS

In India, for much of the 1990s, the state broadcaster seemed as central to the future of commercial broadcasting as it was to that of public service broadcasting. The novelty of the satellite channels and the success of some of them did not mean that the state broadcaster was left behind. In the face of competition from 1990 onwards, Doordarshan managed to grow at a fast rate. But it suffered a fall in revenues in 1993 and after a year of spectacular growth (33 per cent) in 1996–97, it fell back again by 14 per cent the following year. In 1998–99, Doordarshan revenues fell to a point where Zee TV had almost overtaken it, and Sony Entertainment Television, the second ranking revenue earner among the private channels, was getting close.[43]

Table 4.3 TV Viewership by Socio-economic Categories and Income Levels (India)

Channel	A1+	A1/A2	B1/B2	C	E1/E2	MHI up to 1K	2K-4K	4K-6K	6K-10K	10K+
DD1	2.1	15.3	22.9	24.2	17.0	5.9	38.1	18.8	9.3	5.1
DD2	3.5	19.0	24.0	23.4	14.7	3.9	36.7	21.4	12.4	7.8
Star Sports	4.8	24.1	27.5	22.8	9.6	3.2	33.8	23.4	14.8	10.6
ESPN	7.1	30.1	28.2	20.5	7.3	2.1	31.4	24.4	17.4	14.0
CNN	14.3	43.9	26.8	17.4	4.2	0.4	22.3	24.1	22.4	26.1
BBC	8.3	32.8	29.0	20.2	5.8	1.7	27.8	25.3	19.1	16.4
Discovery	7.4	30.0	28.2	20.7	7.3	2.7	30.0	24.1	17.6	14.5
TNT	9.1	34.4	28.3	20.0	5.4	1.7	26.7	25.2	20.0	18.0
Cartoon Network	7.9	31.1	28.1	21.5	6.5	2.1	28.9	24.7	18.1	15.9
Sony	4.7	24.1	27.2	22.4	10.5	2.1	35.3	24.0	14.9	10.6
Zee	4.2	22.9	27.0	22.7	11.1	2.7	35.7	23.4	14.1	9.7
Channel V	8.2	32.7	28.7	20.3	6.6	1.4	28.5	25.6	19.3	16.3
Star Plus	4.7	24.3	27.5	22.6	9.9	3.1	33.9	23.5	14.7	10.6

MHI: Monthly Household Income.
Source: Sandeep Nagpal, Stratagem Media Communications Pvt. Ltd.

This was a major blow to Doordarshan, whose main strength has been its superior reach as the only terrestrial broadcaster. With a slower rate of growth in the advertising industry as a whole in the mid-1990s, all the channels had to fight hard for a larger share of comparatively static advertising budgets.[44] This process resulted in a re-distribution of the advertising cake and Doordarshan lost badly. Advertising was not expanding to match the growth of outlets competing for revenue. This acted as a constraint on the development of plurality in the industry and the programme choice which should accompany it.

Doordarshan—especially its Hindi and local language satellite channels—is still seen as the obvious choice for building a mass brand. For luxury goods, English channels may be more appropriate. Despite the ease of switching channels, advertising spending is very much oriented to the channel rather than the programme. Channels try and build a homogeneous programme profile. Zee's ability to capture advertisements for its mass entertainment channel is not because Zee's programmes are necessarily better but because for most people in northern, central and western India it is the channel they switch to first. In this view, the programmes are important but not usually important enough to drive viewers to switch channels.

In the early 1990s, in response to the development of the satellite channels, Doordarshan realised that it needed to capitalise on its technological strengths. It remained strong on its own ground. But new and distinct audiences were emerging for whom the national network was insufficient. Ashok Mansukhani, deputy director of Doordarshan between 1992 and 1996, explains the genesis of the DD regional channels as a way of bridging the gap between the satellite audiences and those for the Doordarshan national network. If satellite television reached 18 million homes—or 90 million people—there would still be 160 million viewers only watching Doordarshan. Doordarshan executives aimed to turn the network into a major force. The changes started with the inauguration of the Metro Channel (DD2) in 1993. The then secretary for information, Bhaskar Ghose, decided that the best use of the available transponders would be to develop the regional channels. They were regional in their programming but they could be seen across the country. This 'unique concept', as Mansukhani describes it, both recognised the diversity of languages spoken in different parts of India and made services in those languages available to the many ethnic and linguistic communities living away from their 'home' states, for example, Tamils in Mumbai, Bengalis in Delhi or Punjabis in Calcutta.[45]

In this strategy, DD1 was to be the main public service broadcasting channel, leaving DD2 (Metro) to be market-driven, earning revenues from commercially more popular programmes. But advertisers were not entirely convinced by this strategy. Most of them still preferred DD1 because of its extensive reach, although DD2 had been extended to cover nearly fifty towns and a further audience of 30 million through cable networks. In 1997–98, DD2 earned Rs. 12.3 million and DD1 Rs. 34.5 million. A further Rs. 17.3 million came from DD's regional stations, most of it from the five in the South. The regional stations accounted for 38 per cent of Doordarshan revenues in 1995–96, falling to 31 per cent in 1996–97 and 27 per cent in 1997–98. A recession in advertising affected some regional kendras, while national advertising maintained its consistent growth. The existence of strong satellite competition was also a factor. The Madras kendra of Doordarshan remained the most profitable of all regional centres, though its revenues fell from a peak of Rs. 500 million in 1996–97 to Rs. 360 million in the following year. In the same period, however, the Bengali regional channel DD7, which did not face such strong competition, raised its revenues by 10 per cent to Rs. 204 million. In addition to a Bengali speaking audience in many urban areas outside West Bengal, it was also popular in Bangladesh and got advertisements from across the border.[46]

In 1998, DD1 claimed a total of 331 million home viewers; higher estimates of 448 million take viewers outside the home into account. DD2 was seen by 125 million people. Among the regional channels, the highest viewership was claimed by DD5, the Tamil channel, and DD8, the channel dedicated to both the Telugu and Punjabi languages. They each had an audience of over 33 million, not just in their primary service area but across India. They were followed by DD7, the Bengali channel, with a viewership of over 30 million. The other major regional channels were the Kannada channel, DD9, which claimed an audience of 22 million, followed by DD4, the Malayalam channel, with 16 million viewers.

By 2000, the terrestrial reach of Doordarshan was a diminishing though still powerful factor in determining the television audience and advertising market in India. DD1, with a terrestrial reach of 86 per cent, had the largest coverage of all the channels. Its satellite-fed infrastructure of low powered transmitters ensured that it had the potential to reach virtually the entire population of the country. By 1998, in the face of damaging competition, it was focussing its marketing efforts on this primary advantage over all other channels.

DIGITISATION AND REGULATION

With digital broadcasting and even Internet television on the horizon, technology is radically changing the way information is delivered and exchanged. Markets become smaller and there are more players in competition. The need grows for a better understanding of the complexity of the broadcasting industry, an improved quality of information and larger sample sizes. In 1998, there were about 40 channels; by 2000, up to 100 channels were theoretically available to South Asian audiences, though many of them were of very marginal interest. With digital broadcasting, the number of channels could increase to 200 or more.

For a group such as the Hindujas' Indus Group, the development of their InCable network is part of a strategy to build a multimedia communications operation through cable. Their aim is to be a part of the information super highway, not just to operate cable services but to test their ability to supply Internet services, data transmission and telephone services. Until 2000, the government was not ready to allow cable companies to provide competition in telephone services. Though technically quite possible it would cut across the licences already awarded to private or semi-privatised telephone companies. But Indus successfully lobbied the government over a long period to allow them to deliver Internet and data transmission services. The ending in 1998 of the monopoly of the state-owned VSNL in providing Internet services opened the way. By the end of the year both Indus and their cable television rivals Siti Cable were ready to enter the market as Internet service providers.[47]

The marketing and regulatory problems presented by the existing cable and satellite revolution have hardly begun to be solved. Meanwhile, new technologies are presenting a new phase of globalisation and posing immediate new challenges for marketing and advertising professionals as much as for government regulators.

For most of the 1990s, the leading player in this new South Asian marketing and regulatory environment has been the Star group of channels owned by Rupert Murdoch's News Corporation. By creating a predominantly free-to-air service disseminated by cable, Star did much to set the terms for the way in which satellite television developed in India. Star's big project then became the conversion of that new mass market into a profitable vehicle for the broadcaster as well as the cable operator. But its plan to be the first to provide a Direct to Home (DTH) multi-channel service to India was blocked by the Indian government and eventually abandoned. The fear of monopoly and the difficulty in regulating DTH operators was a central issue for the long delayed Broadcasting Bill. As media consultant Sudip Malhotra correctly predicted, the Indian government was playing for time. The aim was to allow it to equip itself to take full advantage of the facilities of the new technology. This was the reason why permission for DTH, with all its implications for the convergence of communications systems, television, radio, e-mail and the Internet, was withheld for a further three years and then provided in 1999 in the first instance only to the Indian state broadcaster.[48]

INDIA AND SOUTH ASIA: MEDIA, ECONOMICS AND CULTURE

International and Indian entrepreneurs have exploited the advertising potential of the new satellite channels to sell their goods and services to the huge Indian middle class. But the enticements of the new consumerism have had an appeal well beyond the borders of India. Indian popular culture on satellite television has attracted very large South Asian audiences and advertisers see this as a basis for a potential South Asian media market. MNCs have usually thought in terms of national, not regional markets. But now a process is beginning of standardisation of products which have appeared in different markets under different names.[49]

Unilever is in the forefront of this process of developing regional markets where previously there were considered to be national markets. In Bangladesh, Aly Zaker of Asiatic Communications argues that '...MNCs see little difference in the markets in South Asia. The major consumer products of South Asia are basically the same, owned by a few companies, such as Unilevers, British American Tobacco, Nestle etc. In the era of globalisation, they are becoming monolithic in their approach to advertising'.[50] A senior manager of Hindustan Lever in India prefers a slightly different take. Turning the catch phrase 'think globally and act locally' on its head, he says: 'We think locally and act globally. We take pride in the fact that we are a multi-local, multinational company'.[51]

But there are significant political and cultural differences between South Asian countries which prevent this potential from being realised for the time being. An Indian company executive told us that many of his MNC clients were not yet aware of the potential. He identified a lot in common between the five countries but also important differences.

> Cross-border media buying is pretty simple. It can work out once the system is in place. But for creating an advertising campaign it is going be difficult because you are violating the principle of thinking globally and acting locally. Sri Lanka and South India are pretty homogeneous, so are Bangladesh and West Bengal, or most of north India, Punjab and Pakistan. So, instead of one single advertisement for the entire subcontinent, I would rather have an advertisement each for these sub-regions, which would also cross borders.[52]

Other media planners, like Vijay Kastoori, accept that some regions of the subcontinent can be treated as homogeneous, particularly where there is a common language. 'Packaged wheat flour can be sold across the northern subcontinent, fish can become a product across Bengal, and perhaps coconut may do the trick for Tamil Nadu and Sri Lanka'. But he does not believe it is possible to treat South Asia—or even India—as one market, now or in the future. The strategy for media buying for each of these markets is different.[53]

Advertising in South Asia evokes cultural and national sensitivities, as it does in Europe. 'In India you can talk of a woman in an office situation and talk of body odour...', says Meenakshi Madhvani. 'In Pakistan, I don't think that may be allowed. In

Bangladesh, too, it may not succeed.'[54] In Karachi, Taher Khan makes the same point: 'Levers are advertising tea in India through dance. This is aspirational in India but taboo in Pakistan.'[55] But while advertising professionals are aware of what works culturally in which market, satellite television, with its relentless focus on India, is less sensitive. Pakistani media professionals recognise that Indian TV is popular and influential. But they say people do not want to see their culture and value system eroded.[56] It is a fact, however, that Zee TV is widely seen in Pakistan, Nepal and Bangladesh, complete with advertisements aimed at the Indian middle class. Despite government discouragement, some Pakistani advertisers even placed advertisements on Zee TV to reach their own customers when one of the Pakistani TV channels went off the air in 1997. National broadcasters, with their superior reach, remain the best means of selling soap and toothpaste to mass audiences, but satellite TV reaches the transnational educated middle class very effectively, even if it does provoke some strong cultural reactions.

Some advertisers with global brands detect what a leading Indian software producer calls 'an emerging synergy in the television market, especially in South Asia and South East Asia'.[57] Kunal Das Gupta of Sony describes his global media company as a 'boutique' which is available all around the world, with the same product, virtually at the same time. Certain products do lend themselves to transnational advertising if the cultural appeal is right. Firms like Coca-Cola and Pepsi have successfully projected their brands across South Asia with the help of well-known cricketers like Imran Khan and Sachin Tendulkar. Cricket always was a passion in South Asia; it has now become a passport to new consumer markets.

Marketing among the South Asian diaspora in the Gulf or Europe has also demonstrated how much there is in common. Bhaskar Majumdar notes that '...in Zee's international operations, the feeling of being a South Asian channel is much stronger. Over here, we are still pretty clear that the focus of our business remains India. Over there, the communities are far more integrated and the programming schedules mix Urdu with Bengali and Tamil language programming.'[58] Outside India Zee markets itself as a south Asian ethnic channel. Bhaskar Majumdar maintains that '...typically, ethnic channels don't merely remain a channel but become a platform for the entire community'. In Nepal, Neer Shah accepts that Zee TV is 'not exclusively Indian' in comparison with the state channel Doordarshan.[59]

Another factor in promoting a common consumer culture across the region is the growing role of Indian advertisers in neighbouring countries. Over the past few years, agencies like IMRB and ORG-MARG have either set up branches or entered into partnerships with local advertisers in Nepal, Bangladesh and Sri Lanka. They have become an important new source of expertise and a means of South Asian coordination for particular campaigns.

Aly Zaker, whose firm is responsible for Unilever advertising in Bangladesh, told us that the growth of regionalisation, both in advertising and in broadcasting, had brought about major changes in his country. He said: 'In view of the added advantage of numerous dialects and ethnic diversity, India is generally considered as the lead for Unilever products. This means that products will be moduled in India by top advertisement agencies which are located in Mumbai.' Regionalisation is a matter of changing the model: 'Because no foreign models can be used for advertising products marketed from Bangladesh, the advertisement is redone using local characters.'[60] But satellite TV can distort even this degree of regional focus. Sometimes, viewers of both terrestrial and cable TV in Bangladesh see two versions of the same advertisement, one aimed at India and another at the local terrestrial market.

Competition for new markets is also increasing competition among advertising agencies. The re-broadcasting of Tamil satellite channels like Sun TV and Raj TV on Sri Lanka television has awakened Indian advertisers to the possible southward extension of their markets. A leading South Indian advertising agency, R.K. Swamy, affiliated to the multinational BBDO, has recently expanded its operations in Colombo to exploit the synergies which are emerging.[61] According to Geeteara S. Choudhury, chief executive of the company with the largest billing for TV adverts in Bangladesh, the entry of cable TV has forced Bangladeshi advertisers into a greater concern for quality. 'In this changed competitive world, an Indian company may easily come and set up office. So we have to stay ahead. We work harder, we are more creative.'[62]

Ramendu Majumdar, who leads the activist Combined Cultural Alliance in Bangladesh, points to the dangers of cultural homogenisation arising from India's leading role in advertising. He accuses multinational companies of saving costs through central control, which has the effect of marginalising local culture. 'MNC advertisements are lead-country based and this automatically leads to monocultural domination of that lead country. In our case this is India.' But Majumdar argues that some products are essentially local culture based. 'Advertisements must be identifiable at a local level to work. Many Indian advertisements don't work here', he says.[63] For Aly Zaker, however, the trend to monoculturalism is inevitable.

Marketing is widely seen as a major force for cultural homogenisation. The perception in Bangladesh is that television is promoting a South Asian identity, one that is defined not by any sense of the cultural or economic distinctiveness of South Asia but by the products the consumer buys. 'South Asian man', according to this view, will be shaped more by the efforts of the Mumbai advertisers than by the politicians of Delhi or Dhaka. At the moment, the satellite footprint over South Asia does not correspond to the market. Political divisions, between India and Pakistan in particular, are holding up the implementation of plans to create a South Asian free trade area. But there is a regional as well as an international trend towards freer trade, despite the political and economic anxieties of India's smaller neighbours.

Satellite TV is at the cutting edge of the development of new South Asian markets. It is creating awareness of new products and lifestyles, even if the goods are not available locally. The lure of the Indian market has persuaded international media entrepreneurs like Rupert Murdoch to 'hindigenise' their programmes and thereby their appeal. Indian companies like Zee TV and Sun TV have used the same new opportunities with even greater commercial success. Powerful new media instruments have been created which not only serve commercial interests but also play a very important role in the wider projection of Indian culture. The influence of satellite TV is not just about new markets: it is about culture and cultural influences and about the role of the market and the state in defining them. In South Asia, satellite TV has cut across the well established boundaries of the nation state and has raised fears for the future of 'national' cultures. It has also raised widely debated questions about the homogenisation of Indian culture itself in an age of globalisation. In the next three chapters, we look at the cultural influences and implications of the satellite revolution. We show how a new popular culture has been created and we examine reactions to it in India and neighbouring countries.

NOTES AND REFERENCES

1. Omkar Goswami, 'The Wasted Years', *Business India*, 9–22 March 1998, quoted in Mayank Bhatt's paper 'The New Media Market', commissioned for the Media South Asia Project, July 1998. This chapter draws extensively on Mayank Bhatt's research.
2. The survey covered 515 cities and towns, 1509 blocks and 182,599 households in urban areas and 820 villages across 410 districts and 99,169 households in rural areas, mapping the ownership and purchasing patterns of 281,768 varieties of consumer durables and 18,730 genres of consumer non-durables. It was updated in 1998. I Natarajan (1998), *Indian Market Demographics Report 1998*, National Council of Applied Economic Research (NCAER).
3. The NCAER has published separate reports on this wealthy class as the demand for information about the market for luxury goods has increased. See, *The Very Rich Whitebook: A Study of Super Affluent Indian Consumers*, NCAER, 1998.
4. P.K. Varma (1998), *The Great Indian Middle Class*, p. 172
5. Cf. Praful Bidwai, *Frontline* , 10 February 1995, cited in Varma, *The Great Indian Middle Class* (1998), p. 173.
6. This was at 1993–94 prices with an adjustment of 50 per cent upwards to allow for unaccounted income or black money.
7. For example, that of the Confederation of Indian Industries, cited in Varma, *The Great Indian Middle Class* (1998), p. 171.
8. Gurcharan Das quoted in *Business Today*, 22 February–6 March 1996.
9. Quoted from 'The New Market Place', *Business Today*, February 22–6 March 1996.
10. Ijaz Gilani, Gallup Pakistan, Islamabad, January 1999.
11. Cited in Herman and McChesney (1997), *The Global Media: New Missionaries of Global Capitalism*, p. 58.
12. S.L. Rao, former director of NCAER writing in *The Economic Times*, 13 July 1998. Other advertising specialists endorse this view (cf. Roda Mehta, O&M Advertising, Mumbai, May 1998).
13. M. Suku, Colgate Palmolive, Mumbai, May 1998.
14. A. Padamsee, Mumbai, April 1998. For a full account of the interview see, *Gentleman*, February 1999.
15. Pravin Tripathi, Associate Regional Director, Chaitra Leo-Burnett, Mumbai, May 1998. For a discussion of the implications of WTO policy in the communications field see Pradip Thomas (1999), 'Trading the Nation', *Gazette*, Vol. 61, pp 275–92.
16. Roda Mehta, Mumbai, May 1998.
17. *Ibid.*

18. M. Suku, Mumbai, May 1998.
19. Roda Mehta, Mumbai, May 1998.
20. D. Sriram, Madison DMB&B(Darcy Masius Benton and Bowles), Mumbai, May 1998.
21. Meenakshi Madhvani, CEO, Carat India, Mumbai, March 1998.
22. *Doordarshan Annual Report 1996.*
23. Ammirati Puris Lintas estimates in *APL Media Guide India*, June 1999, p. 15.
24. In 1998 it was 5.6 per cent according to industry estimates. *APL Media Guide India*, June 1999.
25. The NRS-97 survey was conducted in urban areas only.
26. Sony Entertainment TV, for example. Though its overall audience is much smaller, it delivers an audience with ten times more young people than either of the music channels, MTV or Channel V, which are specifically aimed at a younger audience. Sony also has a much younger audience profile than Zee.
27. 1998 Lintas estimates. Total media expenditure in 1998 was estimated at nearly Rs. 70,000 million (approx. US$ 1,670 million). *APL Media Guide India*, June 1999.
28. For NRS-95, four agencies were appointed: IMRB, MARG, MRAS (which is now AC Nielsen) and MODE. For IRS-95, ORG was the main contractor. Shortly afterwards, MARG merged with ORG to form India's largest market research agency. Two subsequent National Readership Surveys (NRS-97 and NRS-99) were conducted by only three agencies, while ORG-MARG carried out the rival Indian Readership Survey in 1998.
29. For urban areas, each of the 100,000+ towns are sampled. For towns below 100,000+, IRS uses a concept called socio-cultural regions, taking samples that include towns.
30. Ramesh Thadani, President, Indian Market Research Bureau (IMRB), Mumbai, May 1998.
31. M. Madhvani, Mumbai, March 1998.
32. Bhuvan Lall, in *Screen International* (London), 8 October 1999.
33. Kunal Das Gupta, CEO, Sony Entertainment TV, Mumbai, April 1998.
34. NRS-97 shows that even in the more prosperous states more than half the TV sets are black and white only; in all but four states the figure is over 70 per cent. Only in three cities do as many as 10 per cent of households have more than one TV set; one of them surprisingly is Patna, the capital of one of India's poorest states. Unnikrishnan and Bajpai found in their sample of mostly affluent households in Delhi that 35 per cent owned more than one TV set; 10 per cent said they had three or more; one joint family of 15 members possessed no less than six sets. See, N. Unnikrishnan and S. Bajpai (1996), *The Impact of Television Advertising on Children*, p. 48. Sources in the advertising industry in 1998 were not forecasting a rapid move to multi-set households.
35. M. Madhvani, Mumbai, March 1998.
36. Rumy Mukherjee, *Economic Times*, 25 February 1998.
37. Sunil Maloo, general manager, INTAM (Indian National Television Audience Measurement), the research wing of ORG-MARG, notes an increased interest in cable by advertising agencies and multinationals. INTAM figures for December 1997 and January 1998 indicate that the share of cable viewership rose from 16 per cent to 20 per cent in Mumbai, from 10 to 14 per cent in Delhi, from 5 to 8 per cent in Bangalore, and from 3 to 3.2 per cent in Chennai.

An IMRB People Meter study for the week 1–7 June 1997 revealed that the share of cable viewing between 9.30 p.m. and midnight was 51 per cent of all viewership. Sunil Maloo, Mumbai, May 1998.

38. Hiren Pandit, Vice President-Media, Enterprise-Nexus, cited by Rumy Mukherjee; *Economic Times*, 25 February 1998.

39. V. Kastoori Vice President Media Services, Vibrant Media (P) Ltd., Mumbai, June 1998.

40. This profile has been made available by Sandeep Nagpal, CEO, Stratagem Media Communications Pvt. Ltd.; also Interview, Mumbai, May 1998.

41. Cf ., Chapter 3, Table 3.6.

42. The definitions of the categories are given in NRS-97, pp. x–xi and NRS-99, pp. 11–14.

43. From Rs. 5,700 million revenue in 1996–97, Doordarshan revenues fell to Rs. 4,000 million in 1998–99. Zee TV announced revenues from advertising of Rs. 3,850 million in 1998/1999 and Rs. 5,160 million in 1999/2000. Zee website: www.zeetelevision.com.

44. M. Madhvani, Mumbai, March 1998.

45. Ashok Mansukhani, Mumbai, May1998.

46. Ashok Mansukhani, Mumbai, May 1998. Figures updated from *Doordarshan 1998* (Audience Research Unit).

47. Cf. Report by Anita Mani, *The Hindu*, 11 November 1998. InCable worked to a deadline of November 1999 for providing cabled Internet services in Mumbai.

48. Sudip Malhotra, Mumbai, April 1998. An apparent conflict of interest between Rupert Murdoch and Subhash Chandra over DTH, widely reported while they were still in partnership, is believed to have influenced the government's decision not to allow Star to be the first to establish a DTH platform.

49. Taher Khan, Chairman, Interflow, Karachi, May1998.

50. Aly Zaker, Asiatic Communications, Dhaka, April 1998.

51. Irfan Khan, General Manager-Corporate Communications, Hindustan Lever, Mumbai, April 1998.

52. D. Sriram, Director-Media Services, Madison DMB&B, Mumbai, May 1998.

53. Vijay Kastoori, Vice President, Vibrant Media (P) Ltd., Mumbai, June 1998.

54. M. Madhvani, Mumbai, March 1998.

55. Taher Khan, Karachi, May 1998.

56. Cf . Satish Anand, Karachi, May 1998.

57. R. Screwala , UTV, Mumbai, April 1998.

58. Bhaskar Majumdar, Vice President-Corporate, Zee Telefilms Ltd., Mumbai, May 1998.

59. Neer Shah, Kathmandu, March 1998.

60. Aly Zaker, Dhaka, April 1998.

61. S.K. Swamy, Chennai, May 1998.

62. Geeteara S. Choudhury, CEO, ADCOMM, Dhaka, March 1998.

63. Ramendu Majumdar, Dhaka, May 1998.

Five

WHOSE POPULAR CULTURE?

In this chapter we look at the kind of satellite programmes available in South Asia and at public and professional reactions to them. Many of the programmes, particularly English language programmes, are made for global audiences and watched in South Asia largely by the English speaking elites. Our main focus, however, is on reactions to programmes made specifically for Indian audiences, particularly on popular entertainment channels like Zee, Sony and Star, which are watched not just in the metropolitan centres but over a much wider area. We argue that these programmes have helped to create a new South Asian popular culture which transcends national barriers.

The evidence comes from a range of different interviews, discussion groups and surveys which were carried out in the five main South Asian countries over an eighteen month period in 1998 and 1999. The picture it paints is impressionistic, but it is sufficient to show that new electronic communities have been created and that many of the issues raised by the satellite media are shared across the region. These include the propagation of new visions of society, the growth of consumerism, the targeting of children and controversies provoked by soap operas which offer new role models for South Asian women.

In asking the question 'Whose popular culture?' we attempt to probe the ideas and objectives of those making and funding the programmes, whether through advertising or sponsorship. We also examine the interconnectedness of advertising and programme making and its implications for diversity of choice. In analysing satellite programmes which successfully appeal to the new Indian middle class, we explore the terms on which the global and the local meet in putting across a new vision of society.

Our interviews and discussions illustrate the difficulty of disentangling the influence of the satellite media from the growth of television as a mass medium. For many interviewees, the satellite media are part of a general process—the entry of South Asia into the television age—which is having an impact on how people spend their leisure, how they eat their meals, how they relate to each other in families. What our interviews and discussion groups have produced, therefore, are not just reactions to particular programmes or types of programmes but also broader reflections on the state of the electronic media in general.

We begin the chapter with an overview of satellite television, what it offers to the urban middle class and how it differs from the programmes and traditions established by Doordarshan. The rest of the chapter looks at different aspects of the new satellite culture and its reception in India and other parts of South Asia.[1]

NEW VISIONS OF INDIA: THE APPEAL OF THE SATELLITE CHANNELS

After years of state monopoly, the arrival of satellite channels was like a breath of fresh air for India's middle class viewers. Those with cable and satellite connections were suddenly liberated from Doordarshan's paternalistic programming and were offered access first to a wide range of international channels and soon afterwards to popular commercial programming specially made for Indian audiences. The first beneficiaries were the English language-knowing audiences in the large cities. Though only approximately 3 per cent of the population, they are nonetheless an economically and politically influential niche audience. But the main target of the popular channels has been the expanding Indian middle class with Hindi as its lingua franca in the North and other languages in the South. As we saw in Chapter 4, the prospect of selling products to over 100 million consumers has been the main motivation of India's rapidly growing advertising and media industries which have attempted to tap this market with a new mix of programmes. This has included more regular access to films, new kinds of tele-serials, quizzes, fashion shows, game shows, popular music, showbiz and sports.

The new popular satellite channels have been powerful agents of a new consumerism. Unlike Doordarshan, which has traditionally propagated the political and development ideology of the Indian state, the satellite channels appeal to the viewer as a consumer in a liberalised India where personal choice has become a new ideology. With no inherited obligations to the 'nation' or to existing rule books and standards, they have questioned old social and cultural traditions, explored new fusions of East and West, and put materialism much higher up the agenda. Zee TV, in particular, has been the flag bearer of a new vision for middle class India in which money and good looks are the hallmarks of success.[2]

One of the most sophisticated interpreters of these trends, marketing consultant Rama Bijapurkar, argues that liberalisation of the Indian economy was a macro-event which involved a major transformation of Indian cultural attitudes. She says the move to 'freedom of choice' and a philosophy of 'survival of the fittest' constituted 'a whole new way of living' which would gradually become the new culture of India. In an article written with two British market analysts at the beginning of the satellite revolution and using a system of cultural classification developed by them, Bijapurkar divides India since independence into three 'age cohorts'—the first, those who brought independence, the second, 'the Rajiv Gandhi age cohort', and the third, 'the post-liberalisation age cohort: tomorrow's consumer'.[3] She accepts that 'outer-directed culture', by which is meant the new world of consumer choice, changes much faster than 'inner-directed culture', which relates to the home and family and long-established beliefs. In the new world, people will tap into two or more cultures and will have to cope with the contrasts and conflicts between them. But Bijapurkar argues that the 'genetic coding of Indian society', which she defines as 'acceptance, adaptability where essential and an ability to exist on many cultural planes', will ensure that 'India's cultural response to liberalisation and the resultant invasion of foreign culture through branded goods and services will be to accept them, and include them in certain facets of life without subsuming them or being subsumed by them.'

Translating this vision into programmes which will sell new products to the Indian middle class has been the job of advertising agencies, who have worked closely with television companies to achieve this purpose. The culture which has emerged from this collaboration is a mixture of mutually reinforcing lifestyles and commodities, with branded goods acquiring new importance as a distinguishing mark of success. According to Bijapurkar: 'Liberalisation of the mind has occurred alongside liberalisation of the market.... The average consumer is now truly beginning to see what brand choice is.'

Retail is an important part of the post-liberalisation culture. It was relatively undeveloped before the 1990s but by the end of the decade it had grown into a booming industry worth an estimated US$ 180 billion a year.[4] Bigger India's cities have witnessed the building of new shopping malls which are also a focus for the new youth culture.[5] The 'mom and pop' store, like the 'mom and pop' cable operation, is slowly being replaced by national retail houses and, in some cases, retailing and broadcasting come under the same corporate umbrella. The Rahejas, who have been building a chain of retail outlets called Shoppers' Stop, are also developing a national cable network. The Goenkas, who operate the largest cable network in Calcutta, have been investing in food supermarkets.

Satellite programmes are being watched by all sections of the urban community, from the students of elite colleges to labourers in cities like Ahmedabad and Pune. But urban youth are a key target group which have been offered a new image of themselves. Satellite music channels, MTV and Channel V, have played an important role in putting pleasure and consumption much higher up the agenda than in the past. According to Sunil Lulla, formerly MTV India's chief executive: 'Young people today are not inter-ested in rebellion, ideology and such issues. They are interested in moving ahead in life.'[6]

A new emphasis on personal appearance is also fed by American and Indian soap operas and encouraged by a growing cosmetics industry. Social scientist Anjali Monteiro says, 'TV has contributed to the culture of packaging oneself. This comes in the form of beauty contests constituting national pride, middle class girls coming into the profession as VJs, modelling being considered respectable....'[7]

Many critics and artists use the term 'packaging' disapprovingly. For them it is the triumph of form over content, which they see as characteristic of new trends in art and culture. Columnist Shanta Gokhale says money now dominates everything. 'When Vikram Seth and Arundhati Roy's books came out, the news was that the rights had been bought for so much.... Even our contemporary architecture has to show itself. Theatre is showing this trend.

Hyping everything.'[8] Sunil Shanbag, a theatre director and television producer, makes the same point. 'There was a time when "sponsored by" would be tucked in the corner of the advertisement.... It was an embarrassment. Today it is a sign of success.... It is linked to the consumerist way of thinking; packaging is the most important thing.'[9]

In keeping with the emphasis on individualism, many satellite channels have created a new environment in which audiences feel more empowered than before. They discarded Doordarshan's serious discussion programmes with politicians and intellectuals. Instead, they brought the viewers into the studios and used them to call politicians and intellectuals to account. The vogue for seriousness was replaced by showmanship. But with it came a far greater sense of public participation, as evidenced in the huge popularity of musical talent shows like *Antakshari* or political debates with studio participation like *Aap ki Adalat*, both on Zee TV.

This sense that the individual viewer counts is part of the new populism of satellite TV which is having an effect throughout society. Since satellite TV ended Doordarshan's monopoly, TV talent spotting competitions and shows encouraging audience participation like *Meri Awaz Suno, Antakshari* and *Sa Re Ga Ma*, have developed very large audiences all over India, particularly among the young. Hima Vishwanathan, a researcher with IMRB, discovered 'an amazing gleam in the eyes of three girls she was interviewing when she asked them if they would like to participate in *Antakshari*. They said they would love it...the dream is to be part of *Antakshari* even as an audience.'[10]

These influences have gone right down to the district levels in India. The principal of a music college in Latur in southern Maharashtra told us that 'shows like *Sa Re Ga Ma, Alaap* and *Meri Awaz Suno* have created an urge in the minds of the young to learn music. Some of them joined the college with the express desire to appear on these music shows.' A college principal in the same town said that at annual get-togethers the students 'insist on *Antakshari* and quiz programmes centred around film songs and film information. At their request we organise programmes like *Aap ki Adalat*. We interview local government officers in the programme. Student participation is good. They ask studied and oblique questions fearlessly.'[11]

Beyond giving the public more visibility, the agenda of maximis-
ing consumption also involves downplaying Indian caste divisions
and attacking what an executive of Pepsi Cola described as 'the
Brahminical cult of contentment and stability'.[12] Transforming a
historically caste-divided society into one where people are defined by consumption is one of the objectives of the advertisers,
though it does not always go down well with those who support
the status quo. There is some evidence, however, that the promotion of consumer products is also promoting what one commentator called 'a kind of social equality at a banal level'.[13] This is also
the view of Dr. Abhilasha Kumari, who has researched the effect
of television commercials. She discovered, contrary to her own
expectations, that the audience's relationship with commercials
was helping to create 'a secular kind of world where consumption
patterns were shared'.[14]

At the same time, the new vogue for branded goods has generated cottage industries all over South Asia producing surrogate
versions for those who cannot afford the real thing. 'Television is
promoting a fake culture...', said a working class man in Karachi.
'There is no item that cannot be faked. Nobody sells genuine items.
I know the hotel here sells fake Coke.... Most things advertised on
TV are so expensive and out of reach of people like us that there
are cheaper, substandard versions of everything available in the
markets.' Another said: 'There is a vast disparity between our
leaders and people. We are given nothing, no health package, no
educational facilities and yet we are talking about entering the
twenty-first century. What are we going on–a donkey cart?'[15]

Another contribution of satellite TV and its talk shows has been
to promote far greater openness about issues like human rights,
women's rights, questions of choice and career, sexuality and
relations with others. Anita Anand of the Women's Feature Service
in Delhi says: 'There was nothing like that available when I was
growing up: no opportunity to talk about what men think about
women, what they want, what women want from their lives. Half
the things that people invited to TV studios say is pure garbage
but it does not matter; the fact is that they have a platform and an
opportunity to think about these issues.'[16] Academic Sabina Kidwai agrees: 'The best thing about satellite TV is that it has allowed
a lot of people to express opinions.... The last two years' debates

on women's issues on talk shows would have been unimaginable before satellite TV.'[17]

New ideas about sexuality have also been a key element in a new generation of TV soap operas which are one of the main battle-grounds between Doordarshan and its satellite rivals. Doordarshan still addresses far larger audiences than any of the satellite channels, but since it began the metro channel to build a national urban audience to counter the appeal of its satellite rivals, it has been competing directly with them for advertisements aimed at the Indian middle class. As a result, as broadcaster Kiran Karnik predicted, satellite television has had a cloning effect on Doordarshan, which 'affects even those who only view domestic channels'.[18]

In the pre-satellite era, Doordarshan's own strategy for building a mass audience took a very different form. In the late 1980s, it had begun to broadcast what are known as 'mythologicals'— serials which dramatise some of the great religious traditions of India. The first two of these, which were based on the great Hindu epics, the *Ramayana* and the *Mahabharata*, were watched by hundreds of millions of viewers and were seen by many of them not just as entertainment but as a religious experience. For Doordarshan, these serials were a source of professional pride and formidable new revenues, but they also attracted considerable controversy because they were widely believed to have contributed to the rise of Hindu nationalism as a political force. The political context in which they were broadcast has been explored and analysed elsewhere.[19] In terms of Indian popular culture, however, they showed the powerful role that television could play in appealing to the emerging middle class market in religious, and particularly Hindu, terms. As Chakravarty and Gooptu have pointed out: '...with the market driving the growth of the media and the middle class forming its primary target audience, not surprisingly, media productions not only drew upon but also reproduced and magnified middle class notions of the "Hindu" nation in a bid to promote consumerism among these classes.'[20]

The emergence of the BJP and the Shiv Sena as dominant political influences at the national level and in Maharashtra in the mid-1990s contributed to the emergence of a more conservative cultural atmosphere, which the growing importance of market forces to some extent reinforced. As columnist Shanta Gokhale put it when talking about contemporary films and plays: 'You can't separate films from the political process.... It's back to Hindu values. Young people are far more conservative.'[21] For many viewers, however, Hindu mythologicals are a form of education and entertainment, rather than an expression of any overt political sympathies. As another critic has written: 'Morality is passé, but religion, like fast food, is an increasingly popular form of gratification.'[22]

The popular satellite channels have not invested heavily in mythologicals, except in South India, where they are engaged in more direct competition with Doordarshan for a mass audience. The Hindi satellite channels have been aiming at different audiences and offering different visions of modernity. Doordarshan, despite its new dependence on market forces, represents a tradition of state control, paternalism, didacticism and conservative morality, whereas the popular satellite channels are pursuing an agenda centred far more on personal choice and consumption. If liberalisation involves major changes in outlook and philosophy, as Rama Bijapurkar has argued— from isolation to interaction with the rest of the world, from ideology to rationality, from curbing consumption to stimulating demand,...from obeying authority to freedom of choice, from protectionism to survival of the fittest'[23]—the satellite channels are very much more at the cutting edge of change than Doordarshan. For Doordarshan, as we shall see later, the pressures of commercial competition have involved a crisis of identity which has still not been resolved. In many parts of India, it is losing urban audiences and finding it difficult to win them back.

SATELLITE TELEVISION AND THE ENGLISH-SPEAKING ELITES

As far as South Asia's English-speaking elites are concerned, it is often said that they have more in common with each other than with their own compatriots. English language education lost much of its official patronage in the post-colonial period. But the South Asian professional job market has continued to value English and middle class parents have seen it as vital to their children's advancement, whether at home or abroad. In this sense, globalisation is not a new thing; it is an old phenomenon which is becoming more pervasive as a result of improved technology and communication.

Among the English-educated middle class, there is wide appreciation of the extension of choice which the satellite revolution has brought. Whether one is talking to intellectuals in capital cities or teachers in district towns, everyone acknowledges that their access to information and entertainment has improved. Young adults, particularly males, welcome the new access to international news and international sports coverage. There is appreciation for the professionalism of many satellite productions and for better quality documentaries and wildlife programmes. But there are also concerns about the ruthless commercialism of the entertainment channels, the morality implicit in some of the serials, the effect of consumerism on children and the lack of serious programming about India.

The other striking finding of our group discussions is the dramatic decline in viewing of Doordarshan programmes in cable and satellite households. Doordarshan features infrequently in lists of favourite programmes, not only among English-knowing middle class groups but also among Gujarati, Marathi, Hindi and Bengali speakers. Many middle class viewers have switched to Star, BBC and CNN for news, to Zee or Sony for entertainment, to Star and ESPN for sports, and to Discovery for science, environment and wildlife. Doordarshan may be holding its own outside the large conurbations, where its reach is unrivalled, but in the urban areas it is not doing well, except with the older generation.

Discussions held among English-speaking middle class groups in Mumbai indicate that satellite TV has been a means of reinforcing their existing preferences. Young middle class professionals working for multinational employers in Mumbai watched very little television; they worked long hours and returned home late. A majority said they preferred reading to watching TV. What they wanted from television was news and business updates and 'something light' for relaxation. Channel preferences included Star News, Star Movies, CNN and BBC. There seemed to be no following for Doordarshan. In many ways, this kind of group looks outside India for its role models. Asked about Indian culture on television, one discussant said: 'We are not interested in the past.'[24]

Girls and boys of 12 or 13 years of age going to the elite Bombay Scottish school showed a similar preference for international programmes. They liked British comedies, sports, particularly football matches, news and the Discovery Channel. They preferred English horror movies like *The X-files*, saying 'the Hindi ones don't look real'.[25]

Employees of an Indian bank in Ahmedabad were contemptuous of Doordarshan and Hindi soaps. No one with cable watched Doordarshan; they thought the programmes and presentation were too poor. One called Doordarshan 'the pits'; a second said: 'They just don't care.' Mostly in their 30s, they watched cable TV for news, current affairs, sports and the occasional film.[26]

Among a largely Maharashtrian professional group interviewed in Pune, Star news was the most regularly watched programme. 'They have managed to capture the culture we live in', said one discussant. But another criticised Star news—and much of satellite TV—for being centred in the west. 'The basic orientation of TV here is not Indian', he said. 'I am watching more about the USA and UK, not about Andhra and Assam, and I want to know why we are obsessed with the west.'[27]

Though these illustrations come from India, they can be reproduced among English speaking elites in other South Asian countries. Research in Bangladesh indicates a similar divide in viewing habits between the elite or upper class, which follows English language programmes, and the middle class which is happier with Bengali or Hindi. As Afsan Chowdhury puts it: 'The upper class has always felt that alienation from local culture was a sign of privilege, a status symbol. In that way, there is continuity in the perception of their own culture.... Children of the elite regularly request songs on MTV and Channel V. The middle class children only watch, but they prefer Hindi channels. They also can't afford calls to Mumbai. But those who get to watch "serious" channels have a higher level of knowledge than their parents.'[28]

THE MTV GENERATION

It is among the college populations of South Asia that satellite television has made its greatest impact because it tends to be this group which is most affected by new trends in language, fashion or behaviour. Earlier, the incorporation of elites into the international community took place in a more subtle and limited way.

Now satellite television is thrusting the commercial face of western industrial civilisation into almost every metropolitan household and helping to create a new global middle class ethos which affects far larger numbers of people. 'Given certain socio-economic characteristics', said a South Asian advertising executive, 'we are looking at the same kinds of markets. And advertisements are market driven. So the foundation of a common culture is already laid.'[29] Earlier, the gap between the elite and the rest of the middle class was very wide. Now television is playing a part in levelling those differences, particularly among college students in metropolitan cities. As the same executive put it: 'The children of the middle class, with their demand for Nike shoes and Calvin Klein T-shirts, look much the same wherever they live'.

MTV started off on the Star platform offering western pop music to South Asian audiences and being widely criticised as culturally invasive. After Rupert Murdoch took over Star, MTV was dropped and replaced by Channel V, with more Indian VJs and more Indian pop music. It was a programme of Indianisation which brought immediate rewards. Channel V began to grow at 25 per cent per year, helped by the popularity of its road shows, which reached out to college students in the big cities and made its VJs national figures.[30] In late 1996, MTV, which had initially put its faith in a more western product, accepted the logic and re-launched itself with a much more Indian profile, playing much more Indian film music. The style of presentation was the same but the content changed dramatically. What had begun as a largely western music channel appealing to students of elite colleges changed to one carrying 70 per cent Hindi popular music. According to MTV, 1997 brought a doubling of turnover and an increase in penetration from 4 million to over 8 million homes. The following year, the channel was no longer aiming at a metropolitan audience but at over a hundred Indian cities.[31]

A discussion group among 17- and 18-year old students from the elite St. Xavier's college in Mumbai revealed that most of them spoke English at home and watched English language television programmes. None of the group watched Doordarshan and neither did their parents. VJs from the music channels were definite reference points for style and fashion in music and dress, though most of it was western. There was a strong following for English language soaps on Star World. The vulnerable and comically indecisive lawyer Ally McBeal was a particular favourite: 'I like *Ally McBeal* a lot. I can relate to her very well', said one. 'Some of the episodes are really silly but many of them really show the way a girl thinks', said another.[32]

Outside Mumbai, even in large cities like Ahmedabad or Pune, the music channels were less popular and more controversial. In these cities, traditional values are still well entrenched and students displayed more resistance to western role models and morals. Among middle class Gujarati-speaking students in Ahmedabad, the boys expressed a preference for news, sport and quizzes, while girls favoured mythologicals and Hindi satellite serials. However, the girls were openly enthusiastic about TV fashions. 'That is what I am watching each time', said one young woman, '... the hairstyle, the shoes, the clothes.... I watch the music channels only for that.'[33]

A similar group in Pune with conservative leanings expressed worries and some frustration at the moral values reflected in satellite programmes. One participant said: 'We get an inferiority complex...when we see all these serials.... People are having sex at our age.... Why can't we if they can?' The group also differed over the music channels and the role of VJs. Several of them watched the music channels. But one said: 'The VJs are the most irritating souls on earth.... They talk rubbish, wear stupid clothes.' Others said: 'They are copying foreign values.... They are not even imitating...they are aping.'[34]

MTV and Channel V offer young people a vision of a freer, more fashionable world, the promise of more gratification and an entertaining escape from parental and cultural pressures. Cyrus Broacha, a VJ with MTV who has travelled across India from campus to campus, says 'TV has definitely played a role in people opening up.... Girls are free.... Even in Lucknow in an all girls college they are all over me, enthusiastic to speak, to snatch the mike.'[35] But that very prospect also makes them a source of anxiety to parents, who believe they threaten the values they are trying to inculcate in their children. A sociologist who studied the influence of television in Goa found that 'there is a moral panic among parents with satellite channels, especially Channel V and MTV, in the lower middle class, where parents say they are afraid to leave the home and go away because children will turn to these channels.'[36]

The scale of the culture shock which the music channels have caused has also prompted some heart-searching among those involved in marketing the new visions. 'The question that worries me', said one of them, 'is that because of the high aspirations and media floating around...are we going to see class wars? ...When will the servant's son turn around and say: "Why the hell not me?"'.[37]

Anita Anand believes it is the promise of a different kind of sexuality for the next generation that lies behind the anxiety they have caused. She says: 'There is nothing else that is bothering nice middle class people, including myself, more than talk of sexuality and aspirations. Behind the facade of criticising the media for creating aspirations and for not addressing real issues is the fear that...our children will have a sexuality and aspirations that we will not be able to address.'[38]

The same music channels also have a following in the metropolitan centres of other South Asian countries—among college students in Dhaka or Colombo and even in Pakistan, where public opposition to western influences is more marked. According to Farzana Bari, a social scientist at Islamabad university, 'preference for MTV is based on the English-medium school culture', which is already preparing the children of the professional class to absorb western influences. She says 'the germs of western preferences, individualism and materialism are already present in the youth of this class.'[39] A discussion among students attending colleges in Islamabad produced much praise for the Indian channels and many criticisms of PTV. 'MTV has good numbers, good beat, one can enjoy them.... The Pakistani programmes are very dull', said Huma, a recent matriculate.[40] In Pakistan, however, much of this enthusiasm is privately relished and expressed; it has not given rise to the same degree of public activity or display as in Mumbai or Delhi because of conservative pressures within the society.

In most countries, MTV and Channel V are more popular in the big cities than in the districts, but in Nepal many college students in the smaller towns of the terai were aware of the music channels and had opinions about them. Some followed the fashions set by the VJs and were at the centre of a debate about where Nepali culture is going. 'In urban areas, the culture is being taken over by something that is not Nepali', said one student. 'TV has spawned a "punk" culture. From childhood, kids have taken to wearing earrings and singing pop songs. These are the negative effects of TV', said another. Most young Nepalis deny any disloyalty to their culture or disrespect for their parents. But they acknowledge the power of the new influences. 'Nepal TV should also go on satellite', said one student. 'That way other people will also know something of our country.... It also means that just like MTV and V have a strong impact on our society, similarly Nepal TV can promote Nepali culture elsewhere.'[41]

Within India, the channels have had an unexpectedly strong impact in the small, tribal states of the North East. According to Subir Bhaumik, an expert on the region, states like Nagaland, Mizoram or Meghalaya, which are largely Christian, 'see westernisation as giving them strength to face the dominant local cultures of the Assamese and Bengali variety.'[42] Bhaumik reports that separatist rebels in the Imphal Valley in Manipur, a predominantly Hindu area, have banned some Hindi satellite channels and MTV on the grounds of obscenity and 'bad culture'. However, these channels are available in tribal and Christian areas where the Nagas and Kukis are the major tribes. In those areas, he says, 'even the rebel groups have no hang ups and MTV seems to be the most popular channel among the tribal youth in the North East.' MTV is aware of this audience and has produced programmes with local singers in Shillong. It is an interesting illustration of the role channels can play in encouraging a counter-culture beyond metropolitan limits.

SATELLITE TV SERIALS: NEW SPECTATOR POSITIONS

Satellite TV has created its greatest ethical and cultural ripples as a result of a new series of soap operas which broke with the traditions of Indian cinema and offered the public bolder themes, franker treatment of personal relations, and fewer happy endings. In Indian cinema, many heroes and heroines transcended the taboos of caste and community, and relationships which would not have been condoned in traditional society were redeemed by love. In this way, Hindi cinema broadened and democratised ideas of nationhood and played its own part in the project of building an independent country. At the same time it did little to challenge the extended family or the values it enshrined; love may have triumphed over social divisions, but everyone lived happily in the end in the patriarchal family. Many soap operas on satellite television have broken this mould, modelling themselves on the sexual openness of American soap operas and offering new role models to Indian audiences. One major reason for this is satellite TV's more segmented audience. Bollywood films, with a reach beyond the urban conurbations into the rural areas, aim at a nationally inclusive audience; Zee TV, aiming at middle class cable households, can afford to be—indeed aims to be—more challenging and experimental in its approach.

The synopses of some of the most popular teleserials shown on Zee and other satellite channels give a clue to the controversies which they have aroused. One of the first to break the mould was *Tara*, the story of four young women from Chandigarh who set off for Bombay to realise their dreams. The story focused on the cultural shocks they experience as they shift from a protected and conservative existence to a more independent one. Tara is the insecure daughter of divorced parents who works in a Bombay hotel and gets involved with her boss. His daughter, Devyani, never accepts Tara and much of the serial concentrates on their strained relationship. Eventually the father dies and Tara is ousted from the business.

Tara shattered the myth of the 'good Indian woman' and led to an unbottling of feelings of women in similar situations. It proved shocking on several counts: one of the women was raped; they were portrayed drinking alcohol, smoking and swearing; and in one famous episode a girl slapped her own father. But despite the controversies it caused, *Tara* touched a chord with many young women who do migrate to the big cities in search of education and jobs and it played a role in making cable TV popular in the smaller Indian towns. According to Vinta Nanda, the writer of the serial, it was specifically designed to spread Zee's appeal from the metros to the smaller towns.[43]

Hasratein was another controversial serial which set out, in the words of its director Ajay Sinha, to explode ' the life of hypocrisy and double standards' which enabled a man to have extra-marital affairs but made it unthinkable for his wife. 'I allowed the women to reveal their inner feelings and live their life as directed by themselves', says Sinha.[44] The plot centres around Savitri, the young daughter of a well-known classical singer who died of a heart attack when his wife left him for a younger tabla player. Savitri was brought up strictly by her father's sister and married to a man who became suspicious of her loyalty and resented her developing her career. In the end, Savitri falls in love with her boss, Krishnakant Trivedi (KT), who leaves his wife to set up home with her. Much of the rest of the serial portrays Savitri's efforts to balance her love for KT with that for her own daughter, and her tussle with KT's parents and his estranged wife who try to win him back. At the end of the four year series, Savitri's sincerity only brings partial reconciliation as KT flies off to the USA for medical treatment.

Another high profile serial is *Saans*, which was still running on Star Plus in early 2000. N.G. Productions, which makes the serial, describes it as 'the life breath of every Indian woman as it depicts her character, strength, virtue and steadfastness'.[45] *Saans* tells the story of a happy family—Priya, Gautam and their two children—brought to unhappiness by Gautam falling for the attractive Manisha. The heroine is Priya who 'makes innumerable attempts to win back the love of Gautam solely for her children'. She contemplates divorce but does not pursue it. As events unfold, Manisha becomes pregnant and has a miscarriage and Gautam is forced to live with her because of her critical condition.

These sorts of themes marked satellite television out, at least initially, not only from Hindi cinema but also from Doordarshan. But by the mid-1990s, Doordarshan serials were also exploring similar relationships. *Dard*, which was broadcast on the Metro channel as Zee put out *Hasratein*, told the story of Radha, a good looking young woman who had married an older man and later developed an extra-marital relationship. However, in the denouement, which in many ways holds the key to public reactions to such serials, the widowed Radha was depicted devoting herself to bringing up her son, an ending very much in keeping with traditional morality. Though Doordarshan explores some of the same themes, it still manages to retain its reputation as an upholder of family values.

Doordarshan had pioneered soap opera in the 1980s with *Hum Log*, which carried a message of modernity centring on the nuclear family, with two children and aspirations for a better life through education and more consumer goods. That was didactic television intended to serve the development goals of the state, though it was not always construed by the viewers as its producers intended. Later, in the same decade, Doordarshan also broadcast a number of soap operas offering women new role models and exploring their rights. One of these, *Udaan*, about a woman's efforts to become a police officer, proved extremely popular and resulted in more women entering the police academy.[46] By contrast, satellite TV soap operas of the 1990s were tailored more to the demands of the advertisers than to those of the state. They took their cue less from successful media experiments encouraged by international development agencies than from American commercial soap operas like *Dynasty* and *Dallas* with their more direct appeals to materialism. There was some continuity of emphasis on the aspiring nuclear family and its vision of modernity; those who transgressed social norms were often punished for their pains. But the new soap operas also incorporated western preoccupations with the disintegration of the family and offered Indian viewers a range of spectator positions which were certainly not provided earlier by Doordarshan.

Anjali Monteiro and K.P. Jayasankar, who have studied the changing discourses of Indian cinema and television, point out that in its earlier incarnation 'staid, domesticated, educative' Doordarshan was seen as 'a counterpoint to popular cinema', which offered 'an escape into a fantastic larger than life world'. Now, they say, Doordarshan is occupying similar ground to the Indian cinema, while satellite TV is offering 'imaginary spectator positions' which violate its norms. Monteiro and Jayasankar point out that in Indian cinema anything but the monogamous and the heterosexual tends to be disallowed. 'If there is, for example, a love triangle, one of the characters conveniently gets killed towards the end of the film, leaving behind a monogamous, reassuring residue!' But the satellite TV soaps 'with their endless round of extramarital and pre-marital relationships, replete with children born out of wedlock, offer a sharp contrast....' With all this, they say, 'the moral landscape of urban popular culture has become far more complex and problematic, engendering resistance of various kinds.'[47]

The kind of controversy generated by these serials is illustrated by different reactions to *Saans* in discussion groups held in western India. The story line went down well among English educated college students at St. Xavier's in Mumbai, but was much more hotly contested elsewhere. The only Hindi serials mentioned by the St. Xavier's group were the more realistic ones, with *Saans* the best rated.[48] However, a group of Maharashtrian students training to become civil servants at the Chanakya School in Pune exhibited serious differences over the serial. One male student criticised TV soaps and comedies for 'giving the wrong messages', particularly *Saans* for encouraging extra-marital affairs. Another defended the serial as 'so sensitive...the best on Indian television right now.' 'It is because of these serials', the first retorted, 'that divorce is increasing...do you want divorce?' 'If my wife and I didn't get along, then it would be a necessity', replied the second. 'These are just western values', came the reply.[49]

The same serials have been widely watched in Bangladesh and Pakistan and have raised similar controversies there. *Hasratein* was criticised in discussion groups in Bangladesh because it was seen to hold a brief for adultery. One criticism was that the sexual openness of some of these serials was not always relevant to the story. 'On BTV such relationships don't exist', said one discussant. 'On Indian TV only such relationships do.' Many Bangladeshis see satellite TV as offering increasingly adult entertainment and are worried that children are being affected. Discussants said that *Saans* in its depiction of a split marriage caused anxiety amongst children.[50]

A NEW SOUTH ASIAN LINGUA FRANCA

The new satellite culture has also challenged the linguistic orthodoxies of South Asia's nation states by producing its own lingua franca which mixes English and Hindi in ways which reflect the everyday speech of the English educated. This new language, pioneered by Zee TV, which has come to be known as Hinglish and sometimes Zinglish, has caught on with the urban young all over North India and has become a point of controversy with others. One of the reasons for its popularity is its complete break with the style and preoccupations of the national broadcasters. 'TV always reflected the upper class or caste type of language', says John Samuel, Director of the National Advocacy Centre in Pune. 'Zee entered and changed that. It questioned the hegemony of language. The highly sanskritised Hindi and the very formal English...took a beating with the coming of Zee.'[51]

Our districts surveys in India confirm that television has produced 'a perceptible change in the usage of language'. In western India, the Maharashtrian 'middle and lower classes' are reported to be using more Hindi and English words in everyday Marathi language. The 'higher classes''are trying to retain the sanskritised flavour of their language by using 'either Sanskrit or elite English words'.[52]

There are both hostile and pragmatic responses to this pervasive new fashion. Dr. Bhadrinath Kapoor, a linguist and lexicographer at Benares Hindu University, told us that 'the most corrupting language is of Zee and Star news.... The Zee language neither contributes to Hindi nor to the English language.... Zinglish throws grammar and syntax to the winds.... Most of the time, the communication is conceived and written in English and translated. I am not against using English words in Hindi. But the words should not be like pieces of stone in rice.'[53] Others see a more relaxed approach to language as a necessary response to fast-changing times. Professor Ransubhe, a lecturer in Hindi and Marathi in Latur, says that there were no words in either language for many new products, processes and services. TV has given those words. He says: 'The concept of purity of language is humbug. I welcome the new trend.... This language does not make a fetish whether the word is English or Hindi or Marathi, as long as it is understood by the majority of listeners.'

Repercussions beyond India's borders have been coloured by concerns for national sovereignty. Language and culture are seen as inextricably linked and the evident popularity of Hindi satellite television is thought by some to be undermining national cultures. In Pakistan, an old debate about the role and character of Urdu as the country's national language has been revived by Zee TV and by the respectability it has given to mixing Urdu and English. Aslam Azhar, Pakistan's first managing director of television, ridicules this as 'Minglish' and sees it as part of a deterioration in standards, promoted by the Hindi satellite channels and imitated by Pakistan's commercial producers.[54] Others are concerned that children are picking up Hindi words from television and using them in conversation at the expense of their Urdu vocabulary. To this extent, they see satellite TV as undermining the distinctiveness of Pakistan's lingua franca.

Iftikhar Arif, the Chairman of the National Language Board, believes some of the changes in approach to language provoked by satellite competition have improved communication. There has been a tendency to use fewer loan words from Arabic and Persian and to simplify language in order to speak more directly to viewers. Urdu in its pristine form is not only under attack from across the border; it is also changing its character and intonation within Pakistan as it is increasingly owned and spoken by Pakistan's other language groups. Arif says 'No language can remain pure if it is to grow. Fossilised languages cannot live. It is only insecure societies who are scared to accept new things.'[55]

However, there are concerns that the new style is an urban phenomenon which reflects the dominance of the middle class English elite in the new media and a lack of seriousness in communicating with the rest of society, which does not know English well. Some see the new trend as a result of sloppiness—the projection of the linguistic inadequacies of convent-educated trend setters onto the population as a whole. It is a criticism made not just of Zee TV but of many of the new FM radio channels in the big cities. In Sri Lanka, according to television producer Maleec Calyaratne de Silva, 'people with British, American or any other foreign accent gained preference over those with Sri Lankan accents. Entertainment and idle talk became hip over the radio while responsibility was grossly neglected. Foreign investors who were behind these institutions seemed keen to introduce foreign cultures and commercialism through their radio programmes.'[56]

FILM STARS AND CRICKETERS: SCREEN IDOLS AND ROLE MODELS

Though mixtures of English and other languages have become the norm in addressing urban audiences, Hindi satellite entertainment channels have ensured their success with the wider public by exploiting the popularity of commercial cinema. The cinema has always influenced style, language and behaviour and its stars continue to exercise a huge fascination over South Asian audiences. Inter-war American cinema clichés transferred effortlessly into Bombay or Madras movies—from the styles of the stunt men and women to the heavy overcoats and homberg hats of the Chicago gangsters. In the same way, it is the dress and hairstyles of Indian film stars which are still sought after at the fashion boutiques and hairdressers of urban India. The jacket worn by Salman Khan in the film *Maine Pyar Kiya*, the hat Aamir Khan wore in *Dil Hai Ke Maanta Nahin* or the saris Madhuri Dixit wore in *Hum Aapke Hain Kaun* were all available in Mumbai shops soon after the films became popular. Such enthusiasm is largely confined to 'middle India', but on occasion the upper middle class can also be affected. Up-market tailors in Mumbai reported heavy demand from their well-heeled clientele for the 'Kamasutra choli' after the success of Meera Nair's film of that name. A more recent Hindi blockbuster, *Kuch Kuch Hota Hai*, made a direct appeal to the same group by dressing up the stars in designer-label outfits.[57]

Television has never had this kind of impact. According to Hima Vishwanathan of IMRB: 'Television has created no single point hero. Not a single hero or heroine has functioned as a trend setter in fashion or clothing.'[58] The nearest television has come to producing its own cult following is for the VJs on MTV or Channel V. But the intrusiveness of TV has had an impact at a different level. Whereas films remain in the realm of fantasy for many viewers, television projects the stars as human success stories and stimulates interest in their lifestyle, relationships, wealth, clothing and personal likes and dislikes. In this sense, stars are an important element in the commodification of everyday life.

A survey of the impact of satellite television in two districts in India—Latur in Maharashtra and Varanasi in Uttar Pradesh—provided ample evidence that satellite television serials are stimulating a growing interest in personal appearance and beautification. Though many of those interviewed denied they were imitating the styles of the stars, the proprietor of Amrita Beauty Parlour in Latur said her clients specifically demanded hair styles from *Surabhi, Shanti* and *Tara* as well as those of Sonia Gandhi and Princess Diana. Even in Udgeer, a smaller town in Latur district, clients of Jose Beauty Parlour, requested hairdos in the style of Renuka Shahane of the show *Surabhi* and the so-called 'Tara cut'. Its proprietor, Mrs. Dole, believes that 'beauty consciousness is the contribution of TV shows'. She says in Udgeer it has become normal practice to visit the beautician before attending any celebration and she believes TV is the reason why this trend has become entrenched 'in a comparatively backward place'. In Udgeer, five beauty parlours are doing comfortable business. In Latur, there are more than 200 beauty parlours with state-of-the-art equipment. Evidence from dress shops in both Latur and Varanasi suggests that there is a roaring business in dresses popularised in films, with the Mumbai wholesalers dispatching them in volume once the film has become popular. However, Ruby Baranwal of Ananya Designs in Varanasi told us that whereas 'clients from the middle and lower classes mention clothes worn by actresses, higher class women...want their own exclusive designs.' She believes that TV is developing 'fashion literacy'; women are coming into the shop asking for 'hipsters' and 'tight-fit' fashions and she says sales of dresses, including evening gowns, are running at 300 a month.

Staff at Grihasti, a cosmetics shop in Varanasi, reported that sales of cosmetics have increased dramatically since the early 1990s, with lipstick becoming much more fashionable. Equally marked in Benares is the trend among the young towards T-shirts and jeans. The proprietor of Rohit Collections, a general dress shop, said that 'Benares is changing very fast.... The demand is sometimes based on costumes worn by actors and actresses; sometimes it is triggered by advertisements.... In the last two or three years... the turnover of my shop has increased many fold...thanks to TV ads and serials.'

These new fashions encouraged by TV have provoked some criticism from traditionalists. The salesperson at Grihasti, selling sixty lipsticks a day, has had to justify her activities to parents who object to her chosen work: 'We told them that we are doing nothing wrong. Beautifying one's face and body has a long Indian tradition.... The tradition is ancient; only the products have changed.' The proprietor of Guddi Beauty Parlour, which is frequented by followers of Zee TV's beauty show, put up the same defence: 'We do not think we are corrupting the culture of Varanasi. Beautifying oneself has been a long tradition in Hindustan. Temples are testimonies of that tradition. Look at Khajuraho.'[59]

The same programmes are also having an impact among the middle class in Pakistan and Bangladesh. According to informants in Islamabad, local designers not only watch Zee's fashion programme *Khoobsurat*; they also record it for future reference. They say many local designs and colour combinations owe their inspiration to this programme. Indian channels may also be aiding a comeback for the sari, which went into an officially-enforced decline during the days of General Zia-ul-Haq. Pakistani fashion magazines have been featuring saris again and the wearing of saris and bindis has become more common on festivals and social occasions, whereas in India the opposite has happened. Satellite TV has helped to popularise the salwar kameez at the expense of the sari.[60]

Even in smaller towns in Nepal, these influences are acknowledged. Professionals in Birgunj told us: 'TV programmes are really affecting the way our women perceive themselves. We can see it in the number of beauty parlours that have come up after we began getting satellite channels here. These are things that have to be considered carefully. Women's fashion can lead to a strain in relationships for the simple reason that we can't afford the kind of fashion shown on TV.'[61]

Film and TV influences on young men centre on film stars like Shahrukh Khan and cricketers like Sachin Tendulkar, both of whom have lent their names to advertising campaigns for well-known products. Both have acquired cult status with the young, not just for their professional acting and playing but also for their very noticeable wealth. For many young men from unprivileged backgrounds, cricket and films offer a means of identifying with success and the fantasy of achieving the same themselves.

Many working class parents in western India were clear that 'boys were more influenced than girls' by television serials and films. One mother said: 'My kid watches TV like mad...and he couldn't care less about his studies.... The kids are obsessed with Hindi films...they copy the songs and dances.'[62] This idolising of film stars has also brought a new interest in physical development. In the town of Udgeer in Maharashtra, Nilu Damle discovered that health clubs and karate classes had sprung up, something quite new to the culture of the town. 'The youths had seen the well built heroes of the films and wanted to imitate them.' Meeting a group of young men in Udgeer, Nilu Damle noticed 'some had grown their hair long like Sanjay Dutt.... One boy always talked like Amrish Puri.... He felt he *is* Amrish Puri. One boy was imitating a character from *Chandrakanta*. I could see that almost everybody was obsessed by films and serials.'[63]

The other obsession is cricket, which is now preferred to traditional games in rural areas. The owner of Latur general stores said that within three months he had sold 400 bats marketed in the name of Vinod Kambli, the well-known Maharashtrian cricketer. According to school teachers in Udgeer: 'The white Gandhi cap has been replaced by cricket type caps.... Instead of gulli danda they have taken up cricket...the students are addicted to viewing one day cricket matches on the TV.... They know all the cricketers and their records. They know all the terms used to describe the game.' Even in the village of Ekurka, a small village with no satellite TV, 'people are mad about cricket, thanks to televised cricket matches....'

Ekurka also witnessed a lively debate about the influence of television. One man said: 'The young generation has gone astray because of over exposure to TV programmes. They sing dirty songs, gesticulate in a dirty manner. Their ideals are not Gandhi and Nehru but Shahrukh Khan and Sanjay Dutt.' Another retorted: 'I do not agree with my friend. I find TV a good educational device. There are lots of informative programmes. You will find the level of knowledge of the younger generation higher than us. It is a thousand times better to see programmes on TV than to loiter around in the village and get involved in prankstering.'[64]

TARGETING CHILDREN

The need to protect children as a vulnerable group from exposure to unsuitable programming is a responsibility which government and broadcasting authorities take seriously all over the world. Many broadcasters operate watershed policies which keep programmes with adult story lines or excessive violence off the air until children are supposed to be in bed. But such policies are only ever partially effective, even with active parenting. Another area of concern and one which is more difficult to monitor and control is the targeting of children in advertising. The exploitation of 'pester power' is becoming increasingly sophisticated and according to some marketing companies has now spread 'from sweets and snack foods—often linked to film or television characters aimed at the under 12s—to CDs, computer software, and even cars and holidays.'[65]

Shailaja Bajpai and Namita Unnikrishnan, who studied the impact of television advertising on children in India, present a case for real concern at the profound changes which have taken place in cultural attitudes among the television generation. According to their research, young people spend an increasing number of hours watching TV and are enthralled by it. They say TV is presenting consumerism as a way of life. Consumer nondurables are the easiest things to sell because they do not require a big investment. But advertisements for soft drinks and cosmetics boost the market for a whole range of consumer durables associated with 'modern' lifestyles. Selling these goods is the big prize. Advertisers for rival brands, ostensibly in competition with each other, are engaged in a common enterprise of preparing the market for future consumers.[66]

Analysing children's reaction to television advertisements, Unnikrishnan and Bajpai note that the push to individual consumption on a western pattern tends to undermine more traditional Indian habits of sharing. Advertising promotes the nuclear family at the expense of the joint family.[67] They argue that many children have begun to associate happiness with owning or possessing a toy or being indulged by their parents.

Discussions with working class groups in western India support the view that parents are under pressure from their children to buy things. A group of working class women in Pune said they were influenced by advertisements, particularly for cosmetics and toiletries, with their children wanting them to try all sorts of new products. A Muslim broom maker in Millatnagar near Ahmedabad said of her son: 'If he wants, then he wants. There is no stopping him.' One boy in this group had even demanded a mobile phone from his uncle.[68]

Middle class housewives in Pune raised worries that children had become addicted to TV. 'If there is an interruption', said one, 'my child insists I call up the cable guy immediately'. Another mother recounted how her boy had seen a sweet advertisement at 10 p.m. the previous evening and demanded one immediately. 'Finally', she said, 'my husband had to step out and buy it so he would stop crying.' Some of this group were using TV as a means of amusing their children and paying a price for their absorption in the world of advertisements, which many of them knew by heart.[69] A similar group in Ahmedabad revealed that in many houses the television is on all day, though viewing is concentrated at particular times. In these families, the children seemed to control the remote and were 'crazy' to try advertised products.

Many parents argued that satellite television was playing a pernicious role in advertising alcohol and cigarettes. Alka Wadkar, an academic psychologist who studies the impact of TV on children says: 'We as parents say "learn good things", but what has been prohibited for generations is what is highlighted as fantastic by the media.'[70] In a discussion in Benares, satellite TV was blamed for the growing popularity of alcohol among young people, who were going to restaurants on the outskirts of town to drink and smoke. 'TV... has given prestige to drinking', was the view of this group. In Udgeer, in Maharashtra, a professional said: 'In the old films, consumption of alcohol was not prestigious.' 'When the character in the film was not in a normal state of mind he used to consume alcohol. But these days...alcohol is being taken casually as if it's a cup of tea. This is a very dangerous thing...in a small place like Udgeer you will see so many bars have sprung up and the clientele is ever increasing.'[71]

In Pakistan, articulate teenagers from a slum area of Rawalpindi proved to be very familiar with satellite TV programmes.[72] Most of these teenage boys and girls worked part time or full time; some went to the local government school. Several of them saw satellite TV as a strong aspirational influence. 'They show such goodies that we immediately want to acquire them', said Samina, aged 14. 'The only question is where to get the money from...But I still love watching the advertisements and know by heart the names of all the items....' 'I like to watch movies and programmes that show people rising from a low to a high position', said Anthony, aged 15. 'I wish they would show more programmes like this which encourage many like us to continue our struggle.' Bashir, aged 12, said: 'I have learnt that America and England are the best places to be if you can get a job there. Then you can have access to all the things like Wrangler jeans, Nike shoes and of course Kentucky Fried Chicken and McDonalds.'

Unnikrishnan and Bajpai, in their analysis of TV advertising in India, note that in middle class households children also influence their parents' decisions on the purchase of big items such as refrigerators or cars. Advertisers know this and use this in their marketing strategy for adult consumer goods. According to the director of an advertising firm in Calcutta: 'Children are exposed to advertising of products which have no connection to them, yet the parents are under mounting pressure to take their children's opinion into account when making any decision related to the purchase of goods. The advertising agencies have capitalised on this...by coming up with many more advertisements directed at children.'[73]

With the vast majority of households in South Asia only having one TV set, it is not surprising to learn that children spend most of their time watching programmes made for adults. But there is also a shortage of programmes for children, particularly on the satellite channels. The only frequently mentioned children's programme was *Shaktimaan* on Doordarshan, with a central character modelled on Superman. The satellite channels are best known for their western cartoons, whose accessibility to South Asian children has proved a cost effective means of reaching these audiences without commissioning any regionally specific alternatives. Discussions with parents frequently highlighted this inadequate provision and in Sri Lanka there was a detectable demand for more children's programmes. Labourers in Matara regarded many programmes shown during the day as unsuitable for children. Matara home makers argued that 'more programmes that are exemplary to both children and adults should be presented.'[74]

SATELLITE TV AND THE REPRESENTATION OF WOMEN

A great deal of the debate about satellite television has been about its influence on women. A study of viewing habits by the Delhi-based Media Advocacy Group published in May 1994 showed that women are more 'regular' in TV viewing than men and that the lower the income group, whether male or female, the more regular the viewing.[75] Women also view TV for longer periods than men and according to our soundings with women's groups they are more likely to make time to view what they like. They are also heavier consumers of cable television than men, which means that the 'modern' story lines of the soap operas are playing to very full houses.

The story lines of satellite TV serials are of special interest because they project women in different roles from those of wife, mother and home maker. Serials like *Tara* or *Hasratein* have dealt with issues of working women, divorce, extra-marital relationships, sexual harassment, rape and abortion in ways that were unfamiliar in the days of Doordarshan's monopoly. With their depiction of 'the new bold woman', they have offered a variety of new role models to the urban middle class and provoked much controversy in the process.

The evidence from our own discussion groups suggests such new role models have been more influential in the larger cities than elsewhere. A group of women in Latur felt that the serials by and large painted 'an unreal and perverted picture of women'. Two working class women took very strong objection to what they termed 'the misbehaviour of young women in serials'. They claimed that their day-to-day life and reality was never shown in the serials or films. To them the women shown on the screen belonged to a very small affluent section of the Indian society, which is not at all representative [76]

Among the middle class, there is a definite following for the new soap operas. Middle class home makers in Ahmedabad expressed distaste for the new themes but admitted watching *Hasratein* regularly. 'We are now hooked and we want to know the end', was one reaction. Another said: 'It is a different story but such things are taking place in society today.'[77] Middle class students in Ahmedabad were also watching the serial, though it was clear that they did not see Savitri as a radical figure, despite her extra-marital relationship. Asked whether they found *Hasratein* bold, one of them replied: 'It is bold, but Savitri does not act bold. She is like a traditional wife.' 'I like Savi'. said another. 'She respects everyone and teaches me to respect everyone.'

Rama Bijapurkar uses Raymond Williams' description of culture as a series of overlapping ideologies—the residual, the dominant and the emergent—as a means of interpreting changing reactions among women of different generations to the impact of the new media.[78] The residual ideology of self-sacrifice and self-denial, subservience to husband and family, involves a fatalistic acceptance of the woman's traditional status. The dominant ideology is more questioning of tradition, less diffident, keen for more windows on the world, still bowing to authority but negotiating. The emergent ideology is of a woman confident, discerning, living fully in two worlds of home and career, by no means a beast of burden but constantly stressed trying to balance self and family.

In line with this interpretation, Bijapurkar believes that television has played a part in winning acceptability for the idea of the middle class working woman, even if the numbers have not grown substantially over the past ten years. She points out that the matrimonial columns now advertise for working women, which was highly unusual before. In the same way, in her analysis of the Zee TV serial *Hasratein*, Bijapurkar interprets the story line as a sign of the changing moral climate: 'You are actually saying that it is OK to walk out on your husband and get involved with a married man and have a child out of wedlock...and yet the feeling towards the protagonist is overall positive...nobody is banning the second woman...the audience is not rejecting the serial.'[79]

Some serials, like *Shanti* and *Aurat*, both broadcast on Doordarshan, which portray women fighting for their rights rather than exploring new personal relationships, seem to have developed a committed following across a broader social spectrum. As one working class woman in Pune put it: 'The women are strong and fight injustice...they do not believe they are inferior to the men....'[80] One interesting indicator of the impact of such serials is that some husbands try to stop their wives from watching them. This has been established by studies conducted by the Media Advocacy Group and by IMRB and was confirmed in our own discussions with women in Pune. Several participants said their husbands had dissuaded them from watching *Aurat*.

A discussion group in Bangladesh also argued that the portrayal of women in teleserials had had an impact on men. As one discussant put it: 'Men have recognised that women can be strong role models. Cable TV is full of women who take decisions, who manage, who matter. Men are beginning to get convinced that women are capable of much more than they thought. As yet they are not threatened but the future is not certain.'[81]

Whether admiration for TV role models leads to behavioural change is more difficult to determine. Reactions to what is seen on the screen depends on individual circumstances. However, sociologist Anjali Monteiro, who held discussions with Indian women on the impact of some of the new serials, concluded that 'women were using the images in their process of questioning'.

According to Monteiro, 'the imaginary identification...at least offered some kind of revolt against where they were.'[82]

The franker treatment of sexuality in the satellite TV serials is another related area of debate. Vidhyut Bhagwat, Director of the Women's Studies Centre in Pune, believes that the new channels 'are definitely opening up doors of sexuality'. She sees a growing consciousness of the body and greater concern with one's looks. She says: 'Now, a fully body-conscious Indian woman is definitely not unreal.... Even in the serials, the middle aged woman is shown fit, dancing, singing...and this is not only an upper class phenomenon. Even among the lower classes, I see older women wearing brighter coloured saris.... There is a definite zeal about looks and the outer form. This is one area where everybody is touched.'[83] Dr. Neelam Gore of the Stree Adyar Kendra in Pune says, 'women complain that men want more sex. They say men are perverse because they want sex in the day too. Also, a lot of men expect their women to be sexy, to have oral sex...women are not yet comfortable with that.' Sharmila Rege, a sociologist who also works at the Women's Study Centre, feels that pre-marital sex is becoming more common and that there is greater awareness of contraception. But she does not think this is necessarily linked with greater awareness of sexuality; she says it is often due to 'fear of losing the boy'.[84]

Anita Ratnam, the Indian classical dancer and TV personality, believes that 'Indian women are coming into their own', but that this greater assurance is not being shown on the screen. She contrasts some American serials with the general run of Indian ones. 'Take fantastic programmes like *L.A. Law*. You see women equal with men. Not just for sex or comedy. Maybe there is a male boss but the women have voices which are heard.' She says that with few exceptions, the only strong role model for Indian women is 'a modern day Durga who screams and threatens. A regular woman with class and taste who disagrees with her husband is automatically bad.'[85]

Sharmila Rege is also sceptical about satellite TV's progressive credentials. She believes the impact of satellite TV in terms of greater self-awareness has been achieved at the expense of economic and political awareness. She says 'the major impact of satellite TV has been on middle class women in terms of day-to-day behaviour, dressing and language.... On classes lower than that it has led to a loss of critique.... In this media society, for example, I just can't imagine the anti-price rise movement that we saw in the 1970s...because the woman is lacking a sense of critique.' This view is also supported by Vidhyut Bhagwat. She says women are getting more visibility, issues are getting more space, but there is too much stereotypical representation of their problems. In fact she sees satellite TV as subversive of women's fight for political emancipation. She says it is a case of 'give them visibility and kill them' and she holds that invisibility would have been preferable.

The Media Advocacy Group, which held extensive discussions with women in different Indian cities about their response to such soap operas, concluded that 'they appreciated the new bold woman', though they differed considerably over how the boldness was portrayed. An underlying concern among working women themselves was that their portrayal in the serials was 'extremely negative and problematic.... Many of them even felt that there was a conspiracy to malign working women and to project them as home wreckers, divorcees, incompetent parents and often failures as persons....' One conclusion of these discussions was that women's worlds are not reflected adequately on television, except in soaps and serials, and that something needs to be done to correct the imbalance.[86]

Professional women in other South Asian countries voice similar concerns about the failure of the new media to play a more progressive role. Professionals in Islamabad wanted programme editors to take stock of how women were being portrayed and to make more effort to show them playing a variety of roles. 'Women are shown in plays, entertainment and movies and are not much included in current affairs discussions, economic research and political debates', said one participant. 'Television is not showing what our women are achieving', said another. 'Women should appear in the media in a diversity of roles, not a limited and stereotyped one', was a third opinion.[87] According to Farzana Bari of Islamabad University, women's issues gained ground in Pakistan during the 1990s; government and non-governmental organisations gave more importance to them and they were more discussed on television. But she says teleserials and plays are still 'perpetuating the same traditional image of a weak woman living happily within four walls'.[88]

A study on the representation of women in the Sri Lankan electronic media also concluded that during prime time television 'women are represented primarily in their roles within the family and principally confined to the domestic sphere'.[89] Its author, Maithree Wickramasinghe, a lecturer at Kelaniya University, found this to be particularly true of Sri Lankan teledramas. She says many of them are 'rampant with gender stereotypes'. Very few critically consider issues such as oppression of women within the family or problems of domestic violence. Moreover, the few that do, such as the popular teledrama *Nedayo* which raised the issue of unequal marriages, fail to resolve them from a progressive angle.

Wickramasinghe also criticised western films for their 'culture of violence' against women and their representation as sex objects. Hindi and Tamil influences were even more negative. 'I cannot believe they have any positive impact', she said. Wickramasinghe argues in her report that there is a need for 'clear and comprehensive guidelines on gender and the media'. She says television needs to promote role models 'founded on achievement and not on appearance' and that there is a need for more women in television management and more training in gender issues for media staff.

OLD WORLDS AND NEW

Many reflections on the impact of television in South Asia are similar to those observed in other societies entering the television age. People comment on the role of the television set in reconstituting family space, its effect on the taking of meals, its implications for family relationships and the new problems of choice and control which have to be negotiated. As Hima Vishwanathan of IMRB puts it: 'Lives revolve around the idiot box.... All the patterns of the day are determined by what comes on TV.' Beyond that, she detects what she calls a 'loosening up, with TV giving suggestions'.[90]

Many discussants express nostalgia for the loss of social interaction which was a hallmark of city life in the pre-television age. Dr. Satish Kumar, a lecturer at Benares University, says the city used to be full of small restaurants and clubs, whereas today 'most people are before TV sets.... The TV has replaced the banks of the Ganges.'[91]

Discussions in Bangladesh confirm a decline in socialising. Family gatherings have grown less frequent as programmes take priority and social interaction is often determined by what is on TV. 'I know I wouldn't want a guest when the drama is on', said one informant. 'Others won't like it when a countdown show is being shown. I think that is the biggest change in the last few years since we have had so much of TV.'[92]

A common complaint of parents is that children are glued to the television set and neglect their studies, though the supposed correlation between addiction to television and poor exam results is not easy to prove. Some parents have cable TV disconnected as exams approach, though most teachers argue that television, properly used, has widened children's horizons and helped them do better. The viewing and reading habits of parents are in most cases more significant determining factors than the presence or absence of a television set.

In Nepal, it was not just parents who were complaining. School children in Birgunj were annoyed that parents did not bother to sit down with them when they had difficulty with their homework. They would rather watch TV than talk to their children.[93]

Some of the strongest reactions to the new consumer culture come from religious leaders who see it undermining spirituality and with it, their place in society. The Shankaracharya of Varanasi told us that 'an attempt is being made to destroy the balance of the spiritual and the material.... This is a global conspiracy and TV is a part of it.'[94]

Some Muslim clerics are urging their flocks to avoid television entirely, though they know their advice is not generally being accepted. The Imam of the Faruqui Nagar mosque in Benares told us: 'In Islam, only devotional music is allowed; no dancing is allowed; no alcohol is allowed. All this is shown on TV. They show women without *purdah* on TV. This is also strongly prohibited in Islam.' The Imam does not condemn TV outright. But he urges his followers not to see serials and films 'because they are anti-Islam and corrupting'.[95]

The contrast between the world of the Buddhist religion with its emphasis on self-denial and spiritual enlightenment and the new world of commercial television has provided some interesting cultural juxtapositions in Sri Lanka. At the launch of the commercial TV channel TNL in 1993, the sight of Buddhist monks chanting auspicious prayers as the first programme—the cartoon series *American Gladiators*—was broadcast was one such occasion. The chief monk, who was obviously disconcerted, turned to the news director and gently advised her to be more discerning about the programmes the station chose to show.[96]

A well-known Buddhist monk said in a recent Sri Lankan television discussion that 'the public has exceeded the limits of religion—almost to the extent that the clergy can no longer capture the people's interest and imagination.' In the same discussion, Father Cyril Fernando said 'our culture has been built up over thousands of years and these programmes are threatening all this.... We can't place these commercial objectives on top and forget all else.' In reply, Jackson Anthony, the director of a commercial Sinhala radio station, said the younger generation had a different perspective on change. 'We can see the difference between the two cultures but the generations that follow may not be able to make a comparison. They are likely to compare their culture with other contemporary cultures of the world.'[97]

Many conservative reactions to the growth of popular television are in line with Europe's experience, though the contrast between screen society and behaviour and the realities of social and cultural life in the districts of India, Pakistan or Bangladesh seems to have provoked a much higher level of anxiety. South Asian parents of almost all backgrounds express worries about the greater incidence of sex, violence, bad language and bad behaviour on satellite television. There is concern that violence on the screen is producing copycat violence on the streets or in the classroom, that sexual gratification and promiscuity are being encouraged and that certain kinds of more explicit programmes undermine family and traditional values. Parents and grandparents fear that children are losing their innocence by being exposed to unsuitable adult programmes—especially the vulgarity of Hindi film songs and the unnecessary violence and frankness of serials.

Family viewing of programmes with bolder themes or franker treatment of sexuality is a source of embarrassment for many parents and some children. One woman in a working class group discussion in Latur said that television had provoked children to ask all sorts of embarrassing questions: 'Small children ask questions about underclothes, the menstruation cycle, etc. We cannot answer them. They shouldn't show such things on the screen.'[98]

Parents in Puhulwella, a rural settlement in Matara district in Sri Lanka, were equally concerned. 'Sex and violence are things that are not openly discussed in average Sri Lankan families and should not be shown on television', summed up this point of view.[99]

Speculation about the impact of television is common, though most of it cannot be confirmed when specific examples are sought. In discussion groups in Latur, some participants wanted to blame television for girls running away with men of different religions and castes, though others pointed out that such things had happened before. Others talked of girls being raped in colleges, though no one was aware of any specific examples and the police had no records of such crimes. Such examples are symptomatic of general concerns about the impact of television, which is reflecting the fractured world of advanced urban societies to localities with more conservative traditions.

Discussion groups in Bangladesh commonly expressed the view that 'cable TV is responsible for growing promiscuity in society.' TV is seen as the immediate culprit because of its visual presence discussing sex or portraying sexuality-related activities. However, as groups examined the issue in more depth, they would generally modify their verdict, accepting that no media product alone can be responsible for something as basic as sexual behaviour patterns.[100]

Satellite television is part of a complex pattern of social change, but some professionals dealing with social and personal problems see it as a negative influence. Dr. Sunita Krishna, a social worker from Hyderabad, believes that part-time prostitution among college girls has increased, and sees consumerist pressures driven by TV as deeply corrupting.[101] Jayashree Shidore, a family lawyer who runs a counselling centre for children of disputing parents in Pune, says 'feelings of understanding, dependency, mutual trust... are increasingly absent in people now and I see that as a direct result of the images on TV.'[102]

Another worry for parents is the level of violence in Hindi films, teleserials and cartoons. One Pakistani parent said: 'Even cartoons are no longer safe. Some of the characters have become so ridiculously violent that they are losing their suitability for children. Children are learning to kick and punch and use foul language.' A teacher in Islamabad noted that 'the soft spoken and gentle romantic hero of yesterday has been replaced by the uncouth, rugged, angry young man. Today, children and youth like to answer back, be rude and demonstrate aggressive behaviour.'[103]

A similar discussion group in Bangladesh accepted that violence in society had its origins in economic deprivation and social breakdown and could not be blamed solely on the media. But many discussants did blame TV for a process of desensitisation to violence. They held that people are willing to accept a greater degree of violence because of their exposure to it on TV. Some also believed that TV did influence the behaviour of marginal players. Those on the verge of assault or adultery may risk it under the influence of TV.[104]

There seems to be a class dimension to reactions to media violence. Working class women in Ahmedabad were more divided on this question than some middle class groups from the same region. Some of them held TV responsible for an increase in violence; they believed men were copying what they saw on the screen. Others believed that TV had had a pacifying influence on men.[105] Some media commentators also stress these differences of class perception. For the middle class, the level of violence in films is outside their normal experience, whereas for the working class it is not regarded as unusual. Anita Anand says: 'When you take a clip from a TV programme of violence and abusive behaviour and show them, nine times out of ten they say "This is nothing, let me tell you what happened here the other day...." Women in slum areas...are not surprised or shocked to see it portrayed on TV.... They are surprised that we are surprised.'[106]

Some discussants expressed concern that satellite television, which is targeting the middle class with expensive products, may be alienating working class and rural viewers and fuelling social unrest. But our researches among working class families in Ahmedabad and Pune found more evidence of prurience than of frustration and anger. These families, with a purchasing power of less than Rs. 3,000 a month, all confront the dilemma that their children are constantly exposed to advertisements for goods they cannot afford to buy. They were critical of many of the programmes and of the advertisements, but they followed new products closely and exhibited a high rate of sampling, whether of soaps, shampoos, biscuits or chocolates.[107]

All the discussions show that people are worried about the impact on others, not on themselves. The middle class is concerned about other people's children and about the impact on the working class. The working class, significantly, is concerned about what it sees as the growth of corruption in the middle class. A group of boatmen and craftsmen interviewed in Varanasi blamed the parents of rich children for conniving at indecent behaviour. They said they were afraid that their children would be affected by rich adolescents. All of them were of the opinion that 'TV is responsible for the creeping corruption in society'. But they also recognised 'some good effects of TV'. One said he thought the dowry system was vanishing because of media exposure. He said: 'In my home everyone is convinced that this system is bad and outdated. We will try to marry our sons and daughters without dowry. This is the contribution of TV.'[108]

The young are also divided over the new cultural influences, but they are less nostalgic and more open-minded. To that extent, the age cohort theory does have some relevance. A group of students at Chiraigaon near Varanasi told us they enjoyed the new soap operas, 'including the carefree behaviour of young men and women'. They did not find it culturally degrading. But they said they would not express this view to their parents. They felt that their parents belong to the old generation and naturally would not like their views. At a discussion with students at Benares University, some middle class students were as critical as their parents of Bollywood programmes and MTV, which they characterised as 'bad and corrupting', but they showed less inclination to romanticise the past. One said: 'We have a culture and tradition of joint families. Individualism is not liked by us. Slowly young people are leaving their fathers and starting to live separately. But this is due to socio-economic changes in the society and not due to TV.' A second said: 'I agree. But TV has helped this trend, the serials and films on TV show and glorify this trend.' A third interrupted: 'Look, things are bound to change. We have become a global village now. We are taking things from western culture. Some are bad but some are good additions. I think our society is becoming modern.'[109]

REPOSITIONING THE PRODUCT

Our research suggests that most viewers are far from passive in their reactions. As well as appreciating the entertainment, they have tended to take up messages of self-improvement, self-confidence, egalitarianism and participation. But they have also been critical of the shortcomings of satellite TV and its strident commercialism. Many of them, particularly outside the elites of the big cities, have shown themselves to be much more socially conservative than some of the Mumbai-based market research organisations anticipated.

Similar conclusions are also being reached by many of the advertising agencies who have played an important role in shaping the new media market. A recent survey conducted for MTV among 15–34 year olds in Mumbai, Delhi, Bangalore, Chennai and Kanpur/Lucknow showed that the individualism of Mumbai is not reproduced across the country. The survey indicates that MTV has successfully widened its appeal to include the Hindi-speaking urban middle class but that it now needs to adjust its profile to accommodate their more family-oriented view of the world. Over 65 per cent of the sample said they tried to obey their elders 'even if it hurts', with Mumbai scoring lowest on this question. The majority said their ideal music channel would consist of 75 per cent Hindi film and pop music and 25 per cent regional music. The conservatism was balanced, however, by relatively high scores in areas where personal choice has traditionally been limited. Well over 60 per cent thought they should only marry someone of their choice (with Chennai more conservative than other centres) and 31 per cent thought couples should live together before marriage, with males agreeing more strongly than females.[110]

The realisation that Indian youth is more socially conservative than planners anticipated is leading MTV and its advertisers to rethink their strategy. According to Indrani Vidyarthi of ORG-MARG, the problem is that 'in attempting to create youth attitudes borrowed from the west, many marketeers are forgetting to reflect that which already exists in Indian culture.'[111] At the same MTV forum, Vibha Rishi of Pepsi Cola spoke of the new way as 'choice with accountability, utilising material from both sides—Eastern and Western—and buying the brands which fit the new ethos'. However, the commercial objectives remain the same and the concessions seem to lie mainly in the packaging. Rishi summed up the new resolution of the conflict between tradition and modernity as 'youth stating their needs and desires upfront without guilt, hesitation and embarrassment.... It is about more money, power, experiences, sensation, freedom, sex, music, sports...and more from yourself.'[112]

CONSUMERISM AND CREATIVITY

The dominance of advertising agencies in shaping the new media—the evident nexus between sponsors, advertising agencies and programme makers—is an area of particular concern to the artistic community. Some channels manage their own advertising; others market time slots and leave both the programmes and the advertisements to the highest bidder. There are many instances of sponsors influencing programmes and in some cases being involved in the creation of new formats to showcase their goods. For example, the concept for the musical talent show *Antakshari*, one of the most popular on satellite TV, was developed by Hindustan Lever, the leading Indian advertiser, to promote its Close-Up toothpaste. The same company was also influential in the development of new afternoon prime time slots for women viewers, which are a major target audience for its products.[113] In some cases, the interconnectedness of programme and product has resulted in the stars who advertise the soap and toothpaste playing leading roles in the soap operas sponsored by the same companies.

Many creative artists are concerned that this degree of commercial involvement in programme making and the preoccupation of channels with ratings lead to short-sighted assessments of what audiences might appreciate. According to Chandraprakash Dwivedhi, who was head of programming at Zee TV, 'whenever marketing decides, there is no care about artistic capabilities. In fact they are looking for the lowest common denominator.'[114] He believes the dominance of advertising agencies has forced programming down-market and deprived many companies of an opportunity to be associated with good programmes. This is also the view of film director Govind Nihalani, whose serial *Tamas*, a powerful fictionalised account of the traumas of partition, was widely acclaimed when shown on Doordarshan in the late 1980s. Nihalani does not believe he would be commissioned to make the series today. He told us: 'Politics is now more than ever a caste/religious issue.... It is not possible today to make a programme that combines religion, communities and national politics.... The concerns the medium reflects are those of the urban middle class. TV is designed today for them because they have the buying power. All the series have a token salute to progressive ideas but nothing which rocks the boat.'[115]

Sunil Shanbag sees his own experience with a chat show on Zee TV about bringing up children—*Choti Choti Batein*—as an illustration of how the ratings experts can get things wrong. According to Shanbag, it was a low cost sponsored programme which was given a non-prime time afternoon slot. But he says it proved very successful because 'there are any number of people who want value out of TV'. Shanbag says there will always be a viewership for soaps and sitcoms; 'the problem arises when 85 per cent of airtime is devoted to them'.[116]

Both Shanbag and Nihalani see the influence of sponsors on programme making as one of the biggest impediments to creative work. 'The programme should not look like a 23 minute advertisement and that understanding has still to come to sponsors. It is a constant battle', says Shanbag. 'The time of the sponsor dictating content is not far off', says Nihalani. 'If you allow all profits to come from the sponsor, it is bound to happen.'

WHOSE POPULAR CULTURE?

Though Indian market research is making adjustments to accommodate the newly discovered conservatism of the middle class market, for the satellite channels this is largely a matter of fine-tuning. The most successful of them have already established themselves as market leaders for entertainment, news, sports and soap operas, and have undermined the appeal of national broadcasters to their own middle class not only in India but also in neighbouring countries. The English-knowing middle class is now better informed electronically than ever before. The Hindi-knowing middle class has been given a new popular culture, which despite the controversies over matters of taste and decency has a wide appeal across the whole region.

In terms of theories of globalisation, the emergence of this new satellite culture has shown clearly that success in a large market like India requires a high degree of localisation. The transformation of Star TV and of the music channels is clear proof of that; as is the role of Indian creative expertise in the process. The television culture which has emerged draws selectively on American and European programme formats and expertise, and is devoted to economic ends set in many cases by multinational companies: the creation of new consumer markets. But neither in business nor in the media is the field confined to the multinationals. Just as many Indian businesses have held their own in the new era of liberalisation, the success of Zee TV has been copied both by Doordarshan and by international competitors.

Beyond the evident success of localisation, there are important questions about the form and character it has taken. New collaborations between international and national business, with Mumbai and Delhi taking the lead, have generated a culture which matches western-style consumerism with the popularity of Bollywood and reaches audiences well beyond the Hindi-speaking heartland. Its success has raised questions within India about the future of regional cultures, while in neighbouring countries, pleasure at the wider access to information and entertainment has been tempered by concern at the enormous growth of Indian cultural influences. On the mass entertainment channels, it is largely Indian culture which is being projected in a South Asian version of globalisation, with neighbouring countries for the most part passive or not so passive recipients. Consequently, looking at the cultural impact of the satellite revolution in neighbouring countries brings into the picture questions not simply of popular culture but also of inherited political attitudes and relationships.

In Chapters 6 and 7 we look at these issues, as they have emerged in interviews, surveys and group discussions in India and neighbouring countries. Chapter 6 looks at regional reactions to the satellite revolution within India, exploring why north of the Vindhyas the dominance of Hindi programming has left little space for alternatives in Marathi or Gujarati or even in Bengali, and by contrast how the southern states have been so successful in setting up their own regional language satellite channels. Chapter 7 looks at reactions to the satellite revolution in Pakistan, Bangladesh and Nepal, where India-focussed programmes are commanding big audiences, and contrasts the situation in those countries with developments in Sri Lanka, where a proliferation of national channels has resulted in a very different experience for Sri Lankan viewers.

NOTES AND REFERENCES

1. Several sections in this chapter draw extensively on Deepa Bhatia's research in Mumbai and other parts of western India and her paper on 'Cultural Dimensions of the Satellite Revolution', commissioned for the Media South Asia Project, July 1998.
2. Chandraprakash Dwivedhi, Former Head of Programming, Zee TV, Mumbai, May 1998.
3. Rama Bijapurkar, Virginia Valentine and Monty Alexander (1995), 'Charting the Cultural Future of Markets', paper delivered at the European Society for Market Research Annual Congress at Davos (September), in *ESOMAR 47th Congress Handbook 1995*, Amsterdam, pp. 143–61.
4. Quoted in Krishna Guha's report in the *Financial Times*, 21 August 1999.
5. According to the consumer insights director of McCann-Erickson Asia Pacific, 'hanging out' in shopping malls is an important part of youth culture, part of 'rebelling "into" the middle class' which is believed to distinguish the youth of China and India from their counterparts in the West. See Dave McCaughan, 'Hanging Out: Real Media Issues for Asian Youth', an essay on communicating with the teen market based on discussions with Asian youth in six countries in 1996 and 1997.
6. Sunil Lulla, Mumbai, April 1998.
7. Anjali Monteiro, Mumbai, May 1998.
8. Shanta Gokhale, Mumbai, April 1998.
9. Sunil Shanbag, Mumbai, April 1998.
10. Hima Vishwanathan, Mumbai, May 1998.
11. Nilu Damle, Report on Latur District, May 1998.
12. Vibha Rishi, Presentation to the MTV Forum, January 1999.
13. K. Bikram Singh, Delhi, June 1998.
14. Dr. Abhilasha Kumari, Delhi, June 1998.
15. Labourers, Karachi, December 1998.
16. Anita Anand, Delhi, June 1998.
17. Sabina Kidwai, Delhi, June 1998.
18. Kiran Karnik (1993), 'Satellite and Cable TV Invasion: Its Socio-economic Impact', in *Mass Media*, p. 14.
19. See, P.C. Chatterji (1991), *Broadcasting in India*, pp. 209–17; Romila Thapar (1991), 'A Historical Perspective on the Story of Rama', in S. Gopal (ed.), *Anatomy of a Confrontation*, pp. 141–63; Ananda Mitra (1993), 'Television and the Nation: Doordarshan's India', in *Media Asia*, Vol. 20, No. 1; K. Sekhar (1999), 'Emergence of Religious and Regional Language Programming in Indian TV', in *Media Asia*, Vol. 26, No. 1.
20. See Rangan Chakravarty and Nandini Gooptu, 'Imagination: The Media, Nation and Politics in Contemporary India', in E. Hallam and B. Street (eds) (2000), *Cultural Encounters: Representing Otherness*, pp. 89–107.
21. Shanta Gokhale, Mumbai, April 1998.
22. Sevanti Ninan, *The Hindu Folio*, August 1997.
23. Bijapurkar, Valentine and Alexander, 'Charting the Cultural Future of Markets' (1995), pp. 143–61.

24. Professionals, Mumbai, July 1998.
25. School children, Mumbai, May 1998.
26. Professionals, Ahmedabad, May 1998.
27. Professionals, Pune, August 1998.
28. Afsan Chowdhury, 'Media Profile of Bangladesh', commissioned for the Media South Asia Project, July 1998.
29. Geeteara S. Choudhury, Chairperson of the Advertising Association of Bangladesh, March 1998.
30. Julles Fuller, General Manager, Channel V, Mumbai, June 1998.
31. Sunil Lulla, Manager MTV, Mumbai, April 1998.
32. Students, St Xavier's, Mumbai, July 1999.
33. Gujarati students, Ahmedabad, May 1998.
34. Students, Chanakya School, Pune, August 1998.
35. Cyrus Broacha, Mumbai, July 1998.
36. Anjali Monteiro, Mumbai, May 1998.
37. Rama Bijapurkar, Mumbai, March 1998.
38. Anita Anand, Delhi, June 1998.
39. Farzana Bari, Islamabad, March 1999.
40. College students, Islamabad, January 1999.
41. College students, Biratnagar, June 1998.
42. Subir Bhaumik, 'Media Profile of North East India', commissioned for the Media South Asia Project, May 1998.
43. Vinta Nanda, Mumbai, July 1999.
44. Ajay Sinha, Director's note and synopsis, *Hasratein*.
45. N.G. Productions, *Saans*, A brief sketch.
46. For a discussion of these Doordarshan series, see, Sevanti Ninan (1995), pp. 176–85.
47. Anjali Monteiro and K.P. Jayasankar (2000), 'Between the Normal and the Imaginary: The Spectator Self, the Other and Satellite Television in India', in I. Hagen and J. Wasko. (eds), (2000) *Consuming Audiences: Production and Reception in Media Research*.
48. Students, St. Xavier's College, Mumbai, July 1999.
49. Students, Chanakya School, Pune, August 1998.
50. Afsan Chowdhury, 'Media Profile of Bangladesh', commissioned for the Media South Asia Project, July 1998.
51. John Samuel, Pune, July 1998.
52. Interviews with Professor Ransubhe and Professor Maggirwar, language teachers from Latur, May 1998.
53. Dr. Bhadrinath Kapoor, Varanasi, June 1998.
54. Aslam Azhar, Islamabad, November 1997.
55. Iftikhar Arif, Islamabad, March 1999.
56. Maleec Calyaneratne de Silva, Colombo, September 1998.
57. *Business India* (1998), Anniversary Issue, looked at trends in fashion in India, the continuing influence of the cinema across India and the adoption by the wealthy middle class of a mixture of 'ethnic, western and chic'.
58. Hima Vishwanathan, Mumbai, May 1998.
59. Drawn from Nilu Damle's reports on Latur and Varanasi districts, May–June 1998.

60. Tasneem Ahmar, 'Media Profile of Pakistan', commissioned for the Media South Asia Project, December 1998.
61. Professionals, Birgunj, June 1999.
62. Labourers, Waghari tribe, Ahmedabad, May 1998.
63. Nilu Damle, Report on Latur district, May 1998.
64. *Ibid.*
65. *Financial Times*, 'Yielding to the Pressure of Pester Power', 17 August 1999.
66. Namita Unnikrishnan and Shailaja Bajpai (1996), *The Impact of Television Advertising on Children* .
67. *Ibid.*, p. 231.
68. Women labourers, Millatnagar and Padavnagar, May and August 1998.
69. Home makers, Pune, August 1998.
70. Alka Wadkar, Pune, April 1998.
71. Nilu Damle, Reports on Varanasi and Latur districts, May–June 1998.
72. Islamabad teenagers taking part in this discussion included girls and boys between the ages of 13 and 19, live in a *katchi abadi* or slum area in Nurpur Shahan in Rawalpindi town. The discussion took place on 28 January 1999.
73. Shilloo Chattopadhyay, Director, MODE Research Services, Calcutta, March 1998. A survey carried out in 1988 gave three reasons why children were increasingly being targeted: (1) they had more money at their disposal than in the past, (2) they were seen as a major influence on the choice of brand in family purchases and (3) the process of instilling brand loyalty starts young. 'Inside the Child's Mind: Advertising and Marketing' July 1989 (cited in Unnikrishnan and Bajpai 1996), *Impact of Television Advertising on Children*, p. 156).
74. Labourers and home makers, Matara, May 1998.
75. 'People's Perception: Obscenity and Violence on the Small Screen', sponsored by the National Commission for Women, Media Advocacy Group, Delhi 1994.
76. Nilu Damle, Report on Latur district, May 1998.
77. Home makers, Ahmedabad, May 1998.
78. See, Raymond Williams (1977), *Marxism and Literature*; Bijapurkar, Valentine and Alexander, 'Charting the Cultural Future of Markets' (1995), p. 154.
79. Rama Bijapurkar, Mumbai, March 1998.
80. Women labourers, Hadapsar, Pune, March 1998.
81. Social activists, Dhaka, March 1998.
82. Anjali Monteiro, Mumbai, May 1998; see also Monteiro and Jayasankar, 'Between the Normal and the Imaginary' (2000), and for an account of her research in Goa, Anjali Monteiro (1998), 'Official Television and Un-official Fabrications of the Self: The Spectator as Subject', in Ashis Nandy (ed.), (1998) *The Secret Politics of Our Desires*, pp. 156–207.
83. Dr. Vidhyut Bhagwat, Pune, August 1998.
84. Sharmila Rege, Pune, August 1998.
85. Anita Ratnam, Chennai, December 1999.
86. Media Advocacy Group (1997), *The Audience Speaks: Building a Consumer Forum*, Section III, pp. 35–67.
87. Women professionals and activists, Islamabad, May 1998.
88. Farzana Bari, Islamabad, March 1999.
89. Maithree Wickramasinghe, Colombo, October 1998.

90. Hima Vishwanathan, Mumbai, May 1998.
91. Nilu Damle, Report on Varanasi district, June 1998.
92. Afsan Chowdhury, 'Media Profile of Bangladesh', commissioned for the Media South Asia Project, July 1998.
93. School children, Birgunj, June 1999.
94. Shankaracharya of Varanasi, June 1998.
95. Maulana Irtija Hussain, Varanasi, June 1998.
96. Santhini Jayawardena, 'Media Profile of Sri Lanka', commissioned for the Media South Asia Project, October 1998.
97. ITN's regular discussion programme, *Janatha Adhikaranaya*, chaired by H.M.Gunasekara, 12 October 1998.
98. Nilu Damle, Report on Latur district, May 1998.
99. Santhini Jayawardena, Report on Matara district, July 1998.
100. Afsan Chowdhury, 'Media Profile of Bangladesh', commissioned for the Media South Asia Project, July 1998.
101. Dr. Sunita Krishna, Delhi, April 1998.
102. Jayashree Shidore, Pune, March 1998.
103. Teachers and parents, Islamabad, May 1998.
104. Afsan Chowdhury, 'Media Profile of Bangladesh', commissioned for the Media South Asia Project, July 1998.
105. Women labourers, Ramdeo Nagar, Ahmedabad, May 1998.
106. Anita Anand, Delhi, June 1998.
107. Four discussion groups were carried with lower income working women in Pune and Ahmedabad between March and August 1998.
108. Boatmen, Benares, June 1998.
109. Students, Chiraigaon and Varanasi, June 1998.
110. MTV Asia, *Tuning in to Indian Youth*, Part II, Mumbai, 1999.
111. Indrani Vidyarthi, 'The Millennium Generation Speaks...Direct Dil Se', Presentation to the MTV Youth Forum, Mumbai, January 1999.
112. Vibha Rishi, Presentation to the MTV Forum, January 1999.
113. Irfan Khan and Venkatraman of Hindustan Lever, Mumbai, April 1998.
114. Chandraprakash Dwivedhi, Mumbai, May 1998.
115. Govind Nihalani, Mumbai, April 1998.
116. Sunil Shanbag, Mumbai, April 1998.

Six

INDIA: NORTH AND SOUTH

In this chapter, we investigate the influence of satellite broad-casting on India's regional cultures. We have already seen how the lure of the Indian market gave rise to the development of several satellite channels in Hindi, of which Zee and Sony are the most popular. This market reinforcement of the role of Hindi as the lingua franca of northern India had repercussions well be-yond the six core Hindi-speaking states. Zee TV and other Hindi language satellite channels developed large audiences in the bordering Hindi-knowing regions, which include states like Maha-rashtra and Gujarat in the west and West Bengal, Orissa and Assam in the east. In the first phase of the satellite revolution, Indian advertisers successfully reached middle class audiences in these states through Hindi programmes on Zee, Star or Sony, with the result that there was only limited commercial support for regional alternatives in Marathi and Gujarati or even in Bengali. By 2000, however, this situation had begun to change. A number of regional language channels were established to meet the need for regional news and entertainment, which our interviews and discussions had highlighted, though these innovations did not answer other criticisms of the nature of satellite programmes.

Doordarshan, the national broadcaster, with stations in Mumbai, Ahmedabad or Calcutta, has been swept along in commercial com-petition with Hindi satellite channels for the huge Hindi language audience. In comparison to the levels of funding available for popular programmes in Hindi, Doordarshan's regional program-mes in Marathi and Bengali have been poorly resourced, while control from Delhi and a lack of genuine autonomy has contributed to their ineffectiveness. In this chapter, we show that Door-darshan's relative neglect of regional broadcasting has helped to skew the terms of 'cultural trade'against important regional cul-tures instead of acting as a counter-balance to dominant trends.

We do this by looking first at the situation in two important states on the periphery of the Hindi-speaking heartland—Maharashtra and West Bengal, where Hindi programming overshadowed regional cultures throughout the 1990s. We later contrast the situation in those states with the situation in South India, particularly in Tamil Nadu, where satellite channels in regional languages emerged much more quickly to serve local needs. We ask why the South successfully seized the opportunity to develop satellite media, while important cultures north of the Vindhyas remained neglected for much longer.

MAHARASHTRA

On the face of it, one might have expected satellite TV to blossom in Marathi because there is a strong Marathi culture, particularly in the theatre and literature. But in fact it took a long time for any Marathi satellite channels to be launched. When much of the research for this chapter was carried out, there was no commercial Marathi satellite channel at all and efforts to set up local Marathi cable channels had only had any real success in Pune. The Doordarshan Marathi channel was also not doing well, as our discussion groups showed, except with one or two exceptional productions; it certainly did not compare in audiences or revenues with Doordarshan channels in Tamil or Bengali.

One obvious reason for this situation was the widespread knowledge of Hindi among Maharashtrians, who took to watching the many glossy, well produced entertainment programmes on Zee, Sony or Star in much the same way as other North Indians. Nothing available in Marathi matched the production standards of the Hindi satellite channels, though there was plenty of evidence to suggest that better quality Marathi programmes would find a ready audience.

Another factor holding back the development of Marathi satellite TV was the lack of a thriving regional film industry. The success of satellite TV in North India had been firmly based on the popular film culture of Bollywood, while its success in the southern states fed off the profitable commercial cinema in the four main languages. Many celebrity programmes, quiz shows and talent competitions capitalised on the fascination with films, film stars and film songs and—most important of all—many hours of TV time were filled with re-runs of old movies. The importance of film in the economics of satellite TV put regional cultures without such a strong tradition at a distinct disadvantage. Marathi cinema had its 'golden age' in the 1930s and 1940s, but it was never known for the volume of its productions. Today, according to the playwright and screenplay writer Vijay Tendulkar, regional cinema is facing dwindling audiences. It cannot match up to commercial standards.[1] Marathi alternative cinema, which had a reputation in the 1970s, is in poor shape, though there has been a small increase in commercial releases recently.

Bollywood's overshadowing of Marathi cinema is a reflection of Mumbai's dominance of Maharashtra. Mumbai is a cosmopolitan city; it has a diverse population from all over South Asia, including Tamils, Gujaratis, Sindhis and professionals from all regions of the country. It is not only the headquarters of many Indian industries and banks, it is also the gateway to India for the international business community. Mumbai's hinterland is not Maharashtra; it is India itself. Bollywood, the headquarters of India's film industry, reaches out to a pan-Indian audience and Marathi speakers are often caught between a sense of pride in being part of this larger whole and one of regret that their own culture is being overshadowed.

For these reasons, Maharashtra has a complex relationship with North Indian culture. Many Maharashtrians make the point that whatever their pride in their own culture, they do not define themselves in antagonism to Hindi culture as some of the southern cultures do. Maharashtrians, they say, are not chauvinistic about language. Indeed, many of them see knowledge of Hindi as a sign of progressiveness or cosmopolitanism. Ranjit Hoskote, a journalist and poet, says that Maharashtrians aspire to be recognised as Aryans, despite the fact that they have as much, if not more, in common culturally with their neighbours to the south. Hoskote sees this aspiration as a sign of defensiveness about their own culture, something which has taken militant form in the political propaganda of the Shiv Sena party.[2]

In much the same vein, playwright and columnist Shanta Gokhale argues that the Maharashtrian is inhibited by the money-power of North Indians and is insecure in Mumbai. This shows itself in the fact that outsiders were never required to learn Marathi until the Shiv Sena made it the second language in state schools. Until then, after primary school, it had only been an optional subject. At the same time, there is resentment at what is perceived as North Indian superiority towards Maharashtrian culture. As Shanta Gokhale puts it: 'The Maharashtrians feel very disturbed when a non-Maharashtrian says: "We only know Marathi because we speak to our maid."'[3]

Discussions with Marathi-speakers—particularly middle class groups—revealed considerable cultural resistance to the negative stereotyping of Maharashtrians in Hindi films and television. A professional from Pune told us: 'There is a stigma attached to Marathi. The top hero of Marathi films shifts to Hindi films and becomes...some third flunkey or fourth flunkey; Marathi talent is selling out to Hindi films and is doing it cheaply.'[4] Similar resentments surfaced in discussions with a group of Mumbai housewives. 'We want to take this opportunity to point out', said one of them, 'that in serials, especially on Zee...bosses are always shown as Punjabis.... Maharashtrians are always shown as "ghatis" (country bumpkins).... It is very insulting...and this image is going to the whole country.' Another said that she was boycotting one serial for this reason. An interesting feature of this group was that those who had put their children into Marathi medium schools had decided to cut off cable television; they clearly saw it as undermining their own culture.

There was also widespread criticism of Doordarshan for not offering competitive Marathi programming. Only the soap opera *Damini* and the Marathi version of *Antakshari—Tak Dhina Din*—had any appreciable following. 'I see *Damini* because I want to see something in Marathi. I get fed up of Hindi and English...they are boring...', said one Mumbai housewife. Several group members went regularly to the Marathi theatre in Mumbai and to Marathi films. All had seen *Tu Tethe Me*, a recently released Marathi-language family film. Those who were watching *Hasratein* on Zee TV knew that it was based on a Marathi novel and knew too that the novel was different; as one participant put it: 'The serial leans towards vulgarity'.[5]

Working class Marathi-speakers were less resistant to Hindi serials and quiz shows. But they also complained of the lack of a watchable Marathi alternative. One discussant in Pune said of Marathi serials: 'The quality is no good and the timing is no good.

There needs to be a separate Marathi channel, so we can catch it all the time.' Discussions with a similar group in Padavnagar, a slum in Pune, revealed that most houses had cable connections and half had colour TVs. Doordarshan's Marathi channel had some followers for *Tak Dhina Dhin* and *Damini* but most of the group preferred Hindi films and music shows like *Antakshari*. They were critical of Doordarshan's Marathi news for lack of visuals compared with competing Hindi bulletins.[6]

The Shiv Sena, which ruled Maharashtra during the late 1990s, has its own cultural agenda which seeks to rally Marathi speakers in defence of their culture and against those forces threatening to undermine it. It also supports the BJP agenda of making the arts and the media a plank of the Hindutva platform. Pramod Naval-kar, who was then minister of state for culture, told us he believed satellite television posed a serious threat to regional culture, though he also acknowledged that it would be an uphill task to counter the impact of Hindi in urban Maharashtra. He said there is already a decline in the reading of Marathi books, which has affected the library movement and government publications.[7] To counter these influences, the Shiv Sena government inaugurated a number of measures designed to strengthen traditional culture. Scholarships of Rs. 100 a month were established for students or disciples of classical artists or musicians. Grants were made to Marathi film makers. Traditional art forms like *Lavani* and *Tamasha* were promoted. The party also hired thirty minutes daily on DD1 at 6.30 p.m. to project Marathi culture, though the experiment was later discontinued.

Most artists regarded these measures more as a means of cultural outreach for the Shiv Sena than as a means of reinvigorating Marathi culture. Artists not aligned with the Sena—and there are many of them—expressed concern at the climate of repression perpetrated in Mumbai as a result of the Sena's activities and gave many examples to illustrate their case.

In the late 1990s, the Shiv Sena made a number of highly publi-cised and controversial interventions in the fields of music, paint-ing and films, often using bully-boy tactics to intimidate artists for populist ends. In April 1998, the Sena interrupted a concert being given by Ghulam Ali, the well-known Pakistani singer. The *Times of India* in an editorial accused the party of having 'fallen back on cultural bogey-mongering, the last option of the politically bankrupt in the country.'[8] In the same year, the Sena repeatedly attacked the artist M.F.Hussain's portrayal of Sita, the consort of Ram, in protest at what it saw as the trivialisation of her character. But the rhetoric of the Sena has not always been pursued very logically. The same party which protested against a concert by the rock musician Jon Bon Jovi went out of its way to invite Michael Jackson to perform in the city and involved the Shiv Sena leader Bal Thackeray in playing host to him. It was clearly more interested in the manipulation of prejudice for political ends than the consistent pursuit of Marathi cultural interests. As journalist Mukta Rajadhyaksha put it: 'The logical question which arises when the government attacks a rock concert that barely reaches 2000 kids is: Why is Hindi cinema spared?'[9] The answer would seem to be that the Sena is as influenced by economics as everyone else. Critics note that Bal Thackeray's daughter-in-law, film producer Smita Thackeray, has been making Hindi films rather than Marathi ones.

With many Maharashtrians watching Hindi channels, the question naturally arises: are regional languages under threat? Anjali Monteiro, who has studied the impact of television on local culture in Goa, says what is happening is that 'people are absorbing, incorporating...but they are certainly not replacing their regional languages or cultures. It is definitely not a case of wiping out.'[10] Hima Vishwanathan, who does qualitative research for IMRB, is also emphatic that there is 'not a chance of them being threatened. Local languages down to the dialects are very strongly rooted, especially in the rural areas'.[11] Others see a steady erosion of regional culture and language for a variety of reasons, many of them much more long term in their influence. Ranjit Hoskote believes this process of marginalisation has 'more to do with people's aspirations then with channels coming in necessarily.' He points out that 'there has been a distinct move in the last thirty years... away from your own language to education in English.... With that kind of marginalisation already in place, this is a logical cultural trend.'[12]

There is no doubt that the recent economic and political climate of Maharashtra has not been conducive to the flowering of Marathi culture. It remains very strong in certain art forms—notably the theatre and literature—but in a much more commercialised world, in which Hindi satellite television is a prime vehicle for the development of a new consumer society, the terms on which the old culture operates are being superseded by new economic pressures. Marathi theatre, for example, still has a very strong following in Mumbai and throughout the state. It continues to deal with important contemporary social and political themes and there are a number of examples of issues being broached in the Marathi theatre which later translate into commercial success at the Hindi box office. However, Marathi theatre is increasingly under the influence of liberalising India: there is more emphasis on packaging and sponsorship and producers are looking for fuller theatres and larger returns on investment and are less willing to take a chance than they were in the past. According to theatre director Sunil Shanbag, there is now a widening gulf between the experimental and commercial theatre, as there is in the cinema, which is affecting the quality of new work. During the Shiv Sena period, theatres were also less full than before because of the general climate.[13]

At the same time, the success of Hindi commercial television has drawn many creative and talented Maharashtrians away from working in their own language or their own rich theatrical tradition. Vijay Tendulkar, whose *Priya Tendulkar Show* started on Doordarshan and later moved to Star TV, draws a contrast between poorly paid creative work in Marathi and the financial attractions of working for satellite TV. He says: 'Performing on the Marathi circuit is very difficult because it survives on touring. You do not sleep...you suffer bedsores.... It is tough and those who come in have to be determined, unlike in TV, which is a convenient, viable way of surviving.... Writing for theatre has never been lucrative. Writing for TV is frustrating, but it is lucrative. Those who do write manage to buy a car or a house but none of them look on TV writing as serious, creative activity.'[14]

The reverse side of this artistic dilemma is that production and advertising houses do not regard work in Marathi as commercially viable. According to Shanta Gokhale, 'regional language audiences are seen as occupying the lower social rung, even when they belong to the upper class....' Consequently, very little funding is available for productions, which means they are not good. Commenting on Doordarshan's Marathi channel, she says: 'The reason why the local Marathi channel is not popular is because producers think its audiences are lower middle class and so give muck, and people are not willing to watch muck.'[15]

Doordarshan's Marathi channel, which could be an important patron of regional culture, has done little to arrest this decline. The rates which the Doordarshan Mumbai kendra pays for serials in Marathi are regarded as derisory by qualified directors, even if one leaves aside its reputation for poor planning and corruption. Doordarshan also suffers from bad time slots—Marathi serials are shown at 7.30 in the evening when many people have hardly got home from work—and programmes quite often get shifted to accommodate other priorities. Pratima Kulkarni, a director who works in both Hindi and Marathi, told us that Doordarshan's advertising rate for Hindi serials at Rs. 70,000 for 10 seconds compares with a rate of Rs. 4000 for Marathi serials. At such rates, it is impossible to produce quality work in Marathi. 'What angers me', she says, 'is that I want to work in Marathi. I think Marathi, but the economics force me to work in Hindi.'[16]

The fact, however, that a small number of regional programmes—whether in Marathi or Gujarati—have been successful against this general trend suggests that effective regional services in these languages would command substantial audiences. Neena Raut, the producer of *Tak Dhina Din*, a highly successful Marathi version of the Hindi talent show *Antakshari*, developed such a successful format for this programme that it had a higher audience rating in Maharashtra than the very popular Zee soap opera *Hum Paanch*. Neena Raut built the show on the popularity of Marathi music—not just film music but folk songs and religious songs which date back hundreds of years, women's working songs and other local music. In contrast to the glossy shows on Hindi satellite TV, she also made it 'non-glamorous'. She told us: 'Participants came from all stratas of society...farmers, workers, doctors, housewives, government officials, carpenters, bankers. That is something we are proud of: that people came from the remotest parts of Maharashtra from villages whose names we had not heard of....' At its height the programme received 7,000 or 8,000 letters a week from all over Maharashtra, which demonstrated what sort of popular response imaginative regional broadcasting can achieve. Moreover, once its popularity had been proved, there was no shortage of commercial sponsors wanting to be involved. Levers became the sponsor and advertising rates considerably exceeded the normal rate for Marathi programmes.[17]

Vipul Shah, director of the highly successful Gujarati soap opera *Sapna Na Wave Tar*, proved the same point on the even more difficult terrain of Doordarshan's Gujarati regional channel. As he told us: 'Gujarati was even worse than Marathi because Marathi Doordarshan was still in operation but Gujarati was dead.' Because there were no quality programmes and no substantial audiences, advertising rates were very low, which meant that nothing of quality could be supported. Vipul Shah decided, therefore, to ignore sponsorship completely at the beginning. 'We decided to go for 100 episodes without approaching a single marketing agency.... We decided we would not go to the sponsors; we will let the viewership talk. We were sure they themselves would come to us.' The strategy worked. After seventy episodes, they began to command the high advertising rates they had demanded. 'We were getting in the region of Rs. 5,000. That's like a record for Gujarat, which has never happened.'[18]

Vipul Shah's motivation in making *Sapna* was to show that good quality programmes in Gujarati could attract audiences and make money. He saw Gujarat as 'a very good potential market.... I also thought if I can provide you with good entertainment in your mother tongue, which qualitatively may be equal to the Hindi stuff you are seeing on say Zee TV, I think the chances of that becoming a success are very high.' The theme of the soap opera also helped. It looked at the state of the Gujarati joint family and the problem of sustaining it in recent years. It was, as Vipul Shah pointed out, 'basically a family programme which an entire family could view and enjoy.' But making it a success depended on Doordarshan taking a risk and his willingness to sustain heavy initial losses. The gambit paid off. But Vipul Shah also took out insurance. He shot 280 episodes of the soap opera in Hindi as well as Gujarati and on the basis of its success in Gujarati later persuaded Sony to run it on their Hindi satellite channel.

The success of programmes like *Tak Dhina Din* and *Sapna* encouraged a new commercial interest in the Marathi and Gujarati media markets. They were not successful with the sophisticated middle class, but they proved there was a regional audience and a regional market waiting to be developed. In early 1999, Reminiscent Television (UK) launched two regional channels—Gurjari and Lashkara—with an eye on the subscription market among Gujaratis and Punjabis overseas. Then, in the second half of 1999, Zee launched 24-hour regional channels in Marathi, Gujarati, Punjabi and Bengali, with the promise of more to come. Subhash Chandra, lighting the ceremonial lamp to inaugurate Zee Marathi, said it would be 'a channel that Maharashtrians all over the world will feel a part of, highlighting the rich tradition of Marathi culture and literature.' The company's own publicity for the channel made it clear, however, that it would be largely based on the same formula which had worked so well in Hindi. 'Its main content will be soaps, serials, films (both black and white and colour), besides film-based programmes.' However, in an acknowledgement of the thirst for regional news, the schedule also included two news bulletins a day which would 'definitely break the monotony of Marathi news telecasts and cover every aspect of Maharashtra.'[19]

Zee's Marathi channel soon proved the point which Vipul Shah had made with *Sapna*. Within a few weeks, it was claiming to have overtaken DD1 and DD10 in cable and satellite households in Maharashtra in all time slots except those occupied by successful daily soaps like *Damini*. The channel manager, Nitin Vaidya, told us: 'Our basic premise is that Marathi viewers have not had an option.... We also believe that our competition is not with DD1 or DD10 but with all Hindi channels. They have hijacked viewers from Marathi and we have got to get those viewers back.'[20] Vipul Shah maintains that there will always be a difference in the level of finance available for regional channels. 'We are dealing with a pocket audience, so there will always be budget constraints.'But Zee has shown that a 24-hour channel is feasible. Its stress on serving the South Asian diaspora suggests that it sees rich returns in the future from the subscription market in the US and Europe. But it has also proved its point in Maharashtra itself. Zee Marathi is certainly not operating at the same level as the Hindi channels, but it has improved on Doordarshan's parsimonious budgets and has met with a good response from local producers. In this sense, it has only added to the pressures on Doordarshan to improve its performance or to become increasingly irrelevant.

WEST BENGAL

The pride of the Bengalis in their own culture and language, the excellence of their educational institutions and the ccomplishments of their poets, novelists, singers and scholars is well known. Outside the southern states, sensitivity to issues of cultural autonomy has generally figured more prominently in West Bengal than almost anywhere else in India. It comes as something of a surprise, therefore, to discover that the satellite revolution has broken through established cultural barriers in the state and converted many Bengali middle class viewers to a diet of English and Hindi programmes. This is not, of course, to imply that Bengalis no longer have a love of their culture but it does underline the fact that television—whether state-controlled or private—has not been meeting their needs.

As elsewhere in India, school- and college-going students have been most affected, with the music channels firm favourites among the better off and the English educated. Music channel VJs have become role models for a new Calcutta youth culture, which has affected the way people speak and walk, the clothes they wear and the songs they sing. At Calcutta discos, middle class Bengalis request songs in English and Hindi; they no longer turn their noses up at Hindi numbers and will enjoy Daler Mehendi as much as the Backstreet Boys or Celine Dion. Nor is the influence of Hindi confined to the educated middle class. Hindi songs are commonly heard over loud-speakers during West Bengal's most famous religious festival—Durga Puja—providing further evidence of the ubiquity of Bollywood films and music.[21]

The urban middle class is picking up new jargon from satellite programmes and is speaking the Bengali language with more English and Hindi words. Today's young Bengali reads less than the previous generation and is less interested in Bengali literature. A divide has opened up between the culture of the older generation, which still operates largely in Bengali, and a more cosmopolitan, less firmly rooted, younger generation, which gives the English language and the fashions and preoccupations of the Indian elite greater priority.

Bengali middle class girls still come under parental pressure to dress in traditional ways, to wear the sari and to tie their hair in a bun, but western dress is becoming more common and the sari is definitely losing ground to the North Indian salwar kameez. The plethora of advertisements for beauty products has had its effect—women of all ages are more conscious of their looks and are keen viewers of women's programmes like *Paroma* on Doordarshan or

Khoobsurat on Zee. Moreover, changes in fashions are feeding through into purchasing practice. Better off Bengali youth are wearing Levi jeans and Reebok or Nike shoes, subsuming their regional identity in international chic. In Bengal, as elsewhere, there is a new passion for consumer goods, with television in the vanguard of this new trend.

The attraction of these fashions is largely confined to the Calcutta middle class because satellite and cable television is not as extensive in West Bengal as in some other parts of the country— 19.7 per cent in Calcutta, compared with over 30 per cent in Mumbai and Delhi.[22] However, in those middle class households, the penetration of Hindi and English programmes is remarkable. Television rating points provided by a leading research agency for the last week of April 1998 showed that in Calcutta cable and satellite households, there was only one Bengali programme in the top fifty. This is an extraordinarily low figure, even if one accepts that Calcutta plays host to large numbers of non-Bengali speakers. It suggests that like its Maharashtrian counterpart, the Bengali middle class finds satellite programmes, whether in English or Hindi, with their generally better production values and livelier themes, more attractive than what is available in Bengali on Doordarshan. The same TRPs showed that more Hindi films were watched than Bengali films and that there was a big following for Hindi serials on channels like Zee and Sony as well as important sports fixtures on Star Sports and ESPN.

Academics and market researchers confirm that satellite TV— much of it in Hindi—is finding a ready audience among young educated people. Malini Bhattacharya, professor of English at Jadavpur University and a former communist member of parliament, says that younger audiences are turning away from regional cultures and languages to a world of western culture and consumerism.[23] Indrani Sen, Vice President of Hindustan Thompson, the advertising agency, says that by winning over the younger generation, satellite TV is making Hindi the national language and changing the practice of advertisers. Whereas in the past advertisers could rely on Doordarshan's Bengali programmes to reach a cross-section of the community in the state, they now need to use satellite media to reach the professional middle class, particularly young males, and only rely on Doordarshan to reach the mass audience, the urban housewives and the older generation.[24]

Reactions to these linguistic inroads range from condemnation of the new cult of TV consumerism to a defensive recognition that cultural and economic stagnation may have contributed to the ease of the conquest. There is a general acceptance that the Bengali film industry, which had an international reputation in the 1950s and 1960s when Satyajit Ray became a household name in Europe and America, has been in the doldrums for the last twenty years. Its present output matches neither the quality nor the quantity of the earlier period, as is shown by Doordarshan's excessive reliance on old black and white movies. Calcutta is still a very lively city, with its literate middle class, its famous book fair and its many theatre groups, but according to Professor Ananda Lal, twenty years of communist rule has dampened the ardour of leftist writers and sent the theatre and the arts generally into decline. He says: 'Theatre across the world has been at its peak when it has attacked society, not when it has played safe.' But now, 'Calcutta theatre relies more on melodrama, which television can do so much better.'[25]

At the same time, there is considerable resistance among Bengali intellectuals to the growth of Hindi programming, particularly the relentless entertainment on channels like Zee, which they see as more dangerous than the dominance of English as India's link language. 'What is Indian about Zee?', asked Professor Ananda Lal. 'India is too big to be covered by a homogenised Hindi TV programme and that is one danger that I see in satellite TV.... It is going to be as dangerous to the cultural diversity of India as western cultural influences.... With Hindi programmes, there is some kind of cultural hegemony going on and that needs to be curbed.'

Others argue that a lot of Hindi satellite television is simply a translation of western formats into the dominant Indian language. Ashok Surana, whose Channel 8 is one of the few Calcutta production houses to make programmes for the satellite channels, says 'though India has succeeded in countering the invasion from the skies by its own brand of programmes, in actual fact, western cultural values and symbols have been absorbed in the Hindi programmes which are now promoting the same western notions wrapped in an Indian package.'[26]

A lot of the blame for the lack of an adequate television service in Bengali is laid at the door of the Calcutta kendra of Doordarshan, which is seen as poorly run and short of ideas. 'Sadly', says

Professor Lal, 'there is no real policy at Doordarshan, no one to do the programming intelligently.' The main charge against Doordarshan is that it has aped the commercialism of the satellite channels and abdicated its public service responsibilities. Malini Bhattacharya accuses Doordarshan of 'a lack of policy or will' and a 'complete failure' to provide the right mix of education, information and entertainment. Mallika Jalan, the director of a private production company, says: 'Take the case of the Calcutta kendra. Prime time has only serials and one news bulletin. How does Doordarshan claim to have a mandate to inform and educate if the entire prime time is devoted to earning profits for the station?'[27]

In a criticism of the Calcutta kendra which echoes those made of its counterpart in Mumbai, Shilu Chattopadhyaya, the director of MODE Research Services, believes that Doordarshan's professional weaknesses have been compounded by the working of the new media market. He says 'the regional kendra in Calcutta does not have the skill to produce good programmes. The money available to make the programmes is very little, since the Bengali market is very small. Local programmes have to be produced on small budgets and this is reflected in the quality of the productions. This leads to lower viewership ratings and therefore less money available from private sources.'[28]

Thinking people within Doordarshan acknowledge that it has not got the balance right. Ananya Banerjee, its chief producer, says the organisation had to act quickly to counter the challenge of satellite competition in order to maintain its own advertising revenue. But she regrets that instead of going for a good mix of programmes, 'it decided to go totally commercial'.[29] Abhijit Das Gupta, a former director of the Calcutta kendra, is concerned at the declining quality of the broadcasts. In earlier days, he says, well known film directors like Gautam Ghose and Mrinal Sen directed sponsored serials for the Calcutta kendra, whereas today 'serials are being directed by nameless people'. He does not deny that recent productions attract large audiences, but he argues that they lack the 'aesthetic and cinematic value' of earlier ones. 'Those who are managing productions these days', he says, 'are in the business to make a quick buck; they have no interest in understanding Bengali culture.'[30]

Beyond this criticism of commercialism, there is widespread condemnation of the central government's failure to allow space for the development of a worthwhile Bengali television service. The launch of the metro channel as a predominantly Hindi entertainment service to counter the satellite invasion involved a reduction in regional programming, which was only partially restored by the creation of DD7—the Bengali satellite channel. DD7 has a much more limited reach than the terrestrial channels and logically would have been a more appropriate vehicle for reaching the middle class. But national commercial considerations triumphed over the needs of a wider public in the state. Aveek Sarkar, one of the owners of the Bengali newspaper group *Ananda Bazaar Patrika*, argues that 'the mandarins at Mandi House (headquarters of Doordarshan in Delhi) should be held responsible if the country ever splits up because they decided that Hindi programming be carried on both DD1 and DD2 for the larger part of the day.' Aveek Sarkar calls this 'an unmixed evil'. He suggests that DD1 should be devoted to Hindi only, DD2 to regional programmes in Bengali and DD7 to entertainment programmes. This way there would be one terrestrial channel devoted to serving the Bengali audience with a mix of programmes, something singularly absent at the moment.[31]

Zee was the first commercial company to attempt to fill this gap in the market with the launch in 1994 of Zee Bangla, a daily 90-minute slot in the early evening on the main Zee channel. It was similar to other Zee programmes: 'thematically very adult., families breaking up...wives having it off with someone else', as one Zee employee in Calcutta described it. It was also shot in the technically superior Betacam and well funded, with production standards which excelled anything else available locally. Consequently, it did build up a substantial audience very quickly. Zee executives argue that Zee Bangla was responsible for a more than doubling of cable networks in Calcutta in less than a year. But the experiment was soon discontinued. Zee discovered that it was losing its early evening Hindi audience by broadcasting Zee Bangla and that the prospective returns from Bengali were outweighed by its losses in the Hindi heartland.

At that stage, Zee took the view that the West Bengal economy would not support a Bengali channel; there weren't enough big advertisers willing to pay Zee rates to make a special appeal to the Bengali-speaking market. According to Kankan Sen of Mudra Advertising Services, advertising budgets in West Bengal are generally low and advertisers much more cautious than in more prosperous parts of India. She told us: 'Retail outlets like the well-known sari shops...show no interest in expanding their business; they have no farsightedness as far as marketing themselves is concerned.'[32] Moreover, from the point of view of multinationals and of Indian big businesses, there are few products which distinguish the Bengali market from others; according to advertising executives in Calcutta, only hair oils and milk products are consumed in greater quantities. This means that there are no persuasive reasons for devising special advertisements for the Bengali middle class, given the level of Hindi understanding revealed in cable and satellite households.

An alternative scenario examined by media entrepreneurs has been to look beyond West Bengal to the greater Bengali market in Bangladesh, Tripura and among Bengali speakers in India and the Gulf. As the second largest linguistic group in South Asia, with a population of nearly 200 million in the two Bengals, Bengalis should have no difficulty sustaining a satellite service, according to this argument. However, targeting both Bengals is widely seen as problematic on political and cultural grounds. Many Indian Bengalis reject the idea that Bangladesh can take the lead in matters of language and culture, though Bangladeshi scholars are not shy to stake this claim and some Indian commentators endorse it. A Zee representative in Calcutta told us: 'You cannot have a common programme for Bangladeshis and us.... Differences in basic taste and culture mean that it is not going to work on the small screen.'[33] A business executive looking at a similar proposal for an Indian conglomerate came to the same conclusion. 'Although we speak the same language', he said, 'here it is a regional language, there a national one.... Here there is less chauvinism.... Calcuttans are easy with Hindi.... I doubt if we would give our lives for Bengali, whereas the Bangladeshis might.'[34] Moreover, who would manage the news and current affairs? The assumption is that neither side would submit to the decisions of the other.

The Bengali satellite channel ATN launched by a group of Bangladeshi businessmen in the summer of 1998 quickly began to defy this kind of scepticism. The new channel relied heavily on Bengali music, chat shows, quizzes and old Bengali black and white movies, most of them from India. Its production standards were closer to the national broadcasters than to Zee or Star and it pulled in advertising from small businesses and shops rather than big conglomerates. But it did succeed in appealing to the lower middle class in Bangladesh and to some extent in West Bengal, something which the satellite channels with their 'modern' story lines and their largely Hindi programming had failed to do. ATN also overcame some of the divisions across borders by commissioning programmes from West Bengal as well as Bangladesh and by providing current affairs programmes made in both Dhaka and Calcutta. Instead of forcing the two Bengals to come together, it encouraged them to enjoy their differences.

The lesson of ATN's success—that there is an audience outside the big towns which is ready to respond to new kinds of regional programming—is acknowledged by Calcutta's commercially successful producers. Sudeshna Roy, producer of the popular soap opera *Paroma* on Calcutta Doordarshan, draws a distinction between what the Calcutta middle class will accept and what goes down well in the districts. She says Bengali films are doing surprisingly well in the rural and suburban areas, even if they are not well received in Calcutta. The secret of working the Bengali media market is not to confuse it with Mumbai or Chennai. Films in Bengal can be made with a budget of Rs. 3,500,000 and will be counted very successful if they make Rs. 1 million at the box office (approx. US$ 240,000)—a derisory sum by the standards of Mumbai. Bengal is not a market for 'big advertisers' or multinational sponsors, but she says it is possible to attract the support of smaller business houses and to make a decent profit on a sponsored programme.[35]

In 1998, both ATN and DD7, with their low budgets and relatively low production standards, looked poor competitors for the Hindi satellite channels, but two years later the commercial viability of the Bengali market had increased as a result of the spread of cable to the district towns, and the same market began to burgeon with new satellite initiatives. By 2000, ATN, which had lit the way for its own competitors, was already losing ground to channels with deeper pockets.

By the end of 1999, four new Bengali language satellite channels targeted on Bangladesh had been launched, of which one quickly closed down. Potentially, the strongest of the others was Channel I, the product of the country's largest production house, Impress Telefilms. In India, Zee's launch of a new Alpha Bengali channel marked its return to the same market with a different product—

attracting a lower level of advertising but making it available 24 hours a day. Then in April 2000, Bangladesh's first private terrestrial station—Ekushey TV (ETV)—came on air, officially licensed for satellite capacity as well. At the same time, two more Bengali language satellite channels were launched. The first, an initiative of Ramoji Rao's Eenadu group and called ETV Bangla, aimed to position itself as a flag carrier of Bengali culture, with a largely West Bengal focus. The second, called Tara, an offshoot of Star TV, with production and distribution arms in both Bangladesh and India, was more focused on appealing to a cross-border audience.

One obvious uncertainty was whether the Bengali satellite market would support the number of channels which had emerged. In the short term, it seemed likely that some of them would go to the wall. However, the confidence of players like Zee, Star and Eenadu in the long term future of the Bengali market made an encouraging contrast to the bleak landscape of only two years earlier. The arrival of new channels had not stopped the Bengali middle class from watching Hindi entertainment programmes where they recognised their superior production qualities, but Bengali alternatives had emerged, less well funded but in search of ways of serving the wider middle class in its own language.[36] One lesson from these developments would seem to be that where popular Hindi satellite channels are market leaders, a different scale of television aimed at the district towns, or radio aimed at local audiences, is more likely to be commercially successful in reinforcing local cultures than more ambitious ventures seeking to compete with national players and their standards of production and profitability.

As in Maharashtra, these developments in the satellite media have increased the pressure on Doordarshan's Calcutta kendra. The commercialism of its first response to the satellite invasion won it few friends among the Calcutta middle class. However, when it does broadcast quality programmes, it immediately finds an audience, which suggests that a strategic re-think is overdue. The success of *Khas Khabar*, a lively and well produced evening current affairs programme launched in October 1998, proved this point very clearly. An 'out-sourced' programme from Rainbow Productions, *Khas Khabar* was a daily 10-minute sponsored slot which relied heavily on spot reporting from different districts of

West Bengal and quickly became a news source on the state quoted by other channels. Its popularity is best judged by its advertising rates, which at Rs. 15,000 for 5 seconds in mid-1999, were well beyond the regional norm.[37] This kind of commercial success with a programme of regional value showed clearly what Doordarshan could offer in terms of greater choice, variety and quality, if it could overcome its many problems. The arrival of Zee's Alpha Bangla and more recent satellite channels intensified competition in the field of commercial entertainment and news. What remained in doubt was whether Doordarshan, despite its better reach and still comfortable finances, would be able to rise to the challenge.

SOUTH INDIA

In the first phase of the satellite revolution, South India provides a marked contrast to the situation in other regions of the country. Far from struggling to maintain a television presence in the satellite age, South Indian cultures took to the new medium with enthusiasm as a means of affirming their sense of difference. By the year 2000, there were over ten commercial satellite channels in the South, including two in Kerala, one in Karnataka, two in Andhra Pradesh and more than five in Tamil Nadu. Nowhere else in India were the regional opportunities of satellite taken up so quickly and effectively.

This southern efflorescence is explained in part by lack of knowledge of Hindi south of the Vindhyas and by the existence of a thriving film industry which provided much of the raw material in the early years. Unlike in Maharashtra or West Bengal, where familiarity with Hindi opened the door to the new film-based entertainment programmes of Zee and Sony, in the South most people neither understood nor wished to understand Hindi, which had long been seen as a symbol of northern political and cultural dominance. In the South too, Bollywood met its match in a hugely popular southern cinema, whose influence had come to be felt not just in the remotest villages but also in the corridors of state power. In Tamil Nadu, C.N. Annadurai, one of the founders of the Dravidian movement, was the first of a long line of politicians with film industry connections. But in the 1980s, the phenomenon also spread to neighbouring Andhra Pradesh. The emergence at that time of idols of the screen—M.G. Ramachandran and

N.T. Rama Rao—as chief ministers of the two states underlined a unique southern symbiosis of cinema and politics.

Of the four southern states, Tamil Nadu is the most competitive TV market and its capital, Chennai, which has acted as the production centre for southern cinema from the 1930s, has played the same role for the southern satellite channels.[38] Sun TV, the most commercially successful of them, makes most of its profits in the Tamil market, but has also developed channels in other southern languages which depend on their links with its Chennai production centre. Many serials first shown on Sun TV in Tamil are later shown in dubbed versions for other regional audiences. As the Sun TV chief executive put it: 'I can go for big budget serials and split the costs'.[39] Among the southern states, only Karnataka does not permit dubbing, which has involved Sun in more expensive origination of serials for that audience.

This analysis concentrates on Tamil Nadu because of its pivotal role in the South, the importance of its film industry, its longstanding differences with New Delhi over questions of linguistic autonomy and the remarkable success of Sun TV in capitalising on the political and economic opportunities of the new media era. On the basis of interviews and discussion groups in Tamil Nadu, we examine what the growth of Tamil satellite TV has meant for Tamil culture and how Doordarshan has responded to the intense competition.

TAMIL NADU

The avidity with which the opportunities of satellite TV were taken up in Tamil Nadu can only be thoroughly understood in the context of the long and often heated relationship between Delhi and Chennai in cultural and political matters. Nehru's vision of India, which required a strong central government in order to implement his policies of economic development and industrialisation, came to be overlaid in time with a cultural vision of India which emphasised North Indian Hindu traditions and the role of Hindi as a common national language. This cut across Tamil pride in their own language and their own cultural and religious traditions. Attempts to enforce Hindi in Tamil Nadu led to a state-wide agitation and several suicides in 1965 and played a crucial role in the rise to power of the Dravida Munnetra Kazhagam (DMK). Throughout these years, Delhi's suspicions that some Tamil politicians harboured separatist ambitions were resented in Chennai, where Delhi was widely seen as playing a neo-colonial role.

The conflict was made more complex by political and social divisions within Tamil Nadu's Hindu community. The traditional leadership of the community—the small but influential Brahmin caste—gradually lost power to the more numerous non-Brahmin castes as representative government became established. The leadership of the Tamil Nadu Congress, which came largely from the higher castes, found common ground with Nehru and others in putting nationalism before the encouragement of more regional allegiances. This was in part a legacy of the struggle for independence, in part because it served more local purposes; in later years, stressing the pan-Indian and the Sanskritic became a way of reinforcing its own position vis-à-vis the growth of non-Brahmin power. By 1967, however, with the election of the first DMK government in the state, the new political forces assumed power. DMK-led governments have since alternated with those led by the All India Anna DMK (AIADMK), which had its origins as a faction of the same party. The Congress never returned to power in its own right, though it retained power much longer in New Delhi and continued to wield considerable local influence through its control of national institutions.

The role of Doordarshan in serving Delhi's interests in the face of these changing local realities has been a focus of protest on a number of occasions. Mrs. Gandhi's use of the newly established Madras kendra during the Emergency to justify her dismissal of the DMK government and to condemn its politics strongly influenced perceptions of its role. In 1982, when Delhi decided to broadcast Hindi programmes in prime time, the ruling DMK and the opposition joined forces to pass a resolution condemning the move in the state legislature. Ultimately, Delhi had to back down and Tamil Nadu became the only non-Hindi speaking state in India to have a bulletin in its own language in prime time. In 1990, Chief Minister Karunanidhi highlighted continuing dissatisfaction with Doordarshan by publicly smashing a TV set at a protest meeting in Chennai.

Critics of Doordarshan argue that it has propagated a brahminical or sanskritic culture at the expense of the Tamil language and more popular regional cultures; that it has patronised those writers who were against regional autonomy and excluded supporters of the Dravidian movement. As one commentator put it: 'Even Karunanidhi had to wait till 1996 to get his first serial approved by Doordarshan.'[40] Some say this political bias can be attributed as much to the bureaucracy, which provides many of Doordarshan's top administrators, as to politicians. According to a professor of Tamil at Madras University, Doordarshan's very popular adaptations of the great Hindu epics—the *Ramayana* and the *Mahabharata*—were 'divine propaganda for the Indian administrators and the bourgeois class'. Dr Arasu says: 'Programming on Doordarshan is decided by the bureaucracy, which is constituted mostly by upper class brahmins or those kind to the Brahmin ideology. No counter culture can find entrance there.'[41]

In a similar vein, Sashi Kumar, formerly managing director of Asianet, sees the flowering of the southern channels as 'a reaction to Doordarshan's Delhi-centric attitude.... They could not see beyond their noses and they thought everything beyond the Vindhyas was one big Madras. They did not even know there were four states, as far as I can see....'[42] Anita Ratnam, the classical dancer, holds Doordarshan guilty of tokenism in dealing with regional cultures. 'India's...regionalism is completely lost on Doordarshan. We see it once a year in the Republic Day parade.... Even if they do appear, it is always along with a ministerial visit or a foreign dignitary. They are just plucked out for them to see. It is like cultural imperialism within India.'[43]

Given the interconnectedness of southern politics and media, it comes as no surprise that many of the new Tamil satellite channels have strong political links. Sun TV, the most successful of them, is controlled and managed by the family of the DMK leader. His nephew's son, Kalanidhi Maran, is the chief executive, and many other members of the family and party work for it.

The AIADMK has been less successful in developing a media vehicle of its own. Its first venture was JJ TV, which was launched in 1995 by the family of Sashikala Natarajan, a close friend and confidante of J. Jayalalitha, who was then the chief minister of the state. The channel's dependence on her patronage was made very apparent when it folded soon after she lost power in 1996. Subsequently, its management was taken to court over alleged infringements of foreign exchange regulations. After this, the party relied for some years on sympathetic treatment from Vijay TV, a Tamil channel owned by Vijay Mallya's United Breweries Group. However, in 1999, shortly after Vijay TV was sold to a consortium headed by an Indian software company, JJ TV resurfaced as Jaya TV, a transparently party political vehicle, like its predecessor. Public reactions to news programmes on private channels indicate that Sun TV is seen as relatively objective, despite its DMK connections. Discussants interviewed in Chennai and Madurai praised it for covering a full range of political news and for superior news presentation. 'Sun news is very balanced; they do not speak of the DMK alone', said a labourer in Chennai.[44] Some respondents also thought well of Raj TV. As a channel set up by Sri Lankan refugee businessmen, it has tried to keep out of state politics and there is public acknowledgement that it is striving for neutrality. Vijay TV, on other hand, was perceived as biased in favour of the AIADMK, a view which persisted six months after its new owners had relaunched it in April 1999 as an entertainment channel aimed at the youth market. Jaya TV was seen as a party channel. 'Their news is biased', said a retired school teacher in Chennai. 'During elections, Jaya only interviewed AIADMK politicians; Sun interviewed everyone.... I think even Vijay is getting glaringly channelled into AIADMK.'[45]

Sun's chief executive Kalanidhi Maran argues that using the channel for party purposes would undermine its credibility and its revenues. He told us: 'I am a regular watcher of Sun news. It is the number one programme. I don't want anyone saying that it has become a propaganda vehicle.'[46] Director of Current Affairs, Malan, says if the channel had not been genuinely apolitical 'it would have gone the way of JJ TV and other party-linked channels'.[47] However, some commentators praise Sun as much for shrewdness as for impartiality. 'Constantly they are working for their party but with more subtlety than Jaya TV', says media academic Father Joe Andrew. 'For example, some news item about Sashikala, which is not at all needed for the public, will somehow find its way into the daily news programme.'[48] Such critics argue that Sun's credibility is an asset which can be used when required. They say it does help the party by keeping the inadequacies of the opposition in the news and by pitting capable DMK speakers against weaker opponents in studio discussions.

The party certainly benefits from knowing that its point of view will not go by default, though there is no immediate correlation between the existence of a sympathetic channel and performance at the polls. In 1998, despite Sun's strong position, Jayalalitha routed the DMK in the national elections and went on to join the BJP-led coalition in Delhi. According to Sashi Kumar: 'The DMK had spent a lot of money and were preparing to celebrate victory... but lost heavily. It is a big lesson and question as to whether broadcast political propaganda makes any difference at all.'[49]

Satellite TV and Tamil Culture

Discussions in Chennai and Madurai registered relief that Tamil audiences had been liberated from Doordarshan's long-established monopoly and that they now have a choice of channels in their own language offering programmes 24 hours a day. This has brought a new level of affirmation of the regional: more coverage of Tamil Nadu, more interviews with its politicians, more debate about local issues, a greater sense of public participation and more programmes crafted to local cultural tastes. As one political commentator put it: 'DD could never give the feeling to the viewer that it is the medium which belongs to them; instead it gave the feeling that it is an official medium of the state. Private channels have reversed this; this is a positive trend.'[50]

At the same time, there is a lively debate about whether the new opportunities are being well used. Viduthalai Rajendran, general secretary of the Periyar Dravida Kazhagam, a party which remains loyal to the founding principles of the Dravidian movement such as rationalism, atheism and anti-brahminism, regrets that 'the way programmes are done in the private channels does not facilitate the growth of Tamil'. He says: 'In almost all programmes, the Tamil which is used is the Tamil of the urban middle class, with a lot of English words thrown in.... In other words, private TVs are presenting the culture and language of the urban middle class/upper caste as the culture and language of ordinary Tamils.' Professor T.K. Nannan, the educational broadcaster, holds that the new TV ethos represents a much greater challenge to Tamil society than the Dravidian movement itself. 'The challenge that Periyar presented was a positive one, intended to take society forward. The present challenge is a negative one, not intended to advance society. Film culture is vulgar; it is like an epidemic or a dog with rabies.'[51]

Those involved in the new channels take a more pragmatic view of Tamil culture. 'How can a Tamil channel not keep the Tamil identity afloat?', asked Kalanidhi Maran. 'If they are complaining about the spoken Tamil, where our hosts sometimes liberally use English words, it merely reflects the present social reality.' Malan, Sun's director of current affairs said: 'The so-called traditional meaning of Tamil culture is no longer the same. We speak English, drink coffee and dress in western clothes.'[52] Channel owners partially defend the concentration on urban India by arguing that everyone aspires to be middle class in the new India. 'It is very easy to say that we cater to the new middle class', comments Kalanidhi Maran, 'but the fact is we cater to the vast section that wants to move up the social ladder. In Tamil Nadu, the urban-rural divide is not singular. The entertainment industry is essentially both urban and rural. If we screen one film based on urban Tamil Nadu, the other is invariably on rural Tamil Nadu.'[53] Others argue, however, that TV is encouraging a trend it should be doing something to counter. A teacher at the Film Institute said: 'It is like demonstration and effect.... Every villager's ambition is to come here and be a successful city person. This the TV feeds.'[54]

As part of the quest for a Tamil personality for regional TV, Tamil culture is being reflected on the screen in the use of tradition-al art forms. For example, the *pattimandram*, a form of oratorical contest, has inspired many successful TV programmes, including the popular *Aratai Arangam*, which appears to be watched avidly by all social groups on Sunday mornings on Sun TV. Its compere, Visu, is admired for his skill in oratory and his success in training others in the same art, though he is also criticised for propagating his own opinions.[55] Another very popular performer is Valumpuri John, a story teller who appears regularly in *Vanakum Tamzhagam* on Sun TV.[56]

However, it is difficult to detect any direct correlation between the existence of satellite channels with strong links to Dravidian political interests and the propagation of Dravidian culture. Door-darshan is widely held to have propagated pan-Indian and sans-kritic culture and to have encouraged Tamil writers sympathetic to those themes. But the satellite channels, who might have been expected to use their new opportunities to pursue different ideologies, seem to have been more keen to poach successful writers and producers, whether from DD or from the Tamil film industry, than to develop new ones. In fact, some discussion groups criticised the satellite channels for doing less well than the film industry in reflecting the diversities of Tamil society. 'Why should all the stories be about Brahmins? As if there is no other story to tell', asked one Chennai housewife. 'Other castes besides Brahmins, Chettiar, Mudaliyar and Naidus, come only to wash vessels and beg', said another. 'Maybe because they have the money and they are the ones making the serials', said a third. 'At least in the movies, they have been showing other castes.'[57]

Some analysts suggest that the Dravidian parties have reworked their ideology since they assumed state power. They now emphasise their pan-Indian character as a means of underscoring their participation in national alliances and governments and the advantages which the state has derived from the liberalised economy. In the new, more genuinely federal India, concern for economic development has superseded the old preoccupations with social disadvantage. There is some echo of this view in the management style of Kalanidhi Maran, who describes himself as 'federal' in his approach to the Sun group of channels.[58] But even federalism is judged by business criteria. With a degree in business administration from America, Maran places his emphasis on what works in each market, on the economics of the bottom line and on keeping abreast of the latest technology rather than on ideology. These kinds of commercial considerations require tried and tested formulas for success and they draw on past marketing experience. In the South, as elsewhere, advertising agencies have had a powerful influence on the nature of programmes and they have been keen to play down old social divisions and propagate images of material progress accessible to all.

Other commentators point out that whatever the influence of economics, it is neither practical nor desirable to try and isolate either a pure Indian or a pure Tamil tradition. A.S. Panneerselvan, the South India correspondent of *Outlook*, talks of three different forms of *mokhsha* or liberation to which Tamils aspire in the early twenty-first century. One he calls 'Silicon *mokhsha*'—the belief that paradise is situated in California and that happiness consists of obtaining a green card to work in the computer industries there. The second is 'Pan-Indian *mokhsha*', which is represented by the new liberalised culture of Mumbai where money is supreme and everyone wears Punjabi dress. The third he calls 'Tamil *mokhsha'*— an attempt to maintain the purity of a 5000-year old culture in an era of globalisation.[59] His view is that these aspirations co-exist in contemporary urban Tamil society and that that reality has to be accepted. In his opinion, Tamil TV serials do represent contemporary urban life quite authentically but not the rural areas. 'The cultural conflict', he says, 'is in rural Tamil Nadu.'[60]

As far as stylistic influences are concerned, southern satellite television is as hybrid a phenomenon as its counterpart in the North, with the main borrowings from American TV and the Tamil film industry. As a professional in Madurai put it: 'It is now a mixed culture that is seen on TV. All kitsch.'[61]

Kalanidhi Maran admits that many programmes on Sun have been modelled on western programmes. 'In the initial stages, most of them were copies of US television programmes. *Nerukku Ner* was a copy of *Face to Face*. The United States gave me exposure to programming. Even today, all channels are only copying. If you take my *Pepsi Ungal Choice*, it is a copy of US radio shows.'[62] However, he draws a distinction between copying and cloning. He says: 'If in my talk show we deal with questions of domestic violence, it is not aping Oprah Winfrey but taking a cue from her. It is a very thin line that divides learning and cloning. I maintain that thin line and will defend it very carefully.'[63]

By contrast, the new serials and soap operas draw heavily on the Tamil film tradition. Many of them are made by producers who have transferred their allegiances to TV. One of the most successful is K. Balachander, whose video production company, Min Bimbangal, produced *Raghuvamsam*, the first daily Tamil soap opera for Sun. His company worked closely with Sun TV to produce some of the channel's most popular serials, including the new wave horror serial *Marmma Desam* and the soap opera *Premi*, the first to centre on a female subject. *Marmma Desam* was initially planned as a crime investigation or thriller, but the producer, Bala Kailasam, developed it into a horror serial with wider local appeal. His aim was not to promote superstition but to explore traditional Indian belief systems and oppose them with rationality. This format was very loosely inspired by *The X-Files*, which contrasts the scepticism of one character towards the paranormal with a receptiveness on the part of the other. The opposition between superstition and rationality is an early theme of the Dravidian movement which has been reflected in Tamil cinema. In this sense, as film maker Kutty Padmini maintains, the format at its best is a play on this theme without introducing the Brahmin-Dravidian ideological opposition specific to South India.[64] As a genre, however, it is criticised for not living up to this standard and for 'creating a legitimacy for superstition' rather than combating it.[65]

Kutty Padmini works for Vaishnavi Enterprises, another commercially successful production house. Once a child star of the Tamil cinema, she broke new ground by shooting crime serials in Singapore, Hong Kong and Thailand and went on to make a Hindi serial on the same subject for Star TV called *Customs File*. By 1999, she had to her credit 3,000 hours on air and at one point had seven serials on different channels at the same time. When Sun TV and Min Bimbangal fell out in 1999, Padmini came up with the thriller serial *Mandira Vaasal*, which replaced *Marmma Desam* and scored even higher ratings.

Despite TV's debt to the film industry, TV serials have evolved in different ways, with horrors and thrillers the biggest money spinners. Pritham Chakravarty, a specialist on South Indian television, sees the new cult for thrillers as a way of incorporating those long-ignored sections of society who have now found a political voice. 'What better way for the middle class to do this than to move to a rural setting, complete with folk beliefs and tradition... which automatically, with middle class aesthetics, necessitates dark skin and regional locations for the characters?'[66] The purpose, evidently, is to widen the constituency for television programmes in the interests of mass advertising. However, middle class aesthetics remain dominant; there is no voice on the new channels for the under-privileged. Arulmozhi, an avant-garde film maker, says: 'Our individual identities will only come forth when dalits have their own TV, feminists have their own TV. It will happen like the blacks made it happen in USA. Once it does happen, then HTA and Lintas (leading advertising agencies) will come forward with their Ponds and Whisper ads for them too. After all they will realise they have a market there too.'[67]

Some commentators see signs that commerce is slowly forcing image changes on the programme makers. Pepsi Cola, with its ambitions to extend its market into India's villages, has developed some advertisements targeted at village people, including one with

Sachin Tendulkar in a rural setting. But this is an exception in a world of advertising which concentrates largely on the middle class.

Criticisms of the
Tamil Satellite Channels

Given that the new Tamil channels, like popular Hindi channels in the North, draw on western programme formats and style, it is not surprising to discover that they have provoked some very similar reactions among the general public. Discussion groups in Chennai and Madurai evinced very similar concerns about taste and decency, particularly about the way young people dress, speak and treat their elders, as those in the North commenting on MTV or Zee. Vijay TV in particular, which seems to have modelled itself on MTV, provoked critical comments from all social groups, even the young. Its comperes were described as 'foolish and absurd' or 'very irritating' and criticised for wearing skimpy clothes, mangling their Tamil and setting a poor example.[68] 'No one in real life will dare to dress like that', said a housewife in Chennai. 'In the old movies, only "bad" women dressed like that; good women wore saris or churidars', said another.[69] 'All the girls in Vijay are bad. They look and speak so false', said two young sisters from Madurai. 'The language spoken on the satellite channels can only be described as murder', said a professional from the same town.[70]

This resistance to what many regard as tasteless imitation of western fashions is accompanied, however, with popular admiration for those presenters who manage to straddle the modern and traditional without causing offence. Interestingly, the most popular presenters are not dressed according to Tamil tradition but wear either salwar kameez which has come to be associated with pan-Indianness, or some variation of western dress. The young female presenter of *Pepsi Ungal Choice*, a music show on Sun TV, who goes by the name of Pepsi Uma, was the favourite TV personality of many discussants. 'No-one can beat Pepsi Uma in speech or dress', said a housewife in Madurai.[71] Another favourite, especially among students, was Swarnamalya, who presents another request show on Sun. 'She dresses well and chats with the college students, especially boys, with ease', said a group of teenage girls from Madurai. 'She... dresses only in modern clothes but she is so decent', said a grandmother from Chennai.[72] However, while this kind of adulation is itself a sign of respect for hybridity, serious exponents of South Indian culture regard it as worrying for this reason. 'Look at Pepsi Uma. Every girl in the city talks like her', said Gowri Ramnarayan, the culture correspondent of *The Hindu*. 'They think this is the best possible way to speak. Our language will soon die.'[73]

The championing of English in Tamil Nadu and other southern states in the post-colonial period was in part a defence against the encroachment of Hindi. In this particular battle, English and Tamil were natural allies. But considering that the Tamil language was the main badge of identity of the Dravidian movement, it is significant that the satellite channels, which are so closely linked to those political parties, are actually encouraging its dilution and the popularisation of southern versions of Hinglish, variously called Tamenglish or even Tanglish. Gowri Ramnarayan argues that 'once you kill the language, you kill the culture.' Public responses are less pessimistic but criticism of Vijay TV and its comperes is a sign that this sensitivity is widely shared.

Critics of the new satellite channels are also worried that cutthroat competition is forcing down costs of production to the point where the serials which dominate the schedules are made like industrial products and are poor in quality. 'Serial making is like factory work.... There is no space for creativity now', said one commentator. 'People walk in at 9 a.m. like they would into an office and leave at 6 p.m.... It becomes routine work....'[74] The economics are also resulting in longer and longer serials which do not have much dramatic impact. Whereas Doordarshan still runs some thirteen-part serials, other channels are now broadcasting serials which run for several years. Film director Arulmozhi says: 'You are asked to shoot one episode in one day. If the producer is kind, then for the pilot you get two days. No good director who respects his talent will do that kind of work. This is the reason why serials themselves had to go through this shift from three, seven or thirteen episodes to fifty-two episodes or 256 episodes. Your one time costs in the major sets come down and so the bigger the serial, the more money you make.'[75] These pressures have also led to sloppiness among producers. Research effort is cut down, sophisticated literature loses its complexity in the pursuit of a good story line with strong emotional interest, and standards sometimes fall after the first few episodes.

Sashi Kumar refers to satellite TV as a 'clonish subculture of cinema—at times appropriating and at times being eaten into by the dominant celluloid strain.'[76] Others argue that television will only improve when cinema improves. Arulmozhi says: 'Our cinema itself lacks any decent Tamil identity. Therefore, when TV came, the same hybrid format could be adapted here also....' Critics of Tamil TV complain that like the cinema it concentrates on 'syrupy, synthetic, over-dramatic, emotion-soaked programming' at the expense of social, economic or literary complexity.[77] The economics of production ensure that fiction is paramount and that stories are acted out on sets rather than in the real world. Professor Venkatesan of the Film and TV Institute argues that 'the Indian concept of TV or film is fiction'. He says: 'TV need not be used as yet another story-telling mechanism. It can be put to much better use.... Non-fiction can also be made interesting, entertaining.' [78] But so far there has not been sufficient public demand for change.

Some critics attribute the mediocrity of much Tamil television to the system instituted by Sun and copied by others of selling time directly to producers, leaving them with the responsibility of making the serials and selling the advertising. This reduces a channel's overheads but at the same time limits its opportunity to guarantee consistent standards or to encourage more creative or less commercially viable work. Sun itself is sensitive to such criticisms and has been paying greater attention to quality as a means of improving its reputation with more discerning viewers. It commissioned the well-known film maker, Balu Mahendra, to make *Kathai Neeram*, a series of adaptations of Tamil short stories, which became one of the most popular serials on Tamil TV.[79] It was praised by professionals as 'very creative and of course technically the best now' and its popularity challenged the wisdom of 'sausage-machine'economics. [80] But in late 1999, it was very much the exception to the rule.

Rabi Bernard, who was managing director of Vijay TV before its sale to UTV in 1999, told us how his efforts to inject quality into the schedule had fallen victim to commercial imperatives. 'Initially I wanted Vijay TV to be mother and teacher, carrying educational and development programmes.... After eight months, market realities showed me that what mattered was money.... Prime time TV was largely dictated by advertising agencies.... They give me a briefing that characters should not speak pure Tamil but Tamil-English. It is a buyer's market.... The company has to have a return on its investment.' Bernard also said: 'Tamil culture requires that we carry serious programmes...but advertisers don't want to be associated with them. If I produce a documentary on the plight of the untouchables, it can only be shown on non-prime time.'[81]

The Role of the Chennai Kendra

Doordarshan's efforts to combat its commercial opponents have not won it very much applause. Many Tamil intellectuals believe it has been instrumental in its own demise, whether through its historic insensitivity to Tamil aspirations or its abandonment of its wider brief. Doordarshan executives reject this kind of blanket criticism. They argue that they did offer strong support for Tamil culture, for drama, music and the arts but that they were hampered in combating the satellite channels due to lack of time on Doordarshan's terrestrial channels. The station director of Doordarshan's Chennai kendra told us that the satellite channels would not have done so well if Doordarshan had had the time and funds to do more regional programming.[82]

This view is supported to some extent by critics. They point out that when Doordarshan launched its Tamil satellite channel, DD5, more original work was possible than had till then been the case. But Arulmozhi's experience in trying to sell Doordarshan's national channel an idea for a serial about a great Tamil composer illustrates how the market is squeezing out worthwhile reflections of regional cultures. 'When I approached Doordarshan to telecast my serial concept on Muthusami Dikshatar, they said: "No one in Haryana or Bihar will know who he is. Why don't you make a thriller; then all will understand." Doordarshan is not ready to take the risk.... We are asked to develop linear taste.' According to Arulmozhi, even a play by Karunanidhi, with an underlying political message, was transformed in the process of adaptation. 'The serial itself, unlike the text, had to blunt its various political strands and concentrate on human emotions alone.'[83]

Sashi Kumar, himself a former Doordarshan broadcaster, blames Doordarshan for this kind of slavish imitation of its new competitors. 'Instead of doing its own thing, Doordarshan began to imitate what the new channels were doing. They began to get rid of their *krishi darshans* (agricultural programmes) and started showing films. It became one-upmanship on the same terrain.'[84] Most viewers of Doordarshan think its programmes have become worse since it started competing with other channels for advertising. 'Now it has become commercialised', said one critic, 'everybody feels that they should get the maximum revenue to be in the good books of their ministers. They are not interested in the overall national interest.'[85] The fact that government has been pushing the organisation to be more self-sufficient has accelerated the trend.

Doordarshan still has its defenders. The film and television producer, S.Krishnaswamy, refuses to make programmes for the satellite channels. He says: 'Unless you base your programme on popular Indian cinema...there is hardly any scope. Productions which require more than a minimum outlay do not get a return on the satellite channels but continue to do so on Doordarshan. Values have been eroded because of the competition but you can get creative satisfaction.' Krishnaswamy, who comes from a generation of film makers that adopted Nehru's scientific rationalism, criticises Tamil cinema and satellite channels for propagating 'value systems repugnant to the advancement of a mature society. As much as traditional films promoted superstition and heroic, semi-divine images, so-called modern films try to make a virtue out of infidelity; they are promoting images which are not healthy to society.'[86] In 1999, he produced a series for Doordarshan to encourage more critical thinking about the media.

Discussion groups also recognised some residual differences between Doordarshan and its competitors. 'Only Doordarshan gives space for social messages', was one comment.[87] According to a teenager interviewed in Chennai 'Doordarshan is slightly better at showing the poor', though this verdict was not universally supported. 'Doordarshan will not disappear. People know Doordarshan to be a public media. Private channels cannot show themselves as one', said a professional in Madurai. Doordarshan's problem, however, seems to be that it has lost touch with the young. 'Children do not watch Doordarshan. We can only see what they choose to see', said a housewife from Chennai. 'Who is watching Doordarshan?' asked a student at the TV and Film Institute. 'The audience is only for Sun TV.' 'What can they do?', asked a labourer. 'They are owned by the ruling party.'[88]

NATION AND REGION: STATE, SATELLITE AND MARKET

For most of the late 1990s, the experience of South India provided an encouraging counterpoint to the situation in Maharashtra or West Bengal. While Maharashtrians and Bengalis were enticed into watching Hindi satellite channels for want of adequate regional alternatives, southern media entrepreneurs seized the opportunity offered by satellite to break free of Doordarshan's step-motherly treatment, affirm local cultures and, in the case of Sun TV, enjoy runaway commercial success. There were many similarities in the successful formulas of Zee and Sun, notably their common reliance on film and film-based programmes and on quiz and game shows. But Sun TV's penetration of Tamil society went far deeper than Zee's penetration of Maharashtra or Bengal. It capitalised on the advertising needs of small entrepreneurs and shopkeepers and on the thirst for participation at much lower levels of society. The fact that cable has been spreading so fast in the South is explained partly by the success of the southern channels in speaking more directly to the rural areas and small towns. As Sashi Kumar puts it: 'The programmes are aiming at a township level...and this...viewership target is something that is new....'[89]

By 2000 the same trend was becoming visible in the North and West as well. The success of ATN in attracting the Bengali 'township' viewer showed the way for others in that substantial transnational market. But Zee's launch of its Alpha channels in 1999, which played to the needs of regional audiences at home and abroad, followed by other initiatives from Star and Eenadu in early 2000, raised the stakes in Indian regional broadcasting to a new level. Zee's announcement in April 2000 that it was moving into South India in collaboration with Asianet made plain its national ambitions.

These developments look set to temper concerns at the way the new satellite media market had reinforced the dominance of Hindi at the expense of other regional languages north of the Vindhyas.

But the reproduction on a more economic footing of the formula which had worked so well for Zee in Hindi or Sun in Tamil seemed unlikely to answer a wide range of concerns expressed across Maharashtra, West Bengal and Tamil Nadu about the relentless pursuit of profit and the neglect of other kinds of programmes. Until late 1999, leaving it to the market in North India meant that the prime time battle between Doordarshan and its satellite rivals was fought out in the field of Hindi language soap operas with their immense appeal across the whole northern subcontinent. According to Hamid Kidwai, Director of Jamia Millia Mass Communication and Research Centre in Delhi, that involved 'an erosion of cultural diversity in North India'.[90] Whether the establishment of new regional channels in different languages will reverse this trend remains uncertain, but the evidence from Tamil Nadu encourages scepticism. According to a Tamil politician critical of trends in the South: 'Tamil TV channels are putting out the same retrogressive material as Hindi TV. You have so much of religion, you have so much of cinema and you have so little of what would be useful to people. This means that though we have channels in Tamil, they are no different from the ideological thrust of Hindi channels.'[91]

So far, Doordarshan has not risen to this kind of challenge. It has maintained its revenues by adopting the strategies of its competitors, but it has lost ground with middle class audiences, both nationally and regionally. This loss of confidence in Doordarshan is particularly marked among the English educated in the big cities, but it is also noticeable among the younger generation outside the metropolitan areas, who often regard it as a channel for their parents and grandparents. Doordarshan seems to have lost contact with this generation.

Doordarshan's regional language services have also been found wanting by middle class viewers. Its kendras in Calcutta, Mumbai and Ahmedabad have had some success with commissioned soap operas and current affairs programmes, which has demonstrated what could be achieved in the right conditions. But viewers are very critical of its poor standards and its reliance on soap opera. There is a definite strand of opinion which believes that Doordarshan should be offering a different and more varied service to the public.

Awareness of Doordarshan's strengths as a regional news provider came through in many discussion groups in western India. There was an evident preference, particularly outside Mumbai and among the older generation, for regional news in regional languages, a service which Doordarshan is providing through its satellite channels and which was not being offered until recently by any commercial competitor. Zee's new Alpha channels, which aim at just this audience, will put pressure on Doordarshan here too.

Our surveys suggest that Doordarshan still retains some respect as a 'safe pair of hands' in what many regard as an increasingly dangerous moral universe. As a working class father in Pune put it: 'Doordarshan is much more natural'.[92] Doordarshan may lose points for being official or dull, but it wins over others for its residual commitment to serving the whole community, for its acknowledgement of regional and linguistic differences, for its relatively greater independence of commercial interests, and for avoiding extremes of voyeurism and sensationalism. These are all assets of value if it ever chooses to reposition itself in relation to its satellite competitors.

No one questions the need for Doordarshan to be as entertaining as its rivals, but if the experience of Tamil Nadu is anything to go by, head-to-head competition in the production of prime time soap operas is likely to diminish its level of public support. The issues are more clearly appreciated, even in government, than is sometimes understood. The launch of Doordarshan's regional satellite channels was an imaginative response to the emergence of satellite competition, which seemed to reflect a more federal spirit in newly liberalising India. But the idea was not followed through effectively; as we have seen, these channels have not been funded well enough to generate the kind of quality programmes viewers would like to see. Defending 'national' audiences in Hindi has been given greater priority than developing workable strategies for the regions. According to our research in Tamil Nadu, even among those who criticise Doordarshan for its lack of professionalism, there is a wistful recognition of what it could achieve if it were reformed and given more regional autonomy, accompanied by disappointment that it has not been able to deliver.[93]

With the development of private satellite channels in Bengali, Marathi, Gujarati and Punjabi, the battleground has moved from

Hindi broadcasting to Doordarshan's more vulnerable regional language services. The state broadcaster still retains very large audiences beyond the cable networks, particularly in the poorer states, but its hold over regional 'township' audiences in the North is now being put to the same test which it seems to be failing in the South. If it pursues the same policies, there is a danger that it could be marginalised with the regional middle class as well as in the metropolitan areas. In this sense, the satellite revolution in the regions is not just about Doordarshan's competitiveness but also about what sort of state is appropriate to India's diversity.

NOTES AND REFERENCES

1. Vijay Tendulkar, Mumbai, May 1998.
2. Ranjit Hoskote, Mumbai, July 1998.
3. Shanta Gokhale, Mumbai, April 1998.
4. Professionals, Pune, August 1998.
5. Home makers, Mumbai, August 1998.
6. Marathi-speaking workers, Padavnagar, Pune, August 1998.
7. Pramod Navalkar, Mumbai, June 1998.
8. *The Times of India*, 30 April 1998.
9. Mukta Rajadhyaksha, Mumbai, April 1998.
10. Anjali Monteiro, Mumbai, May 1998.
11. Hima Vishwanathan, Mumbai, May 1998.
12. Ranjit Hoskote Mumbai, July 1998.
13. Sunil Shanbag, Mumbai, April 1998..
14. Vijay Tendulkar, Mumbai, May 1998.
15. Shanta Gokhale, Mumbai, April 1998.
16. Pratima Kulkarni, Mumbai, April 1998.
17. Neena Raut, Mumbai, August 1998.
18. Vipul Shah, Mumbai, July 1999.
19. Zee Network press release, 16 August 1999; www.zeetelevision.com December 1999.
20. Nitin Vaidya, Mumbai, October 1999.
21. This assessment is based on Anuradha Mukherjee's media profile of West Bengal and on discussion groups with professionals, school children, college students, and home makers.
22. IRS-98.
23. Malini Bhattacharya, Calcutta, June 1998.
24. Indrani Sen, Calcutta, May 1998.
25. Ananda Lal, Calcutta, July 1998.
26. Ashok Surana, Calcutta, May 1998.
27. Mallika Jalan, Calcutta, May 1998.
28. Shilu Chattopadhyaya, Calcutta, March 1998.

29. Ananya Banerjee, Calcutta, April 1998.
30. Abhijit Das Gupta, Calcutta, May 1998.
31. Aveek Sarkar, Calcutta, March 1998.
32. Kankan Sen, Calcutta, May 1998.
33. Manas Chatterjee, Calcutta, May 1998.
34. P.K. Bose of RPG Group, Calcutta, May 1998.
35. Sudeshna Roy, Calcutta, July 1998.
36. We are indebted to Indrani Sen of Hindustan Thompson Associates for a briefing on the West Bengal media scene as the book went to press in April 2000.
37. Soma Mukherjee of Rainbow Productions, May 1999.
38. The following information on the history of the main southern channels draws extensively on a 'Television Profile of South India' commissioned from Lata Ramaseshan, March 1999.
39. *Business World*, 7–21 September 1998.
40. A.S. Panneerselvan, Note on satellite TV in Tamil Nadu, written for the Media South Asia Project, December 1999.
41. Professor Arasu, Chennai, November 1999.
42. Sashi Kumar, Chennai, February 1998.
43. Anita Ratnam, Chennai, December 1999.
44. Labourers, Chennai, November 1999.
45. Senior citizens, Chennai, November 1999.
46. *The Week*, 23 May 1999.
47. Malan, Chennai, December 1999.
48. Father Joe Andrew, Chennai, November 1999.
49. Sashi Kumar, Chennai, May 1998.
50. Viduthalai Rajendran, Chennai, January 2000.
51. Professor T.K. Nannan, Chennai, May 1998.
52. Malan, Chennai, December 1999.
53. Kalanidhi Maran, Chennai, November 1999.
54. Professor Venkatesan, Chennai, November 1999.
55. Professionals, senior citizens, teenagers, labourers, Chennai, November 1999. But Dr. Arasu holds that 'the diction used is gibberish, part brahminical, part de-politicised'.
56. A professional interviewed in Chennai described this as 'the only useful programme on Tamil TV'. Professionals, Chennai, November 1999.
57. Home makers, Chennai, November 1999.
58. Kalanidhi Maran, Chennai, November 1999.
59. A.S. Panneerselvan, London, December 1999.
60. A.S. Panneerselvan, Note on satellite TV in Tamil Nadu.
61. Students, Madurai, November 1999.
62. *The Week*, 23 May 1999.
63. Kalanidhi Maran, Chennai, November 1999.
64. See, Workshop on Tamil Cinema: History Culture Theory, 15–19 August 1997, Madras Institute of Development Studies, Chennai, p. 54.
65. Professionals, Chennai, November 1999.
66. Pritham Chakravarty discusses recent trends in film production in a report on the cable industry in South Chennai commissioned for the Media South Asia Project.

67. Arulmozhi, Chennai, November 1999.
68. Labourers and professionals, Madurai, November 1999.
69. Home makers, Chennai, November 1999.
70. Students, professionals, home makers, Madurai, November 1999.
71. Home makers, Madurai, November 1999.
72. Students, Madurai, and senior citizens, Chennai, November 1999.
73. Gowri Ramnarayan, Chennai, November 1999.
74. Father Joe Andrew, Chennai, November 1999.
75. Arulmozhi, Chennai, November 1999.
76. *TV and Video World*, July 1995.
77. Anita Ratnam, Chennai, November 1999.
78. Professor Venkatesan, Chennai, November 1999.
79. In an interview in November 1999, Kalanidhi Maran argued that the search for TRP ratings was forcing Sun to constantly upgrade its technology and its programme form and content.
80. Ravi Raj, Professor of Direction at the Film and Television Institute, Chennai, November 1999.
81. Rabi Bernard, Chennai, May 1998.
82. Natarajan, Chennai, May 1998.
83. Arulmozhi, Chennai, November 1999.
84. Sashi Kumar, Chennai, February 1998.
85. Raadhu, Chennai, May 1998.
86. S. Krishnaswamy, Chennai, May 1998.
87. Senior citizens, Chennai, November 1999.
88. Students, senior citizens, labourers, Chennai, November 1999.
89. Sashi Kumar, Chennai, February 1998.
90. Professor H.R. Kidwai, Delhi, June 1998.
91. Viduthalai Rajendran, Chennai, January 2000.
92. Lower income groups, Padavnagar, Pune, August 1998.
93. This is the assessment of Pritham Chakravarty on the basis of her interviews for the project.

Seven

THE SOUTH ASIAN FOOTPRINT

In some respects, reactions to international satellite programmes among India's neighbours are not very different from those in India itself. As in India, they focus on their role in introducing new images of social choice and behaviour, particularly for young people, their influence in promoting cultural homogenisation and their effect on national and regional languages. Responses are both positive and negative, displaying a high degree of critical discrimination among audiences towards the programmes offered. Satellite channels are seen as providing a counterpoint to state TV and a stimulus to better production values. At the same time, the state is assumed to have a regulatory responsibility, which it often fails to exercise.

In so far as English-educated metropolitan elites in Karachi or Lahore, Colombo or Dhaka share the aspirations of their counterparts in Mumbai or Delhi, many satellite programmes find the same sort of welcome in those cities. However, the popularity of Hindi language entertainment channels has given rise to apprehensions that the culture of Bollywood is swamping other national cultures and even destroying the ideological boundaries of the nation state.

Such ideological worries have been most intensely felt in Pakistan; less so in Bangladesh or Nepal, though the popularity of satellite channels has presented a challenge to state broadcasters in those countries as well. In all three countries, those speaking for national cultures see Hindi satellite channels as carriers of an Indian culture which threatens to break down the sense of difference which the state and state broadcasters have been trying to reinforce.

Sri Lanka is the only country in South Asia where these issues have not featured so prominently. Sri Lankans also watch satellite programmes—including both Hindi and Tamil soap operas imported from India—but on their own terrestrial channels, not via cable or satellite. The argument that a more diversified national media is the best defence against globalising media interests is one which Sri Lanka's experience enables us to put to the test.

BANGLADESH

In Bangladesh, initial responses to the satellite revolution were as negative as in India. The government was resistant to the invasion of its air space and worried about possible political repercussions. The fact that only the very rich had access to satellite images made satellite TV all the more questionable; there was a perception that the rich enjoyed culturally alien and, by implication, decadent entertainment. These reactions were transformed, however, by the development of Dhaka's cable systems, which were servicing up to 40 per cent of the city by the year 2000. Satellite had been democratised: it was plainly popular and the debate about cultural invasions gave way to a scramble for connections.

By 1998, after a relatively slow start compared to India, cable had become well established and Bangladesh Television (BTV) was beginning to lose its urban middle class audience. In Dhaka, cable operators were offering over twenty channels; in district towns the number was closer to ten. According to cable operators and advertising agencies, the Star group of channels, Zee, Sony, TNT/Cartoon Network and ESPN were the most popular of the 'foreign' channels, with the Bengali language channels, DD7 and ATN Bangla, among the market leaders. At that stage, some seasoned media observers were predicting 'a situation where cable TV will actually replace our national media'.[1] Others were pointing to divided audiences, the well to do watching cable and the poor in rural areas relying on national TV and radio services.

As a result of the spread of cable TV, Indian film stars and cricketers became as familiar to the Dhaka middle class as they were in India. Chinmoy Mutsuddi, the editor of *Binodon Bichitra*, had to transform his film magazine into a TV journal, featuring Indian stars and their lifestyles, because of changing popular tastes. 'My readers watch cable, so I have to cover Ruby Bhatia and Nafisa and Meghna.... The new generation especially are very keen.... As things are going, we shall soon become an extension of the Indian TV market. We shall grow up watching others.'[2]

Indian influences were also seen at work in fashion, music and a wider knowledge of Indian politics and culture. Boutique owners in Dhaka admitted to following Mumbai TV fashions, though their own offerings were tailored to less adventurous local tastes.[3] Outside Dhaka, pressures to conform remain strong, whatever individuals might personally wish. A young woman interviewed about TV fashions in Jamalpur, 100 miles from the capital, said: 'If I wear a skirt and dress, they will say bad things about my father, about my family. I have to live according to the norm of my town....'[4] But both in Dhaka and Jamalpur, beauty care programmes like *Khoobsurat* on Zee TV had a wide following and were affecting women's perceptions of themselves. 'What has happened', said one boutique owner, 'is a heightened sense of personal beauty care. They are more sophisticated, more concerned about elegance rather than garish make-up. They are looking for and asking more about how to look nice and confident.'[5]

A limited survey of 100 households in the Dhaka area carried out in February 1998 put entertainment, information and sport among the main reasons for watching cable TV. Satellite programmes were also commended for their good production values and for discussing critical issues. On the other hand, cable TV was criticised for being 'very sexually suggestive', 'culturally alien' and for assuming a low level of audience intelligence. Fifty per cent of those questioned thought cable TV was 'a threat to national culture'; 60 per cent thought national culture had already been affected.[6]

Comments made in discussion groups helped to amplify these perceptions of cultural change. The popularity of sports channels and their commercial effectiveness was confirmed by a university student who relished this new access to international matches: 'We never got a chance like this before. It's great to see countries play. I think it will also influence us to drink more Pepsi and Coke and to carry bags on our shoulder, but that's how time moves.'[7]

The discussions revealed that Indian films were both very popular and a cause for concern on account of their 'embarrassing scenes' and violence. According to one home maker: 'Hindi movie violence is the worst influence.' Others believed western stars were more powerful role models than Indian ones and commented adversely on the 'half naked women' appearing in western soap operas. Except among religious conservatives, however, there was a sense that 'people are getting used to it'. What had been embarrassing initially, was being tolerated more easily after a few years.[8]

Many discussants rejected the idea that foreign television programmes were undermining their culture. One housewife said: 'If a society's cultural base is strong, external influences can't have much of an impact. In the last twenty-five years there has been a lot of cultural confusion. There are numerous ideologies and young people don't know what is right. Hindi cinema did not make society corrupt. Politics did.' A university student said: 'The influence of foreign channels is over-estimated. It has influence at the popular level.... In marriage ceremonies, traditional songs are disappearing and are being replaced by Hindi movie songs. That is a loss.... But our culture and politics is too linked to be overrun by foreign influences.'[9]

Others were seriously concerned about existing media imbalances. A development worker told us: 'Cable TV is destroying traditional culture.... More than influence, what it's doing is replacing what existed. Punjabi dances can be seen in rural Bengal now.'[10] A professional said: 'People don't stop to think about cultural influences. It becomes inevitable when one culture becomes weak. Our culture is still strong but our inputs are relatively weak. If it get's weaker, we may not have a culture of our own. Hindi cable culture will become our culture.' Another professional said: 'Indian channels will overwhelm local TV because the investment in Indian TV is so high.' But he also argued that the absence of attractive programming in Bengali was the key factor.[11]

For some critics of satellite TV, the successful marketing of Mumbai lifestyles in advertisements encourages damaging social divisions. For them, changing fashions in dress are not superficial but indicative of deeper alienation. As one development worker put it: 'I think you can't separate dress from the other parts of lifestyle they subscribe to. They know Madonna but they have never heard of Abbasuddin Ahmed. They can dance like the movie stars but don't know the traditional dances that exist in our society. They have no stake, no vested interest in what we have. That's why it's so easy to migrate to USA without a thought for their country. When have they had an opportunity to see their country?

They have grown up seeing India and the USA. In their minds Bangladesh doesn't exist.'[12]

Such a view does not go uncontested. Geeteara Choudhury, chief executive of a leading advertising agency, sees much that is positive in the new television role models. She sees nothing offensive in the fact that the Dhaka middle class youth wear sweatshirts and jeans and takes an interest in new music. 'In fact', she says, 'the present crop of girls are more confident than any that I have seen and I think the regional mass media has helped in creating such a space for our children.'[13]

Others, however, believe that satellite television has done very little to reinforce the efforts of non-governmental organisations in empowering women. One development worker told us: 'A major change in our society is the higher status that women now enjoy. That was possible through the work of non-governmental organisations. But very little of that comes through cable TV.' Another development worker told us: 'The influence has been on the upper middle class who have now become product driven. They want more and more and although our society can't afford that, they still want consumer items.... The class which was the pride of Bangladesh now only want washing machines and dandruff removers.'[14]

In Jamalpur district, where cable systems are restricted to eight or nine channels, the dominance of Hindi channels is proportionately greater.[15] The main channels available are Zee, Star, Sony, MTV, DD7 and ESPN. Respondents to the questionnaire gave more or less the same analysis of benefits and disadvantages as their counterparts in Dhaka. In Jamalpur, more than in Dhaka, having a cable connection and aspiring to know Hindi are taken as signs that people were 'intellectually or socially advanced'.[16] But there was also a recognition that the window on the world offered by satellite TV was limited: 'We only get Hindi channels; we don't know what is happening elsewhere...', was one comment.[17]

The perception of change was greater in Jamalpur than in Dhaka. Seventy per cent of respondents thought culture had already been affected, compared with 60 per cent in Dhaka. However, fewer respondents took it as a threat—50 per cent said it was not a threat compared with 20 per cent in Dhaka. Proportionately, satellite TV has made a greater impact on media services in the districts, though the sense of social control is greater at that level than in the bigger cities. Urban viewers, on the other hand, despite a more westernised lifestyle and greater addiction to satellite, are more concerned about what they see as cultural intrusions.

One measure of the sense of marginalisation induced by satellite TV was the eagerness with which the return of ATN Bangla, the only satellite channel run by Bangladeshis, was greeted in mid-1998, particularly among the lower socio-economic groups in Dhaka. Elite and middle class viewers were less enamoured of ATN, which they saw as a bad Bangladeshi copy of Mumbai culture, but it caught on very well with others, simply because it was in the local language. TV producers like Syed Borhan Kabir criticise ATN for its lack of originality: 'We should not try to compete with Mumbai. It is absurd to think it is possible. We should produce our own kind of programmes.'[18] But it proved that there was a strong demand for Bengali programming. It also attracted considerable advertising and encouraged the launch of new Bengali channels in 1999, which to some extent undermined its position.

The popularity of Doordarshan's Bengali satellite channel DD7, particularly outside Dhaka and with the older generation, underlines the same point. Though it does not match the Hindi satellite channels in terms of production standards or entertainment value, it is seen as a more culturally acceptable option.

Another significant result of the surveys carried out in Bangladesh is that despite disillusionment with Bangladesh Television (BTV) there is widespread recognition of its national cultural importance. Surveys carried out in Dhaka and Jamalpur among those with BTV and cable connections revealed that 90 percent of the respondents do watch BTV and the vast majority spend about a third of their viewing time looking at it. The programmes they like are drama (in Bengali), dubbed Hindi serials, musicals and two local current affairs programmes—*Ittihadi* and *Poriprekhit*—which are modelled on satellite programmes. Asked what qualities they appreciated on BTV, respondents mentioned its coverage of 'national culture and news', its drama and its relevance to their problems. When asked whether they believed BTV news, 75 per cent said 'No'. Asked if they wanted it to continue, 100 per cent said 'Yes'. Despite the limited character of the surveys, they show a sophisticated awareness of both the weaknesses and strengths of the institution. Despite its long history as the mouthpiece of different political parties, BTV does have a constituency on which it can build, given the right conditions.

According to soundings in Bangladesh, many viewers see a better BTV as the only viable cultural response to the marginalisation process which they are facing. In 1998, when Hindi satellite channels faced only limited Bengali satellite competition, some even went as far as to say that this must happen in one generation. They argued that the next generation of elite decision-makers had already been alienated from mainstream national culture and had little enthusiasm to sustain traditional cultural idioms and forms.[19]

The head of Bangladesh television, Salahuddin Zaki, acknowledges the problem. But he is not as worried as some of the 'cultural conservatives' about the impact of satellite TV. In his view 'traditional societies can withstand a bit of singing and dancing.' But he says 'we must recognise that unless there is cultural input, the young generation will have no idea about their own culture and that will create intellectual and social alienation.' He sees better programmes on BTV as the answer.[20]

The obstacles in the way, however, are considerable. Despite its language advantage and its unrivalled reach, BTV has lost much of its middle class audience to the cable channels because its entertainment programmes are seen as hackneyed and its news lacking in credibility. It remains an instrument in the hands of the Ministry of Information and Broadcasting, without the financial or creative freedom to make programmes in the wider public interest. Despite manifesto promises of a freer media by the Awami League, the recommendations of the Autonomy Commission it set up on entering office were not implemented, though it did take the important step of licensing a terrestrial commercial channel. At the end of the 1990s, despite the urgency of the cultural issues thrown up by the satellite era, the perennial conflict between the instincts of bureaucrats and politicians and the requirements of an effective electronic media remained unresolved.

NEPAL

The growth of satellite TV intensified the competition which the Nepalese media already faced from across the border in India. Most Nepalese had their first experience of TV by tuning in to

Doordarshan and concern about Indian dominance of the electronic media was the chief spur to the development of a Nepalese
television service in 1985.[21] But satellite TV has proved more influential than Doordarshan, particularly with the middle class, and
has put Nepal Televison (NTV), which does not use satellite for
its own transmissions, at a double disadvantage. In the early 1990s,
by comparison with either Bangladesh TV or Pakistan TV, NTV
was still a fledgling organisation for which the challenge of satellite
was much more daunting.

As a cultural phenomenon, however, the arrival of satellite TV
proved less controversial in Nepal than in either Bangladesh or
Pakistan. Indian films and television programmes were already
popular in Nepal. The Hindi language was very widely understood and cultural resistance to Hindi satellite channels initially
very low. The first general manager of Nepal Television, Neer
Shah, identifies the close relationship of Indian and Nepalese cultures—the shared Hindu traditions—as a reason for this relaxed
attitude.

Partly because of this low cultural resistance, satellite TV has
had a 'tremendous impact on young minds'—in their use of language, their dress and behaviour, and in the popularity of music
channels. In Neer Shah's view 'pop singers on MTV and Channel
V already have an influence and the impact will grow.'[22] A group
of 13- to 14-year olds in an elite English-medium school in Kathmandu confirmed this assessment. Like their counterparts in
similar schools in other South Asian capitals, they showed great
familiarity with English language satellite channels and with the
presenters and performers on Channel V and MTV India. Music
headed the reasons why they watched TV; news, sports and films
came close behind. Sports commentators and VJs figured among
the people they most admired. A majority of them thought that
their friends were influenced by TV in what they wanted to be,
what they wore and how they spoke.[23]

As elsewhere in South Asia, satellite TV has helped to popularise
Hindi music, Indian film stars and South Asian cricketers. Many
college students in Biratnagar, Birgunj and Pokhara followed the
music channels and accepted that they had been influenced in
their speech and dress, though there was considerable debate
about what such fashions meant in terms of their commitment to
their own culture. 'If we are to be fed the kind of stuff that we get

on satellite channels, our entire perception of society will change. There will be nothing left of our society if this goes on...', said one male student. 'How can you say that we learn only the bad things from TV and not the good ones...', retorted a girl. 'I have learnt a lot of things from TV such as becoming self-dependent, how to deal with people....'[24] School children in Birgunj were thoroughly up to date on Hindi and Nepali film songs. Even more interesting, satellite TV appeared to have ignited a passion for cricket in a country which has not traditionally played the game. Birgunj school boys said their favourite cricketers were Sachin Tendulkar and Sanath Jayasuriya. The girls did not watch cricket, but some of them enjoyed football and wrestling.[25]

As in Bangladesh, discussion groups raised concerns that satellite television which projects foreign film and sports stars is cutting the urban viewer off from his own roots. As a professional in Birgunj put it: 'Everyone will recognise a picture of Bruce Lee or of Sridevi, but there will be very few who would recognise any of our heroes, like the poet Bhanubhakta or the boxer Dal Bahadur Rana Magar.' In urban areas, 'culture is being taken over by something that is not Nepali', said a professional in Biratnagar. 'That is why it is important for the electronic media to reflect Nepali culture.'[26]

There are also concerns about language. Hindi is already widely understood in Nepal and the growing popularity of Hindi satellite channels is seen as undermining the role of Nepali as the national language. A professional in Birgunj told us: 'My Hindi language skills have improved through watching TV, since most of the programmes beamed to South Asia are Hindi based. In the same way, my English has also become better. On the other hand, since we spend most of our time watching TV rather than in studying, our Nepali is suffering.' Another man in the same group criticised what he saw as the growth of a 'Star culture' instead of Nepali culture. 'I am not at all in favour of this. Although we may have gained in terms of language, language is not a matter of priority. Our Nepali culture is a symbol of our nationality and of our originality. That is why the TV culture we are seeing is definitely not something that we should be happy with. At the moment we hardly watch NTV. And those of us who have cable TV surely don't watch NTV at all.'[27]

Commentators on media developments in Nepal strike a balance between appreciating the informational benefits of satellite TV and warning of possible social and cultural damage. Rupa Joshi, a media consultant, says: 'On the positive side, it gave us a feeling of being part of the world and made real the term "global village".... On the negative side, the reality depicted on satellite TV is not our reality.... It portrays a western culture completely different from ours. This "living" with two realities could cause psychological and other problems.'[28] Durga Ghimire, a human rights activist, says: 'Because of the low level of education in our society, good and bad programmes cannot be differentiated, and because of the absence of any other sources of healthy entertainment, satellite television has brought about an erosion of values.'[29] Others believe that audiences can look after themselves. Audiences are not passive in deciding what programmes to watch, says Keshab Sthapit, mayor of Kathmandu City. 'Slowly they will start watching the good ones only. They can choose between good and bad. Earlier there were no alternatives to Radio Nepal and NTV. Now there are and this is a positive development.'[30]

The sociologist Dipak Gyawali thinks the impact of satellite TV is mostly superficial; he says the 'soul of Nepali society' will not be affected. He argues it is wrong to blame foreign channels for corrupting Nepali youth without accepting that the Nepali media and regulators share some of the responsibility. Commenting on Nepali practice before the ban on tobacco and alcohol advertising, he said: 'Many countries do not allow cigarette and liquor advertising on private channels in their countries but we do. While we allow such things, how can we blame multinationals for corrupting our culture?'[31]

Publisher Kanak Mani Dixit agrees that the negative influences are 'only superficial, like wearing clothes shown on TV, and are experienced in parallel with Nepali culture. This is shown', he says 'by the fact that while they watch *Baywatch*, they also conduct esoteric religious rituals.' But he is not complacent. In the long run, he believes satellite TV will have an effect and that a counterstrategy is necessary. This should include: improving NTV, using satellite for Nepali purposes, educating children about how to watch the media and publicising its negative aspects through the press.[32] Bandana Rana, NTV newsreader and coordinator of the Women Journalists Group, also places her emphasis on media awareness. She says in the name of progress 'globalisation and centralisation is on the rise in satellite channels. Those who can't judge the media...have had to bear its autocracy.'[33]

Many commentators see an improvement in NTV programmes as the best way to combat the influence of foreign channels. Bandana Rana says: 'Because NTV gives priority to political broadcasts, good programmes take a back seat.... Here state broadcasters cannot have any objectives. Even if they have, it doesn't matter. The bureaucrats and politicians control everything.' According to Rupa Joshi: 'Public broadcasting means everybody getting a chance to voice their opinions and concerns, which helps in empowering the people. Since NTV and Radio Nepal have not fulfilled this role, their credibility has declined.' Joshi would like to see NTV taking positive action to counter the new cultural influences. She says: 'Grandparents and elders should inform children about Nepali culture and traditions through stories. Schools should provide children good books and make them interested in plays, poetry and sports. Teachers should recommend TV programmes to children and tell them about the negative impact of television.... We should generate interest in our culture.'[34] Others argue that NTV should dub more films in Nepali.[35]

Some Nepalis—particularly those who are not familiar with Hindi—do watch NTV out of a sense of patriotism. Among a group of home makers in Birgunj, close to the Indian border, three women from the hill country said they watched and liked NTV because they were Nepalis.[36] But most discussion groups recognised that foreign channels were taking away NTV's audiences and that something needed to be done about it.

One of the problems for Nepal TV is that resources may never be sufficient to produce the kind of exciting programmes available on satellite. As a schoolboy in Birgunj graphically explained: 'Nepali programmes are so bland. Indian programmes have real scenes. Houses are blown up, trains are exploded, planes blow up. Till now not a single plane has been blown up in a Nepali programme.'[37] But most discussants agree that they would watch good Nepali programmes if there were more of them. The very popular NTV comedy programme *Hijo Aaja ka Kura* which commands very large audiences on Friday evenings is proof of that. Unfortunately, the generality of programmes does not reach this standard. 'NTV programmes are not good at all', said a discussant in suburban

Kathmandu. 'NTV seems like the 16th century compared to others. Even the news is difficult to accept as true. Nepal needs other private channels.' Another said: 'There are very few good programmes on NTV, but when they do come, not many people miss watching them.... The problem is our TV programmes try to copy Hindi programmes and these turn out bad. That is the problem with both TV and FM. Too few genuine Nepali programmes.' For the moment, however, the mood is one of resignation. As another participant put it: 'There are very few foreign channels that suit our culture and traditions. But we are slowly getting used to it. This was not so earlier when watching these channels with our youngsters would be embarrassing. The foreign channels have not actually affected our society but they will do so in the long run.'[38]

PAKISTAN

The coming of satellite television has posed peculiar problems for the official custodians of Pakistani culture because it has breached the ideological boundaries of the state in a much more intensive way than ever before. This is particularly the case with the Hindi language satellite channels which have found a ready audience in Pakistan because of their easy intelligibility. As Zahid Malik, Editor of the *Pakistan Observer*, put it: 'Our culture is threatened by the invasion of two cultures—the Western and the Hindu culture—and the latter is more dangerous than the former *because it is Pakistan-specific...*'. (our emphasis)[39] The availability of these new channels has intensified debate within the country about what constitutes Pakistani culture, while the popularity of channels like Zee TV has shown up the inadequacies of state-controlled television.

One of the problems for those trying to define Pakistani culture too narrowly is the love affair between the Pakistani public and the Indian film industry. As a contributor to a Pakistani newspaper put it: 'Indian films have always been and still are the most sought-after cultural product in Pakistan.... Even for the generation that saw the partition riots and misery, old Indian movies remain its first love....'[40]

Indian films continued to be shown in Pakistan after independence and it was only at the time of the 1965 war that they were banned, which left many fans disconsolate once the ardours of patriotism died down. In the 1960s and early 1970s, many Pakistanis travelled to Kabul to watch Indian films, but once India put up a television station at Amritsar, with programmes more or less visible in Lahore, that city became the weekly venue for Indian film fans. A columnist in the *Nation* newspaper of Lahore recently recalled the first film to be shown—*Pakeezah*—and the reaction among the general population. 'On the day *Pakeezah* was to be shown, we witnessed hundreds of people carrying large antennas to catch Amritsar. Every other scooterist, every other motorcyclist, every other motorist was carrying an extra-long antenna....'[41] Popular films like *Pakeezah* and *Mughul-e-Azam* could turn Lahore into a ghost town until the video era made it possible for smuggled cassettes to be watched at leisure.

This cultural traffic was not entirely one way. Pakistan Television's drama serials, which achieved very high standards, were widely appreciated across the border. They were watched regularly in Indian Punjab and marketed as videos in Delhi and elsewhere. However, they were appreciated more by the middle class than the masses, whereas Indian cinema appeal to a very wide audience in Pakistan.

In the 1990s, through the satellite channels, Hindi films became in normal times an integral part of local culture. Most Pakistani newspapers now publish the schedules of satellite channels like Zee and Sony, if not of Doordarshan. Video shops carry Indian film posters, bookstalls display Indian film magazines and Indian songs are played regularly at Pakistani weddings.

On occasion, the passion for Hindi movies is interrupted by a bout of India-Pakistan hostility. When both countries exploded nuclear devices in May 1998, Indian videos disappeared from the shops in Lahore and shopkeepers vowed to stock them no more. Within two months, however, all the empty shelves had been refilled with new movies.[42] According to Tahir Mirza, Resident Editor of *Dawn* in Lahore: 'Over the years, through videos and TV, there has been an acceptance of Indians as similar people, so it would be very difficult to eliminate Indian videos and TV programmes from our viewing habits.'[43]

One result of the opening of the skies—and this can be put down more to television than films—is a more extensive exposure to Indian culture, artists, politicians and ordinary people, which has helped to break down the barriers of misunderstanding erected by years of propaganda. Those who had previously been demonised in the official media were suddenly seen to be very similar to Pakistanis themselves. In the words of one media professional: 'Satellite has demystified the differences between India and Pakistan.... It has taken away the 'them' and 'us'. Alienation and hatred are crumbling away. We are all human beings.'[44] However, as we shall see later, some of the advantages of greater familiarity are offset by the one-way nature of the media traffic.

Those who wish to see better relations with India welcome the greater openness because they believe the demolition of stereotypes makes war less likely. Others see the proliferation of Hindi entertainment programmes as an Indian charm offensive designed to undermine and ultimately destroy Pakistan's raison d'etre. In March 1998, the Urdu daily *Nawa-i-Waqt*, a mouthpiece of the Punjab establishment, took a Lahore police band to task for playing Indian film songs at a local sports function. It was clearly worried that the Punjab police had gone over to the enemy.[45]

The popularity of Indian satellite channels has become a bone of contention between 'Islamists' and 'Liberals' within Pakistan. With few exceptions, Islamists resent the popularity of Indian films and film songs and believe Pakistani culture, which they identify almost exclusively with Islam, is threatened. On the other hand, liberals welcome the greater access to other sources of information and entertainment, which they believe strengthens their own cause.

A prominent Islamic scholar, Dr. Anees Ahmed, who directs the Dawah Academy, which is part of a new international Islamic university in Islamabad, argues that Pakistan's Islamic culture provides a complete code of life and its protection is as important as the defence of the country. He warns that in the name of globalisation the West is trying to impose its culture on Pakistan through modern means of communication.[46] He criticises satellite TV programmes for putting across unfavourable pictures of Muslim civilisation, even in cartoons. He says that 'the Aladdin series and others project Muslims in a comic manner; they show them as extravagant, with big harems, with a desire to tease and be unjust to women.' He would like the Pakistan government to curb the violence and obscenity shown on the satellite channels. But he has no confidence that it will. He says: 'The way I look at our so-called policy planners, they have no mind, no eyes and no ears; they sit blankly and imitate their western models.... If the West has a Michael Jackson approach, they have their own Ali approach, who in the name of a very great Muslim hero sings and jumps and behaves no different than Michael Jackson.'[47]

In June 1998, in the wake of the nuclear standoff between the two countries, Islamic activists called for an end to 'Indian cultural pollution' to safeguard the ideological frontiers of the country. The influential Jamaat-i-Islami party demanded a complete ban on the sale of all Indian films, songs and books, and the leader of its student wing in Punjab, Atiq ur Rahman Tosi, called on video and audio shopowners and bookstores to remove Indian material on pain of 'dire consequences'. According to press reports, Jamaat student activists threatened to remove posters of Indian actors and actresses themselves if the shopkeepers did not take action. Cinema owners were also urged not to display hoardings of actresses and there were threats of attacks on offending cinema houses.[48]

Islamists are not the only critics of satellite channels. Other media commentators complain about their explicit treatment of sexuality and violence and the bad example they set young people. Uzma Gilani, a television artist and advertising executive, says educated girls in India take up modelling with the blessing of their elders, whereas in Pakistan 'these areas are still considered taboo. Most of the girls who enter these professions are not from good families, neither are they educated. They try and follow the styles and fashions of Indian models, minus the grace and sophistication. The result is more obscene and more dangerous.'[49]

Reactions among the public are more mixed. Middle class professionals in Karachi robustly rejected suggestions that the government should put a ban on satellite dishes The general response was that the government has no business to do so. Though not uncritical of the quality of some satellite programmes, the group dismissed as 'rubbish' suggestions that dish culture is undermining their Pakistani or Islamic identity. A woman travel agent said: 'There is something wrong with your value system if it can be destroyed just by watching somebody else's culture.'[50]

American and Indian teleserials were the subject of a lively debate among wealthy home makers in Karachi which revealed both a strong following for them and concern about the moral climate they create. Commenting on American serials, one participant said: 'Imagine the kind of relationships that are shown in them—father and son having an affair with the same girl, women having babies out of wedlock. There are no moral values and that is why I wouldn't want my girls to watch this kind of rubbish.' Another participant thought that Indian soap operas were more corrupting: 'These kind of relationships are also shown in Indian soaps like *Banegi Apni Baat*, *Tara* and many others.... I feel more threatened by these Indian plays as the characters look like us, speak our language and have more or less the same cultural and social values.'[51]

At the same time, there seems to be a class dimension to such reactions. A survey in three distinct socio-economic localities of Rawalpindi district—a middle class suburb of Rawalpindi, an area of government housing for clerical staff and a village on the periphery of the capital, Islamabad—confirms impressions elsewhere in South Asia that the middle class, particularly parents, despite their greater access to satellite television, are more concerned about questions of cultural influence than the less well off. The survey took place in Westridge, a colony of ex-army officers, Ilyas colony and Saidpur village. It revealed 90 per cent access to satellite in Westridge and 55 per cent access in the other two areas. Among favourite programmes, middle class Westridge was markedly more interested in sport, Ilyas colony in the news and Saidpur in music. A significant difference between Westridge and the other two localities was its higher negative ratings for the social impact of television. A majority of respondents from Westridge thought that the impact of television on women and children and on the arts and music was negative, whereas respondents in Ilyas colony and Saidpur welcomed TV influences in these areas.[52] The fact that Westridge is a colony of ex-army officers may account for some of the scepticism. Army families might be regarded as natural repositories of Pakistani values, appreciating the sport but worried about the spread of Indian culture, whereas the villagers of Saidpur seemed to be more concerned to enjoy good music than to examine its origins.

The Role of the State in Defining Pakistani Culture

The debate about Indian influences, which intensified after the arrival of Hindi satellite channels, has highlighted the role of the Pakistani state in defining national culture. Many liberals argue that the narrowness of government approaches to culture has handed the Indian channels their advantage. Those in the entertainment industry and the performing arts, who have suffered from the discouragement of their professions over the past twenty years, are particularly bitter. Agha Sajjad Gul, the owner of Lahore's oldest film studios, says: 'Although the media is the most important thing in today's world, in Pakistan there is no acknowledgement of the importance of film, TV, radio or any form of art.' As a result of Zia ul Haq's suppression of Pakistani film writers and directors, talented young people are not opting for the profession and the visual arts are suffering. Sajjad Gul believes it is this lack of government policy which explains why Pakistan was overwhelmed by the satellite revolution. In his opinion, 'Pakistan has lost the cultural war. Patriotic and nationalist feelings were there during the 1965 war. Today the scenario is different. There are no institutions left. All have degenerated and the situation is deteriorating.... Today, Pakistan has no culture except for preaching Islam and Kashmir....'[53]

One reason why the satellite experience has been seen as threatening is because it has shown how much Indian and Pakistani cultures have in common and how difficult it is to distinguish between them. Dr. Mehdi Hasan, a former professor at Lahore University's Department of Mass Communication, argues that there are overlapping cultural norms in Pakistan, and that 'in 50 years we have not been able to decide what Pakistani culture is.'[54] According to Sheema Kirmani, a classical dancer ,whose art has been officially targeted as 'unIslamic': 'We have conflicts within us. The issues of nationhood, denial of past linkages with India, ignorance of cultural heritage, the blocking out of certain attachments are all part of this conflict. I am asked not to wear a sari while performing, as it is an Indian dress. We are told not to offer sitar if India is also offering that. It is basically not being able to define what is Pakistani culture after disowning a huge chunk of cultural heritage... .'[55]

This is also the view of Kishwar Naheed, who was appointed director general of the Pakistan National Council of the Arts during the People's Party government. She says: 'Tell me of any nation that does not have a taste, a liking , an urge for music, fine arts, for fun and laughter....' But she admits that in Muslim countries, what she calls 'dual cultures' exist. What people actually want is not promoted by the state, but it goes on in some form anyway. 'This hypocrisy is there in many Muslim countries and that is why culture and the performing arts have not been promoted....'[56]

Because of these inhibitions, many performing artists in Pakistan envy the artistic freedom available in India. They feel embattled in their own country and resent the government's failure to support their profession. Theatre director Khalid Ahmed says Pakistan exhibits what he calls an 'anti-performing arts culture': a bias against theatre and dancing, no support for them either from the state or the private sector and no academies to teach them. He believes that the current vogue for economic liberalisation has set up new conflicts in Pakistan because it naturally brings with it cultural liberalism which provokes resistance from the conservatives. He sees India, on the other hand, as comfortable with economic liberalisation as it has a liberal policy on culture as well. Like many performing artists in India, however, Khaled Ahmed criticises the satellite channels—American and Indian alike—for their relentless commercialism and their failure to project serious culture. He says: 'A certain universalisation of culture is taking place but it is very vulgar. The Americans are the biggest exporters of junk culture, followed by the Indians, who get their cue from the Americans and are exporting the same junk culture. So we receive junk from both ways.'[57]

The case of the Pakistani pop group, Junoon, which attracted official condemnation for undertaking a tour of India in the aftermath of the nuclear tests of 1998, illustrates the dilemmas of Pakistani artists who choose to put artistic expression before officially approved notions of national culture. Junoon had earlier resisted PTV's wishes that it should change its appearance and tone down its lyrics. But its visit to India and its appearance on Zee TV at a time when Indo-Pakistan relations were extremely tense brought charges of treason against the group and a ban on all TV or public performances. The group also received death threats and warnings that they would be killed if they performed again. In an outspoken interview in the *Dawn Review* at the height of this experience, Junoon's Salman Ahmed challenged the government to play any of the group's songs on TV and 'let the people of Pakistan decide how patriotic or anti-Pakistan we are.' Asked why other Pakistani artists who toured India had escaped accusations of disloyalty, Salman Ahmed replied: 'We are outspoken. We call our leaders corrupt.... We write songs about the economic disparity, social and economic turmoil and violence. We reflect it in our art.'[58]

I.A. Rehman, the secretary general of the Pakistan Human Rights Commission, argues that the treatment of Junoon showed the Pakistani state displaying 'paranoia in an advanced stage'. According to Rehman, the people have swallowed the myth of the state's fragility and have been led to believe that 'a Pakistani woman dancing abroad or a singer praising peace away from home will bring down the roof on them'. By contrast, Rehman argues that restrictions on contacts with India and Bangladesh have been 'fatal to our intellectual, literary and artistic interests. The partition of 1947 was a division of territory.... It should not have divided culture. But that is what happened and there have been colossal losses on both sides.' Rehman points out that the state's own role is central to the question of artistic freedom. His concern is that in Pakistan 'the rights and status of artists, instead of receiving higher respect, are being increasingly encroached upon not only by the unlettered and the uncultured in society but also by the state, whose primary purpose is to protect them against the former.'[59] No view could be more diametrically opposed to the position taken by those on the Islamic right, who look to the state to enforce one nationalist ideology.

The Challenge for PTV

As early as 1996, a survey conducted among satellite television viewers for *Dawn's* 'Tuesday Review' demonstrated that even at that stage, Star TV and Zee TV were developing a strong following for their news as well as entertainment programmes.[60] One question asked of a sample of 300 people in six of the country's largest cities was: with the option of watching Star TV, does Pakistan Television News (*Khabarnama*) still hold your attention? The answers given were: 'No' 68 per cent and 'Yes' 32 per cent, with the percentage of 'No' being over 85 per cent in Hyderabad and Karachi, both towns with substantial populations originating in India. The survey also revealed an interesting regional break-down in responses to the question: do you base more credibility on *Khabarnama* or Zee news? Fifty-three per cent rated Zee more credible, while 38 per cent voted for *Khabarnama*, with *Khabarnama* scoring highest in Lahore (80 per cent) and lowest in Karachi and Hyderabad (10 and 12 per cent respectively). The survey showed that *Khabarnama* was still being watched every day by what it called 'a more than respectable 42.5 per cent', but it also indicated the scale of the credibility problem posed by satellite competition.

The disillusionment of respondents in Karachi and Hyderabad with the official Pakistani media clearly reflects the political crisis in relations between the Urdu-speaking Muhajirs, who were in the vanguard of the demand for Pakistan, and the political parties running the Pakistan state for most of the 1990s—Benazir Bhutto's People's Party and Nawaz Sharif's Muslim League. The inability or unwillingness of either of these parties to conciliate the MQM, the political organisation which represents the Muhajirs, resulted in a state of permanent crisis in Karachi and thousands of violent deaths during that decade. In these circumstances, many alienated Muhajirs not surprisingly turned their backs on official news broadcasts and found refuge and entertainment on the satellite channels.

But if disillusionment with PTV news has been greatest in Karachi, Pakistanis everywhere have been making comparisons between their own didactic television and the programmes on offer on satellite channels. As the journalist Khaled Ahmed put it: 'Domestic audiences are tired of ideological TV and crave enter-tainment.'[61]

Zee TV, which is the market leader among the Indian channels, has successfully appealed to many Pakistani women with pro-grammes which treat issues of interest to them more openly and more seriously than PTV. A housewife in Westridge told us: 'Some Indian programmes are very informative; ours are not so up to date. Programmes on sewing and cutting are redundant and should not be produced any more.' Women in Westridge praised *Purushshetra* and *Helpline* on Zee TV in particular, though they felt some of the issues raised were 'too bold for our public'.[62] Well off home makers in Karachi described the same programmes as

welcome relief from PTV's diet of cookery and beauty programmes. 'Housewives are not always as...dumb as TV people
think', said one. 'They need good talk as well—things to think
about. Zee has a programme called *Purushshetra* which does touch
on important issues. There should be Pakistani programmes made
on those lines too to analyse issues from our perspective.'[63]

It is clear that many young Pakistanis are hooked on the satellite
channels and look down on PTV in much the same way that young
middle class Indians look down on Doordarshan. A discussion
with college students in Islamabad revealed a strong following
for the music channels and very little interest in PTV. Recently
graduated Nadia said: 'PTV programmes can be defined in just
one word—horrible. They are boring, repetitive and monotonous.
There is nothing new, no variety...I want PTV to have more cartoons and more English movies. I like to watch only these two
things on television.'[64]

A discussion group among teenagers from working class
families in a slum area of Rawalpindi showed extensive familiarity
with satellite TV programmes at this level too, despite parental
disapproval, and some cynicism about such strictures. Nasreen,
aged 18, detected some hypocrisy in the elder generation. 'I am a
little confused', she said. 'Why do people say that watching Indian
movies and listening to Indian songs is not good for us? They say
that being a Pakistani one should not watch these because they
are our enemies. But then why do we have our TV commercials
copying popular Indian songs? If you listen carefully, so many
ads are a copy of Indian music and they run on our state TV.'[65]

SHARED PERCEPTIONS OF MARGINALISATION

There are striking similarities between the reactions of some of
India's regional cultures to the dominance of Hindi satellite television and those of India's neighbours. Issues of sovereignty add
to the levels of apprehension experienced in Pakistan, Bangladesh
and Nepal, but everywhere there are concerns that better financed
and better produced Indian programmes aimed at the mass market
have reduced the space for other cultures. There is concern that
Indian heroes will become better known than those of Nepal or
Bangladesh. There are worries that efforts to develop national

languages will be undermined by the growth of 'Zee Nepali' or by greater familiarity with Hindi and English.

These fears among opinion-formers in neighbouring countries have been reinforced by the failure of satellite channels to take any serious notice of what is going on in the region. 'Why should Star TV only broadcast Indian news if the satellite is supposed to be a regional one?', was a common complaint in discussion groups held in Dhaka and Jamalpur. 'Zee TV and other channels have excluded us', was another comment. 'Bangladesh TV doesn't show any problems and Indian TV only shows Indian problems', was a third.[66]

Satellite TV has created a sense of marginalisation among the thinking middle class in these countries. Many commentators criticised the whole satellite TV experience as uni-directional. 'Many Bangladeshi kids speak Hindi well', says Chinmoy Mutsuddi, 'but no Delhi kid knows much about Bangladesh. This is neither desirable, nor sustainable, nor beneficial for the region.'[67] The same view was also reflected in Kathmandu, where Kanak Mani Dixit deplored the fact that '...there is almost no Nepali news or programmes related to Nepal on satellite TV.'[68]

Several Bangladeshis noted that Star TV had recognised the existence of Pakistan with its *Postcard from Pakistan* weekly programme. But no such concession had been made to Bangladeshi sensibilities. In mid-1998, world interest in India and Pakistan's nuclear tests was adding to this sense of neglect. In Pakistan, however, the paucity of coverage of Pakistani affairs is seen not just as a matter of neglect but as evidence that the prime purpose of the channels is one of cultural assault. 'The way Indians are projecting their religion, their national identity, is an eye-opener for us', said a multinational executive in a Karachi discussion group. 'What they have sold to Pakistan', said Khalid Hassan, then head of Shalimar Television Network, 'is a highly glamourised image of India, unnatural and untrue.... These channels can become links, but at the moment they are used negatively.'[69]

Reservations about the impartiality of the satellite media increased dramatically as a result of the coverage of two important events in 1999: the Kargil conflict in Kashmir in the summer and the hijacking of an Indian airlines plane to Kandahar in December. Our own research in Tamil Nadu (the only part of it to be carried out after these events) indicates that opinion in the south of India was divided over media coverage of the Kargil hostilities. Some discussion groups praised TV's role in awakening a sense of patriotism. Others criticised it for 'pumping patriotic messages'. 'Do what you want for the rest of the time but stamp yourself as patriotic', was how one Madurai professional summed up the profile of the new commercial channels.[70] Professional media-watchers agreed that the southern channels had covered the conflict in much the same way as Doordarshan, often using footage provided by the state sector for their own programmes. According to Father Joe Andrew: 'Everything became a government version of it. Even Star—not just DD—became a pro-government mouthpiece.... The pain and misery was never reflected in any of the channels, be they private or public.... Kargil revealed that we don't have a free media.... All the channels were pro-war, pro-government, glorification of the war and demonisation of Pakistan.'[71] Another critic said: 'TV told me that I should revive my narrow patriotism, which I don't have at all. I feel as sorry for the Pakistani who is shot as for the Indian.'[72]

Pakistani viewers of satellite media saw little of this heart-searching on their screens. According to Kunda Dixit of Panos South Asia, 'the Indian media—especially Zee news and Star—behaved much like the American networks and CNN during the Gulf War and the Indian military used and manipulated satellite television much as the American military did in Kuwait.'[73] On the Pakistan side, PTV behaved no less jingoistically, though it was less successful in carrying the public with it, which led some commentators to argue that a diversified media would serve the country better. As Mir Jamil ur Rahman put it: 'People are no more a captive audience. They have the choice to turn over to a dozen channels at the push of a button to test the veracity of the PTV version.... Even if it was to tell the truth, the credibility gap would not narrow down. Therefore it is imperative to allow private TV channels in this country.'[74]

The hijacking of an Indian airlines plane by Kashmiri separatists from Kathmandu via Amritsar and Lahore to Kandahar in December provoked similar concerns, both in Pakistan and Nepal. According to a cover story in *Newsline*, a Pakistani political journal with a track record for independent reporting: 'Zee TV, Star News and Doordarshan abandoned all pretensions of the ethics of independent journalism as they waged a virtual media war against

Pakistan.' 'Though one might expect some journalistic legerdemain from the state-run Doordarshan', wrote Samina Ibrahim, 'to hear the so-called independent channel Zee TV indulge in the same hyperbole came as a surprise.'[75] The article accused the satellite media of supporting India's efforts to get Pakistan declared a terrorist state and of broadcasting stories to implicate Pakistan in the hijack, which were subsequently proven to be groundless.

In the case of the hijacking, Nepal also came under media fire because it began in Kathmandu and the Indian government and media accused the Nepalese government of being too sympathetic to Pakistan. Kunda Dixit of Panos South Asia says: 'Zee TV has probably done more to harm Nepal-India relations at the people level than anything else in recent times.... Satellite broadcasting, instead of bring people closer is polarising them, and the reason is that Zee and Star are regional broadcasters but operate as if they were solely broadcasting to India.'[76]

Satellite channels like Zee and Star looked initially as if they aspired to cover South Asia as a whole but they are now perceived by many Pakistanis as Indian channels with Indian slants to their coverage. According to Mahommed Malik of NTM: 'In the early days of Zee, there was some pretence of striking a balance, but when they realised their biggest marketing was coming from India anyway, they openly took on Indian colours because it helped with their marketing.' Malik thinks 'the biggest threat...is from Star News...but there again they have made the mistake of making it an Indian channel.... There again, Pakistan has been left out... whereas they should have started with an impartial hue to it.... People are not stupid...the slants are there.'[77]

Some Bangladeshi commentators, seeing the extent to which international channels have been 'Hindigenised' to appeal to the Hindi market, are resentful that the so-called Hindi channels have made no efforts at regionalisation to accommodate viewers in Bangladesh. Parveen Rashid of the Social Marketing Corporation (SMC) says: 'The need to have the local stamp, the local colour and the local creativity is very important'. But she finds less and less of it in MNC advertising. She echoes other social marketing experts in expressing her concern that India-based channels are oblivious to the existence of other cultures and believes this will have a negative impact even if no resistance is noticed.[78]

Official reactions to these cultural intrusions have been largely defensive: hiring satellite transponders or aspiring to do so. Both Pakistan and Nepal use commercial arguments to support their thinking—the opportunity to tap the purchasing power of their nationals in other countries—but it is also a form of diplomacy by other means. In a world threatened by homogenisation, nation states feel the need to employ the same weapons as their attackers.

Beyond these defensive reactions, there is a more fundamental problem: how to build a more genuinely South Asian media which reflects the realities of the region. In its early years, the South Asian Association for Regional Co-operation (SAARC), tried to stimulate programme exchanges between the different countries in order to make viewers more regionally aware. But the initiative was largely confined to non-topical subjects and was not taken up with much enthusiasm by the national broadcasters.[79] An Asian news-pool, which made national news footage available by satellite for wider regional use, was more successful. However, both were designed to strengthen regional coverage on national television. They did not address the issue of regional balance on the new commercial satellite services.

Kanak Mani Dixit, whose *Himal* magazine is one of the few successful South Asian media ventures, had no illusions about the difficulties of building an effective regional satellite media, even before the hijacking episode. He does not believe satellite channels will change until people in neighbouring countries make them more aware of their South Asian footprint. He says: 'It is not enough for people to lobby in Delhi; it must be south Asia wide.'[80] Nepal's leading TV professional, Neer Shah, believes that public-private financial partnerships might be a means to get smaller countries onto satellite and the same technique could perhaps serve a wider purpose.[81] Much depends, however, on the regional satellite channels themselves. What is clear is that unless they address the sense of marginalisation they are helping to foster and take their regional responsibilities more seriously, they will continue to be seen as Indian rather than South Asian broadcasters.

SRI LANKA

In Sri Lanka there is far less sense of cultural threat from the satellite media than there is in Pakistan, Bangladesh and Nepal. Unlike in those countries, where the satellite revolution brought direct access to a wide range of foreign television programmes for viewers accustomed to a diet of state-controlled broadcasting, in Sri Lanka lively competition among terrestrial channels was already delivering greater choice to the public before some of these developments took place. To that extent, the satellite revolution has not acted as the prime agent of change. Change came first from the introduction of competition in the domestic media market.

This pre-existence of terrestrial competition is of particular interest to this study. If the satellite revolution has been less of a shock to society in Sri Lanka, it is partly because Sri Lankans watch what Sri Lankan editors have decided—for cultural or economic reasons—might be profitable or interesting to show them. There is a greater sense of ownership of the process and even channels with high proportions of foreign programming present a strong national profile.

In Sri Lanka, as in India, the appetite for English language programmes is mainly confined to the large conurbations. Maharaja TV's marketing director, Shevanthi Jayasuriya, estimates that 98 per cent of those who watch English programmes live in Colombo or Kandy.[82] Advertising agencies distinguish between the urban middle class, which includes people of all communities, and accounts for 6 to 7 per cent of the population, and the mass market, which operates largely in Sinhala. According to Deepthi Senanayake of J. Walter Thompson, the affluent middle class 'appear to have little time to sit and watch TV. They are highly sociable...plus they are exposed at various other places—like backlit advertisements in public places or direct mailers....' In her experience, advertisers don't spend too much time reaching those exposed to western magazines; they assume they have already got the message.[83]

The commercial dominance of the Sinhala market is confirmed by an extensive survey of media habits conducted in 1995 and 1996 by the International Centre for Ethnic Studies in Kandy. Forty-eight per cent of the sample declared Sinhala TV programmes their first preference, 12.3 per cent Tamil programmes and only 3.1 per cent English language programmes. The authors confessed to being surprised by 'the relative unimportance of the English stream in mass media'. They wrote: 'While English radio and TV programmes may be important because they cater to the elite, they definitely do not reach appreciable numbers. Only the English TV programmes, watched as they are by some for what they convey pictorially...could be regarded as a partial exception to this generalisation.'[84]

International English language programmes have a marked influence, however, on local programme formats, whether in entertainment, news or current affairs. TNL's *Always Breakdown*, a satirical puppet show modelled on a long running British commercial television programme of the 1980s *Spitting Image*, pointed the finger at all the leading politicians in the country and enjoyed great success. MTV executives admit that they have actively remodelled their news style and presentation on those of BBC World. The channel has grown increasingly professional in recent years, rejecting Rupavahini's preoccupations with ministers and officials, using more live reports and interviews, more human interest stories, and giving international stories a Sri Lankan spin.

Western influences are also evident in a new crop of programmes on the private channels which have greatly extended the scope of political debate in the media and held politicians to account in new ways. TNL set a new trend in political discussion programmes with *Jana Handa* which also went out of the studio to obtain information and responses from representatives of various interest groups. For the first time on Sri Lankan television, opposing political elements confronted each in a series of explosive debates which were watched by large audiences in the run up to the 1994 election. Four years later, the same presenter, Chandana Sooriyabandara, launched another successful programme format for rival channel Swarnavahini. *Rathu Ira* enabled people throughout the country to put difficult questions to politicians in the studio and sometimes led to long and vituperative debate, interspersed with advertisements.

Such innovative programmes give a somewhat deceptive impression of liberalism. It is largely the Sinhala public sphere that is affected; the Tamil electronic media have not developed to the same extent. Moreover, gathering and broadcasting news about the war in the north in whatever language is subject to rigorous constraints, including at times military censorship. Nevertheless, these current affairs programmes have broken definitively with the paternalistic style and pro-government bias of the state-monopoly era. Whatever the inspiration, they have taken distinctively Sri Lankan forms and have attracted large audiences. However, beyond their success in popularising political debate among the different parties, they have also been criticised for bringing more heat than light to the political arena. The late Professor A.J. Gunawardena told us he thought political debates were becoming a form of popular entertainment. 'They are rude and crude—a lot of flash about them, a lot of energy. People enjoy the cut and thrust of the debates, but they won't illuminate political problems.... I can foresee a situation where politicians who appear in these debates will ask for a fee'[85] Ajith Sameranayake, Editor of the Sri Lanka *Observer*, says the media 'has made its own contribution to the trivialisation of the political and intellectual debate in society.' He laments the fact that 'there has been no lobby, interest group or public watchdog to compel the media to adopt higher standards.'[86]

The Growth of Indian Cultural Influences

Sri Lankan channels show a wide range of foreign programmes, principally from American, British, Australian, Indian and Japanese sources, though western programmes tend to be confined to those channels aiming at the Colombo and Kandy elite. In its early years, Sri Lanka's state-run channel, Rupavahini, used to import BBC programmes to show to urban audiences, but with the spread of television to rural areas it abandoned elite programming and relied increasingly on Sinhala teledramas for its popular appeal. Rupavahini now broadcasts teledramas every day of the week and two on Sundays, the vast majority made by independent producers, a model followed by other Sinhala channels. These teledramas attract very large audiences and constitute the bedrock of Rupavahini's continuing commercial success. In 1998, however, Rupavahini launched a second channel and signed an agreement with Discovery to re-broadcast its programmes outside peak hours. This second channel was intended to provide more space for sport and education and for locally produced Tamil programmes, though in this last field it proved slow in fulfilling expectations.

In the new, highly competitive, mass market, many Sinhala channels are supplementing their programmes outside prime time with Indian films and serials. This is partly on grounds of cost and partly because the themes of these Indian productions are more immediately accessible to local audiences. As a commentator on the Sri Lankan media scene put it: 'Western cultural interests have now been replaced by eastern cultural interests and whether India's cultural interests or Japan's cultural interests are always good for us, I don't know.'[87]

Though state-controlled Rupavahini and ITN maintain a high percentage of local programming, many of their rivals rely more heavily on imported programmes for their commercial appeal. MTV, the first successful commercial channel in Sri Lanka, began as a largely urban channel relaying English language films and serials and BBC World Service television news bulletins. Later, it came to agreements with ESPN to strengthen its sports coverage and with the Indian Tamil language channel, Sun TV, to improve services for the country's Tamil minority. In 1998, in an acknowledgement of the growing importance of the Sinhala television market, MTV launched a Sinhala TV channel, Sirisa, to build on the remarkable success of its sister radio station.[88]

TNL, another of the early commercial TV channels, tries to cater both to the educated middle class and the wider Sinhala-speaking audience. Its relay of MTV, the international music channel, has a substantial following among young people in Colombo, particularly school and college students. TNL also provides the main platform in Sri Lanka for the programmes of Young Asia Television, a recent media initiative with NGO backing, which has a young staff, many of them women, putting across serious subjects in an accessible way for the new generation.

Swarnavahini, which started in 1995, relies more heavily than others on Indian television imports. It shows Hindi films regularly and has an arrangement with Raj TV of Tamil Nadu to re-broadcast its Tamil programmes, often complete with South Indian advertisements. Rosmand Senaratne, the programme manager of the station, defended this practice in terms of ease of operation, but it seems the advertisements have created some interest in South Indian goods, which is welcomed by traders in both countries.[89] The station's reach improved significantly after it bought the rights to telecast the 1999 Cricket World Cup and decided to upgrade its transmission system.

Sinhala audiences watch Hindi films without dubbing or subtitling, though most foreign soap operas require sub-titling to attract large audiences. The Indian soap opera *Shanti*, which was bought by MTV from Doordarshan for its Sirisa channel, attracted huge audiences in Sri Lanka and advertisements to match. Another somewhat unexpected success was the Japanese serial *Oshin*, which was dubbed into Sinhala. Dubbed English language films have not attracted big audiences. It seems the story lines are less engaging for Sri Lankan audiences.

Commercial channels capitalise on the popularity of Indian films and serials by inviting stars to visit Sri Lanka. When MTV brought the star of *Shanti*, Mandira Bedi, to Sri Lanka, she was mobbed by hundreds of fans. Swarnavahini advertises its Hindi films on cinema hoardings in Colombo and has sponsored visits by film stars and concert performances in the largest sports stadium in the country.

Public Responses among the Sinhalese

Group discussions in Colombo and in the southern district of Matara confirm the popularity of Hindi films and teleserials. Advanced level students interviewed in Matara told us they thought Hindi films were 'more watchable' than Sinhala films. 'The stories in Hindi films may be naive', said one student, 'but the acting ability of Hindi film stars is far superior to that of Sinhala film stars.'[90] Labourers in Matara also preferred Hindi films to Sinhala films, though they said 'some of the love scenes...make you feel uncomfortable when you are with the family.' Many parents said their children 'tend to imitate the Hindi songs and dances at home and even in school.' Some said children neglected their homework in order to watch Hindi films, even watching them after their parents had gone to sleep.[91]

Evidence from the smaller settlement of Puhulwella some 16 miles away from Matara told the same story. Most people under the age of twenty-five seemed to be hooked on Hindi films and film songs. Sinhala teledramas or Hindi films dubbed or sub-titled in Sinhala were the favourite television programmes of the overwhelming majority of women and quite a few of the men. As one home maker commented: 'We can identify much more with Hindi films than with English films.' At the time of the survey, the Indian soap opera *Shanti* was very popular. It was shown five days a week on MTV and young women admitted to being addicted to it.[92]

Discussants in Colombo seemed less interested in Hindi films. A group of young middle class schoolchildren, aged between 10 and 13, interviewed in the suburb of Boralesgamuwa, admitted that they had found Hindi films and songs totally absorbing two or three years earlier but said they were no longer impressed. They felt they had more to learn from locally produced teledramas, which were more accurate reflections of real life with their story lines on drug addiction and family and social problems.[93]

University students in Colombo turned out to be more interested in radio than television—a tribute to the impact of Sri Lanka's new FM stations which are targetting younger people. They agreed that Hindi films were extremely popular but they felt 'there was too much of it and lots of it was of poor quality.' One student described Tamil films as 'unbelievable, but sometimes quite amusing'. They accepted that 'some people are dressing up in very "filmy" ways but they said that more "sophisticated" young people would prefer to look like TV presenters.' The group was also critical of the commercialism of the new media, particularly the introduction of 'gimmicks' like Valentine's Day, which through the influence of television was becoming a part of Sri Lankan urban culture.[94]

In many discussions, Hindi film stars and South Asian cricketers were bracketed together as idols of the rural young. Development workers in Matara spoke of the 'almost unbelievable' enthusiasm of the young for Hindi films and cricket matches. They had taken to planning their meetings to avoid clashes with popular programmes. 'To get either the adults or children to participate in workshops at the time of weekend Hindi films or cricket matches is extremely difficult', said one development worker.[95]

Some media commentators are concerned that behind the glitzy and melodramatic story lines, Bollywood is exerting a retrogressive influence. 'Thanks to television stations falling over themselves to dish out Hindi films', says Raine Wickremetunge, features consultant for the *Sunday Leader*, 'we have spawned a whole new Bollywood culture...with everyone from children to adults hooked on a make-believe world of beautiful women being saved from the clutches of the ugly villain by a handsome hero.... Being good-looking seems to be the number one priority.'[96] Madhubhashani Ratnayake, writing in the *Sunday Times*, paints a more apocalyptic

picture: 'Given our proximity to India, our small size and our mis-
trust of the strength of our own roots, shouldn't some danger signal
be going off in all of us?' She is particularly disturbed by the role
models provided by Hindi films for relations between men and
women and by the cult of violence they encourage. 'Everyday',
she says, 'a new vision of life... a powerful, false message...is being
given to our youth and the undiscriminating viewer.'[97]

Adults and parents, whether in Matara or Colombo, shared
some of these concerns, though the level of anxiety in Sri Lanka
about foreign influences seems to be less than in India or Pakistan.
Home makers in Colombo and Matara all said they enjoyed Hindi
films and series. Some were worried about the impact on their
children, but the majority saw them as fads which were distracting
children from more sensible activities.[98]

Satellite Services and Sri Lanka's Tamil Community

Among the different communities in Sri Lanka, the Tamils have
benefited more than most from access to satellite programming,
whether directly via the dish or indirectly through re-broadcasts
of South Indian programmes on MTV, Swarnavahini and other
channels. The community now has access to a wide range of Indian
Tamil programmes, whether films or quiz shows or cultural programmes, which has helped to compensate for the recent poor
performance of the Sri Lankan state media.

The war with Tamil militants in the north took an early toll on
broadcasting and affected the state's ability to deliver an adequate
service to the Tamil minority, particularly on television. A great
number of Tamil broadcasters left the island in the years after
1983 and it proved difficult to replace them with qualified people.
Many Tamils came to regard the state media as the voice of the
Sinhala majority, which affected both recruitment and credibility.

Through those difficult years, state radio proved more resilient
than television. There are two state Tamil channels, a 'national'
channel which includes news, drama, discussions, music programmes and religious programmes, and a 'commercial' channel
which is heard not only in Sri Lanka but also in South India. These
two channels offer 35 hours of Tamil programming a day. There
is also a Muslim service of the SLBC, which broadcasts in Tamil.

The greater decentralisation of radio offers opportunities to serve regional Tamil communities. The station at Kandy carries special programmes for the 'hill country' Tamils working in the tea industry. However, reception in the Tamil majority areas of the north and east of the island has not been good. Tamil Tiger attacks on transmitters cut the north off from most television and radio broadcasts during their domination of the Jaffna peninsula in the 1980s and 1990s. The government's recapture of Jaffna brought a resumption of radio relays from the army camp at Palaly. But both electricity and batteries have been in short supply. Reception in the east of the island has also been poor, which has militated against an effective service to this politically sensitive region.

State television never gave Tamils the sense that they were equal partners, not least because with only one channel, prime time tended to be devoted to programmes for the Sinhala majority. Many of the more important television programmes aimed at the Tamil community, particularly news bulletins, had a translated quality about them. Ensuring that everyone was told the same story acted as an impediment to the pursuit of more sensitive programming. Professor Thilillainathan, a board member of the SLBC, says this continues to be a problem; Tamil news, being a translation of the English and Sinhala bulletins, often includes material of little relevance to Tamils of the north and east. Media minister, Mangala Samaraweera, has acknowledged the problem and promised 'additional news of interest to the Tamil people'.[99] But such an innovation would break with a long established practice in Rupavahini, which has become more rigid on account of the war and the censorship of war news.

Because of these inadequacies, in the late 1980s the opportunities of satellite were taken up by the country's Tamil-speaking population to access programmes from a wider world. According to the leading commercial dish manufacturer in Sri Lanka, 'most people—over 75 per cent of them–who have bought and continue to buy these dishes are Muslims.'[100] Most of Sri Lanka's wealthy Muslim trading community speak Tamil and have bought dishes to access Indian channels. Once the cost of dishes came down, the popularity of dishes also spread to the hill country, where Tamils working in the tea industry grouped together to buy them.

The way in which private television channels like MTV and Swarnavahini have catered to local Tamil audiences by rebroadcasting South Indian programmes is a positive reflection of the working of the commercial market. Satellite television has compensated for the rigidities of bureaucratic control and the weakness of the local market. Moreover, in servicing the local community at minimal cost, relays of Indian Tamil broadcasts have demonstrated that the audience exists and have helped to raise its profile and expectations.

In the space of two or three years, several Sri Lankan channels have upgraded their Tamil broadcasts. MTV introduced twice-daily bulletins in Tamil for the first time in 1998. Subsequently, ITN also started a Tamil bulletin and other non-news programmes. Shevanthi Jayasuriya told us MTV would like to start a Tamil channel and had applied to the government for a licence for this purpose. The chairman of Rupavahini, D.E.W. Gunasekere, told us he would like to do so too, though for the moment he is concentrating on increasing Tamil programming on the second channel.[101] These are all responses to expectations raised by the availability of satellite services.

While the Tamil public seems to have welcomed access to Indian programmes, the Tamil middle class has voiced similar reservations about imported Tamil programmes as those expressed by others about Hindi films and serials. Dr. Selvy Thiruchandran, Director of the Women's Education and Research Centre in Colombo, who was herself a board member of Rupavahini, is concerned about 'the oppression of women which dominates South Indian Tamil films.' This is treated as 'a de facto part of their life in India', though she says it is 'alien to the Sri Lanka Tamil culture'. Her worry is that through these films, such social oppression—for example, the way that widows are treated in South India—will become influential in Sri Lanka. One sign of change is that themes from these films are now being taken up in short stories written by Sri Lankan Tamils. There are even indications that some Tamils are trying to treat widows differently. Another area where she detects a significant South Indian influence, both among Tamils and Sinhalese, is in the growth of religious cults. She believes South Indian television is popularising the cult of 'God men', of seeking salvation through a guru, which was not prevalent in Sri Lanka in mid-century. As far as Thiruchandran is concerned, the influence of South Indian Tamil culture is in a different league from any influence wielded by western culture. She says: 'When a Sri Lankan Tamil watches a western film, he or she is prepared to accept it as part of a western tradition. There is no effort to imitate that to the extent that a Tamil Sri Lankan is likely to be influenced by a South Indian film. The penetration level is definitely more. There is a hegemonic influence that is impacted on the Sri Lankan Tamil audience by South Indian films and programmes.' [102]

A related concern is that imported Tamil programmes will be seen as a substitute for funding local productions. Commercial channels are not producing many programmes aimed specifically at Sri Lankan Tamil audiences, except for news bulletins. Sri Lanka never had a thriving Tamil film industry and it seems unlikely in present circumstances that one will develop. Even Rupavahini relays South Indian Tamil films to meet audience needs because it has not been easy to find commercial sponsors for Tamil tele-dramas. [103] However, the state sector has made considerable investments in Tamil programming, even if quality has deteriorated because of the war. An important question is how such services could be improved and whether employing commercial criteria makes sense in this area.

MEASURING THE BENEFITS OF TERRESTRIAL COMPETITION

A salutary lesson from Sri Lanka's experience is that a policy of licensing terrestrial channels does ensure a relatively high proportion of local programming, even if the quality is not always high. Sri Lankan audiences see a wide range of foreign programmes, but competition for local advertising ensures that local programming remains dominant on most popular channels, particularly during prime time. A survey of a week's broadcasting in late 1998 on all eight terrestrial channels available in Colombo produced figures of 80 per cent for local programming on ITN, 52 per cent for Rupavahini (reflecting the start of the second channel and the re-broadcasting agreement with Discovery), 62 per cent for TNL and 49 per cent for the new MTV Sinhala channel, Sirisa. Swarnavahini, at that time the terrestrial channel with the poorest reach, scored 34 per cent; Indian imported programming made up 49 per cent of its schedule. The only channels with a much lower ratio of local programming were those aimed at the English-speaking middle class. MTV's main channel, which relies largely on western and Indian imports, scored 17 per cent, while ETV,

Swarnavahini's sister channel which relays Sky TV and other English programmes, scored 100 per cent.[104] These figures are only indicative, but they do illustrate an important trend.

How the editorial process in Sri Lanka has worked in selecting foreign programmes for re-broadcast on local channels is a particularly interesting area of enquiry, though finding out what has not been broadcast is more difficult than finding out what has. Damayanthi Pathirana, programme manager at MTV, says for their niche English audiences they mostly buy comedy programmes and sitcoms, which generally defy subtitling or dubbing. For Sirisa, the Sinhala channel, 'the programmes we buy...are mostly action-oriented. The popular belief is that action-oriented programmes with straightforward plots are the popular choice.' Shan Wickremesinghe of TNL says he is mainly looking for family entertainment. 'This is what our clients want and are willing to buy. Movies that the entire family can watch are popular.' Cost is a definite factor which makes them look to small US suppliers rather than the big names. 'And of course', he adds, 'we need to make sure that there will be no adverse reactions from anyone to any of them.'[105] Nalaka Gunawardene, who is campaigning for more space for documentaries on Asian television, makes the point that local gatekeepers very often play safe and this makes them a conservative influence. 'Channels which are basically here to make money for foreign or local investors...would rather avoid controversy', he says. This means that they tend to avoid subjects such as poverty or social issues. They take the view that the middle class sees poverty on the street; they don't want television to make them miserable.[106] Maleec Calyaneratne de Silva, a television producer, also has the impression that Sri Lankan editors are not very selective. She says: 'You get the feeling that they often go for the cheapest stuff—which could mean inferior quality or relatively old programmes.'[107]

What the policy of diversification has achieved, however, is a sense that Sri Lanka itself remains at the centre of the media agenda. The public clearly appreciates the greater range of local programmes and the new sense of participation, even if there are some criticisms of programme content, quality and accuracy.

The vast majority of people in Puhulwella who took part in a questionnaire about the media agreed that the diversification of the media had ensured better representation of different viewpoints and better access to information. Many people felt that despite the many foreign programmes, there was more space for local artists. 'Although there are lots of programmes of other cultures, there are quite a few programmes about ours as well'. said a government employee.

Most villagers seemed resigned to the fact that Rupavahini or SLBC news broadcasts would be somewhat biased and would not always tell the whole story. But this did not stop them from listening to government-controlled channels. Some people even suggested that the government should handle broadcasting in the way it thought appropriate; they did not want to criticise the government when it was fighting a war to keep the island intact.[108]

Though Sri Lankans exhibit some similar reactions to foreign programmes as those in evidence in Pakistan, Nepal or Bangladesh, anxiety levels are lower and there seem to be fewer worries about their social divisiveness. The high incidence of public education and literacy in Sri Lanka, which is well ahead of levels achieved nationally in the other countries, undoubtedly plays a part in this. Another reason is that all Sri Lankans are able to watch the same programmes. There is less differentiation between viewing experiences and responses at different levels of society than in other countries. The Colombo middle class, particularly the English-speaking middle class, is certainly more cosmopolitan in its tastes and less interested in Hindi films and serials than the Sinhala-speaking middle class elsewhere. But even in Puhulwella, parental concern at the craze for Hindi films is balanced by a shrewd awareness of the commercial objectives of the channels and an appreciation of the strengths and weaknesses of the new media environment. To this extent, Sri Lanka's satellite revolution has not reinforced divisions between town and country or even between large town and small town, which has been a feature of the reliance on cable systems or satellite dishes elsewhere.

The other advantage of managing the process of change within the framework of terrestrial competition is that Sri Lankans are in a position to address the central issues themselves, whether through public pressure or through legislation. As we shall see in the next chapter, the rapid expansion of terrestrial broadcasting in Sri Lanka has brought other kinds of problems, but at least in relation to the satellite media there are none of the complaints of marginalisation that are so widespread in Pakistan, Nepal or

Bangladesh. The framework of broadcasting already established in Sri Lanka ensured that there was less of a sense of 'them and us' in Sri Lanka's new relationship with the global and regional media.

NOTES AND REFERENCES

1. Chinmoy Mutsuddi, Dhaka, March 1998.
2. *Ibid.*
3. Fashion boutique proprietor, Dhaka, March 1998.
4. District survey, Jamalpur, June 1998.
5. Fashion boutique proprietor, Dhaka, March 1998.
6. This survey was organised by Afsan Chowdhury in the Dhaka area in early 1998. It involved a simple checklist interview of 100 households with both BTV and cable. Despite the small sampling size, the results were more or less in line with the findings of advertising and research agencies.
7. University students, Dhaka, February 1998.
8. Home makers, Dhaka, February 1998.
9. University students, Dhaka, February 1998.
10. Development workers, Dhaka, March 1998.
11. Professionals, Dhaka, March 1998.
12. Development workers, Dhaka, March 1998.
13. Geeteara Choudhury, Dhaka, March 1998.
14. Development workers, Dhaka, March 1998.
15. This survey of opinion in Jamalpur district took place in June 1998. It employed the same questionnaire and methodology as the Dhaka survey conducted in February 1998.
16. Home makers, Jamalpur, June 1998.
17. Young males, Jamalpur, June 1998.
18. Syed Borhan Kabir, Independent television producer, April 1998.
19. Afsan Chowdhury, 'Media Profile of Bangladesh', commissioned for the Media South Asia Project, July 1998.
20. Syed Salahuddin Zaki, Dhaka, March 1998.
21. Durga Nath Sharma, Deputy DG, Nepal TV, Kathmandu, March 1998.
22. Neer Shah, Kathmandu, March 1998.
23. Schoolchildren, Kathmandu, March 1998.
24. College students, Biratnagar, June 1999.
25. Schoolchildren, Ages 9–13, Birgunj, June 1999.
26. Professionals, Biratnagar and Birgunj, June 1999.
27. Professionals, Birgunj, June 1999.
28. Rupa Joshi, Kathmandu, May 1998.
29. Durga Ghimire, Kathmandu, May 1998.
30. Keshab Sthapit, Kathmandu, May 1998.
31. Dipak Gyawali, Kathmandu, May 1998.
32. Kanak Mani Dixit, Kathmandu, May 1998.
33. Bandana Rana, Kathmandu, May 1998.

34. Rupa Joshi, Kathmandu, May 1998.
35. Professionals, Biratnagar, June 1999.
36. Home makers, Birgunj, June 1999.
37. Schoolchildren, Birgunj, June 1999.
38. Mixed group, Lokhantali, Kathmandu suburbs, May 1998.
39. *The News*, 14 June 1998. Report of a speech by Zahid Malik at a workshop in Islamabad on 'Cultural Invasion and Role of the Media'.
40. Ashfak Bokhari, South Asian Cultural Bazaar, *Dawn*, 23 May 1998.
41. Maxim's column in *The Nation*, 19 March 1998.
42. As observed by Tasneem Ahmar on visits to Lahore in 1998.
43. Tahir Mirza, Lahore, May 1998.
44. Raana Syed, Islamabad, November 1997.
45. *Nawa-i-Waqt*, 12 March 1998, quoted in *The Nation*, 19 March 1998.
46. *The News*, 14 June 1998. Report of speech by Dr. Ahmed at a two-day workshop held at the Dawah Academy.
47. Dr. Anees Ahmed, Islamabad, March 1999.
48. Report by Saeed Ahmed, *The News*, 12 June 1998.
49. Uzma Gilani, Lahore, May 1998.
50. Professionals, Karachi, June 1998.
51. Home makers, Karachi, June 1998.
52. The Rawalpindi survey work was carried out by Tasneem Ahmar between mid-May and mid-June 1998.
53. Agha Sajjad Gul, Lahore, May 1998.
54. Dr. Mehdi Hasan, Lahore, April 1998.
55. Sheema Kirmani, Karachi, July 1998.
56. Kishwar Naheed, Karachi, February 1999.
57. Khalid Ahmed, Karachi, July 1998.
58. *Dawn Review*, 29 October–4 November 1998.
59. I.A. Rehman's article entitled 'Tunnel Vision' was the cover story of the *Review*.
60. *Dawn Tuesday Review*, 5–11 March 1996.
61. Khaled Ahmed, Lahore, January 1999.
62. Mrs. Asif Kitchloo, Rawalpindi district survey, May 1998.
63. Home makers, Karachi, June 1998.
64. College students, Islamabad, January 1999.
65. Teenagers, Islamabad, January 1999.
66. Afsan Chowdhury, 'Media Profile of Bangladesh', commissioned for the Media South Asia Project, July 1998.
67. Chinmoy Mutsuddi, Dhaka, March 1998.
68. Kanak Mani Dixit, Kathmandu, May 1998.
69. Khalid Hassan, Lahore, May 1998; Professionals, Karachi, June 1998.
70. Senior citizens and professionals, Chennai, and Professionals, Madurai, November 1999.
71. Father Joe Andrew, Chennai, November 1999.
72. Gowri Ramnarayan, Chennai, November 1999.
73. Kunda Dixit, Telephone interview, February 2000.
74. Mir Jamil ur Rahman, 'Let's look forward', *News*, 17 July 1999. Jamil ur Rahman is a member of the family which owns *Jang* and *News* and has been bidding to start its own satellite channel.

75. Samina Ibrahim, 'Eight Days of Hysteria', *Newsline*, January 2000.
76. Kunda Dixit, Telephone interview, February 2000.
77. Mahommed Malik, Islamabad, March 1998.
78. Parveen Rashid of SMC, Dhaka, March 1998.
79. See, H.M.Gunasekara (1997), *Media as Bridge Maker*, pp. 34–39. The SAARC Audio Visual Exchange Programme (SAVE) was established in 1987.
80. Kanak Mani Dixit, Talk to Media South Asia group, Kathmandu, July 1998.
81. Kanak Mani Dixit, Kathmandu, May 1998; Neer Shah, Kathmandu, March 1998.
82. Shevanthi Jayasuriya, Colombo, April 1998.
83. Deepthi Senanayake, Colombo, July 1998.
84. See S.W.R. de A. Samarasinghe, 'Reading, Listening and Watching: A National Sample Survey of the Sri Lankan News Media' in G.H. Peiris (1997), *Studies on the Press in Sri Lanka and South Asia*, International Centre for Ethnic Studies, Kandy, pp. 290 and 293.
85. A.J. Gunawardena, Colombo, June 1998.
86. Ajith Samaranayake, *Lanka Guardian*, May 1998.
87. Nalaka Gunawardene, Colombo, July 1998.
88. This material on the development of the independent TV sector in Sri Lanka draws on Santhini Jayawardena's 'Media Profile of Sri Lanka', commissioned for the Media South Asia Project, October 1998.
89. Rosmand Senaratne, Colombo, June 1998.
90. Students, Matara, May 1998.
91. Labourers and professionals, Matara, May 1998.
92. Survey Puhulwella, Matara district, July 1998.
93. Schoolchildren, Colombo, April 1998.
94. University students, Colombo, June 1998.
95. Development workers, Matara, June 1998.
96. Raine Wickremetunge, Colombo, October 1998.
97. *Sunday Times*, 2 August 1998.
98. Home makers, Matara, May 1998; Home makers, Colombo, June 1998.
99. S. Thilillainathan, Colombo, June 1998.
100. Vasant Guruge, Colombo, March 1998.
101. Shevanthi Jayasuriya, Colombo, April 1998; D.E.W. Gunasekere, Colombo, March 1998.
102. Selvy Thiruchandran, Colombo, May 1998.
103. S. Thilillainathan, Colombo, June 1998.
104. The week in question included a religious holiday, which may have increased local programming to some extent. Calculations by S. Jayawardena based on TV Guides of the *Sunday Island* and *Sunday Leader* for the week starting 29 November 1998.
105. Shan Wickremesinghe and Damayanthi Pathirana, Colombo, September 1999.
106. Nalaka Gunawardene, Colombo, July 1998.
107. Maleec Calyaneratne de Silva, Colombo, September 1998.
108. Survey Puhulwella, Matara district, July 1998.

Eight

THE RESPONSE OF THE NATION STATE

INTRODUCTION

The similarity of inherited models of broadcasting institutions across South Asia has meant that the satellite revolution has posed a broadly comparable challenge to the role of the nation state in all countries. The way the different South Asian states traditionally managed the electronic media had a significant influence on issues of government, national culture and identity, beyond the field of information and broadcasting policy. Broadcasting was an instrument of cultural autarchy, a means to literacy and an educational resource. Using a technical infrastructure built with public resources, it was a vehicle for setting out the preferred ideology of the state as articulated by the government, a means of building a national identity and promoting a national culture.

For these reasons, the response of the state to the challenge of satellite broadcasting was not a peripheral matter. It involved a re-thinking of a whole range of activities and policies at the heart of government and social organisation. As broadcasters, the state institutions were concerned about their own survival. They were not strangers to commerce or advertising; advertising already brought them a substantial income. But competition was unfamiliar territory.

Conditions for broadcasting had radically changed. Governments were presented with a new set of issues for which they were unprepared. What was needed was a regulatory system to take account of the new media institutions and technologies and to harness them to national objectives. This was not such an empty hope as appeared at first sight. The nature of satellite technology and the financial power of the media giants who dominated it seemed to consign the idea of national regulation to the history books. It seemed that regulation could never catch up with the ability of new technologies to circumvent whatever controls were devised. But the free-to-air beginnings of satellite TV in South Asia disguised the true costs and practicalities of distribution for a mass market.

By the mid-1990s, the marketing lessons from the expansion of satellite television had demonstrated the attraction of programming in local languages over the international. Fears of cultural invasion receded as the big audiences followed the channels geared to local popular cultural interests. Within the South Asian region and even within India itself, the perception of an external global cultural threat was replaced by an apprehensiveness regarding regional cultural homogenisation.

If the responses of the state involved decisions on questions of national policy beyond broadcasting, the broadcasters themselves, deprived of their monopoly, had to make immediate adjustments to their own schedules. The initial aim was to fight off the competition without surrendering control of sensitive areas of programming. What was not questioned was a belief in the power of the media and its capacity to influence society for good or ill. But a determined defensiveness was not a long-term solution to the issues thrown up by the new media environment. Questions of competition and control, of taste and decency and of the wider public interest in broadcasting needed to be addressed. Government had to assume the role of regulator more seriously than before. This chapter looks at the measures taken by South Asian governments in response to the new situation and examines how far they have been successful in meeting the challenges they face.

MEDIA LAW IN SOUTH ASIA

The antiquity of the laws governing the media in South Asia reflects a lack of change over many years and the dominance of security issues in government thinking. Some of the key instruments of media law and regulation were passed under British colonial regimes and are over 100 years old. The *Indian Telegraph Act* of 1885 is still in force in India and actively used. Though modified by subsequent legislation in Pakistan and Bangladesh, much if it still holds good there. Under this Act, governments have wide powers to intervene in the interests of public order or to protect the sovereignty and integrity of the country and the security of the state. Because the electronic media have been directly controlled by the government, radio and television have been insulated from the need to regulate them as private activities. But once they move out of government hands, the legal framework for their activities acquires a new relevance.

Libel and privacy laws and those affecting public morals and public policy are fundamental constraints on the media, though not necessarily specific to them. Even older than the *Indian Telegraph Act* of 1885 is the *Public Order Act* of 1860, which is still the basis of current legislation in India, Pakistan and Bangladesh. In India the Act defines as acts of 'sedition' attempts to bring the government into hatred or contempt.[1]

A free press is no guarantee of social and political responsibility. By extension, it would be idealistic to assume that an open broadcasting system would never be used in a socially irresponsible way. In all the countries of South Asia, concerns that the media will be misused have been a powerful brake on the process of liberalisation. Sri Lanka, despite the prolonged conflict in the north and east, appears to be an exception. The apparatus of general and specific controls on its media is in many ways more restrictive than in India, especially for the print media.[2] But this has not prevented bold measures of diversification of broadcasting.

The weight of social and security legislation borne by the media should not have a defining influence. But it helps to explain why the state's responses to new media technologies have been slow and why the development of regulation has been marked by uncertainty, hesitancy and political controversy. State broadcasters and media observers in both India and Bangladesh agree in describing the responses of their governments as 'confused'. In India, there was a shift from official denial of the significance of the international satellite phenomenon to a radical reinterpretation by the state broadcaster of its broadcasting strategy. The balance between commercial imperatives and public service obligations came under close scrutiny.

Beyond this was a general awareness of the need for a new communications strategy, more suited to the new technologies which had made obsolete much of the old regulatory framework.

Liberalisation, planned or unplanned, needed a framework. According to one media analyst, echoing the television coverage of Saddam Hussein's 'mother of all wars', the uncharted and unplanned entry of multi-channel TV in the Indian market started the 'mother of all confusion'.[3]

INDIA

The initial reaction of the state in India, as elsewhere in South Asia, was that the state monopoly should be enforced by any technical means available. P. Upendra, the Minister of Information who steered the Prasar Bharati Bill onto the statute book in 1990, paints a picture of bureaucratic frustration as the implications of open skies were becoming evident. 'A file was put up in the Ministry as to how to counter the satellite invasion. What steps should be taken to stop it? I wrote back saying you cannot stop the sun shining by holding an umbrella. The more you try, the more you encourage people to watch. It was better to allow them to operate from India under control rather than allow them to operate from Sri Lanka or some other foreign country.'[4]

There were two areas in which a degree of control of foreign satellite channels might be exercised. One was through administrative control of the business interests of the companies and advertisers whose market or manufacturing base was in India. An attempt was made to limit advertising by Indian companies on satellite channels by requiring advertisers to finance their advertising by export earnings. The second—which took longer to materialise—was through control of the mass distribution cable system. The *Cable Television Networks (Regulation) Act* of March 1995 followed an earlier ordinance in establishing a system of licensing which made the cable operators responsible both for the provision and content of the broadcasting channels. They could not be controlled directly by other means.

Both advertisers and cable operators have criticised this. Some argue that what is expected of the cable operator is unrealistic and meaningless.[5] Others acknowledge the value to government of the powers the Act provides where national interest or security issues are at stake. 'Cable provides an opportunity to the government to weed out what is undesirable. So the argument that international broadcasters can beam whatever they want into India is not strictly speaking true. For instance, the police commissioner may order us to shut down BBC, and we will be obliged to do so'.[6] During communal disturbances in Bombay, there were informal instructions to cable operators from the Bombay police not to relay Pakistan TV. PTV was banned again in July 1998, when the Union Minister of State, Mukhtar Abbas Naqvi, made a public announcement, and in early June 1999 during the Kargil conflict. Cable operators are clear that an informal request is sufficient for them to respond, but the police have the right to issue more formal instructions if necessary.[7] The legislation has been a constant subject of protest, especially as larger companies have gained control of small cable operators and brought an all-India influence to bear.

The Cable Act represented a first attempt to control the phenomenon of the new satellite media. As part of it, the government aimed to influence cable distribution in favour of Doordarshan. The cable law specifies that cable operators have to show at least two Doordarshan channels on the prime band. But 80 per cent of homes with cable and satellite cannot receive more than twelve channels. As encryption becomes more common, the cable operators' margins are decreasing and their agreements with the broadcasting channels increasingly specify prime band allocation. These technological and commercial constraints have resulted in Doordarshan being removed in some places from the prime viewership market. Most cable operators show DD1, the national channel, and DD2 but ignore newer services intended to capture cable and satellite audiences. Patchy relaying and poor technical quality in the cable sector have also played a part in Doordarshan's urban decline.

The draft Broadcasting Bill of 1997 incorporated legal provisions aimed at putting responsibility for the content of broadcasting more firmly where it belongs, in the hands of the broadcasters rather than the distributors. But the range of technical and legal issues, the commercial interests involved and the instability of governments proved an effective brake on action.

The state broadcaster in turn found it had little support from government or the courts in reinforcing its public role. The financial provisions of India's Ninth Plan reversed the established proportions of financial subsidy to the state broadcaster. Previously, 80 per cent of funding had come from the government and 20 per cent from earnings from advertising and sponsorship.

From 1992, the requirement was the other way round. Though Doordarshan was confident of its ability to attract advertising, the leap was an enormous one. The autonomy provisions protected the jobs of staff as government employee, so few savings could be made in that area.

After the initial shock, two innovative officials, Information and Broadcasting Secretary, Bhaskar Ghose, and Director General of Doordarshan, Rathikant Basu, with the encouragement of Information and Broadcasting Minister, K.P. Singh Deo, masterminded a vigorous response. Between 1992 and 1995 they took the battle into the camp of their rivals, especially Zee TV. They launched the Metro Channel, DD2, which was designed specifically to attract advertising revenue, and rescheduled programmes on DD1. Doordarshan also floated the 'Movie Club' as part of its efforts to compete with Zee Cinema.

Next appeared DD India, an international channel consisting of the best programming culled from all Doordarshan channels. This channel broke new ground when the government decided to hire a transponder on a foreign satellite PAS-4 to transmit it. Doordarshan also started a new elite information and educational channel, DD3. Targeted at the top 10 per cent of the population of the major cities, it eventually foundered from technical problems and inadequate funding. It was ultimately closed down in January 1998.

The launch of a whole new range of regional satellite language channels which were accessible throughout the country proved a much more successful development. The interest shown by cable operators in these channels, responding to pressure from customers living away from their 'home' states, helped to create this success. A combination of regional languages and local distribution was forging a new kind of national identity.

While the government attempted to put its own house in order, the satellite media business was left to grow on its own. The survival of satellite channels hinged on the commercial disciplines of profit and loss, without the regulation which governments, and to some extent the industry itself, wanted. The existence of any kind of choice was a new and welcome development both for the TV viewer and for the advertiser. The release from a government monopoly for those who could receive satellite or cable transmissions was a kind of liberation. It gave rise to the anarchic ideal that satellite technology had not only made existing regulations redundant, but that all regulation of international and national broadcasting would in future be impossible to enforce. Ideological libertarians welcomed this development; to others, who mistrusted the new purveyors of information and entertainment, it was a nightmare.

Faced with a steady reduction in government budgetary support, the ministry took a closer look at the system for marketing commercial time on Doordarshan and All India Radio. It set up an expert committee headed by Siddhartha Sen to examine the existing system and suggest ways to improve it. The Sen Committee focussed on the needs of the consumers, both advertisers and viewers. Its report was sharp and outspoken.[8] It condemned much of the output of the private channels in Hindi and other regional languages as 'trite nonsense'. But it was optimistic about the ability of Doordarshan and AIR to improve significantly as broadcasters.

The Sen Committee firmly endorsed the need for both Doordarshan and AIR to be commercial. It was confident that commercial broadcasting did not in itself mean a lowering of standards. It made detailed recommendations for a more transparent system of charging for advertising spots to make information more accessible to advertising agencies. It urged greater control by Doordarshan of its own software and the sale of its own air time. But above all it set out to change the preconception that marketing was for 'hucksters and charlatans'.

The Sen Committee's work overlapped with that of the committee set up in December 1995 under Dr. Nitish Sengupta to make recommendations on the structure of Prasar Bharati. The Act had lain dormant for five years. To the increasingly pressing need to respond to competition from the new satellite channels, a new urgency had been added by the Supreme Court judgement of February 1995, declaring the airwaves or frequencies to be 'public property'.

That judgement is much quoted as spelling the end of the government monopoly of broadcasting. But it was not a privateers' charter. The judgement specifically warned against 'the privileged few—powerful economic, commercial and political interests' which would come to dominate the media if it were not regulated.[9] Far from being required to dismantle controls, the government was told to take immediate steps to set up 'an independent auto-nomous public authority' to control and regulate the airwaves 'in the interests of the public and to prevent the invasion of their rights'.

The Supreme Court's direct charge to the government to do something about the regulation of broadcasting also stimulated thinking about policies towards the print media and film. The role of broadcasting had to be placed in the context of a broader nation-al media policy. A working paper on national media policy, drawn up for a committee under the chairmanship of Ram Vilas Paswan, endorsed the aim first set out by the Joshi Committee in 1983 of achieving an 'Indian personality' for Indian broadcasting. The paper said one of the ways in which the Indian ethos could be served was to enable universities and other educational institu-tions, as well as state governments and local bodies such as pan-chayats, to set up non-commercial broadcasting services to further developmental and public service aims. But the report was not specific about the institutional and financial support that it recog-nised would be required to implement the idea.[10]

This draft national media policy also argued in favour of strict regulation of satellite channels. George Verghese, on the other hand, put the case for a more relaxed view, which the Sengupta Committee shared, at least in relation to fears about a threat to national security. 'For the last several years', Verghese said, 'all the satellite channels broadcasting to India are unregulated except by goodwill. It is now argued that firm regulation is needed to see that they don't get up to mischief. But you have given them a free run for six years and nothing terrible has happened. On the whole they have shown respect for our concerns.' However, he acknowledged that there had to be a regulatory framework. As time passed and nothing was done, more players came into the market and '...it was more difficult to ensure a level playing field'.[11]

The action of Minister of Information and Broadcasting, Jaipal Reddy, in bringing into effect the bill giving autonomy to state broadcasters was a big step forward. But Reddy's priority when he became minister in May 1997 had been a more radical one. 'My whole idea was to minimise the power of the ministry. On the day I became minister, I made a statement which was then being dismissed as romantic and rhetorical. It was "my objective to liberate the Ministry from the Minister and the media from the Ministry".'[12]

Within a week, a bill for setting up a Broadcasting Authority of India was introduced in parliament and referred to a joint select committee. The policy framework had been decided by the previous Cabinet of Prime Minister H. Deve Gowda. In drafting the Broadcasting Bill, Reddy left that framework intact. Only after introducing the Broadcasting Bill did Reddy take steps which led to the implementation of the seven-year-old *Prasar Bharati Act*, through an ordinance promulgated on 29 October 1997. Reddy had hoped to have the Broadcasting Authority set up to regulate a new system by the end of 1997. 'If I had one month more, I would have introduced the Broadcasting Bill'. But time ran out and I.K. Gujral's United Front government fell.

For a further three years, the draft Broadcasting Bill remained a major piece of unfinished business. The Bill set out a procedure for granting licences, initially in seven different categories of broadcasting services. It laid down the terms under which private stations would be allowed to uplink from Indian territory, the extent of foreign ownership permitted in companies licensed in India, and specific restrictions on cross media ownership by both foreign and Indian entrepreneurs. It proposed a new pattern of organisation for the cable television industry to supersede the Cable Act of 1995. It also spelt out the conditions for licensing Direct to Home (DTH) satellite television services, following the general ban on such services by special notification in 1996. All these activities were to come under the authority of a newly constituted independent Broadcasting Authority of India.

Major media entrepreneurs were insistent that without a regulatory framework investment in the development of broadcasting would be blocked. But the terms of the bill as published were heavily criticised. While there was a common determination to prevent monopolies, enterprises like the Indus Group were concerned that the proposals to prevent cross media holdings would be unworkable. Attempts by their own group and others to create media synergies would be ruled out.[13] Following the refusal of permission for DTH in 1996, Star attempted to persuade the authorities of the benefits of the system. However, the decision in 1999 to award the first DTH license to Doordarshan excluded Star from operating it.

The election of the BJP-led government in 1998 meant that broad-casting issues were put on hold. But the expectation that the BJP would try to reshape the media in the BJP mould were not ful-filled.[14] The criticisms of Prasar Bharati that the BJP had expressed in opposition were concentrated, once they were in government, on the personalities and political backgrounds of individual members of the Prasar Bharati board. Their criticism of Jaipal Reddy's amendments to the original *Prasar Bharati Act* seemed a secondary issue.

The BJP argued that members of the board were all close associates of the former Prime Minister, I.K. Gujral, and for that reason could be assumed to be politically biased. They criticised the waiving of the age limit for senior officials of the board and in particular for the chief executive, S.S. Gill. However, their handling of the issue increasingly demonstrated a lack of commitment to the survival of the autonomous broadcaster. The Ministry of In-formation was also hostile to the new organisation. Its officials complained that they were being held responsible for state broad-casting when they no longer had any authority. Behind the conflict was a growing perception that the satellite revolution had changed conditions for the state broadcasters so radically that the argu-ments for relaxing state control were no longer so convincing.

In the end, the BJP government played a waiting game. It relied on the fact that unless parliament ratified the 1997 Prasar Bharati ordinance within six months, it would lapse. So the legislation continued in the form in which it was originally passed in 1990, but without the later amendments. As a result, the chief executive officer was deemed to be over age and was dismissed, though the decision was challenged in court. These uncertainties in the legal position hampered the functioning of the Prasar Bharati organ-isation and the government's own actions made matters worse. When the Board's chairman, the veteran left wing journalist Nikhil Chakravarty died, no move was made to replace him. However it might be disguised, the reality appeared to be that the government did not wish to see an autonomous public broadcaster.

The BJP coalition government explained its reluctance to pro-ceed with a new Broadcasting Bill in terms of its shaky parlia-mentary position. Information Ministers Sushma Swaraj and Pramod Mahajan faced difficulties in drawing up broadcasting regulations which would satisfy foreign investors, domestic industry and their political allies and opponents. Pramod Mahajan argued that the controversial provisions of the bill, such as restrictions on cross media ownership, were not likely to pass through parliament. But the BJP did take up other aspects of the bill in a piecemeal fashion. Sushma Swaraj successfully pushed a decision on uplinking through Cabinet. Pramod Mahajan also left his imprint within a few months of being allotted the portfolio. His stated priority was for the government to be seen to encourage the flow of foreign investment and new technology. But the establishment of autonomous broadcasting institutions did not play a part in that vision. The appointment of a serving government official, R.R. Shah, as acting CEO of Prasar Bharati in mid-1999 was taken as confirmation of the closer control that the government had been exercising over the autonomous corporation since the dismissal of Mr. Gill.

On the future of radio, the BJP-led caretaker government took more far-reaching action than any of its predecessors. The time slots allocated to private operators on AIR FM channels were abruptly cancelled in June 1998 in the wake of a legal challenge to the terms on which the licenses were to be renewed. A year later, in July 1999, it was announced that private companies would be allowed to set up 150 independent FM stations in forty cities.[15]

But an independent Broadcasting Authority of India was no nearer realisation. Despite the Supreme Court judgement that the airwaves were public property, the terms and conditions for the new FM licenses were to be set by government. The century old *Indian Telegraph Act* of 1885 and the *Indian Wireless Telegraphy Act* of 1933 provided the means. As a leading media journalist wrote: 'Privatisation has preceded autonomy. So enabling legislation effectively seems irrelevant....'[16]

PAKISTAN

The fact that Pakistan has enjoyed a much less democratic political history than India has inevitably influenced the management of its media. More than 25 years of military rule added substantially to the armoury of repressive legislation available to the state and though many of these laws were repealed after the demise of General Zia ul Haq, civil society is a good deal less robust than across the border. After 1988, when the country returned to democratic government, the press became much more free. But successive democratic governments proved unwilling to end the well-established pattern of political control of the electronic media. The country experienced four elections and four separate civilian governments after 1988, but it was still a long way from establishing a constructive political consensus on the role of the media in civil society when the Army took over again.

The return to democracy in 1988 ushered in some hopeful changes in the field of human rights and the media, though the minority character of Benazir Bhutto's administration meant that she was obliged to make compromises with the country's military establishment. With Javed Jabbar as the minister of state for information and broadcasting and Aslam Azhar, the country's leading television professional, as chairman of Pakistan Television and Radio, efforts were made to open up the media. Fairer ground rules were established for the reflection of government and opposition views, whether in the coverage of parliamentary proceedings or the compilation of news bulletins and current affairs programmes, and there was a palpable public welcome for the new spirit of openness. But after only four months, both men were forced to give up their responsibilities.

This reversion to long-established patterns of government control set the tone for the next decade. Nawaz Sharif's Muslim League complained loudly about its exclusion from the airwaves but practised the same policies itself when returned to power in 1990. Benazir Bhutto's second administration was, if anything, more proprietorial in its management of the media than the first. In the first four months of 1995, PTV news gave the opposition only 5 per cent of the coverage given to the government.[17] In the words of one media professional, there was a 'complete blackout' of all criticism of government policies.[18]

It was only when Nawaz Sharif came to power for a second time in 1997 that a more sophisticated style was developed, with former newspaper editor Mushahid Hussain as the minister of information. The new administration began relaying parliamentary question time, including criticism of government from the opposition benches, and it launched a programme called Open Forum, in which ministers and officials were subject to questioning by members of the public from all over the country. In substance, however, little changed. While the Nawaz Sharif government recognised that too much propaganda could be counter-productive, it showed no sign of surrendering control in this key area. [19]

The decision by Benazir Bhutto's first administration to set up a second television channel, originally called the People's Television Network but later renamed Shalimar Television Network (STN), offered the welcome prospect of greater choice for viewers and more opportunities for independent producers. However, the award without a proper tendering process of a monopolistic contract for the supply of programming and advertising to NTM, a Karachi-based consortium created by an advertising agency, undermined some of the potential of the scheme. [20] Competition was artificially restricted and the dominance of advertisers in the consortium, contrary to international practice, militated against independent programming.

This did not prevent NTM programmes from becoming both popular and profitable. As a commercial commissioning agency, NTM did not suffer from the degree of official interference or bureaucratic caution which characterised PTV. It was able to appeal more successfully to the young and to the urban middle class, to sail closer to the wind in terms of themes for teleserials and other programmes. However, STN remained under firm, if indirect, government control; government retained a majority shareholding and appointed the board of management. It was also obliged to broadcast the same news bulletins as PTV; it had no independent remit in this field.

A similar lack of transparency also surrounded the award during Benazir Bhutto's second administration of contracts for pay-TV and commercial FM Radio to Javaid Pasha, a friend of the prime minister's husband. [21] In 1995, the contract to establish the country's first commercial FM stations in Islamabad, Karachi and Lahore was awarded to Mr. Pasha without any tendering process or legislative enactment.

All these contracts were challenged in the Pakistani courts, though for many years no judgement was given in any of these cases. In January 1993, fourteen advertising agencies filed a petition in the Sind High Court against the NTM contract, arguing that it had been awarded in an improper manner and created an unhealthy monopoly. This matter was still *sub judice* during Benazir Bhutto's second administration when the NTM contract was extended on the same basis for a further ten years and to another ten cities. In May 1996, Javed Jabbar and Dr. Mubashir Hasan, a former federal finance minister and a founder of the People's Party, filed a public interest petition in the Supreme Court requesting it to declare the country's airwaves a national asset which could only be utilised on the basis of equity and transparency. But after admitting the petition for a regular hearing, the Supreme Court returned the case to the pending files; it was still awaiting judgement three years later. The judiciary in Pakistan has not made the same kind of bold interventions in media matters as the supreme courts of India and Sri Lanka.

With both main political parties determined to retain political control of the electronic media, efforts at reform often came during the interim administrations which punctuated the functioning of democracy for much of the 1990s. These short-lived non-party governments which held office between the dismissal of one government and the election of another, attempted to introduce what they and the country's creditors regarded as desirable reforms prior to handing government back to the politicians. In most cases, however, such reforms proved short-lived; they began life as presidential ordinances but were later allowed to lapse.

Such was the case with the Electronic Media Regulatory Authority Ordinance, which was promulgated by President Farooq Leghari just before the February 1997 election which returned Nawaz Sharif to power for the second time. This ordinance, known as EMRA, offered a much more liberal future for the electronic media in that it made the award of licences for broadcasting the prerogative of a new authority chaired by a retired judge of the Supreme Court, with a majority of non-government members. The ordinance also struck a liberal note in its declared objective 'to enlarge the choice available to the people of Pakistan in the media for news, current affairs, religious knowledge, art, culture, science, technology, economic development, social sector concerns, music, sports, drama and other subjects of public and national interest.'[22]

The inclusion of news and current affairs in the preamble to the ordinance marked another break with previous government practice. However, after the election of February 1997, despite some early promises, this liberal initiative lapsed.

Despite the challenge of the satellite channels, democratic governments in Pakistan were not persuaded to modify their control of the news agenda. But the fact that television programmes made for Indian audiences were widely seen in Pakistan inevitably led to comparisons of content and standards, entertainment and news, production and presentation, and relative degrees of official control.

Senior media professionals in Pakistan believe that greater access to other sources of information is gradually eroding the government's monopoly. Agha Nasir, a former managing director of PBC and PTV, told us: 'At one time, the two organisations had a complete monopoly.... In radio, people used to listen to the BBC but on a small scale for news and current affairs, maybe for half an hour a day. But with the technological revolution, the coming of the super-highway, computers and the Internet, there is no more possibility of continuing the monopoly as it was....' [23] In his experience, however, government is 'very possessive' about news and particularly wary of opening up this field.

The first well thought-out Pakistan government response to the challenge of the satellite channels was very slow in emerging, partly because of the superior reach of the official media and partly because of the pressures of conservatism unleashed during the military dictatorship of Zia ul Haq. Of the two main Pakistani political parties, Benazir Bhutto's People's Party was more liberal in its approach to culture than Nawaz Sharif's Muslim League, which drew its support from conservative and Islamist forces. After the repressive years of Zia ul Haq, Benazir Bhutto's first government brought a welcome extension of artistic freedoms. Her replacement in the next election by Nawaz Sharif saw a re-imposition of a more conservative policy. During her second administration, by which time the impact of Hindi satellite channels was more strongly felt, Benazir Bhutto appointed Raana Sheikh, a dynamic and well-connected bureaucrat with television experience, as managing director of PTV and allowed her a free hand to develop programmes to win back the middle class youth audience. Raana Sheikh was later criticised for being over-ambitious and for putting PTV into serious debt, but she was largely successful in her main objective. The heavy-handed preachiness of PTV was replaced by a more upbeat, more modern, more youth-oriented menu.

Many of these innovations were discontinued when Nawaz Sharif returned to power with a substantial majority in 1997. Raana

Sheikh went the way of most political appointees and in response to criticism from the Islamist lobby, what one media professional described as 'preposterous', restrictions were imposed on the representation of relations between men and women.[24] However, this strictness was relaxed after some months as a result of a strategic review of PTV's falling popularity and growing indebtedness. It had become clear that something needed to be done to make PTV commercially viable in the new environment.

A number of factors were responsible for this change of strategy: financial mismanagement at PTV, loss of advertising revenue due to over-restrictive cultural policies and concern at the growing appeal of Hindi satellite channels not just to the public but to Pakistani advertisers as well.

The voice of the advertising community was most clearly heard in 1997 when the government terminated NTM's contract and its programmes went off the air for more than a month. According to some estimates, as much as 10 per cent of TV advertising budgets moved to satellite, with Zee TV the favourite destination. Commenting on this at the time, Khalid Rauf, the managing director in Pakistan of Lintas, the in-house advertising agency of Lever Brothers, thought that it might not be just an interim measure. As he put it: 'The quality of programmes on local TV channels has declined considerably and advertisers have realised that satellite channels are where the audiences are. Viewers are just not watching PTV and NTM as much as they used to.'[25]

PTV's total dependence for revenue on advertisements made it very vulnerable to shifting audience reactions in an increasingly competitive world. PTV had taken advertisements from its inception, but for much of the 1970s and 1980s it also received state subsidies to pay for public interest programmes, including news and current affairs. These were discontinued under General Zia ul Haq when it became clear that revenues far exceeded expenditure. The fact that Nawaz Sharif's administration inherited a corporation in debt in 1997 did not initially affect its thinking, but when it became clear that the neglect of entertainment was playing into the hands of the satellite channels and seriously affecting the bottom line, a decision was taken to counter the satellite channels with their own weapons. Yusuf Beg Mirza, a marketing specialist who had previously worked for Zee TV, was recruited as the new managing director with a brief to re-examine the programme mix.

The aim was to make it more competitive and commercially viable while at the same time maintaining a distinctively Pakistani flavour.

The result was the re-launch in July 1998 of PTV's satellite channel as PTV World with a new schedule which followed satellite competition in terms of programme genres but was less permissive in its handling of relations between the sexes. It included more popular music, more film-based programmes, more talk shows, but the emphasis was on 'family entertainment'—a watchword with Pakistani critics of Zee TV. Talking to the *Nation* before the launch, the managing director said: 'We are beginning with a unique selling point since all other satellite channels are reflecting a culture that does not correspond to our own social and cultural values.... Our message is that we are the only family entertainment channel available on satellite.'[26] The new strategy retained PTV1 as the main terrestrial channel and treated PTV World as a channel for middle class Pakistani audiences as well as for expatriates in the Gulf and Europe.

The new management also decided to farm out the collection of TV licence fees which had previously been managed inefficiently by PTV itself. In 1996, according to television licence receipts, there were only 2.5 million television sets in the country, whereas according to reliable estimates, the figure was probably closer to 9 million.[27] This gap represented a huge loss of revenue for PTV, which was also losing money on the collection of much higher fees for videos and satellite dishes. As a result of a tendering process, a private agency paid Rs. 440 million for the contract, a distinct improvement on the Rs. 250 million collected by PTV itself the previous financial year. Yusuf Mirza Beg offered the contract for one year only in the first instance, confident that the potential might be much greater.

These efforts to make PTV more market-oriented also had implications for the organisation's professionalism and autonomy. As one commercial broadcaster put it at the beginning of the process of change: 'Now the government doesn't have any money, they have to start operating as a professional organisation and the sooner they do it the better...because when you start operating professionally a lot of other things fall by the wayside.'[28] By mid-1998, Satish Anand, one of the country's leading film and television producers, told us: 'Autonomy is already there for practical purposes, except for news and current affairs. Other segments of programmes are virtually for sale; even formerly reserved prime time from 7–9 p.m. is now available for sale.' But autonomy in news and current affairs remained some way off. According to Satish Anand, whose company produced *Pakistan Business Update* for Zee TV, news and current affairs could have a market in the right conditions, but ' if it is controlled and restricted it is a non-starter'.[29]

By the beginning of 1999, PTV had become a commercially viable organisation once more. Packages offering incentives to companies wishing to advertise on both channels had successfully pulled back many of the lost advertisers. Better scheduling had boosted advertising revenues by creating new prime time slots for audiences in Pakistan and the Gulf.[30] PTV had begun to invest in new equipment and recruit new producers for the first time in several years. Morale improved.

PTV executives told us that there was less bureaucratic interference than previously, though the way this had been achieved was a peculiarly Pakistani compromise which reduced interference by officials but left political control intact. The government had appointed a powerful new chairman of PTV, Muslim League politician Senator Pervaiz Rasheed, who acted as an effective bulwark against routine bureaucratic interference.[31] With the chairman and the minister of information working closely together, the organisation had been galvanised into meeting a new set of commercial objectives, but political direction had become more direct and more detailed in the key areas of news and current affairs.

Improved control of the media agenda was also the key to the resumption of air time previously allocated to STN. In mid-1999, the Nawaz Sharif administration peremptorily ended STN's contract and used its transmission facilities for a third government-controlled channel, PTV-3, dedicated to news and sports. The involvement of NTM as the programme provider for STN was also ended, effectively removing the rationale for the public interest cases still pending concerning the legality of its contract. The government strategy was designed to combat satellite channels in the critical fields of news and sports, but it made government even more dominant than it had been before. Satellite TV had become a new battleground between Pakistan and India, which justified the elimination of the only other television broadcaster in the country. In the late 1990s, it looked as if PTV might face satellite competition from Pakistani entrepreneurs. At that time, several satellite channels were planned, but none got off the ground. The efforts of the *Jang* newspaper group to launch a channel called GEO, which was the most promising of these ventures, lost impetus as a result of a confrontation with the Nawaz Sharif government over political reporting.[32] Those planning the channel aspired to attract both Indian and Pakistani audiences and were exploring collaborations with Indian software houses. However, a key element in the schedules was to be independent news and current affairs coverage of Pakistan. 'Given the suffocation of the official media', said Imran Aslam, one of the architects of the channel, 'there is a thirst...and we look to viewership of news and current affairs as circulation-building rather than earning revenue directly.'[33] The government denied that it was opposed to the channel, but its own revamp of PTV effectively pre-empted *Jang*'s strategy.[34] All business interests exploring the commercial potential of a satellite channel agreed that the Pakistani market would only support one and PTV World took that slot.

In early 2000, with the army back in power, Pakistanis were looking once more to a non-elected regime to introduce media liberalisation. In his first speech to the nation, General Musharraf said he would like to see the establishment of private television channels. He appointed Javed Jabbar as adviser on information and media development, who drew up a broadcasting policy providing for a new regulatory body to award broadcasting licences. A draft ordinance announced in April 2000 provided for commercial competition for PTV and PBC; if implemented it would give Pakistan the most decentralised media in South Asia. But as with EMRA in 1997, the test of its longevity will come when democracy is restored.[35]

BANGLADESH

Nothing in Bangladesh's institutions or laws had prepared the ground for the technological and regulatory demands brought by the onset of the satellite revolution. But the political environment was one in which media issues were assuming ostensibly crucial importance. Both in the movement which led to the overthrow of President Ershad in 1990 and again in the agitation which brought down the government of Begum Khaleda Zia in 1996, the demand for a more independent broadcasting media played a prominent part.

The *Special Powers Act* of 1974, passed within three years of Bangladesh gaining its independence from Pakistan, was at the centre of complaints about restrictions on the freedom of the media. A wide definition of 'prejudicial acts' which could threaten security or public order was paired with a ban on reporting, whether true or false, which could incite or promote such acts. This and some other restrictive sections of the Act were amended in 1991 after the overthrow of President Ershad.[36] Article 39 of the constitution guarantees freedom of thought and conscience, but the 'reasonable restrictions' applied in practice have effectively nullified those constitutional guarantees. There has been an 'overall trend' to use mass media laws to curb the freedom of the press, which democratic governments since 1990 have not fully corrected. The constraints have been political. But in the judgement of Bangladeshi lawyers, the superior courts could play a vital role 'in the materialisation of golden expectations' for media freedom.[37]

If freedom to publish has been limited in relation to the print media, the state-controlled broadcasting media have lagged still further behind. The demand for media autonomy for TV and radio was a prime issue in the agitation against the BNP government of Begum Khaleda Zia, and when the Awami League came to power in 1996 and pledged to introduce it, a serious attempt was made to look at how it might be achieved. In its report, the National Broadcasting Autonomy Commission recommended setting up a permanent authority, to be called the National Broadcasting Commission, to supervise the broadcast media. The Commission would be responsible to a parliamentary committee. It would have an active responsibility towards the management of the state broadcast media, as well as laying down guidelines, setting standards and awarding licences for private television and radio broadcasting.

The report was a radical one, whose recommendations, if adopted, would have transformed the national media. Though members of the commission were known as supporters of the ruling Awami League, the report in general was seen as an impartial and considered move towards improving the quality of broadcasting. For six months little was done about implementing the report's recommendations, either on management reform or on the wider issue of autonomy. The minister for information described it as too ambitious and said that it could not be implemented immediately. Whatever the difficulties, the broader implication seemed to be that implementation would require a larger investment in transparency, neutrality and accountability than Bangladesh's political culture could be expected to accommodate. In opposition, major political parties including the Awami League, have been the strongest advocates of media autonomy in Bangladesh. But as in India and Pakistan, the interests of the party in government have always seemed different.

Successive director generals of BTV have taken the view that talk of autonomy is premature. But if the government has not been willing to reduce state control, the issue of privatisation has proved less controversial, following a Sri Lankan rather than an Indian example. Pressure to open up television to the private sector began in the mid-1990s as a response to the plurality of choice offered by satellite channels. The government itself identified a need for an additional channel or channels, whether in the private sector or the public sector, to meet social and economic demand. Following the report of the Autonomy Commission, the Bangladesh government decided to go ahead with licensing a private terrestrial channel, without the need to create an autonomous institution to regulate it. It set up a committee to lay out the guidelines for applicants for a licence for the second channel, which the government later decided should be in the private sector. At first, this committee excluded news and current affairs from the remit of a private channel, but this was subsequently revoked in favour of a requirement to relay BTV's national news bulletins. Permission was given for local news to be originated, but government announcements were to be carried free of charge. Conditions were also set out for the granting of radio licences: a medium wave slot was allocated for a local radio station in Dhaka and applications were invited for FM licences.

The legal basis was provided through amendments to the *Indian Telegraph Act* of 1885. There was a requirement to broadcast special programmes on important national days and religious holidays. Advertisements were limited to 20 per cent of transmission time, but no limits were set on the amount of indigenous programmes that would be required. On this basis Ekushey TV or Channel 21, named after the martyrs of the 1952 Bengali language movement in East Pakistan, was given a licence both to operate the second terrestrial channel and to uplink a satellite service from within Bangladesh. There was to be no further terrestrial competition for at least two years, an assurance which was criticised both by potential rivals and by a lobby within the government.

Despite open scepticism about the government's commitment, the pressure for autonomy for the media continued. In December 1998, the government set up an inter-ministerial committee to review the Commission's report.[38] Other committees were to be appointed to frame laws relating to issues like service rules, revenue and financial powers, and a code of ethics. The expectation was that government would take action to implement reforms before the election due in 2001.

But before institutional changes could be brought about, the realities of competition were driving the state broadcasters to re-define their own role. In the area of news, criticisms of the state media long pre-dated the competition from cable and satellite. Here the important factor is credibility. The government set up its own informal 'media advisory group' which recommended a more professional approach to news making. As the capacity of the state media to produce news is restricted, a solution has been to commission news programmes from outside production houses. In this respect BTV is following a policy similar to India's Door-darshan, where news and current affairs programmes made by independent companies played a part in restoring the state broad-caster's credibility.

Bangladesh TV has commissioned programmes which include a type of investigative journalism. Many of them have been in-spired by the satellite news channels. Without threatening the government, they advance the credibility of the state media. The most popular one—*Poriprekhit*—began as a project to improve the quality of reporting. Originally funded by a non governmental agency, it was later taken up by a private production house. It is well received in general and its ratings outside Dhaka are very high.[39] Another programme—*Ghotonar Antorale*—was run on simi-lar lines, but it was less successful and was dropped in 1999. Those responsible for both programmes are prominent journalists known to be sympathetic to the government. Their objective has been to make news programmes more entertaining. Balanced and objective news reporting is not seen as the main aim.[40]

On the quality of news on the official media the Autonomy Commission report's own survey found a surprisingly high percentage of the audience (50 per cent) expressing satisfaction with the national news. But the report said that news making was determined by protocol rather than news priorities. The commission recommended that the guidelines for news production be changed. Parliamentary reporting should be extended, including allowing opposition views to be heard. As in India and Pakistan, politicians' outspokenness has proved an attraction for live parliamentary reporting on television, though the MPs themselves have not always welcomed the results. In the South Asian context, the televising of parliament offers a useful and relatively unmediated forum of open debate on current issues in public life.

The director general of BTV, Salahuddin Zaki, argues that those who criticise BTV or compare it unfavourably to the cable and satellite channels show a lack of understanding of the role of a national media outlet. 'Cable channels exist to entertain and earn money. BTV exists to provide a national perspective and not earn money.... BTV is driven by national concerns while cable by concerns for money. The approaches of both are quite different.'[41] State broadcasters in Bangladesh are unwilling to accept the maximisation of revenue as the criterion by which they should be judged. The purposes of rival commercial cable and satellite channels are seen as significantly different.

But if BTV does have a special role as a national public broadcaster, it is also a mirror of government priorities and popular expectations which are often in conflict with each other. Critics complain of its lack of public accountability and the organisation's focus on job security for its own staff, which is at odds with the service the public expects. Creativity cannot survive very well in a highly bureaucratised culture.[42]

BTV has been financially very profitable, though its management has little or no authority in the spending of its still-growing revenues. In that sense, BTV has not been forced, as Doordarshan was, into an acceptance of commercial realities to make up for reduced government subsidies, though the budget for television was cut in 1998. Like the Calcutta station of Doordarshan, BTV has had unrivalled reach in the rural areas and assured revenues to match. But the establishment of a second terrestrial channel changes that position. Its performance could also affect the future of satellite language channels serving both Bengals. The advertising market for Bengali television is growing, but the arrival of Ekushey TV looks set to test BTV where it is most vulnerable. The Bangladesh government faces a similar predicament with radio, though radio is cheaper to set up and there may be scope for more competition. The government may hope that both Bangladesh Radio and TV will be galvanised into more effective broadcasting by the new competition, but if government control remains as firm as ever, it is by no means certain that will happen. The government could face considerably higher bills to maintain the existing system.

NEPAL

Before 1990, India's brand of democratic party politics may have been an implicit threat to the Nepalese political system. But Doordarshan, as seen in Nepal, did not pose an alternative model to government control of television. In Nepal, politics rather than technology was the trigger for a new questioning of the role of the broadcast media. The rethinking of a new democratic order, following the constitutional reforms of 1990, also questioned the legitimacy of maintaining a tight grip on TV and radio. The satellite television revolution was a coincidence, providing an opportunity for more radical measures.

The pressures of democratic politics did stimulate broader strategic thinking. For the first time in Nepal, a task group was appointed in May 1992 to draw up a new communications policy. As a result of its report, the accelerating convergence of media and communications technologies was recognised by creating a combined Ministry of Information and Communication. This is a reform which Indian communications strategists have been recommending, so far without success, to their own government.

The report recommended that radio and television should be combined into a single National Broadcasting Authority. This authority was to be made autonomous but subject to parliamentary control—not only to a parliamentary committee but also to a board of governors made up of parliamentarians. However, when the report was submitted to the Nepali Congress government, it decided that the board of governors should be appointed by the government. According to Shailendra Raj Sharma, member secretary of the task group and a former head of Nepal Radio, the committee was also in favour of licences being given for commercial TV, but the published recommendation was confined to allowing private productions on the state channel.[43]

The National Communications Policy report was firmly in favour of autonomy, both for the electronic media and the Nepal Telecommunications Corporation. But setting up a truly autonomous institution proved more difficult. The National Broadcasting Act passed in 1992 left government in control of Nepal Radio and TV. Former Secretary of Communication, S.K. Jha maintains that 'autonomy has already been given'. The ministry does not interfere in programmes, but because Nepal does not have a long history of democratic practice, it cannot be full autonomy.[44] According to Sharma, 'in this part of the world, autonomy means less government control.'

At an early stage in the satellite TV era, it seemed that Nepal might be ahead of the field in being the first country to allow facilities to foreign broadcasters. Shailendra Raj Sharma believes that if it had played its cards right, Nepal could have become an uplinking centre for satellite TV on the Singapore or Hongkong model. It seems Business India TV had been given permission by the Nepal Congress government to uplink (though this is still disputed in some quarters), but once the Communists came to power they put tough additional conditions.[45] Sharma argues that this was a wasted opportunity.

One major problem faced by Nepal TV is that it cannot reach all its potential viewers because of the mountainous character of much of the country. It is therefore at a disadvantage compared to the satellite channels. Bandana Rana makes the point that many Nepalis can access satellite TV but cannot view Nepal TV. According to her, putting Nepal TV on satellite could double the number of viewers and is essential in order to develop a genuinely national audience.[46] Hem Bahadur Bista, journalist and former chairman of NTV, says even with satellite, as many as 40 per cent of Nepalis will not be able to access NTV in 10 year's time because of lack of electricity in some parts of the country. Even this may be an underestimate. But Bista argues strongly that the state broadcaster needs to be on satellite to combat the channels run by multinational media companies. Such an operation would also reach the large Nepali minority living in India. Raghuji Pant, former journalist and Communist Party of Nepal (United Marxist-Leninist) member of parliament, sees it as a means of creating international political pressure in favour of Nepali interests. 'For example, the Bhutan issue can be made as big as the Tibet issue', he suggests.[47] But the first hurdle is raising the money to make it happen. A feasibility study had been done but the costs were beyond NTV's existing budget.[48]

Pant is also in favour of developing the role of the private sector, both on Nepal TV and with separate private TV channels. Others agree on the benefits of private programming, but are conscious that the sector has a long way to go. Political analyst Dipak Gyawali is cautious about the viability of private TV, which he says would initially need government help to run.[49] Kanak Mani Dixit, publisher of *Himal* magazine, agrees that private sector TV standards are not rising: 'It is shameful to say that satellite TV is corrupting our society but not improving NTV programmes.' Kanak Dixit argues that NTV should be given more freedom, but crucially believes that it should be government-controlled for the time being.[50]

Nepal TV faces similar dilemmas to other national television stations in the satellite age. It is being deserted by the urban middle class, though it retains its audiences in the rural areas where cable has yet to penetrate. It is not in a very healthy financial condition. Advertising revenues are not expanding very fast; facilities and funds are limited and government finances are already being cut back.

Efforts to develop a private television sector have not met with great success. Several companies won licences for time-slots on Nepal TV in 1994, but not all of them proved profitable enough to continue.[51] According to S.K. Jha, the idea of allowing private TV channels in Nepal has been ruled out, but it is doubtful whether the market would support a second channel anyway.[52]

Radio Nepal is doing much better than Nepal TV. It has expanded the number of languages in which it broadcasts, from Nepali alone in 1990 to nine languages at the end of the decade. It is also making money renting out its transmitters and airwaves to foreign broadcasters and NGOs, including several UN organisations. But its revenues from advertising are under attack from the FM services to which it hired out its own airwaves and this trend seems set to continue as competition increases.

Radio has proved a much more promising field for diversification. For Kantipur FM, licensed time-slots on Radio Nepal served as a launch pad for the establishment of an independent station, which began broadcasting in 1998. The Kathmandu Municipality won another licence. There have also been some striking experiments in community radio, which are explored in the next chapter.[53]

The Nepalese government has been more innovative in its thinking about radio than any of its neighbours. But that has not prevented its licensing decisions from coming under careful scrutiny. Neer Shah, whose Shangri La television distribution company finds itself in very tough competition with a cable company which has been given special advantages, argues that there is a lack of transparency in administration and decision-making. Shah is one media entrepreneur among many in South Asia who argue for a level playing field. 'The private sector is prepared for any kind of media undertaking providing their interests are safeguarded. There has to be a bilateral and binding agreement between licence holders and the government'.[54]

Looking to the future, conditions seem ripe for an expansion of radio but much less so for TV. Cable TV seems the big growth area, which means the middle class in Nepal is mainly going to be fed a diet of imported programmes, whether Hindi or English. Indian companies aiming at the mass market continue to use Nepali TV, dub their advertisements in Nepali and in rare cases make Nepali adverts on location. But the Hindi satellite channels have provided them with a new means of reaching the Nepalese consumer market.

SRI LANKA

Sri Lankan governments retain wide-ranging reserve powers from the colonial period to deal with issues of national security and public order. These have been employed extensively to curb the media during the war against Tamil separatists in the north and Sinhalese insurgents in the south. Media liberalisation, which began in 1992, did not initially allow for any independent programming in news and current affairs. That began after the assassination of President Premadasa in May 1993. His successor, the patrician Dingiribanda Wijetunge, relaxed controls on the media as the political situation improved. The provincial elections of 1994, which gave the opposition Sri Lanka Freedom Party (SLFP) its first taste of power in seventeen years, provided the new commercial media with a chance to assert their independence. Significantly, there was no enabling legislation to usher in these changes.

The SLFP's gradual assumption of power—first at the provincial and then at the national level—was strongly backed by the Free Media movement, an organisation of journalists which had been courageously campaigning against abuses of state power and the victimisation of journalists during UNP rule. The SLFP itself, as the most prominent political victim of state control of the media, pledged in its manifesto to give greater independence to all media, particularly state radio and television, and once it had assumed office showed every sign of redeeming the pledge.

In October 1994, the minister of information in the new People's Alliance government, Dharmasiri Senanayake, submitted a note to the Cabinet which constituted a radical break with the past. The first policy statement on the media made by any government in Sri Lanka, it promised a major overhaul of previous government practice. It argued that media freedom was an integral part of the renewal of democracy and outlined a series of steps to create a 'new democratic media culture', including freeing existing media from government control and creating new institutions to guarantee media freedom and to raise quality and standards. All electronic media were to be granted the right of gathering and disseminating news, subject to a voluntarily agreed charter.

The same note to Cabinet also promised reform of existing legislation to strengthen freedom of expression and the right to information. To give effect to these promises, the minister appointed a committee which included leading lawyers, human rights activists and supporters of the Free Media movement to draw up a programme of legislative reform. The committee's report, which was completed in May 1996, is a model of liberal thinking on these issues which could stand comparison with any in the world. It proposed that an independent broadcasting authority oversee the implementation of broadcasting policy. This body, and not the government, would award and review licences to radio and television stations and be responsible for technical and programme standards. It also proposed that the editorial independence of state broadcasters be guaranteed by law.

The government's reaction to these liberal recommendations was a major disappointment to its media supporters. In March 1997, it gazetted new legislation establishing a Broadcasting Authority which disregarded most of them and left government with the last word in the awarding and renewing licences and general supervision of the media. This revelation of its hand prompted island-wide protests, not only by media organisations but also, ironically, by the UNP. Both these groups protested that the proposed authority would be dominated by officials and that no media personnel were included on the board. The then UNP media spokesman, Dr. Sarath Amunugama, said the bill was 'not only a violation of fundamental rights but also shows dictatorial tendencies.'[55]

The minister, Dharmasiri Senanayake, offered to accommodate amendments proposed by media groups, but most journalists were of the view the bill was so bad that it could not be amended and should be withdrawn. They demanded that the authority be independent of political control so that it could function in a manner that would protect the public interest and the independence of the media. [56]

These critics of the government had their hand strengthened in May by a judgement of the Supreme Court which struck down the proposed legislation as unconstitutional. This meant that the government would require a two-thirds majority of parliament and a referendum to get it passed into law–an impossible condition for the People's Alliance coalition. On 6 May 1997, quoting extensively from US cases on freedom of expression, the court held that the unfettered discretion given to the Authority could lead to a violation of the freedom of thought and information of individuals.[57]

As a result of the Supreme Court judgement, the government withdrew the proposed legislation and in the following year set up a select committee of parliament, chaired by a new minister of information, Mangala Samaraweera, to look into the formation of a Broadcasting Authority and a Media Council, and to reform existing legislation inhibiting freedom of expression. The brief given to the committee and the inclusion of leading opposition figures suggested strongly that government had climbed down, but in reality the whole process of reform had been put on ice. Pressure for reform from the Sri Lankan media continues. In 1998, a symposium on media freedom and social responsibility, supported by many leading media organisations, produced a 'Colombo declaration' which called for an end to the state control of broadcasting services and the establishment of a 'genuinely independent' Broadcasting Authority. But faced with an intensifying war in the north, growing opposition to its constitutional reform proposals and a testing period of provincial and presidential elections in 1999, the government opted for the status quo until these uncertainties were out of the way. President Kumaratunga, her own media honeymoon long since over, concentrated her fire more on the irresponsibility of some of her television critics—notably Shan Wickremesinghe's TNL—than on the inadequacies of existing systems of regulation. As elsewhere in South Asia, the increasing diversification of the media has come to be seen as a justification if not for a reversal of policy at least for a period of procrastination.

Diversification also continues, sometimes without much apparent thought for what the market will stand. What the UNP began, the People's Alliance government has speeded up, and state-controlled radio and television networks are now competing with an ever growing number of stations. In 1993, there were four terrestrial television channels; by 2000, this number had grown to eight.

During the same period, SLBC, the state-run radio with its different national and regional channels, had to face competition from four other radio stations, offering ten different services in Sinhala, English and Tamil. MTV's radio arm, MBC, is responsible for two pop music stations—Yes FM in English, and the Sinhala Sirisa FM—which have revolutionised radio programming with their enthusiastic, upbeat and participatory style of programming. State-controlled SLBC responded by launching its own FM pop music channel, Lakhanda. TNL, the television station, has its radio counterparts in TNL Radio and Isira, with some US affiliations. Colombo Communications had three radio channels—in English, Sinhala and Tamil—which were taken over and renamed at the end of 1999 by the owners of the terrestrial TV channel Swarnavahini. A later arrival, Sunrise Radio of the UK, has set up a joint venture with Sri Lankan partners to run a further three radio services.

In this process of diversification, the state has tended to favour its own and put its competitors at a technical disadvantage. As Graham Ironside, director of programmes for MTV, pointed out: 'This has meant that all television stations are not operating on a level playing field. Private channels have had to incur huge expenses to improve transmission quality and reach.'[58] An island-wide survey of television viewing completed in 1996 showed that Rupavahini was by far the most popular channel in the country, with 100 per cent coverage, followed by ITN with 96 per cent. This compared with 63 per cent for TNL and 56 per cent for MTV. Fourteen per cent of the respondents could only get Rupavahini and 18 per cent preferred it because of superior reception.[59] Gradually, however, successful commercial stations have extended their transmitter networks. By 1998, MTV claimed to cover 85 per cent of the country outside the war-affected north and east and to offer a better signal than Rupavahini in some parts of the south.

As a result of this commercial competition, Rupavahini and ITN have revamped their transmission network with Japanese aid and technology. They continue to have superior reach and larger audiences, but their share of advertising revenue is under pressure from competitors. According to Survey Research Lanka, Rupavahini's share of television advertising went down from 44 to 34 per cent between 1996 and 1997, while MTV's share went up from 22 to 25 per cent and newcomer Swarnavahini, with coverage of less than 30 per cent, weighed in at 14 per cent. These figures are contested by Rupavahini, which claims an increase to 45 per cent over the same period, but the pressure shows in the increasing commercialisation of its schedules.[60]

According to the Chairman, D.E.W. Gunasekera, 80 per cent of its programmes are now aimed at the commercial market and only 20 per cent are of a public service character. Gunasekera has said that he would like to see changes 'from the top down' to enable Rupavahini to compete more effectively with its commercial rivals. He told *TV Asia* magazine: 'We cannot continue to operate in the current framework. We need to be more flexible if we are going to be commercially successful. We have to operate more like a business.'[61]

In the field of radio, the dominance of SLBC has already been seriously undermined. The extraordinary success of Sirisa radio, which the Maharaja group claims has a 70 per cent market share, has put the SLBC on the defensive. Survey Research Lanka, which gives Sirisa a less pronounced lead, says SLBC's share of radio advertising declined from 25 per cent to 19 per cent between 1996 and 1997, while Sirisa and its English sister station, Yes FM, remained at over 50 per cent. Colombo Communication's three channels witnessed a rise to 23 per cent. SLBC's efforts to win back younger audiences by starting its own FM pop music channel—Lakhanda—seems to have eaten into its own revenues rather than those of its competitors.[62]

Unrestricted competition has had negative results, particularly in television. There has been an extension of choice and more scope for creativity, but severe financial pressures have affected standards, particularly in the less well-established stations. Shevanthi Jayasuriya, the marketing director of MTV, told us: 'We welcome competition…but now it is getting a bit too suffocating…. What is going to happen is that everyone will get cluttered screens plus low quality programming…. Stations don't have the money to buy quality programmes….'[63] With eight terrestrial channels operating in a relatively small market in a time of economic stagnation, the result has been a price war. Deepthi Senanayake, Media Director of J. Walter Thompson, told us: 'It's only with Rupavahini that we stick to rates; even with ITN, to a great extent, we negotiate. Negotiating is now the game.'[64]

The intensity of the competition has put state-funded broadcasters under acute financial pressure, particularly SLBC, which has lost market share faster than Rupavahini and ITN. In 1997, with revenues from licence fees relatively static, SLBC Chairman, Janadasa Peiris, had to put the organisation on a crisis footing to make ends meet. Regional stations were set new financial targets and they began to actively canvass local businesses to raise more revenue. Plans were also drawn up to slim down staff drastically over the next few years. At that time, Peiris estimated that SLBC could run on half its staff and offered generous redundancy packages to cut the wage bill.[65]

What has been lost in this increased commercial competition is any distinct sense of a separate purpose for the state sector. According to the late Professor A. J. Gunawardena, an influential literary

critic and media watcher, 'public service broadcasting is by and
large drying up in this country—not only the format but also the
philosophy.' Gunawardena regarded the preservation of the
licence fee in these circumstances as 'totally immoral and ille-
gitimate'. It was merely a residual reminder of Sri Lanka's colonial
broadcasting tradition, which he dubbed 'the British model...
without the independence of the BBC'.[66]

Meanwhile, the ground on which the debate is taking place is
beginning to shift. The working of the commercial media has
convinced some intellectuals that there is now a case for government to retain a channel of its own. Sunil Bastian, a political
scientist who has worked extensively on the island's ethnic conflict,
believes that citizens will benefit if the government does have its
own voice. Bastian points to the private media's treatment of the
government's constitutional proposals to solve the ethnic problem
as proof of his contention. 'If we had a situation where only the
private media existed', he says, 'it is quite possible that extreme
Sinhala opinion, supported by a section of the private media,
would have been able to bury it immediately'. Bastian argues that
the state has to step in to cover the interests of those who cannot
compete in the market.[67]

One significant outcome of discussion groups in Sri Lanka is
the residual respect in which government media are held, even in
the news field, where their shortcomings as purveyors of government propaganda and the lack of credibility of the state media in
reporting the war in the north and the east are widely understood.
Almost all participants in group discussions, asked to indicate
their preferred viewing, listed Rupavahini in the first three, and
the majority, particularly those outside Colombo, put it first, with
news and teledramas the favourite programmes. 'Although the
news is still presented in a somewhat traditional manner', said
one discussant, 'people still have faith in the national TV and ITN....
They are aware of business and political interests behind the
private television companies.'[68]

The need for a new regulatory authority in Sri Lanka, which
will balance the market and the public interest, ensure a level playing field for competition, respect for the pluralities of language
and region, and minimum standards of excellence and accountability is now widely accepted. The difficult issue is the role of the
state in the new dispensation and the extent to which it is prepared

to yield power to a new body. However, delay is only accelerating the trend towards unrelieved commercialism, despite the urgent need for greater clarity on questions of public interest.

CONCLUSION

In this chapter we have looked at different dimensions of the challenge to South Asian broadcasting systems posed by the new media and at the responses of the different nation states. We have argued that the dilemmas of competition and control go beyond media policy, raising questions of the nature of state institutions, the responsibilities of the state to its citizens and the space allowed for the development of local, regional and national differentiation.

There has been a high degree of continuity in law and practice in the management of state-controlled media. But the new media have required an approach to regulation which is not easily accommodated within the established framework. The problems are recognised and South Asian governments have set up committees to recommend how to tackle them. The speed of technological developments, however, has tended to outstrip the ability of governments to catch up with their administrative and legislative implications.

The attractions of commercial revenue for state broadcasters were accepted and exploited long before they faced competition from the satellite channels. The value of radio as a medium of advertising was shown by Sri Lanka in the 1950s and India followed suit. That precedent established that in order to attract advertising, attitudes to programming had to be re-thought, at least on commercial channels.

In facing the challenge of satellite television, it was natural for governments to expect that state broadcasters should take full commercial advantage of a broadcasting infrastructure built up over thirty years or more. Their monopoly of terrestrial broadcasting gave the state broadcasters an unrivalled reach, which the advertisers valued and were prepared to pay for. But exploiting this advantage to its full revenue potential, as the Indian government did from 1992 onwards, involved paying a price that had not been fully calculated. It challenged the whole ethos of broadcasting.

Where the state broadcaster in India had rationed the diet of Hindi films, film-based programmes, quiz shows and other programmes, its commercial competitors had no such inhibitions. The state broadcasters responded to this kind of competition by selling time to independent producers and by re-broadcasting foreign channels. Doordarshan brought MTV into its schedules. PTV and BTV allowed time in theirs for foreign news channels, both CNN and BBC, to win back the English speaking audience for international news. Rupavahini came to an agreement with Discovery.

India avoided playing host to foreign news channels, but commissioned independent Indian producers of news and current affairs programmes to bring a fresh look and more attractive production values into their output. This helped to develop a resource and expertise which was also available to the satellite channels. Programmes first seen on the state channel could move to the satellite sector. Presenters and television journalists who had established their reputations on Doordarshan became available for Star and Zee TV as they extended their output into regional news and current affairs.

Many aspects of the satellite revolution can be brought under a degree of control. But where market forces were working most powerfully, the state monopoly of news or the control of news by direct censorship ceased to be a realistic option. India is now extremely well covered by the satellite media and the competition has had a galvanising effect on Doordarshan. But coverage of other parts of the region is less systematic and the arguments for accepting new realities with good grace and allowing competition in this field have not proved so convincing. Even in India, the government has specified that the new independent FM radio stations should not carry news. Only in Sri Lanka, where the broadcasters themselves seized the initiative in 1994, have private terrestrial radio and TV stations successfully broken this ground.

The resilience of the nation state in defending its broadcasting territory is a marked feature of the 1990s. The legacy of bureaucratic and political control remains extremely influential and the whole process of re-appraisal has been marked, in the words of one broadcaster, by '...confusion, benign neglect, and hoping the matter will resolve itself'.[69] The state has embraced the market but it has been reluctant to tackle the key issues of public interest which the market has raised. At a time when both the state broadcasters and the new private channels were looking for clear guidance on the bounds within which they should operate, this lack of political will left commercial pressures by default as the determining factor in their development. Sri Lanka's experience is a clear illustration of the benefits and dangers of unfettered competition but the government has chosen not to intervene.

In the absence of a clear vision from the states themselves, the strength and independence of the judiciary has been an important influence in furthering broadcasting reform. In India, since the 1995 Supreme Court judgement declared the airwaves to be public property, successive Indian governments have been under an obligation to divest themselves of direct regulatory responsibilities. The United Front government made an unsuccessful attempt to do so with the publication of the Broadcasting Bill of 1997. In Pakistan, despite public interest appeals to the courts, several years passed without any judgements being given. The courts in Sri Lanka, on the other hand, have shown that they have a role to play. Though generally conservative on media issues, the Sri Lankan Supreme Court's rejection of the status of the Broadcasting Authority proposed under the 1997 bill on the grounds that it was not genuinely autonomous, showed its potential to redirect the terms of the broadcasting debate.

In India, Bangladesh and Sri Lanka, governments are faced with an expectation, fostered either by their own political commitments or a judicial and constitutional obligation, that they will take steps to devolve some of their own powers. But governments have preferred to come up with piecemeal solutions under existing legislation, while retaining political control. Bangladesh has taken a major step in licensing a second terrestrial TV channel but has side-stepped the central recommendations of the Autonomy Commission report. The drawback to this approach has been that the awarding of licences has come under the suspicion of political cronyism. Contracts awarded in Pakistan, Nepal and Bangladesh have incurred this suspicion, and even in India the government that created the autonomous Prasar Bharati is accused by its critics of having packed the board with its own sympathisers.

In the new accommodation between state and market which has characterised the last decade, those cultures which correspond most closely to viable markets have had the best chance of exploiting the new broadcasting media. India's largest and most prosperous economic regions have generated successful satellite television services; the smaller and less prosperous, including some accounting for tens of millions of people, have had a sense that the running was being made elsewhere.

Nepal TV's struggle to compete against the powerful resources of the Hindi satellite channels for urban audiences in its own country is a good example of the scale of the challenge faced by smaller states and countries in this new world. How Nepal TV should respond is a question of wider relevance. Does a small and relatively poor country have to accept that it will be overwhelmed by the media products of its larger and more powerful neighbour? How can a state broadcaster in such a country play an effective role? It is clear that for Nepal, as for other countries, the reform of state television is a key element in any strategy for the future. It is also a matter of judging which medium is best suited to which objectives. This study has shown that at least in its initial phase, except in South India and Sri Lanka, the satellite revolution has tended to reinforce a well-established process of centralisation in the management of the state media. It is arguable, however, that a more effective defence of culture and community could be mounted with other media at other levels of society. In the next chapter we look at the role of television and radio in providing a voice for community in different South Asian states and at the scope for decentralisation in the future.

NOTES AND REFERENCES

1. Section 124A.
2. Selvakumaran and Edrisinha's view is that there is 'a fundamental weakness in most of the laws dealing with media freedom (in Sri Lanka)': N. Selvakumaran and Rohan Edrisinha (eds) (1995), 'Excessive Deference to the interests of the State', *Mass Media Laws and Regulations in Sri Lanka*, p. 60.
3. Siddhartha Ray, Editor, *Cable Waves*, Delhi, May 1998.
4. P. Upendra, Delhi, July 1998.
5. E.g., M. Madhvani, Mumbai, May 1998.
6. J.S. Kohli and Y. Radhakrishnan, InCable Network, Mumbai, April 1998.
7. *Ibid*.
8. 'It could be argued that Doordarshan programmes before the commercial age were so poor that they could scarcely get any worse. There is no truth in the story that this channel (DD3) was so named because only three people would see it.' Report of the Expert Committee on the Marketing of Commercial Time of All India Radio and Doordarshan: Recommendations for the Adoption of Suitable Strategies (The Sen Committee 1996).

9. Summary of the judgement delivered by Justice B.P. Sawan Reddy of the Supreme Court of India; cited in Sengupta Report, Annexure 3, p. 42.
10. National Media Policy, A working paper submitted by the Sub-committee of the Consultative Committee of the Ministry of Information and Broadcasting, Government of India, March 1996.
11. George Verghese, Delhi, June 1998.
12. Jaipal Reddy, Delhi, July 1998.
13. Ashok Mansukhani, Mumbai, May 1998.
14. Anjan Mitra, *Business Standard*, 31 December 1998.
15. For a fuller discussion of the development of FM radio in India, see, Chapter 9.
16. Sevanti Ninan, *The Hindu*, 18 July 1999.
17. Information provided by the minister of information and broadcasting on 28 June 1995, quoted by Javed Jabbar in *News International*, 16 July 1995.
18. Sabih Mohsin, Former Director of Programmes, Pakistan Broadcasting Corporation, Karachi, March 1998.
19. Mushahid Hussain, Islamabad, January 1999.
20. For an account of the award of the NTM contract, see Javed Jabbar and Qazi Faez Isa (eds) (1997), *Mass Media Laws and Regulations in Pakistan*, pp. 118–22.
21. *Ibid.*, pp. 124–25.
22. For the text of the ordinance see *Ibid.*, pp. 424–31.
23. Agha Nasir, Islamabad, January 1999.
24. Aslam Azhar, Islamabad, November 1997.
25. Interview quoted in Naween Mangi's article in the *Friday Times*, 13–19 February 1998.
26. *The Nation*, 10 June 1998.
27. Ijaz Gilani, Islamabad, January 1999.
28. Mahommed Malik, Islamabad, March 1998.
29. Satish Anand, Karachi, May 1998.
30. Taher Khan, Managing Director, Interflow, Karachi, November 1997.
31. Akhtar Viqar Azim and Shaukat Parvez, Islamabad, January 1999.
32. The *Jang* group resisted demands by the Muslim League government that some of its senior journalists should be dismissed and subsequently found its access to newsprint restricted and its commercial operations under investigation by a number of government departments. For a period, until these political problems were resolved, it was obliged to produce its main titles in a severely reduced form.
33. Imran Aslam, Karachi, May 1998.
34. Mushahid Hussain, Islamabad, January 1999.
35. The Ordinance, announced by Javed Jabbar on 7 April and due to be promulgated in May 2000, was to set up a Regulatory Authority for Media Broadcast Organisations (RAMBO) with powers to licence broadcasters at the national, provincial, district and local levels. Interview, Javed Jabbar, London, 13 April 2000.
36. Articles 16, 17 and 18 of the Act were omitted. Abu Nasr and Md Gaziul Hoque (eds) (1992), *Mass Media Laws and Regulations in Bangladesh*, p. 245.
37. *Ibid.*, pp. 38–39.
38. *Daily Sangbad*, 30 December 1998.
39. Syed Borhan Kabir, Dhaka, April 1998.

40. Media South Asia discussion with members of the media advisory group, Dhaka, May 1998.
41. Syed Salahuddin Zaki, Dhaka, March 1998.
42. Chinmoy Mutsuddi, Dhaka, March 1998.
43. Shailendra Raj Sharma, Former Head of Nepal Radio, Kathmandu, May 1998.
44. S.K. Jha, Secretary of Communications, Kathmandu, March 1998.
45. Cf. Jamim Shah, Space Time Network, Kathmandu, May 1998. Jamim Shah maintains that BITV never had uplinking permission and that their float on the stock market on this basis was a deception.
46. Bandana Rana, Kathmandu, May 1998.
47. Raghuji Pant, Kathmandu, May 1998.
48. Hem Bahadur Bista, Kathmandu, May 1998.
49. Dipak Gyawali, Kathmandu, May 1998.
50. Kanak Mani Dixit, Kathmandu, July 1998.
51. The evening franchise dropped out quickly. The morning one continued. It was run by a TV software production company with fewer overhead costs. Advertisements remained scarce.
52. S.K. Jha, Kathmandu, March 1998.
53. See, Chapter 9, pp. 330–32.
54. Neer Shah, Kathmandu, March 1998.
55. *Sunday Times*, 13 April 1997.
56. *Sunday Times*, 4 May 1997.
57. Article by Kishali Pinto Jayawardana, *Sunday Times*, 11 May 1997.
58. Graham Ironside, Colombo, March 1998.
59. See S.W.R. Samarasinghe, 'Reading, Listening and Watching: A National Sample Survey of the Sri Lankan News Media', in G.H. Peiris [see p. 291]. The statistics on the coverage of the different channels are from Victor Gunawardena (1996), 'More Responsive and Responsible Media', unpublished manuscript, ICES, Kandy, as quoted in the same survey report.
60. *Survey Research Lanka Fact File*, January 1998. For an analysis of trends for 1998, see, Ananda Rajapakse, *Lanka Monthly Digest*, April 1998.
61. Interview with D.E.W. Gunasekere, *TV Asia*, July 1997.
62. *SRL Fact File*, January 1998.
63. Shevanthi Jayasuriya, Colombo, April 1998.
64. Deepthi Senanayake, Colombo, July 1998.
65. Janadasa Peiris, Colombo, February 1998. Peiris later told the *Sunday Times* that 65 per cent of SLBC's revenues were being spent on salaries and he wanted to bring staff numbers down from 2000 to 750. See *Sunday Times*, 24 May 1998.
66. A.J. Gunawardena, Colombo, June 1998.
67. Sunil Bastian, Colombo, December 1998.
68. Traders and technicians, Matara, May 1998.
69. Syed Salahuddin Zaki, Dhaka, March 1998.

Nine

BROADCASTING AND COMMUNITY

Earlier chapters of this book have looked at the economics of the new satellite market, the emergence of powerful new satellite media in North and South India and at the implications of the growing dominance of these media for the state's control over broadcasting and for its wider responsibilities. One of our conclusions is that the working of the satellite market, particularly in the northern subcontinent, has reinforced the national at the expense of the sub-national or regional. Satellite programmes in Hindi have been undermining the popularity of other Indian regional language services, as well as the appeal of state broadcasters in Pakistan, Bangladesh and Nepal to their own urban middle classes. At the same time, most states have reacted defensively to these commercial challenges; they have sought to maintain their centralised broadcasting systems and in doing so have contributed to the process of homogenisation. These trends raise important questions about the future articulation of regional and community cultures, while the growing concentration of broadcasting services on the middle class market raises other concerns about the failure of the new media to address the problems of those South Asians who live below the poverty line.

In this chapter, we examine the past efforts and future potential of both radio and television to serve regions and communities. We have interpreted 'community' very broadly to include everything from the requirements of development at village level to the needs of large cities to have their own electronic media for information, public participation and entertainment. Such an approach is justifiable only because the centralisation of government in almost all South Asian countries stands in the way of achieving such objectives, whether the creation of community radio or of local radio for the urban centres. A growing lobby is emerging in South Asia for more decentralisation of the media as a means both of strengthening civil society and promoting effective development. We argue in this chapter that tackling this issue has to be at the centre of any programme for change, whether it is pursued through the creation of autonomous institutions or the reform of existing government and broadcasting structures.

TV AND DEVELOPMENT: EARLY EXPERIMENTS

It was symptomatic of how India's political masters saw the role of television in the early days that it was first used systematically for development purposes. The famous SITE experiment, which was managed by the Indian Space Research Organisation (ISRO) at Ahmedabad, deployed satellite technology to encourage farmers to improve food production. There could be no better illustration of Nehru's vision of the 'scientific temper' in action.[1]

Elsewhere in the world, television was targeted first at the middle class—those with the purchasing power to buy the sets. It was not targeted according to need. In India, the government decided to develop a different model. As P.C. Joshi, who chaired the 1983 enquiry into the future of Indian broadcasting, put it: 'We said that we must break that vicious circle; we will make it possible for TV to reach the poor. We will defy the logic and limits set by the market.'[2]

Bridging the gap between the satellite and the poor farmer involved setting up television sets in community centres in a range of different locations throughout India. Many of those involved had never seen TV before. They gathered for the programmes at particular times of day in conditions supervised by others. It was a didactic experience. It was successful up to a point, carried along on its novelty value and the enthusiasm of those directing it. But it also illustrated some of the problems of using television for development.

One of the lessons learnt was that television programmes need to be followed up on the ground. There needs to be close co-ordination between programme makers and schedulers and the agricultural extension workers in the field. This lesson also has implications for the scale on which programmes are conceived. In a vast country like India, national programmes about practical farming do not work well. Farmers need to be addressed in their own language; they need to see their own kind taking up new methods in order to be convinced themselves.

George Verghese, who chaired the report into Indian broadcasting which eventually led to the creation of Prasar Bharati, makes the point that SITE also met with political obstruction. The state government in Gujarat did not like the fact that scientists, sociologists and anthropologists 'were making people aware of their rights'.[3]

What killed it off, however, was the growth of India's ordinary television services. Once the regional station at Ahmedabad started broadcasting prime time entertainment, the community sets were switched to those programmes and the special SITE agricultural programmes began to lose their audiences. Television for development in a vacuum was one thing; competing with mainstream entertainment was another.

In a competitive commercial environment, any programme that does not make money tends to be broadcast at inconvenient times. South Asian state television traditionally saw development as a key area of broadcasting, but this sector has suffered from relative neglect in the new era of satellite competition. Each country can point to some outstanding programmes. But neither the timing nor the production standards of the general run of development programmes have attracted large audiences.

In India, the SITE experiment never became a blueprint for television nation-wide. It was followed by other important local initiatives managed by the Indian Space Research Organisation. In Kheda district in Gujarat, which had been part of the SITE scheme, a TV service was set up broadcasting half-an-hour a day which introduced weekly teleserials in local dialects, as well as specific programmes for farmers, for landless labourers, women and children. The project also developed village writers and made some progress in evolving 'a people-oriented participatory TV system'.[4] It did raise conscientiousness on social issues but it underestimated the importance of entertainment and there were problems of access to TV for the poorest viewers.[5] Another television service, the Jhabua Development Communications project, was broadcasting two hours a day to 150 villages in Madhya Pradesh in the late 1990s. By that stage, the range of programmes had widened to include entertainment as well as watershed management, health and local self-government. There was also more emphasis on interactive training using modern video equipment.[6] It proved difficult, however, whether on grounds of cost or logistics, to replicate these experiments in TV stations across the country. As George Verghese puts it: 'Individual stations have been innovative.... But this has been a one-off kind of success... dropped when the station director is changed...not institutionalised....'[7]

The situation in Bangladesh is very similar. A BTV producer told us: 'The Government doesn't have any specific plan to produce development programmes in any given year. What they have is a broad idea that a large part of their programmes will be devoted to projection of government activities. And producers are assigned accordingly. Neither research nor felt needs are a factor.' A senior producer in the same department said: 'We don't get any freedom to be creative nor any support to produce quality programmes. We have to follow orders.... We can serve the people but our institution puts great limitations....'[8]

THE ROLE OF NON-GOVERNMENTAL ORGANISATIONS IN TELEVISION PROGRAMMES

The involvement of non-governmental organisations (NGOs) in the making of development programmes shows what can be done with adequate resources and commitment. Bangladesh, with its very large NGO sector, is a good example. NGOs were kept out of the official media in the 1980s. There was a feeling that it was the government's responsibility to handle development communications, even though it worked with NGOs on particular projects. In the 1990s, this government attitude began to change and NGOs in Bangladesh invested heavily in communications. By the end of the decade, some NGOs were ahead of the government in communication technology and its use. They were beginning to use audio-visual techniques for training, for programme communication and advocacy. Government remained jealous of its prerogatives, but some NGO productions, particularly those funded by international agencies, were accepted for re-broadcasting on state television. A small number of NGOs also emerged as trend setters in communication hardware, with on-line editing and other digital facilities.[9]

One public service success to emerge from this sort of collaboration was the *Voters Education Programme* broadcast before the national elections of 1996. These programmes, which were funded by UNDP and made by independent production houses, were designed to encourage women to vote and aired for a month before the polls. They were also backed up by the activities of NGOs in the field. According to Salahuddin Zaki, the managing director of BTV: 'This was one of the great moments of BTV. We inspired many women to vote.'[10] Though no independent evaluation was done to show the exact influence of TV on the issue, the women's vote in 1996 was the highest ever and the agencies judged the content, quality and scheduling a success.[11]

Another acknowledged success was *Shabuj Shathi*, a 13-part drama serial which was intended to enhance the social status and visibility of family planning service providers in rural areas. The serial was written by Humayun Ahmed, one of the country's most successful playwrights, and paid for by the Family Planning Department. *Shabuj Shathi* was perceived as a drama serial and not a family planning programme and that is why it appears to have been successful. It worked at the creative level, unlike many other programmes which are didactic and unimaginatively produced. It was voted one of the ten best programmes irrespective of categories in 1998 and led the ministry of information to approach international agencies for support for other series on similar themes.

These successes in Bangladesh reflect the scale of the NGO sector, the relatively homogeneous nature of the society and the fact that BTV was still in a comfortable monopolistic position. Across the border in West Bengal, NGO investment in television is much less dramatic. According to Anuradha Mukherjee of TVE, development agencies in West Bengal have not tried to use the media, except on occasions when a minister is invited to inaugurate or speak at a workshop or project. UNICEF has shown some spots on Doordarshan, but has found it extremely difficult to maintain its foothold in the new financial climate.[12]

West Bengal's share of the Indian development budget certainly does not compare with resources available across the border and NGOs in West Bengal are not big enough to be able to afford the mass media. If they use the audio-visual medium, they prefer to restrict their communication activities to low cost measures like organising public screenings of films. Only when there is a specific campaign which incorporates a budget for media intervention is the mass media used.[13]

In Pakistan, the working of the new media market has also reduced the space for development programmes on state television. In the days before PTV decided to revamp its schedules to take on the satellite competition, it gave more space to development messages paid for by NGOs, and even made development programmes free of charge at the request of particular ministries. As one NGO media specialist put it: 'There was plenty of loose time and not too many sponsors.' As soon as it decided to tackle its financial crisis, it ceased to carry programmes without sponsorship, even programmes suggested by government departments, and finding space for development programmes became more difficult.[14] Development had been a priority in principle but there seems to have been little thought about how to find space for it in a new, more commercially driven environment.

There are some countervailing trends. Some of UNICEF's global messages are now being carried on BBC and CNN. Raana Syed, a development communications expert, told us: 'BBC has set the trend in social issue programming and others are following. There is also a trend to take up and cover special days like UN Environment Day. These are positive signs.'[15] However, there are dangers too. In the new financial climate, the fact that some international NGOs can afford to pay competitive prices for TV exposure means that they are seen as fulfilling a revenue as well as a development requirement, and in the process are acting as a substitute for the devotion of state sector resources to development issues.

TV TRENDS AND THE REQUIREMENTS OF DEVELOPMENT

Satellite television itself has done very little for the social sector. Most satellite channels, particularly in the highly competitive Hindi language area, are involved in an intensive battle for the mass audience which relies on films, serials and other entertainment programmes as its main weapons. Ashish Sen of Action Aid told us that the only satellite channel he had managed to interest in making programmes on development issues was Business India TV, which subsequently folded because of the pressures of the market place.[16] Though there is scope for teleserials to deal with development issues, most of them aim at the urban middle class and most concentrate on love, sex and personal relationships in that setting.

Satellite television has provoked copycat programming from the state sector and a diversion of resources away from public service broadcasting. In Pakistan, for example, the challenge of satellite television has led to a concentration of the resources of the state sector on combating foreign broadcasts. More money has been spent on entertainment and less is available for serving regional audiences or development purposes. Ataullah Baluch, a senior producer with a development brief in the Quetta station of PTV, says the focus on entertainment is irrelevant to the needs of most the population of Baluchistan. 'The majority of our population lives...below the poverty line. Their priority is access to safe drinking water, health care facilities, education.... TV is a luxury for them.'[17] What he would like to see is greater opportunity to tackle these issues in the languages of the local people. This is something which radio is doing and can do more successfully than television, not least because 40 per cent of Baluchistan's villages still have no power supply.

Some development agencies have now written television off as too expensive and too unfocussed for effective development communication. Rajive Jain of CENDIT, an Indian charity which has been working to democratise communication since 1973, believes that television is not really working as a development tool. He says: 'Broadcasting is centralised. Only to the extent that you can develop interactive two-way communication is broadcasting and narrowcasting technology useful and relevant and helpful for development'.[18] Jain even goes as far as to say that 'broadcasting is anti-development'. CENDIT has given up broadcasting and is concentrating on narrowcasting. It is promoting the use of video in rural situations linked to discussion and dialogue. It is also promoting localised production.

There are well-established regional language television services in India, with localised production and distribution, even if they are not competing very effectively with the satellite channels. But they have never been used effectively for rural development. P.C. Joshi says: 'Decentralisation has never been tried...there was hardly any development communication on TV. Radio did much more.'[19] In Pakistan, regional language television is still in embryo. It does not exist at all in Nepal, Bangladesh or Sri Lanka and there seems little prospect of television being decentralised in any of these countries in the foreseeable future.

The Sri Lankan case is an interesting example. Had Sri Lanka not been plunged into civil war, Jaffna could have been an alternative television centre. But the war destroyed much of Jaffna and neither state radio nor television operate there, except on a limited scale under military supervision. The companies with existing TV franchises do not think it makes commercial sense to decentralise TV production. Shevanthi Jayasuriya of MTV says: 'You can't decentralise media too much here. We are not like the USA. Even the provincial radio stations aren't too successful. I think it's a waste of money.'[20] Nalaka Gunawardene of Television Trust for the Environment, who favours decentralisation in principle, also believes there is only 'limited potential...I doubt if there is enough market capital, enough demand in terms of regionalised media production, for it to be viable.'[21]

CABLE AND COMMUNITY

The spread of cable television in South Asian cities has provided a new system of distribution which is already being used in some areas for limited community services. These cable networks have drawn on a wide range of local skills and given a neighbourhood focus to the new media. By the end of the 1990s, however, the community potential of cable was threatened by the growing pace of consolidation. In India particularly, small operators were being taken over by bigger businesses and three or four national cable networks had emerged as the dominant players. In this situation, the role of government became crucial if the potential of cable for community purposes was to be realised.

The Development of Cable in Pakistan and Bangladesh

In Pakistan, cable has only developed significantly in Karachi, where local initiatives have brought entertainment within the reach of even the poorest households. In working class Karachi, the cable operator is running a system which depends on a range of illegal activities for its survival, from unauthorised connections to blatant infringement of copyright. The fact that many Pakistani cable operators design their own schedules, drawing on the best of Hindi satellite programmes and their own TV and film culture, demonstrates a sensitivity to audience requirements which PTV took much longer to emulate. A survey carried out in 1998 in working-class Lyari district brings out the inventiveness of cable operators in providing their own special mix of entertainment.[22] In some places, cable operators were acting as censors on behalf of their customers and changing their menus during religious festivals to provide more sober programmes. But there has been very little generation of local programming.

The same is also the case in Bangladesh. Investigations in Dhaka produced some evidence of cable operators broadcasting local cultural programmes, videos of local cricket matches or variety shows put on by children from the neighbourhood. But these were exceptions. Most Dhaka cable operators confine themselves to relays of entertainment and sports channels and show little interest in making local programmes.[23]

The cable industry in Pakistan remained in a kind of legal limbo until early 2000, when the military government introduced a system of licensing and announced plans to decentralise the media. In Bangladesh, the government had earlier produced a draft memorandum of understanding which specifically forbade cable operators to do more than relay satellite feeds. It was an area in which government seemed determined to ensure compliance and the inhibitions of the operators were reinforced by the prospect of such activity becoming a punishable offence.

Media commentators in Bangladesh believed that the government was making a mistake in forbidding neighbourhood broadcasting.[24] In a globalising media world in which the middle classes are hooked on international channels and spurn BTV, they argued that cable offered a means of reinforcing local culture. Chinmoy Mutsuddi of *Binodon Bichitra* magazine went as far as to say that '...the future of Bangla culture lies in...community or neighbourhood TV.' He told us that Bangladeshis 'are getting used to the glamorous productions of Mumbai. The local culture has been forced to retreat and if money is going to be such a factor, we may end up with these cable units as our suppliers of local culture.'[25] Mutsuddi accepted that cable operators were not professionally equipped to make neighbourhood programmes. But he argued that the government should make space for them to do so.

Consolidation and its Consequences: The Case of Chennai

In India, where cable networks are more extensive and more profitable than elsewhere, a process of consolidation now threatens the survival of the smaller operator. As channels and suppliers try to maximise their profitability, franchisees are often caught uncomfortably between the demands of the supplier and the intractability of the subscriber. Moreover, where franchisees do not co-operate with the supplier, others can be set up to take their place.

In Chennai, smaller cable operators have put up spirited resistance to the encroachments of big companies in order to preserve their own independence. A number of operators got together and set up a head-end to serve all their franchisees and any others who wanted to join. They became a jointly-managed Multi System Operator (MSO) with a single control room giving feeds to their customers. Within a year of the first arrangement, ten such head-ends had been established, enabling them to compete more effectively with the pan-Indian companies.[26]

According to reports from Chennai, once Siti Cable and Rahejas entered Chennai, they tried to eliminate the other MSOs. The strategy was to sponsor rival operators from the same locality and offer them the link free of charge. Jayastree, one of six partners of the Cable Vision Network (CVN), the head-end of the entire Adyar area, complained that she had cables cut and signals jammed constantly by the cable operator of a neighbouring area. Because the police were unwilling to intervene, she was obliged to concede some of her connections to him.

As part of their counter-strategy, most MSOs in southern Chennai launched their own cable channels in the first nine months of 1999. Earlier, local operators occasionally disconnected a vernacular language channel or sports channel and screened a film instead. What is now happening is more systematic, with much more emphasis on the local, which has met with a positive viewer response.

The programmes broadcast include game shows and quiz shows recorded in local schools, coverage of local religious activities, and soap operas bought from software producers. Most local channels have clearly defined times for particular audiences. Typically, early morning is for the older generation when programmes on religion, yoga, health and astrology are broadcast. Though telecasting of news bought from agencies like PTI and UNI is illegal, some cable head-ends have started local news programmes covering events in south Chennai. News broadcasts generally cover local robberies and thefts, transport stories, shop openings, special events, visitors, local personalities and obituaries. The news programmes have become popular and local residents call in and pass on important messages. Some cable operators carry more ambitious programming. PHS Cable and CVN relayed a one day cricket match between India and Pakistan along with locally generated advertisements. PHS Cable even advertised and relayed a popular Tamil soap opera—Min Bimbangal's *Marmma Desam*—just as it went off air on Sun TV.

Most of these cable channels earn their revenue through local advertising. The recovery is slow but steady. Some cable operators produce advertisements for their local clients. Others, like CVN, have managed to attract additional advertisements from significant local businesses. Only multinational companies like Citibank have kept aloof from the local cable advertising market and this is a sign of the progress it has made in a short period.

Though south Chennai has witnessed some innovative developments, the speed of technological convergence and the need for substantial investment put the new MSOs under constant pressure. Their next challenge is the introduction of the Internet. Those cable networks with the funds to invest in fibre-optic technology will be able to offer subscribers telephone and Internet connections through the same system. The Tamil Nadu state government called meetings with cable TV operators in mid-1999 to discuss their involvement in the Internet, but only Universal and Rahejas were ready for the high investment involved.

In the competition between the larger consortia and the smaller operators, the legal fragility of the cable industry is another disadvantage. Though the Cable Act of 1995 provided recognition for their operations on payment of a licence fee, the absence of full legal recognition of their status as an industry hampers the efforts of smaller MSOs to fight off competition. According to reports from Chennai, banks are not yet willing to give loans for the small scale industry sector.

The growing dominance of the large consortia poses a serious threat to the use of cable for community purposes. It is a sign of the urgency of the situation that no cable operator we interviewed in Chennai believed that they would be able to hold out against 'the big sharks', not even those who had so far managed to survive by combining their operations. The draft Broadcasting Bill of 1997 stipulated that cable operators should only relay material; they were not to be allowed to generate their own programmes. These stipulations show even a relatively liberal government's instinct to re-establish control and to eliminate whatever cable has contributed to media diversity, rather than to nurture it and make it viable. If cable is to be utilised for community purposes in the long term, government will have to create a more hospitable environment for smaller cable operators. If the government fails to act, as it did during the late 1990s, the market will do the job for it and an important opportunity will have been lost.

SOUTH ASIA STATE RADIO

In terms of its geographical spread, national radio is far better placed than TV to serve regional or local purposes in South Asia. In 1999, India had nearly 200 radio stations and only forty-three television stations. Pakistan had twenty-four radio stations and five TV stations. Bangladesh had six radio stations and one TV station. In most South Asian countries, the tentacles of national radio networks stretch down to much lower levels of society than TV, offering services in a far greater variety of languages, with the potential to be focussed to a greater extent on community and region. Because of the costs involved, television tends to aim at wider audiences at national level. In the case of radio, the principle of regionalisation is accepted as valid even in smaller homogeneous countries. Radio is acknowledged to be a more versatile medium than television and a more suitable and affordable means of providing local communities with a voice of their own. It is less one-way, more interactive and more suitable for community development.

Radio and television are not inherently centralising technologies, as the early enthusiasm for radio in India shows. There are many countries of the world—the USA among them—where radio and television have been developed as a focus for community. Brazil at the last count had nearly 3000 radio stations.

In South Asia, early experiments in radio and television were absorbed into highly centralised bureaucratic structures, leaving little scope for local initiative or experiment. Despite India's huge size and development problems, no community radio station was sanctioned during the first fifty years of independence. The same holds true of Pakistan and Bangladesh. Equally significant, despite the extraordinary problems of the great metropolitan cities of South Asia, which are growing at alarming rates and are studied at conferences all over the world, state radio stations in those cities are not seen as 'local' but as voices of national government. Commercially driven FM channels have captured the local more effectively, but so far mostly with music shows aimed at young audiences. What follows is an assessment of the reasons why state radio has not been more successful in this important field. It is based largely on interviews with retired senior radio professionals, who provide some insights into the direction change must take if these institutions are to be reformed.

Bangladesh and Pakistan: Problems of Politicisation and Bureaucratisation

Syed Mohiuddin Ahmed, who was director general of Bangladesh Betar until 1996, puts radio's ineffectiveness down to the suffocation caused by political and bureaucratic control. 'From the peons to the DG, they are all government servants, all controlled by the ministry of information...and if you do not put the prime minister at the top of the news bulletins, whatever the quality of the event, the minister will be informed...that you are anti-government.' In his view: 'People are getting fed up with the monotonous programmes of BD radio.... They are made by civil servants and they go on the air like a file.' Mohiuddin Ahmed believes that a lot of the problems come from the method of recruitment. He says: 'Broadcasters are recruited as civil servants by the Public Services Commission and they go to the National Institute for Mass Communication, which is where they are taught how to please the government in power.' Following the liberation struggle against Pakistan, jobs were also seen as rewards for freedom fighters, some of who were still on temporary contracts twenty years later.[27]

The director general of the Pakistan Broadcasting Corporation (PBC) emphasised the role of radio in reaching different linguistic groups. 'There are twenty-three languages spoken in Pakistan and TV simply cannot afford to service them. Radio can do so. It is inexpensive. It reaches places where there is no electricity and it speaks to people in their own language.'[28] Sabih Mohsin, a former director of programmes at PBC agrees that the performance of some of the smaller stations shows radio at its best. He says: 'The regional audience is a captive audience, so there is two way communication which is what you need in radio.' But he points to serious staffing difficulties in maintaining a quality service across the country. He says nationally recruited broadcasters do not want to serve in remote places and political interference can make it impossible to post them there. 'Suppose I posted someone to Larkana. Even before he is relieved of his duties...I used to receive telephone calls from members of the national assembly, ministers, saying, please do not transfer him.' One possible solution would be to recruit more staff locally, though this would not work for senior staff who need to have wide experience. Another possibility would be to break with the bureaucratic tradition of promoting according to seniority and to give more weight to professionalism. Sabih Mohsin argues that the organisation needs to be restructured to be effective. He says: 'Its administration is top heavy and it is following programme practices which have long been abandoned elsewhere.'[29]

Sri Lanka and India: Ineffective Decentralisation

In Sri Lanka, no attempt was made to decentralise radio until April 1979, when a station was opened in the North Central Province at

Anuradhapura. Soon afterwards, two more radio stations were opened at Matara in the southern province and at Kandy in the central province. These stations are distinct from those set up in connection with Sri Lanka's ambitious Mahaweli irrigation project; their purpose is to serve existing communities rather than to facilitate the creation of new ones.

The rationale was to bring broadcasting closer to the regions. But Colombo has continued to maintain strict control of the agenda and regional news and current affairs programmes have not been encouraged. A visit to the Anuradhapura station in August 1998 revealed that the station only had three telephone connections and that the newsroom had neither telephone nor fax. The station broadcast two regional bulletins each day, one in the morning and one in the evening. Some of the news items from regional stringers arrived by post and payments were extremely low.[30]

Far more staff time was devoted to regional culture. The station had a music producer and a nine-piece orchestra which generated four hours of music each week. It also had an agricultural producer. There were strong links with the Farm Broadcasting Service in Colombo and a daily drama was sponsored by the Rice Research Institute.

Sri Lanka's regional stations are over-manned and their costs are high. In 1998, under new guidelines issued from Colombo, medium wave broadcasts were discontinued and the station was only broadcasting on FM. New road-shows to the districts had raised Rs. 80,000 from regional businesses. But most of the advertising money came from national banks and insurance companies. The business manager told us: 'Some jewelry shops advertise, but most shops are not rich enough.'[31] The other trend is towards sponsorship of programmes. Previously, the station broadcast religious programmes free; now they are being sponsored. In a predominantly agricultural area, one serious problem is that advertisers are not interested in farming programmes.

The Matara station faced similar problems, though the area's greater prosperity made it easier to generate local funds. In a period when they had managed to double their income, expenses had tripled due to increases in electricity and telephone charges. Controller Neel Weeratunge told us: 'One of the reasons we cannot be more competitive is that unlike private companies...we cannot make cuts in staff. We have seventy-eight people here.... How are we going to be more efficient...with this kind of large staff?'[32] As at Anuradhapura, the Matara station had begun road-shows to raise money in different districts, taking advertisements from shopkeepers and reflecting the culture too. This has added to the popularity of the station outside the regional capital. But regional management still felt hamstrung by continued controls from Colombo.

A former station director of Radio Chennai made similar criticisms of the centralisation of Indian broadcasting. Faced with the greatly increased output of South Indian news and current affairs from the satellite TV channels, Vijaya Thiruvenkatam had argued for 'the localisation of current affairs broadcasting' in Chennai to meet the competition. But it proved difficult to achieve because of resistance in New Delhi. His main suggestion had been to bring Tamil language news staff from Delhi to Chennai in order to expand the local news operation. He said: 'Today, technology has given us so many opportunities; you need a correspondent in Delhi but not a unit.' But he failed to carry the day and the old situation continued. Only one current affairs programme a week was produced by the Chennai station. The centre's wish to control the national news in different languages stood in the way of giving more responsibility even to its own organisation in the state.

The structure of AIR tends to work against effective broadcasting to the localities. Stations broadcast in many local languages but the objectives are set in Delhi, very often for political reasons. According to Vijaya Thiruvenkatam, many broadcasts to schools and factories have audiences too small to justify them. He argues that it would be possible to cut back on some staff, to re-deploy budgets to make stations more effective, to expand the number of producers, to improve and increase revenue. But persuading Delhi to adopt such a strategy is not easy.[33]

One important question in India is whether the establishment of Prasar Bharati will lead to greater decentralisation of operations. George Verghese, one of the first board members, takes the view that it is implicit in the legislation.[34] However, the act makes no specific mention of decentralisation and George Verghese acknowledges that the resources for local radio are limited. 'Local stations don't have the funds and the personnel. At local and community levels, there is virtually no broadcasting at all.' He sees the possibility that in due course Doordarshan and AIR will be the facilitators and private agencies will be the broadcasters. But the reluctance of BJP-led governments to accept the degree of autonomy for Doordarshan and AIR already on the statute book indicates the resilience of old attitudes.

Prerequisites of Decentralisation

The experience of senior radio managers points to a number of barriers in the way of effective decentralisation. Political control from the top creates an ethos in which producers play safe, avoid controversy and do not take risks. Many staff are hired for political reasons, to provide employment rather than expertise. Overstaffing is a common problem; most senior radio administrators admit that their organisations could run on half the staff. But there are political problems in reducing the wage bill.

Systems of staff recruitment also work against lively local radio. Throughout South Asia there are national cadres of broadcasters. Many staff are recruited not by the broadcasting organisations themselves but by public service commissions. They see themselves as civil servants rather than broadcasters. They enjoy the perquisites of civil servants and they are promoted according to the same rules: seniority is the key. One of the main barriers to the establishment of an autonomous Prasar Bharati organisation in India has been the unwillingness of staff to give up this government status. In an insecure world, it is highly prized.

Whether broadcasting organisations need to be autonomous to achieve improvements in their operational efficiency at the local level is debatable. Autonomy should insulate broadcasting from political interference and the long arm of the public service commission. But the Indian case has shown that continued attachment to government purse strings ensures continued influence and control. Arguably, it might be easier to persuade governments to decentralise broadcasting than to give up their influence entirely.

In the 1990s, most governments only relaxed their grip slightly on radio broadcasting. They acknowledged that the growing South Asian urban middle class needed alternative entertainment. But for the most part they did not wish to give radio a wider brief than this commercial objective. The first fruits of radio liberalisation were FM channels aimed at the younger generation. Only in Sri Lanka and Nepal did economic liberalisation bring a more generous dividend for civil society.

RADIO IN THE ERA OF LIBERALISATION

Liberalisation of the radio airwaves in South Asia followed the same pattern as the liberalisation of television. Where states were slow to liberalise TV, they only made limited and grudging concessions in the field of radio. Where they encouraged competition in television, they did so in radio too. In the 1990s, Pakistan made the fewest concessions; India and Bangladesh more; Nepal and Sri Lanka most of all. Almost all of these innovations took place in FM broadcasting; only in Bangladesh was competition with the state sector licensed on the medium wave.

In India, tendering for commercial FM licences took place in 1993 and broadcasts began the following year. In the first phase, the government restricted itself to the franchising of time slots on All India Radio's FM frequencies in Mumbai, Delhi, Calcutta, Chennai and Goa. Franchisees used AIR studios and equipment and their compliance with the terms of their contracts was monitored by AIR staff. Different commercial concerns took over different time slots, with Times FM, a radio subsidiary of the *Times of India*, a major player in the four main metropolitan centres from the start. Radio Midday, an offshoot of the *Inquilab* newspaper group, became an important player in Mumbai.

Most of these commercial FM programmes targeted young people with a menu of Indian and western pop music and chat. By the terms of their contracts they were not allowed to broadcast news. Current affairs programmes were not ruled out in principle, though such programmes required clearance by AIR management forty-eight hours in advance.[35] The new commercial ventures employed young college-educated disc jockeys who spoke to their own generation in the same mixture of English and their mother tongue which was used on the satellite music channels. The programmes were heavily criticised by the older generation for triviality of content and flippant presentation, but they were refreshingly different from All India Radio and they caught on well among the young urban middle class.

A report on FM in Calcutta in 1998 described it as 'young, confident and very innovative'. According to a city-based survey by Raycon Consultants, in one year FM listenership rose in Calcutta city by 75 per cent and in Greater Calcutta (including suburbs) by 90 per cent. Its success was attributed to the friendly and familiar relationship its presenters had established with listeners and to the attraction of stereo broadcasting. FM in Calcutta is popular among teenagers, who request Hindi and English songs with personal messages for their loved ones, and among their parents and grandparents, who ask for old favourites.

In Pakistan, Benazir Bhutto's government permitted the establishment of independent commercial FM stations in Islamabad, Lahore and Karachi in 1995. The contract was awarded in controversial circumstances to a friend of the prime minister's husband, Javaid Pasha, and was subsequently contested in the courts.[36] What emerged in all three cities was FM100, a station targeted at Pakistan's urban middle class in very similar style to its Indian counterparts. A limited survey in three socio-economic sectors of Rawalpindi and Islamabad in 1998 indicated that it had quickly established itself with the public. FM100 got higher ratings than Radio Pakistan in all three sectors.[37] FM100 relied largely on Pakistani music, with different time slots for different audiences. Though it caught on with urban youth, it successfully appealed to other age groups as well. As in India, it was forbidden by the terms of its licence to broadcast news and current affairs.

Bangladesh began to introduce commercial competition in radio as part of a limited exercise in liberalisation implemented by Sheikh Hasina Wajid's Awami League government in 1999. The Awami League had come to power promising autonomy for state broadcasting, but ultimately decided to retain political control of these institutions and to subject them to competition from the private sector. In 1999, the Unidev Group was granted a licence to set up a private television channel and was given air time for a medium wave radio station in Dhaka called Metrowave. Tenders were also invited for up to fifteen private FM radio stations, excluding news and current affairs from their brief. The terms of the tenders made it clear that the government wished to continue to control the news agenda, though the restrictions were relaxed for TV once the contract had been awarded.[38]

In 1995, Nepal began the liberalisation of its airwaves by hiring out time slots on Nepal Radio FM frequencies. Three years later, it moved to the next stage: licensing independent commercial FM stations with their own transmission facilities. As elsewhere in South Asia, FM in Nepal soon made an impact. ORG conducted a media survey in 1996 which looked at readership, viewership and listenership in the Kathmandu valley. Based on a sample of 700, it showed that 63 per cent of younger people (15–35 year olds) were listening to FM, compared with 62 per cent listening to Radio Nepal. These were very high figures so soon after the new FM band was started. The data indicated that 70,000 households in the Kathmandu valley were capable of accessing FM.[39]

Of the commercial stations, Kantipur FM, a radio offshoot of the successful newspaper group, commanded the highest audiences during the first phase. At that stage, the group had a three hour slot on Radio Nepal FM—from 7 to 10 a.m.—which attracted sufficient advertising to convince them that expansion was commercially feasible. In 1998, Kantipur FM was licensed to set up its own station. The group managing director, Kailash Sirohiya, said it aimed to provide 'infotainment'—music for young people, plus the kind of social education programmes which they had offered on Radio Nepal. But the licence specifically ruled out political programmes. Advertising had to be kept to 10 per cent. Sirohiya was confident that the radio advertising market in Nepal would pick up. In the meantime, profits from the newspaper would subsidise the venture.[40]

Like urban FM stations elsewhere, Kantipur and other Nepali stations are criticised for the negative use of the Nepali language. Discussants in suburban Kathmandu held that FM had been affected by the satellite television music channels—Channel V and MTV. They complained that the radio presenters were 'young, immature and frivolous boys and girls'.[41] S.P. Singh of Kantipur FM thought radio was following rather than creating these trends: 'Take the example of the use of 'Nepinglish' or whatever you call it. FM did not create that kind of language; all it did was reflect what was happening in society.'[42]

In radio, as in TV, Sri Lanka liberalised ahead of the rest of South Asia. It has permitted the establishment of more commercial radio stations than any other country and put the state-controlled Sri Lanka Broadcasting Corporation under considerable competitive pressure. At the end of 1999, Sinhala-speaking audiences had a choice of more than six different radio channels. Tamil audiences had a choice of two SLBC channels and two FM channels. There were also four commercial FM radio stations broadcasting in English. Moreover, in Sri Lanka, private radio stations are permitted to broadcast news and current affairs. As in the case of Sri Lankan private television, this has greatly extended the appeal of the new stations, even if the inexperience of the staff and a number of reporting gaffes have affected their level of public credibility.

The most successful commercial radio station is Maharaja TV's Sinhala language channel, Sirisa, which claimed 70 per cent of the market in 1998. Sirisa led the way in creating a new colloquial language for broadcasting and has given the public a new sense of ownership of the medium through the exploitation of the telephone. In many telephone boxes, there is now a 'Sirisa button', which enables listeners to make direct contact with the station without paying a fee. One media professional paid this tribute to the impact of the station: 'For decades...radio in Sri Lanka was stagnating; it was formulaic with very little experimentation. Sirisa radio changed all that. The telephone—the expansion of the tele-communications network—was cleverly exploited by the radio station. The programmes were based on dialogue, discussion, debate and they got the youth involved. Young people have started discussing personal problems, they are using call boxes, ensuring their anonymity, and often turning to the presenters as if they were friends or counsellors. Radio is being used as an outlet for emotions, a medium to discuss and dissolve their problems.'[43]

Our own survey of opinion in the rural settlement of Puhulwella in Matara district confirmed Sirisa's impact. About 90 per cent of those interviewed started their day with Sirisa. The older generation and government employees still listened to the morning bulletin of the state radio but even in those houses, the young switched over to Sirisa when the news was over. Several older women told us they would have liked to listen to the SLBC regional station but were compelled to listen to Sirisa because of their children or grandchildren.[44]

IMPACT ON THE STATE SECTOR

In most South Asian countries, governments have encouraged private sector commercial radio without thinking too much about what kind of programmes the new channels should broadcast. Beyond the prohibition on news broadcasting, they have made few stipulations, except in the area of taste and decency. Only in Nepal has government set out to licence a variety of different FM stations, serving different audiences.

Because of tight government finances, most governments have seen commercial radio as a means of making money for the exchequer, which has reinforced the primacy of the profit motive among radio entrepreneurs. The management of commercial FM radio in India is the best illustration of this kind of motivation.

When the FM sector was started in India in 1993, the government set the licence fees at Rs. 6,000 per hour in prime time and Rs. 4,000 at other times. These fees were later brought down by 50 per cent owing to complaints from the licensees that they were too high. By 1998, however, commercial FM had established itself and Times FM in particular was making considerable profits because of its national profile. AIR attempted to increase the rates to as much as Rs. 30,000 per hour in prime time but the FM sector resisted the new terms. The *Times* group did not deny its profitability, but it argued that it had had to invest substantially in the medium over several years to reach that situation. The *Times* group took the matter to the courts, but in June 1998 the Supreme Court ruled against them, stating that the proposed auction of FM slots was in the public interest. As a result, the old licences came to an end and AIR resumed control of the commercial FM slots.

The clash between the government and the FM sector was well ventilated in the press, with the *Times* group of newspapers taking the lead in criticising the government for monopolistic behaviour. Ranged against the *Times* was the *India Today* group, which had contended for one of the new licences and accused the *Times* group of profiteering.[45] The *Times* argued that the government was creating 'an artificial scarcity' by restricting FM radio to its own airwaves. It was possible to have a hundred FM transmissions in the available bandwidth; all that was needed was the capital.[46] The paper published a poll which supported the view that AIR should stick to public service broadcasting and leave entertainment to the private sector.[47] Another article argued that 'government indecision' was costing Rs. 250 billion (nearly US$ 600 million) a year. According to Ashish Mullick, this was the potential value of the FM radio market, which was being stunted in its growth by government attitudes 'Clearly the need of the hour', he wrote, 'is the immediate opening up of additional frequencies so as to cater to the emerging needs of a multi-ethnic and multi-linguistic society.'[48]

Tariq Ansari of *Midday*, whose group had pioneered FM radio in Mumbai, criticised the government for its 'highest bidder' approach to FM licences. He argued that this would only produce 'ten clones of Vividh Bharati', AIR's pop music service. What he wanted to see was a qualitative approach: 'Take the instance of London. You just cannot get a licence to run another channel of popular music. They feel they already have too many.... But you can get a licence to run a jazz channel, western classical music, folk music.... There is recognition that there are different segments that need to be served.'[49]

By the end of 1999, the *Times* group had largely won its argument but Tariq Ansari's point did not seem to have been addressed. In November, the re-elected BJP-led national government issued tenders for the establishment of 150 independent commercial FM stations. This was a major step forward in that it broke the government's monopoly of radio airwaves. The four metropolitan cities were to have ten or eleven stations each; the remainder, different numbers according to size and spectrum availability. However, the revenue-earning dimension of the exercise remained paramount. Beyond stipulating that no religious or political organisation and no advertising agency could apply, the tender document was unspecific about the kind of organisations it hoped to encourage. There was no specific mention of educational institutions, non-governmental organisations and community radio stations which had been mooted at an earlier stage.[50] Nor was there any suggestion that successful applicants for commercial stations would have to meet any public service obligations. As before, news and current affairs programmes were specifically ruled out.

Evidence from elsewhere in South Asia makes it clear that the creation of commercial competition for state radio on such terms does expand the advertising market but it also tends to draw revenues away from the state sector and provoke a financial crisis. What makes the crisis more intense is the fact that many governments had already begun to expect state radio to fund itself from advertisements. As a result, state and commercial sectors are put at each others' throats for the same revenues. This frequently leads to the state sector mimicking the private sector in order to win back its market share. To this extent, radio liberalisation has provoked similar developments as satellite competition has provoked in television.

In Sri Lanka, where radio competition is at its most intense, SLBC set up its own FM station called Lakhanda, and gave it a semi-autonomous existence, better facilities and better pay in order to compete with Sirisa and other private channels. But it failed to win back revenues. By 1997, SLBC's share of radio advertising had declined to 19 per cent, whereas the MBC group, which includes Sirisa, remained at over 50 per cent.[51] As a result, the management of SLBC had to embark on a programme of intensified commercialisation. It required regional stations, as we have already seen, to increase revenues and to cut back on staff by offering redundancy packages.[52]

In Nepal, the government had already cut its subsidy to state radio from Rs. 80 million to Rs. 30 million a year before the competition from FM began to bite. In 1998, of Nepal Radio's budget of Rs. 150 million, about Rs. 50 million came from national advertising, Rs. 60 million from renting out the airwaves to international broadcasters or NGOs and just over Rs. 10 million from the rented FM channel.[53] According to commercial FM sources, the government lost advertising to commercial channels but made up the balance from rent.[54] However, with the expansion of FM in Nepal, the pressures on Radio Nepal looked set to intensify.

In Pakistan, the state radio network expanded its own youth-oriented music service to combat the appeal of FM100. Initially, this was the responsibility of individual stations in the big cities but from 1998 it became a co-ordinated national service which was re-branded FM101. Asked if PBC had thought of reshaping its services to serve the big cities in a more dedicated way, the director general responded: 'In 1994, when they gave licences to private radio operators, we thought they might be doing this kind of thing, but they did something different. And unfortunately, I have now launched something in the same direction. The public sector organisations, under financial pressure from the government, have gone into the same market.'[55]

The picture is not entirely bleak. The stimulus from commercial competition has provoked some worthwhile improvements in state radio. The Matara station of the SLBC has developed a range of new participatory programmes which has improved its profile with the public. There is a weekly programme in which listeners can put their questions by mail or by phone to regional officials in the police, health or immigration departments and have their problems tackled. Controller Weeratunge says: 'Villagers get identity cards; fishery problems at particular harbours are sorted out.... Good things like that happen through the programme. People find solutions to their problems.' By mid-1998, such popular programmes had boosted Matara's advertising income to Rs. 600,000.

In Peshawar, Station Director Nisar Mohammed Khan increased live programming, inviting different sectors of the community to take part in special evenings at the station, and planned to broadcast the station's daily output from other district towns in the North West Frontier. More flexible use of staff was improving performance and revenues were rising, though, as elsewhere, a lack of real financial autonomy was holding up progress.[56]

In Calcutta, after a study was conducted on listener reactions to FM, AIR's primary channel also introduced phone-ins, which met with a good listener response. But the station director, Dr. Amit Chakravarti, made it clear that in the new financial environment, maintaining a public service mandate was more difficult. He claimed that 'while other FM channels mainly broadcast entertainment and music, Calcutta was the only one which had tried to experiment with...meaningful discussion.'[57]

Audiences for FM services are often wider than programme planners imagine. A survey undertaken by AIR's Calcutta station discovered that awareness of FM in the surrounding villages was much higher than in the city and that these rural listeners wanted more programmes in Bengali, more folk music and more discussions. Listeners demanded specific programmes for children, career counselling courses for young people and women, and more general knowledge and quiz programmes.[58]

In Bangladesh, where state radio was only exposed to commercial competition in early 2000, financial pressures from government had already resulted in changing programme formats and a substantial increase in advertising revenues. With cable TV attracting the middle class, Bangladesh Betar began to broadcast more live programmes and to concentrate more on rural audiences.[59] Despite its limited resources, it managed to produce a nightly programme called *Nishuti* between midnight and 3.30 a.m., which became very popular, especially among night workers, passengers and students. Offers of commercial sponsorship had to be turned down because under existing regulations it was not permitted.[60] There were also reports from NGOs that Bangladesh Betar was paying more attention to development. 'Its staff are willing to learn the trade and produce programmes on their own', said June Kunugi of UNICEF in Dhaka.[61]

Many improvements have come from the energy of individual station directors and the stimulus of commercial FM competition. But there are similar worries about the ethos of commercial radio broadcasting as there are about satellite TV. Tilak Jayaratne, a leading Sri Lankan educational broadcaster, argues that the dominance of the market is working against the interests of the majority of Sri Lankans. 'In Sri Lanka, about 70 per cent of the people are poor, and the majority of them are from rural areas. They barely have the necessities of life. Private media are exploiting this—tempting the public to give in to artificially created consumer desires.'[62]

Sri Lanka's highly competitive radio market illustrates both the weaknesses and the strengths of a system which relies entirely on the market to determine what sort of services the public needs. Commercial radio has won a large audience in Sri Lanka. In fact, radio accounted for 22 per cent of all media advertising at the beginning of 1998—a far higher figure than in India or Pakistan.[63] It has brought competitive news and current affairs as well as entertainment, and it has given radio a new lease of life with its inter-reactive character. But in radio, as in television, unrestricted competition has concentrated resources on the most lucrative sorts of programmes to the neglect of other needs.

COMMUNITY RADIO IN INDIA: A CASE STUDY IN CENTRALISATION

Community radio in South Asia is a term which is generally used to describe radio for the benefit of the community rather than radio which the community runs itself. Most community radio in South Asia is managed by the state with the participation of local communities, and even this sort of community radio has been a rarity until recently. The long and difficult pursuit of the community radio ideal in India is a reflection of these realities. The central government has viewed development as one of its prime tasks and All India Radio as its natural media supporter. But it has generally directed change itself; it has been very reluctant to encourage any real autonomy at the local level.

AIR has had some historic successes in development. In the 1950s, following a Canadian model, it set up a network of farm radio forums in five districts of Maharashtra, which was very successful in communicating knowledge of agricultural techniques and encouraging participation in decision-making.[64] In the 1960s, AIR played an important role in popularising the green revolution and providing a link between the agricultural extension service and the farmers. M.S. Gopal, one of the pioneers of this radio service, began experimental broadcasts for farmers from the Trichinopoly station in 1966 to persuade them to adopt new high yielding varieties.[65] The success of these broadcasts, which were launched in the most fertile rice growing areas of Tamil Nadu, led to the new variety becoming known as 'Radio Paddy'.

All India Radio's service for farmers is still very popular. As one AIR official put it: 'It is perhaps the only service which is fully utilised by listeners because it closely relates to their life.'[66] Efforts to use radio for education have met with less success. One reason is that co-ordination with the education department has not been as good as with the agricultural extension service. In the 1990s, a survey of schools in Tamil Nadu discovered that 'hardly 2 or 3 per cent were making use of the programmes.'[67] As a result, AIR in Tamil Nadu, which had boasted 50 per cent of radio schools in India in the 1970s, made a decision to abandon broadcasting educational programmes during school time.[68] Instead. they were broadcast in the mornings and evenings, relying on parental rather than educational support, which was inherently less satisfactory.

Serving the localities was the prime purpose of the expansion of AIR's network of stations into the districts. In the 1970s, an experimental FM station in Nagercoil district in Tamil Nadu successfully encouraged listeners' participation and for a time was thought to be a viable model for other FM stations. Pioneered by the broadcaster, K. Anjaneyulu, it worked to a prescription very different from the normal AIR top-down philosophy. Anjaneyulu said: 'Local radio should identify itself so completely with the interests of its local population that the heart of the people beats in every pulse of the programme it broadcasts.'[69] But the formula proved difficult to reproduce in stations managed and staffed by an all-India cadre of broadcasters with only temporary local affiliations.

In 1998, there were 187 radio stations in India, nearly a hundred of which were small district stations broadcasting in local languages as well as re-broadcasting national programmes to local audiences. By that time, critics of AIR were arguing that it was neglecting its development brief under pressure to be financially self-sufficient. It was still broadcasting many programmes with educational and development goals, but a new ethos was taking hold.

At Bangalore in September 1996, an Indian NGO called Voices called a meeting of interested broadcasters, NGOs and policy planners who signed a declaration calling for an extension of community broadcasting. With some support from within AIR, they advocated that AIR's local stations should allocate regular air time for community broadcasting. They also requested the government to grant licences to set up community radio stations to NGOs and other non-profit making organisations.[70]

All India Radio agreed to the first request in April 1997, though it proceeded with infinite caution. Two years later, it permitted a thirty-minute pilot programme on one station in Karnataka on the second Thursday of every month, an experiment which was discontinued after four programmes.[71] AIR had not adopted community radio with any enthusiasm.

The failure to set up a procedure for licensing private local or community stations, as envisaged in the 1997 Broadcasting Bill, and the terms of the tenders issued in 1999 for commercial FM stations, meant that the need for highly localised information was not being met. In Medak district in Andhra Pradesh, UNESCO had helped set up a small local radio station with a 100 watt transmitter, which was to be run by rural women members of a local NGO—the Deccan Development Society. But as media commentator Sevanti Ninan pointed out: 'Until the law of the land changes, the transmitter at this radio station will not be used.... The women tape programmes, edit them on their editing equipment in the studio, and play them back on tape recorders at gatherings of village folk, thus using a community listening system, in the absence of legally permitted broadcasting.'[72]

RADIO SAGARMATHA AND RADIO
FOR DEVELOPMENT IN NEPAL

Rather more progress has been made in Nepal. Nepal's policy of liberalising its media has led to the granting of licences not just to commercial operators like Kantipur FM but also to non-governmental organisations operating on a charitable basis and to local government institutions like the Kathmandu Municipality. There has been a recognition in Nepal that regulators need to look beyond the dichotomy between government and private sector and facilitate the use of radio for more varied purposes.

One distinctive new voice in the Kathmandu valley is Radio Sagarmatha, which is mainly funded by local and international NGOs. It is attempting to offer an alternative vision of public service broadcasting which competes both with Radio Nepal and with the new music-dominated FM stations. With Nepal's state broadcaster copying its commercial competitors and placing more emphasis on western and Indian popular music, Sagarmatha is trying to offer more authentically Nepali music and is trying to reach out for the first time to some of the capital's minorities. Its weekly programmes in Tamang have created a new radio constituency in that community and there are plans to develop other programmes for other linguistic groups. Though Radio Nepal instituted news bulletins in a range of different languages after the revolution of 1990, most of those programmes were translated from Nepali; there has been little creative programming in other languages and no opportunity for exchanges with new audiences.

Sagarmatha is under the same restrictions as all independent broadcasters in the news field. It has to re-broadcast Radio Nepal bulletins; it cannot make its own news. However, it does provide summaries of what the newspapers say and it re-broadcasts some BBC programmes in English and Nepali. It also generates discussions on matters of topical interest and puts considerable emphasis on reflecting local voices, through vox pops, phone-ins and recordings in the community. Despite strictures on news broadcasting, stations like Sagarmatha attempt to respond creatively to audience demands for information without breaking the letter of the law.

The station was initially on air for two hours a day, but this later expanded to twelve hours. According to Binod Bhattarai, the station's first director, the emphasis in the first phase was on 'good programmes: informed talk radio, including local news and community information...to examine arguments and strengthen standards of good journalism'.[73] But with the expansion of time, there was more room for entertainment, for Nepali folk music and programmes targeted at minorities. Bhattarai acknowledged the station's inexperience in development reporting but hoped to build up this expertise by importing trainers from other countries.

Sagarmatha had its origins in an FM project conceived by Worldview International in the mid-1990s. The ultimate objective was not one station in Kathmandu but a network of stations throughout Nepal with small simply equipped studios. In this scheme, Sagarmatha was to act as a resource and training centre for community broadcasters elsewhere. According to Bharat Dutta Koirala, a leading Nepali journalist who was involved in the project from the beginning, the aim was 'to show government that radio can be viable'.[74]

By the end of 1999, the first steps towards the creation of a small network had been taken. As a result of government decisions the previous year, two new community stations were created, one near Butwal in the Terai and the other near Tansen in the hills. The first was known as Lumbini FM and the second as Madan Pokhara FM. The licences were granted when a Marxist-Leninist, R.K. Mainali, was minister of information and broadcasting. The Communist (ML) Party sees community radio as a way of pushing the cause of greater village autonomy in development matters. The Lumbini licence was granted to a local co-operative at Manigram and had a potential coverage of 25–30 km in a well populated urban and rural area. In Madan Pokhara, the licence was given to the Village Development Committee. It covered the Tansen valley, a rich agricultural area. In both cases, the leaders of the local community were well represented on the management committee, with journalists playing an important part. Though the licences permitted advertising, the local communities were clear that they wished to use the stations for information purposes. In Madan Pokhara, one member of the FM committee described the station as an exercise in 'barefoot journalism'.[75]

Though much of the funding for these new stations was raised locally, there was a recognition that outside help was needed in a

number of areas: in the selection of sites for transmitters, in engineering skills and in the training of broadcasting staff and volunteers. Radio Sagarmatha helped to raise additional funds for
community radio training. It offered an engineer on loan for site
selection, training fellowships for broadcasters and as well as help
with programme planning and scheduling. It also started a mobile
radio unit, which visited the new stations, as well as recording
material elsewhere. By the end of 1999, there was an awareness
that Radio Sagarmatha was not just a metropolitan station; it was
part of a growing radio movement in which the three stations were
learning from each other.

SRI LANKA'S MAHAWELI COMMUNITY RADIO

Sri Lanka has more than twenty years of community broadcasting
experience as a result of the involvement of SLBC in the ambitious
Mahaweli Irrigation project. This project, which began in the late
1970s, involved the building of several large dams to divert the
Mahaweli river northwards and to irrigate nearly a million acres
of previously arid land in the north west of the country. About a
million people from the overpopulated south of the island were
resettled and radio was used as a tool to create a sense of community, to ease the process of adjustment and to improve agricultural
productivity. Mahaweli Community Radio (MCR) was set up with
support from UNESCO and DANIDA, the Danish development
agency, and it has become one of the most studied examples of
the use of radio for development anywhere in the world. What is
perhaps most remarkable about it is that it did succeed in mobil-
ising and serving the new communities and in creating radio with
a different voice. Victor Valbuena, who assessed it in 1988, concluded that it had empowered local people to take charge of their
lives and to participate in the implementation of programmes
affecting them.[76] This was a considerable achievement in the highly
centralised, monopolistic broadcasting system of that time.

The MCR philosophy was to involve the listeners directly in
the making of programmes. It reckoned that settlers would adopt
new techniques more readily on the advice of their own kith and
kin than on recommendations from outsiders.[77] In the initial phase
of the project, the community radio production team was based

at SLBC's Kandy station and the programmes were broadcast for an hour each day to the entire settlement area. It is estimated that the Mahaweli Community Radio production teams had visited about 1500 villages up to 1989. After that, field visits were reduced due to the escalation of political violence in the north and east of the country.

Smaller Scale Community Radio: Broadcasting from within the Community

From the late 1980s, a number of smaller local community stations were set up to serve particular sectors of the Mahaweli scheme. The first three were established at Girandurukotte (1986), Mahailuppalama (1987) and Kotmale (1988). Ten years later, a fourth was added at Pulathisiravaya (1998).[78] The notion that 'small is beautiful' has been a governing principle in designing and conceptualising these small stations. Most of the stations have very few staff and depend almost entirely on community participation.

Examining the kind of work carried out at the first station at Girandurukotte gives an insight into how MCR has worked in practice. One of the key areas of activity has been 'project broadcasting' which backs up a specific activity in the field. Producer K.M. Weerasinha initiated the first project in which agricultural extension workers provided technical information and the farmers fed back their experiences into the programme. The producer visited the farmers regularly and served as a mediator between them and the agricultural extension workers. Field activities, such as demonstrations, were organised through the programme. But the project was constrained by lack of input from the hardpressed Mahaweli agricultural unit.

In a subsequent community health project at Divulapalassa, efforts were made to achieve closer co-ordination with extension workers. At the end of the project, the results were impressive. The entire village had dug waste disposal pits. The number of people who were drinking boiled water had significantly increased. By the time the project ended, some of the basic health problems had been solved and the settlers themselves had started thinking about how to tackle unsolved problems.

The most recent station at Pulathisiravaya in Bloc B of the Mahaweli system has only three staff members. The other staff are volunteers recruited from the area. The station covers a large area, including the districts of Batticaloa, Polonnaruwa and Matale. The station is situated in an 'uncleared' area where civilians are caught between the Sri Lankan armed forces and Tamil Tiger guerrillas. Because this area has been isolated by the on-going civil war, it has met an urgent need for a local information infrastructure.

In 1999, the Kotmale radio station also became the focus for a new project, funded by UNESCO, to make the Internet available to rural listeners. Users include farmers seeking information on market prices, people looking for jobs and students compensating for limited educational resources. The aim is to help to correct the existing informational imbalance between town and country.

M.J.R. David, a Sri Lankan broadcaster who has been involved in setting up many of these smaller stations over the past fifteen years, draws a number of lessons from the experience. One crucial lesson is that community participation is essential, though this does not come of its own accord. There are a number of other pre-requisites. An adequate radio signal is 'of paramount importance'. A good location for the station is also vital, as is a well-defined target area, so that programming and other activities do not lose focus. The 'most influential factor' is the commitment of the volunteer community broadcasters and the maintenance of their morale. A final requirement is the right programme mix, which has changed dramatically as a result of competition from Sri Lanka's commercial radio sector. David says: 'In the initial years, our focus was largely on development.... Today the younger generation of community broadcasters are faced with a more complex situation. The emergence of private broadcasting has undoubtedly influenced the programme orientation of community broadcasting. Today about 30 per cent of the programme content on community radio is entertainment oriented.... A shift towards entertainment is necessary to keep listeners drifting towards the private broadcasters.'

Some media analysts point out that to call MCR a 'community radio' project is really a misnomer 'because by definition community radio should be something driven by and managed by the community', whereas MCR has been 'basically administered and run by the government station with some tokenistic participation of some members of the community.'[79] M.J.R. David takes this criticism. He says: 'There is no doubt that the centre-based bureaucratic management structure of a large organisation does not fit community radio.' He would like to see the Sri Lankan government adopt a new national media policy which facilitates community radio independent of the state broadcasting sector. But his criticism of government is not that it is using community for political ends but that it is keeping it artificially non-political. He says: 'A decade or two ago the rural population would have been satisfied with apolitical programming. However, it is hard to think in the coming millennium that a community radio station that does not deal with issues in a realistic manner could be effective.'

CONCLUSION

One conclusion of this assessment of the potential of television and radio to serve community purposes is that television no longer looks as viable as it did before. As a result of the commercial pressures from satellite television, state television has become more focussed on entertainment in order to retain its mass audiences. The pressures of competition have squeezed the time for public service programming and left state services to the regions under-resourced. Though the encouragement of regional television in India and Pakistan would be an effective strategy for countering globalising influences, neither state has shown a strong commitment to it.

In the straitened circumstances of national finances throughout the region, radio seems a far more suitable medium for serving community and locality. Radio broadcasts in many more local languages than television. There are radio stations in all the main urban centres and some remote, rural ones too. Yet, radio is also in the grip of centralising bureaucracies which stifle initiative at the local level and do not give the localities the tools to do their job effectively.

In radio, as in TV, the pursuit of greater financial self-sufficiency in the state sector has brought more emphasis on entertainment and comparative neglect of other programmes. The introduction of commercial FM stations has greatly exacerbated this trend. But financial pressures have also brought welcome innovation and more audience participation. In Sri Lanka, in particular, radio has been given a new lease of life as an interactive medium. Sri Lanka has also led the way in community broadcasting, though Nepal has broken with tradition in licensing community broadcasting outside the state sector.

Some of these exciting developments point to what could be achieved if governments were to adopt decentralising policies and a new vision of radio in the service of community. To do this, however, they need to abandon their proprietorial approach to the electronic media and take on a new role as regulators in the public interest. They need to redefine where the public interest lies in the new, more commercial era of economic liberalisation.

NOTES AND REFERENCES

1. See, Chapter 2, p. 65; also A. Singhal and E. Rogers (1989), *India's Information Revolution*, pp. 62–64.
2. P.C. Joshi, Delhi, August 1998.
3. George Verghese, Delhi, June 1998.
4. See, E.V. Chitnis (1983), 'TV Creativity for Rural Growth', *India International Centre Quarterly*, Vol. 10, No. 2, pp. 145–60. We are indebted to Pradip Thomas for this reference.
5. See Sevanti Ninan (1995), *Through the Magic Window*, pp. 70–75.
6. See, *Pursuit*, a report on the Jhabua Development Communications Project, published by the Development and Educational Communication Unit of ISRO, Ahmedabad, 1998.
7. George Verghese, Delhi, June 1998.
8. Bangladesh TV producers, Dhaka, April 1998.
9. This account of television and development in Bangladesh draws on Afsan Chowdhury's 'Media Profile of Bangladesh', commissioned for the Media South Asia Project, July 1998.
10. Syed Salahuddin Zaki, Dhaka, March 1998.
11. Donor agency official, Dhaka, February 1998.
12. Anuradha Mukherjee, 'Media Profile of West Bengal', commissioned for the Media South Asia Project, July 1998.
13. *Ibid.*
14. Tariq Saeed, Director of Programmes, PTV, Peshawar, June 1999.
15. Raana Syed, Islamabad, November 1997.
16. Ashish Sen, Bangalore, February 1998.
17. Attaullah Baluch, Senior Producer, PTV, Quetta, August 1998.
18. Rajive Jain, CENDIT, Delhi, May 1998.
19. P.C. Joshi, Delhi, August 1998.
20. Shevanthi Jayasuriya, MTV, Colombo, April 1998.
21. Nalaka Gunawardene, Colombo, July 1998.

22. Star and ESPN have since ceased to be free-to-air and are no longer generally available. This description of the cable network in Karachi is based on a report by M.F. Memon commissioned for this book.
23. Afsan Chowdhury, 'Media Profile of Bangladesh', commissioned for the Media South Asia Project, July 1998.
24. On Bangladesh cable regulation, see Chapter 3, pp. 93–95.
25. Chinmoy Mutsuddi, Dhaka, March 1998.
26. This account of developments in Chennai is based on a report by Pritham Chakravarty on 'Cable Networking and Satellite Television in South Chennai', commissioned for the Media South Asia Project.
27. Syed Mohiuddin Ahmed, Dhaka, May 1998.
28. Anwar Mahmood, Islamabad, January 1999.
29. Sabih Mohsin, Karachi, March 1998.
30. They were paid Rs. 40 (less than US$ 1) for a 'hot' news story, Rs. 25 for something which made a headline and Rs. 10 for an item.
31. Hemanta Abeyakoon, Business Manager, Anuradhapura station, August 1998.
32. Neel Weeratunge, Controller of Broadcasting, Matara station, May 1998.
33. Vijaya Thiruvenkatam, Chennai, February 1998.
34. George Verghese, Delhi, June 1998.
35. Raadhu, FM radio producer, Chennai, May 1998.
36. J. Jabbar and Q.F. Isa (eds) (1997), *Mass Media Laws and Regulations in Pakistan*, pp 124–25.
37. Survey by Tasneem Ahmar in Rawalpindi district, June 1998.
38. Syed Mohiuddin Ahmed, Former DG, Radio Bangladesh, Dhaka, May 1998.
39. Piyush Mathur, ORG, Kathmandu, May 1998.
40. Kailash Sirohiya, Managing Director, Kantipur Publications, Kathmandu, May 1998.
41. Mixed group, Lokanthali, near Kathmandu, May 1998.
42. S.P. Singh, Kathmandu, June 1999.
43. Anoma Rajakaruna, Freelance television producer, Colombo, September 1998.
44. Report of survey in Puhulwella, Matara district, by Santhini Jayawardena, July 1998.
45. See for example, Sumit Mitra's article in *India Today*, 13 July 1998.
46. 'Scarcity of Airwaves: Myth and Reality', *Sunday Times of India*, 28 June 1998.
47. *Ibid*.
48. *The Times of India*, 24 June 1998.
49. Tariq Ansari, Mumbai, July 1998.
50. See, for example, *The Economic Times*, 7 July 1998.
51. *Survey Research Lanka Fact File*, January 1998.
52. Janadasa Peiris, Director General, SLBC, Colombo, March 1998.
53. Shailendra Sharma, Former Managing Director, Radio Nepal, Kathmandu, May 1998.
54. Kailash Sirohiya, Managing Director, Kantipur FM, Kathmandu, May 1998.
55. Anwar Mahmood, Director General, Pakistan Broadcasting Corporation, Islamabad, January 1999.
56. Nisar Mohammed Khan, Peshawar, June 1999.
57. Dr. Amit Chakravarti, Calcutta, March 1998.

58. This information is from Anuradha Mukherjee's 'Media Profile of West Bengal', commissioned for the Media South Asia Project, July 1998.

59. M.I. Choudhury, Director General, Bangladesh Betar, Dhaka, March 1998.

60. This information is taken from Afsan Chowdhury's 'Media Profile of Bangladesh', commissioned for the Media South Asia Project, July 1998.

61. June Kunugi, Dhaka, April 1998.

62. Tilak Jayaratne, Director, Training/Research/Education and Sinhala National Service, SLBC, Colombo, June 1998.

63. *Survey Research Lanka Fact File*, January 1998.

64. See, J.C. Mathur and Paul Neurath (1959), *An Indian Experiment in Farm Radio Forums*, especially pp. 105–10.

65. M.S. Gopal, Chennai, February 1998.

66. Vijaya Thiruvenkatam, Chennai, February 1998.

67. *Ibid.*

68. In 1977, school broadcasts covered a little over 50,000 schools, of which 29,000 were in Tamil Nadu. See, *Verghese Report* (1978), Vol. I, p. 131.

69. Sucharita Eashwar and Philip Mathew (1998), 'What Works for Radio? The Indian Experience', *Voices*, Bangalore.

70. *Ibid.*

71. Sucharita Eashwar, Bangalore, November 1999.

72. Sevanti Ninan, *The Hindu*, 21 November 1999.

73. Binod Bhattarai, Kathmandu, May 1998.

74. Bharat Koirala, Kathmandu, May 1998.

75. This information on the establishment of the two community stations is based on a report by Ian Pringle, a Canadian community broadcaster working with Radio Sagarmatha, in March 1999.

76. See, V.T. Valbuena (1988), 'The Mahaweli Community Radio Project: An Evaluation'.

77. W. Hewage (1990), 'Experiences in Field Production', Paper presented to a regional workshop on South Asian community broadcasting, Kandy.

78. This account of community broadcasting in Sri Lanka is based on a paper commissioned for the Media South Asia Project from M.J.R. David, one of Sri Lanka's leading community radio practitioners.

79. Nalaka Gunawardene, Colombo, July 1998.

Ten

REDEFINING THE PUBLIC INTEREST

In all the diversity and uncertainty of the responses of South Asian governments and state broadcasters to the 'satellite invasion', the need for institutional self-preservation, financial viability and continued government control has loomed large. The actions taken by governments have, to a great extent, been dictated by immediate commercial imperatives. But beyond the need to retain existing institutions lies the broader question—what is broadcasting for? We need to ask the question both in relation to the state broadcasters, the commercial channels and, most importantly, the audience for which they are competing. The answer has always included some of the elements of the West European public service broadcasting legacy: the provision of a comprehensive service to a national audience, the obligation to provide a range of programming to reflect different interests and tastes, a general mandate to provide for diversity and pluralism, a role in promoting social integration and a sense of national identity both in the political and cultural sphere, and independence both from sectarian and commercial interests.[1]

Such public service obligations have been characteristic of the broadcast media in contrast to the print media. As a monopoly utilising a scarce resource, broadcast media have been perceived above all as carrying a commitment to serve the public interest. So long as newspapers could be commercially and politically competitive, their open biases and self-interest could be countered by other voices and other interests within the print media. As far as the press was concerned, the obligation was for governments to allow the free expression of opposing views, rather than to provide a single platform which would reflect a national consensus.

A definition of the public interest will vary substantially according to the economic and political circumstances of a state and its people. It would have to take account of the level of development and degree of social cohesion. From the point of view of the governments of South Asia, their own claim to reflect the interests of society as a whole, over the whole range of security, welfare and developmental needs, gave them a leading role, almost a sole legitimacy, in defining what the public interest should be. The growth of the concept of civil society and the advance of a more pluralistic view of legitimacy have widened the concept. Laissez-faire liberalism and free market theory have presented a more fundamental challenge to its validity. But the concept of public interest implies the existence of a common social purpose and a collective policy within society, which can be a reference point for discussion and analysis and a benchmark for an assessment of the broadcaster's role.[2]

Public broadcasters are expected specifically to be guardians of the public interest. But in a mixed broadcasting environment, a regard to the public interest is no longer their exclusive domain. Commercial broadcasters have a stake in showing that they serve the public interest as well. The public have a stake in monitoring how their interest is served.

THE PUBLIC INTEREST AND THE MARKET

The neo-liberal free market ideology professes confidence in the ability of a totally free market to meet all public service needs. In maintaining that '...all provision for the consumer on a competitive basis in a non-distorted market is a public service',[3] its advocates would make this confidence virtually self-fulfilling. It is widely acknowledged that the market has an important role to play in making state-funded organisations more efficient. In South Asia, private commercial channels have provided welcome competition. They have raised awareness of superior production values. They have introduced new and livelier programme formats, many of them skilfully adapted from western originals to appeal to local tastes. They have drawn on the highly successful elements of commercial popular culture—especially music and film—to create a hybrid that is unmistakably local and regional in its content. It may be criticised for vulgarity and bad taste, but it is acknowledged to have improved the level of popular entertainment even in countries that '…have cultivated a philosophy of public service inseparable from an idea of high culture to which all citizens should be raised.'[4]

But the virtually unregulated market in satellite broadcasting which emerged in South Asia in the 1990s, has also demonstrated the negative influences of commercial pressures on programme quality and standards. Entertainment, sport and even news programmes have been shown to attract advertisements. But in focussing on these, there are important aspects of public service which are neglected both by private channels and by competing state broadcasters. Advertisers show little or no interest in documentaries and issue-based programmes or programmes for minorities. Leaving the entire sphere of broadcasting to the market does not demonstrably increase the range of programme choice.

The importance of low income urban and rural communities, by virtue of their sheer numbers, as customers for low value branded consumer goods is not neglected by the advertisers. But their social needs are not catered for, nor is the choice of programming always appropriate to their region and culture. Sohail Hashmi of Sehmat, an Indian drama group working in development, says: 'In slum areas people may prefer to use toothpaste; it is a change promoting hygiene…. But the point is that people do not have houses or medical facilities, schools, clothes…. A medium as powerful as TV should be playing a more constructive role and should be used as an instrument of social transformation.'[5] In this, their predicament is similar to the lack of real choice confronting all TV viewers, but greater in degree. Throughout South Asia, advertising tends to aim at the urban well to do and to neglect the very large percentage of people who are illiterate and poor and living in the rural areas.

George Verghese argues that because 'a large section of the Indian people is outside the market…only a public service broadcaster whose charter is to serve all people and which is not wholly dependent on ratings and commercials can really do so.'[6] It is an argument which is strongly supported by most professionals working in development in South Asia. Dr. Mohan Man Sainju, former Vice-Chairman of the Nepal Planning Commission, told us of his concern that lifestyles and products are being promoted, even for the poor, which are imported, costly and inappropriate. He said: 'Coca-Cola at Rs. 10 a bottle is a status symbol, whereas it would make more sense to buy a small loaf and two eggs for the same money. This consumerism involves a de-prioritisation of basic needs. Once the Kathmandu valley could barely support one beer factory; now there are eight. Fifteen per cent of the population may be doing better; but 85 per cent are not.'[7]

SPEAKING FOR THE NATION

In the countries of South Asia where broadcasting had been a government monopoly from the start, the loss of the monopoly has brought real change. It has challenged the identity and sense of purpose of the public broadcasting institutions. In one perspective, the national broadcaster has been the voice of the government. Attempts to change that aspect of the colonial legacy have met with only limited success. It could not claim to be the voice of the people, which is surely too large a claim to make for any broadcaster in an open society. But the national broadcasters in the countries of South Asia have always been expected in some sense to be the voice of the nation. In the early years after independence in India, Pakistan and Sri Lanka, broadcasters saw themselves as engaged in a political building project, helping to construct the idea and identity of the nation.

The state in South Asia has been seen as the one institution which affects the life and welfare of every one within its borders. Its responsibilities for government and society are so broad in range that no other private or public institution can pretend to match its authority or representative legitimacy. Even if the idea of the state and the alternative concept of civil society have been to some extent the product of a consensus, the state media has played a dominant role in the production of that consensus. A commitment to the broadcast media's nation-building role has been combined with a belief in the almost omnipotent power of the mass media to form and educate opinion by conveying information and approved messages.

Nilanjana Gupta has argued that radio and TV in independent India were used to 'coerce a national unity rather than to evolve a public sphere through debate'. In this analysis the historical narrative of Jurgen Habermas, in which the media contribute to the creation of 'public space', does not hold good for India as a post-colonial nation. The national programme created by the satellite network of the early 1980s is seen as an effort, centrally directed if not actually coercive, to build a consensual cultural narrative of the nation.[8]

Critics of this approach are not necessarily opposed to the idea of nation-building in itself. Dr. Abhijit Pathak of the Jawaharlal Nehru University in Delhi argues that in India the idea of 'public space' in which the public broadcaster operates should be defined in a different way to Europe. In Europe 'public space' is contrasted primarily with the private or commercial sphere. He advances a different notion of public space, in which attention is drawn both to different regional cultural traditions and to the local or 'subaltern' activism of ordinary people. 'Let our media people, and also academics, not only be sensitive to them as individuals but let the local struggles and local issues expand their horizons'. This is not, he says, to accept an 'extreme kind of post modernist vision which fragments the world', but to urge the relevance of the story of fishermen's struggle in Kerala to the horizons of someone in West Bengal. 'His understanding of his own local issues is enriched and a feeling of solidarity is created.' The challenge for the media is one of 'learning from differences', which can be offset against what Dr. Pathak sees as the homogenising (and 'culturally imperialist') influence of global consumerism and its local offshoots.[9]

The role of nation-building has not by any means been abandoned. In Britain it was required of the BBC, especially in the 1920s and 1930s; it is still a requirement in Canada. Governments and the public are particularly sensitive to this role in a time of military conflict. But to some observers it seems dated. It arouses suspicion as a government-directed enterprise, one that does not allow sufficient scope for different regional perspectives, or is even designed to obscure them. In India the idea still has strong advocates, but some will argue that the nation-building project was important at the time of independence but should not now be a priority. Television producer and media journalist Indrajit Lahiri says 'I have not seen beyond Doordarshan's concept of nation-building, but I do perhaps see other ways to build nations which may not necessarily be influenced by politics or by vested interests'.[10] Chandan Mitra, editor of the Delhi English language newspaper *The Pioneer*, argues that 'the "old-fashioned" type of nation-building has had its day (though I approve of it) and a new type of multicultural nation-building has taken its place.'[11] A veteran Tamil educationist maintains that the distinctiveness of Tamil culture is best served by a decentralised concept of the Indian nation.[12]

Some editors and political observers argue that the job has already been done effectively and that what is required today is something different reflecting the pluralism and diversity of the nation. Others, aware of the fragility that goes with the diversity, reject that view. But in general, broadcasters are more cautious about claiming to voice a national consensus and societies are less certain what it is they want.

Whether or not a TV or radio channel is effectively operated by government, the way in which the government presents its own policies, and the publicity it gives to its own initiatives, is bound to have a major influence on the media. Beyond that, the responsibility and power of governments to establish a framework for national communications and broadcasting is accepted virtually everywhere. It is not in itself incompatible with freedom of speech or other constitutionally protected rights. However, in most South Asian countries the public media have been or are used by governments for partisan purposes. So the public is as sceptical about governments exercising the public service broadcasting role in their name as they are about private channels.

State broadcasters in South Asia are often seen as vehicles for public messages formulated by government departments to back up their policies. But it is a misconception to see this as the main substance of public service broadcasting which demands (to quote a British formulation of the 1980s) 'knowledge, culture, education and experiment'.[13] The survival of public service broadcasting and the institutions which can promote it depends as much on enlightened regulation as on an absence of regulation. But it cannot be sustained if there is no new thinking about what its aims and content should be. Public interest and the institutional means to support it is as necessary in an era of multiple choice as it was in the monopoly era. What is true for other areas of economics and social welfare is also true of broadcasting.

A definition of the public interest in the new media environment in South Asia can still draw on the traditional obligations of the public broadcaster—to educate, inform and entertain. But, according to S.S. Gill, these objectives have acquired the status of a mantra without real meaning: 'The three words everyone repeats, they mean virtually nothing. Give it flesh and blood.'[14]

ATTITUDES TOWARDS NEW TECHNOLOGY

Government attitudes towards converging communications technologies will be crucial in determining the future shape both of broadcasting and the newer media. The resources released by digitisation carry a huge potential for commercial exploitation, for revenue raising by governments and, with imaginative regulation, for public benefit. Television sets will continue to be distinct from personal computers as long as the users see them as fulfilling different purposes. But television technology cannot be separated from the provision of other telecommunication services. The cable television network which offers a wide choice of entertainment channels is set to provide Internet access and a range of new interactive services: sound and vision as well as text and data. Mobile telephone services can also provide access to the Internet. Information shops or computer kiosks are being set up to make these services more widely available in rural areas. In Bangladesh non-governmental organisations are taking a leading role; in India some state governments have drawn up their own blueprints. The task of government in regulating this profusion of new services is different, but no less challenging than their previous role as monopoly providers. The private and public sectors have moved into competition in old and new areas of technology, with government setting the terms of competition for both.

To a great extent, India has learnt to come to terms with multi-channel television distributed through the cable system, though a full regulatory system is not in place. But the next technological leap forward—Direct to Home satellite transmission—still causes apprehension commercially, culturally and above all politically. The conditions in India and South Asia as a whole would seem favourable for DTH, which can provide a high quality digital service with a choice of 200 channels across the whole region. But global experience indicates that profitability is uncertain. In most markets it is unlikely that more than one or two DTH consortia can break even.

The advantage that DTH gives in reaching a dispersed rural market is neutralised if the programmes are offered at a price the rural consumer cannot afford. The message from the cable operators is that though Indian viewers may watch television on average for 3 to 4 hours a day, most of them are unwilling to pay for extra channels. Pay-TV through the cable system has been slow to work for this reason. Cable operators are in cut-throat competition with each other and conditions have not yet seemed right to invest in the technology required to provide a different service to different customers—the means of addressability.

In India, it is not so much the fear of DTH which holds back investment in new cable technologies as lack of clarity as to how broadcasting regulation will affect the future of cable operators. The draft Broadcasting Bill stipulated strict controls on the ownership and operation of different parts of the television production, broadcasting and distribution chain. It limited the licensing of cable operators to two for each telephone licensing area, though these areas bore no relation to the way in which cable systems had been set up.

One likely effect of DTH would be to give a boost to local content creators—programme and software producers. With India's proven capacity to produce successful indigenous television programming, it may be resistant to the introduction of more foreign material. For established broadcasters, success in DTH will depend on effectiveness in their core business and their capacity to retain audience loyalty and income from advertising and sponsorship while developing the new services. DTH seems likely to benefit strong traditional players and lower barriers to talented newcomers. It will be a fruitful field for entrepreneurs in film and production to develop high quality local language programming. Like its Hong Kong and Hollywood counterparts, the Bombay film and television production industry should do well.[15]

Banking analysts see DTH as an option for long-term players with deep pockets. The confidence that DTH will make money should encourage international players if they are given an opportunity to provide a service for the upper-end of the market. But initially, DTH is not expected to be a very large market. About 1 million households will get into DTH; the balance of around 20 million cable and satellite homes in India will remain with cable and the free-to-air format.[16]

Conventionally, cable is supposed to compete with DTH, but leading cable operators do not see it as a threat. The common objective is pay per view television; beyond that cable and DTH are different means to the same end. The Hindujas' InCable company policy is to concentrate on distribution, though it has plans to take part in DTH if allowed. Star TV, which had been pressing for early permission to take advantage of its technological lead, withdrew from the field after the Indian government reserved the first DTH licence for Doordarshan. InCable's Jagjit Singh Kohli argues that DTH has not been a threat to cable even in developed markets like the US and that the price sensitivity of the Indian consumer will make it impossible for DTH to compete with the present rates for cable connections.[17]

THE STATE AS REGULATOR

The debate about DTH and other new technologies underlines the government's crucial role in establishing a viable framework for development. Its decision to block Star's DTH ambitions and to privilege Doordarshan in this new field illustrated the Indian government's sensitivity to the power of multinational media conglomerates. In less nationally sensitive but culturally important areas like the development of cable television, it has been less decisive in identifying where the public interest lies.

In the complex new world of media, technology and broadcasting, one role of the state should be to provide enabling regulation—a regime that allows varied and creative programming to flourish. Governments acting in their executive capacity can set out the principles which form the basis of a broad accountability, though parliaments are a better choice, especially if they can establish institutions which reflect a diversity of political views. Other public bodies with a tradition of autonomy can have roles as guardians of a public broadcasting system. The judiciary has a constitutional role in protecting freedom of speech. A university governing body is well equipped to oversee an educational purpose, or newspaper editors to promote independent journalism. Religious institutions may have a role, as in the Netherlands, in safeguarding traditional religious values. But they are all specialised bodies in their own field; and there are drawbacks to all of them. A governing board of bankers, businessmen or accountants, essential as they are to any venture, would be equally limited; though this may be the reality in the world of commercial broadcasting. Broadcasting has a remit that touches all of these concerns but goes beyond them.

This is where the concept of a board consisting of people of independence and distinction in a variety of fields has attractions. Serving for a limited term as representatives of the public, they are expected to serve a dual purpose, both to protect the independence of the broadcasting institutions from political pressure and to provide a counter-weight to the professional broadcasters' own assessment of the public interest. This solution depends crucially on the strength of values of civil society and the willingness of government to select such people in the first place, rather than packing the board with their own political supporters and sympathisers. Variations of the system are practised in Britain, France, Germany, other European countries and in Japan.

In South Asia, there has been very limited progress in giving the public, or their representatives, such a role, except in India, where the Prasar Bharati Act set up a governing body which was supposed to serve this purpose. Satellite channels have not taken any such initiatives and have shown no interest in doing so. Some media watchers are now looking for ways of influencing the impact of the market, which they see as just as ruthless in its own way as the old state monopoly. 'People used to complain about state oppression', says Anjali Monteiro, 'but the market, equally, erases certain voices or prevents certain programmes from appearing.'[18] Anthropologist Veena Das believes that the community has to be brought into the equation to hold the balance between the market and the bureaucracy. What she would like to see is the creation of 'a new kind of space involving participation between government, community and the private sector', so that censorship operating through the market or through the bureaucracy is avoided and the public has a say, whether through communities or individuals of independent stature.[19]

Giving the people a voice is also an issue in Sri Lanka, where unfettered competition among terrestrial broadcasters is affecting programme range and quality. For Nalaka Gunawardene, the key question is: 'How do we gradually nurture and nudge the broadcasting culture towards an era where there is more discerning programming on the part of programme managers and producers?' His answer is that 'viewers and listeners should mobilise themselves and start exerting legitimate pressure on broadcasters.' Such pressure should be exerted, he says, on both private and public broadcasters, but particularly public ones, because in Sri Lanka they get a licence fee.[20]

The Centre for Advocacy and Research in Delhi has initiated the most systematic attempt anywhere in the region to mobilise public opinion on television issues. In 1993, as the Media Advocacy Group, it began by researching viewing habits and encouraging discussion among media practitioners on the representation of women. As a result of this work, it started promoting consumer intervention in media matters more systematically and encouraging qualitative feedback from viewers to broadcasters. In November 1996 it launched a 'Viewers' Forum' 'to conduct public advocacy with the government and the media industry'.[21] Later, it widened its focus to include the interests of those with disabilities and the poor. Akhila Sivadas, the director of the Centre, can point to important changes in the attitudes and agendas of broadcasters as a result of regular exchanges of this kind. As one example, in early 2000, there were three soap operas running on television featuring disabled characters, a change from the neglect of earlier times.[22]

In Pakistan, Javed Jabbar, a leading advocate of autonomy for PTV and radio (and later media adviser in General Musharraf's government), played a central role in setting up the Citizen's Media Commission in 1997. Its aim is to represent the public to the broadcasters, to campaign for autonomy for state broadcasters and a fairer system of media regulation. In promoting the commission, Jabbar argued that 'democratic governance' in broadcasting would contribute significantly to the democratisation of society and that the mobilisation of public opinion was the key to change. 'These media, when truly free and independent of government control', he said, 'enable participation, articulation and representation of people's viewpoints.'[23] The Commission, which is chaired by a retired chief justice of the Supreme Court, has since gone on to organise public meetings and to campaign for these objectives.

BROADCASTING AUTONOMY UNDER REVIEW

In India, even before the state broadcasting monopoly was broken, the idea of determining who speaks for the nation had crystallised in the concept of an autonomous broadcaster. The Prasar Bharati Act was passed with all party support in 1990 after years of public debate. But by the time the act was brought into force seven years later, the whole broadcasting media environment had changed. Yesterday's key question—autonomy or not?—had been replaced with a new set of questions which needed new answers. After the United Front government was defeated in 1997, political commitment to broadcasting reform ebbed away. The thirteen-month administration led by the BJP under Atal Behari Vajpayee, in its open opposition to the composition of the Prasar Bharati board in general, and to its chief executive in particular, did nothing to enable the institution to strike roots. The BJP did not seem to be interested in autonomy for the state broadcaster; the Congress as the main opposition party was no more enthusiastic.[24] Twenty years of debate on the place of broadcasting in society had been sidelined. S.S. Gill, the ousted chief executive, said of the position during the Vajpayee government: 'No spokesman either of government or opposition will say openly that Prasar Bharati should be wound up. There will be public opposition and the media would not tolerate it. But actually nobody wants it. So they try silently, quietly to strangle it.'[25]

Since the end of the monopoly, for some politicians and officials there is a straightforward answer to the question: what should be done about the national broadcaster? Technological advances and commercial competition are now providing a platform for alternative voices and lively sources of entertainment. It is therefore unnecessary for the national broadcaster to be either autonomous or comprehensive in its coverage. According to this argument, which has been heard in Sri Lanka, Bangladesh and in India, autonomy without financial self-sufficiency is in any case an unreal objective. The government's responsibilities in South Asian societies mean that it needs its own channel and that the national broadcaster can now concentrate on performing this role. Pramod Mahajan, information and broadcasting minister in the BJP-led interim government in 1998–99 maintained that the government needed 'a medium to propagate its messages and counter foreign propaganda'.[26] S.S. Gill argued that this was a double-edged weapon. Firstly, no one would watch a government channel, so the purpose would be defeated. Secondly, a party out of power would not be happy at the way another government expressed its views.[27]

NEW FINANCIAL REALITIES

Another important factor in the present situation is the state broadcaster's increasing dependence on advertising. The realities of the new media market have undermined the financial basis of the existing system and raised questions as to whether public service broadcasting in the wider sense—not just officially sponsored information—can be sustained in the changed circumstances of today.

Even before the satellite channels had begun to establish themselves in serious competition for a mass audience, Doordarshan was being pushed into paying its way. Until colour television became widely available in towns and cities throughout the country, television had hardly been considered an advertising medium. With the creation of a national TV network in the early 1980s, Indian advertisers could capitalise on Doordarshan's extensive reach. Marketing became the skill for the 1990s, though the national broadcaster was unpractised in marketing skills.

Initially, there was a steep, and in many ways very successful, learning curve. Doordarshan had a major advantage both as the sole operator of a terrestrial channel and with its own satellite network of regional language services. But private satellite channels have been catching up. They have their own pitfalls and uncertainties; few of them are profitable. Despite some loss of ground to its competitors, India's national broadcaster is far from written off. But for Doordarshan, as for other national broadcasters in South Asia, some repositioning seems to be inevitable.

The problem of funding for public service broadcasting dominates every area of debate. For those who attach primary importance to public broadcasting as a service of education and information, with a key part to play in national development, it ranks with health and basic formal education as a high priority for a full state subsidy. On the opposite side are those who argue that the market is the best judge of what the public wants and needs and that broadcasting does not need state funds.

All South Asian countries started by charging a licence fee for radio and television, but several governments later abolished them because the costs of collection were outweighing the returns. Radio is much more dependent on government subsidy than TV and the radio licence has tended to be the first to be abolished. India abolished it for one and two band receivers in 1980; Pakistan in the budget of 1999. However, as state television has attracted substantial funds from advertising, governments have increasingly seen this as the most obvious means of funding these services. India abolished its TV licence in 1985, before the advent of satellite television, when commercial returns for Doordarshan looked very secure. In Pakistan, the government stopped subsidising PTV in the early 1980s but did not abolish the licence. In 1998, PTV was able to bring in private tax-collectors to try to improve returns. The following year licence fees for satellite dishes were withdrawn.

In West Bengal, the ruling Communist Party (Marxist) suggested a form of public funding for Prasar Bharati, for which tenders or shares could be floated, to supplement a government-subsidised trust fund.[28] The Sengupta Committee Report on Prasar Bharati in August 1996 recommended the restoration of a licence fee, or a one-off tax on the sale of new television sets.[29] Many broadcasters are in favour. Siddhartha Ray, one of the accredited marketing agents of Doordarshan said: 'Absence of licence fees makes it extremely difficult for Doordarshan to take its role as a public service broadcaster seriously. There are limitations to public funding. It is not easy to find advertisement support for a lot of programmes like chat shows, educational and children's programmes and awareness drives. The only alternative is higher budgetary support.'[30]

The public does not seem to be averse to this idea. At a group discussion organised as part of the Media South Asia Project, a group of ex-soldiers in the North Indian town of Mathura told us that they were ready to pay licence fees in the range of Rs. 200–Rs. 500 a year if they were assured of meaningful and useful programming.[31] But an annual licence fee is expensive to collect. Trade unionists are against it. Politicians in and out of government fear that it would be a political embarrassment. No such proposal is on the agenda of any Indian political party. Other forms of taxation, either on the sale of hardware or on cable operators and subscribers, might be less controversial.

But it seems unlikely that Doordarshan or any public broadcaster is going to be able to rely solely on public funding again. In March 1996, the expert committee set up by the Indian government to recommend the adoption of suitable marketing strategies for AIR and Doordarshan advocated a more market-oriented approach by the state broadcaster.[32] The idea was implicitly accepted that the established public broadcaster had something to learn from its commercial rivals. Revenue could be earned from exploiting archival material as well as non-broadcasting activities such as radio paging on the FM network. In 1999, with the appointment of a further three-man expert committee, the newly elected BJP-led administration seemed to be thinking along much the same lines.

In Pakistan, a more market-oriented strategy, combined with the farming out of licence fee collection, brought about a major improvement in finances within a two-year period. This might also be an option in Sri Lanka, where radio and TV licences still exist but provide only limited revenue because of collection problems. The licensing of private channels, or of time on air to private radio stations, is a further potential source of revenue. It could become a method for subsidising quality public interest broadcasting either by the state broadcaster or on private channels. In practice, the solution to funding is a mixture of sources, with a licence fee or a subsidy, subscriptions and commercial revenues balanced in a way that satisfies the government, the public and other intermediate stakeholders.

MANAGING THE INFRASTRUCTURE

Part of the obligation that a public service broadcaster in the European tradition assumes is to provide universal accessibility. One aspect of this is the reliability and quality of reception, which is both a public service objective and a commercial asset. TV advertisers and sponsors will only pay for programmes that can be seen and heard. The reach of Doordarshan has ensured that it gets a major, though declining, share of advertising. But where cable is a mass distribution system, as it is in urban India, the state broadcaster is in the same boat as its competitors in wanting to ensure good reception quality for its programmes. In India it has the law on its side. But as Doordarshan has discovered, the provision in the Cable Act of 1995 that cable channels must carry at least two Doordarshan channels, does not always ensure the quality it hopes for. The cable operators have become de-facto gate-keepers for the state broadcaster, and that sometimes means that viewers receive Doordarshan services in poorer quality by cable than they would by direct reception. Other Doordarshan satellite services have to take their chance alongside private channels, competing for the available slots in the cable operators' schedules. Unfavourable and potentially damaging comparisons of reception quality are then made between the public and private channels.

The national broadcaster may find it is required to share technical infrastructure with private companies. When this sharing involves a service which is not in competition with broadcasting, like AIR's use of its extensive and under-used FM network for a radio paging service, the additional revenue acts as a welcome addition to shrinking government subsidies. Controlling the infrastructure can also bring competitive advantages. The Sri Lankan government permitted private FM stations to broadcast in Colombo with their own studios and transmission facilities. But the most effective sites and most powerful transmitters for island-wide reception are reserved for SLBC as the state broadcaster. In Pakistan, before the military takeover, the semi-government second channel, Shalimar TV, was not allowed to have a national network.

The infrastructure of broadcasting built up over more than seventy years represents a large public capital asset and national investment, managed by the state broadcaster on behalf of the state. In India it was estimated (in 1998) to be worth Rs. 550 billion (US$ 13 billion).[33] The reach of the terrestrial television service is 86 per cent of the population. No private broadcaster could begin to match Doordarshan for size or reach. Nor would it wish to match the weight of administrative and staff costs that come with it. The challenge for the public broadcaster is to make the best use of these capital assets on behalf of the public.

Critics argue that capital expenditure in the expansion of the broadcasting network in India had been influenced by political and employment considerations. Kali Prasad, general secretary of the Doordarshan Producers' Association, argues that the need to make use of a large engineering staff was a factor and that the huge investment in low-powered transmitters from the 1980s was an unnecessarily expensive use of the Insat series of broadcasting satellites.[34]

Where the public broadcaster plays host to private stations using its own facilities, as AIR and Radio Nepal have done, this also demands a judgement as to what kind of programming should be expected from the private broadcasters. But institutions are not always the best arbiters of the terms on which their competitors can operate. The technical infrastructure of national broadcasting is a public asset, whose use is best allocated by an independent regulatory body.

CATERING FOR MINORITY INTERESTS

A second aspect of accessibility is an obligation to cater for minority as well majority interests. For the public broadcaster, the single-minded pursuit of a niche market is not a long-term option as it is for the private channels. It is an important and defining difference in their respective roles. Yet, the commercialisation of the media market in India and Sri Lanka has also affected the range of programmes offered by the state sector and illustrates the restriction in choice involved if commercial criteria become dominant. Our own research has highlighted a shortage on satellite and state channels of children's programmes (except for cartoons), documentaries, scientific features, as well as programmes on development issues and the performing arts. It is also notable that when Doordarshan extended its prime time band, it was at the expense of minority programmes like those on the performing arts. Accommodating minority interests on mass entertainment channels is not easy, but intelligent regulation can create spaces for them.

Television coverage of the performing arts in India provides an interesting example of different approaches by the commercial and public sectors. Satellite television has done a great deal to make music popular, including some classical music, but not on traditional terms. Since satellite TV ended Doordarshan's monopoly, TV talent spotting competitions and shows encouraging audience participation like *Meri Awaz Suno, Antakshari* and *Sa Re Ga Ma,* have developed huge audiences all over India, particularly among the young. The principal of a music college with over 400 students in Latur told us he believed as many as half of his students had come to the college because of the impact of TV. He told us: 'The Taj Mahal Tea advertisement (featuring one of India's most accomplished tabla players) has inspired many young boys to learn tabla and become Ustad Zakir Hussain....'[35]

At the same time, the thoroughgoing commercialism of satellite TV has demanded shorter, more popular treatments of music or dance which seem to many classical artists a prostitution of their art. As one classical dancer from Orissa told us: 'Fast action is now the buzz word of all entertainment.... In their efforts to sensationalise everything, they are even presenting Odissi classical dance as a break dance mix.'[36]

The reputed Bharatnatyam dancer Mrinalini Sarabhai and her daughter Mallika are refreshing exceptions in their espousal of the new media, despite concerns that some satellite programmes are popularising the mediocre. Mallika Sarabhai believes that TV offers great opportunities 'to make people excited and knowledgeable about dance', even if some compromises are involved. She says with telling use of language: 'We need to develop and package dance and still keep its integrity, so we remain mistresses and TV becomes our genie.'[37] Mallika developed a pop music opera called 'The Adventures of Krishna Gopala' which aimed 'to package classical dance in a way...applicable to the MTV generation'. She was later commissioned to develop a popular children's programme for Star TV. She told us her aim was to be 'entertaining with value'; she said it is a myth that to entertain you need to aim at the lowest common denominator.

Commercial television in its pursuit of the mass market cannot devote substantial sequences to classical music, which only appeal to a minority of viewers. But this is an area where publicly-funded broadcasting can make a valuable contribution, particularly if a number of channels are available. Dr. Kiran Seth, director of an organisation promoting Indian classical music among young people, believes that television—not just satellite TV but Doordarshan as well—have so far played a very superficial role in this field. He says television has tended to 'literalise' art rather than stimulate the imagination. In his view, 'there is not much difference in how they film a political rally or a dance programme.'[38]

The view that Doordarshan lacks the expertise to fulfil this important role is widely expressed. The great Odissi dance guru, Kelucharan Mohapatra, told us he regrets the lack of exposure for young talent on television and the shortage of television producers with the knowledge to project his art sensitively.[39] A similar criticism came from the Bharatnatyam dancer Anita Ratnam. She said of Doordarshan producers that 'their insensitivity...and lack of knowledge of the area they are covering is abominable.... This is not just the attitude of Doordarshan; all TV channels are the same. Today I don't allow any of them to cover my dance festivals. If you are a performer, you don't want some uncouth fellow walking in front of you with a hand-held light.'[40] Dr. Seth says television may not be able to play a major role in maintaining the classical tradition but he would like to see it treat classical music with more respect so that 'young people have an opportunity to see the best in the best way'.

NEWS AND CURRENT AFFAIRS

News and current affairs programmes have become a testing ground for the merits of state and private broadcasters. Despite the presence of international news broadcasters such as CNN and the BBC, state broadcasters continued to monopolise locally-originated news and current affairs for a few years after the satellite invasion. Private Hindi and South Indian language channels were initially seen as purely devoted to entertainment. But after 1996, the barriers were comprehensively breached. Both Star TV and Zee TV carry news coverage more widely watched throughout South Asia than established international channels such as BBC or CNN. Star's coverage of the Indian elections in 1998 and 1999 won particular admiration. Discussion groups conducted for this book confirmed that Star News carried high credibility.[41]

The importance which private channels have come to attach to their news services may indicate their own political agenda or need for visibility to advance other corporate aims. Some of the Indian channels have open political affiliations. But there is a sensitivity to political bias on the part of the audience which applies to all channels. TV journalists are judged by journalistic criteria and professional standards; their own professional reputations are at stake, and they can carry them from one channel to another, public or private. It should be in the interest both of the public and private broadcaster to have an objective standard by which they can expect their credibility to be judged.

Doordarshan responded to the challenge, first of video news magazines and then of the satellite channels, by commissioning current affairs programmes produced by outside producers. They were previewed and pre-censored, creating real problems in keeping a fast-moving story up to date. But they enhanced Doordarshan's credibility, the more so when Prasar Bharati was created in 1997 and the pre-viewing requirement was lifted. The expertise in independent TV journalism brought in from the print media and fostered in the state channel became a resource for the whole industry to draw on.

Doordarshan can also take credit for its contribution to the growth of what Sevanti Ninan calls an 'appetite for political accountability' on television.[42] The probing television interview, pioneered by the video news magazines *Newstrack* and *Eyewitness*, was initially feared by the then Congress governments. But these programmes were adopted by Doordarshan itself in 1994, and they and other independently produced news programmes brought a sharper element into media political discourse.

Rajdeep Sardesai has pointed to the special character of television news reporting, which differentiates it sharply from that of the print media.[43] Live television reporting introduces an immediacy missing in the print media. Events in remote parts of the country can rapidly become the focus of major national news interest. A study of the 1998 Indian elections argues that the weight given by the television medium to the role of personalities in politics is particularly evident at election time. Print journalists have also played a major role in television coverage, commenting on elections and on issues of national political importance. Though television news reporting has produced its share of trivialisation and sensationalism, the report says that at election time, to a surprising extent, all television channels identified important national issues.[44]

Doordarshan's greater openness to outside talent, combined with its reach and the fact that it was the first in the field, helped it to begin repairing the confidence that audiences want to have in the national broadcaster. There was also some reduction in direct political pressure, as politicians began to appear on satellite channels as well. If liberated from an agenda dictated by the ministry and the government of the day, a state broadcaster has valuable assets as a provider of news. The belief that the state broadcaster has irredeemably lost credibility is disputed vigorously, not only by the state broadcasters themselves but by other independent observers in the media.

In India, Doordarshan implemented significant reforms in news coverage in response to the challenge of satellite competition. Pre-censorship of news and current affairs programmes was lifted by Prasar Bharati's chief executive officer, S.S. Gill, almost from the first day of his tenure, and this made for an acknowledged improvement in the environment for independent producers working on these programmes.[45] Prasar Bharati News had some key advantages. Its monopoly on uplinking, which was only ended in 1998, gave a speed of coverage not available to the private channels. Nor could they match the wide range of the state broadcaster's reporting network, especially in the north east. Access to the National Informatics Centre's satellite-based computer communication network (NICNET) has also given Doordarshan an advantage in the reporting of elections.[46]

Compared to the private channels, Doordarshan claims to have different expectations of its news producers, characterised positively by one presenter as 'a greater sensitivity to what is perceived to be the healthy development of society.'[47] But according to a senior news editor in Calcutta, its lopsided recruitment patterns can lead to production problems. For example, a 'good-looking graduate' is too often put as a requirement for a television newsreader, though this is a trend on the satellite channels as well. There are also bureaucratic difficulties. The news units in the Doordarshan's Calcutta station are headed by people from the government information services. They are wary of changing established systems and averse to taking risks. They find it difficult to resist pressure from opposition Congress party leaders in West Bengal to cover specific news items, or from the CPI(M), as the dominant party in the ruling coalition government.[48] It is significant that *Khas Khabar*, Calcutta's successful current affairs programme, is a private production for the station.

By bringing in talent from the press, however, Prasar Bharati has significantly improved its performance. Arvind Das, a print journalist who presented a daily news programme on Door-darshan, told us he thought Prasar Bharati news was now 'so good that with the BBC World Service it provides sufficient news coverage'.[49] Others regarded this an exaggerated claim. M.J. Akbar, the editor of *Asian Age*, who had his contract as a presenter of a weekly current affairs programme on Doordarshan terminated at short notice, argues that 'Doordarshan was not and is not a free medium', though he accepts that it has improved.[50] Chandan Mitra, editor of *The Pioneer*, believes that 'satellite TV has extended the scope of news and current affairs and forced Doordarshan to pro-fessionalise'. As a result, Doordarshan has involved private pro-ducers, acquired better equipment, pays more and is more quality conscious. Mitra says 'it has come a long way but it still has a long way to go'.[51] Several of our discussants made unflattering com-parisons between Doordarshan and Star, whose coverage of the 1998 national elections won it considerable praise. Despite its unrivalled infrastructure and news gathering network, Door-darshan was thought to be less effective than its less well staffed rival. Star News, which recruited many of its managers and profes-sionals from Doordarshan, had shown what they could deliver if freed from Indian bureaucratic constraints.

Despite such comparisons, the potential of Doordarshan to make serious news programmes, whether in English or Hindi, should not be underestimated. Mrinal Pande, the Hindi language broad-caster who was one of Star TV's anchors for its ground-breaking bilingual coverage of the 1998 elections, later broke off her relation-ship with Star because she felt that it was not taking Hindi broad-casting seriously enough. There was a sense, she told us, that the channel thought in English and was not well placed to speak to the vast Hindi audience on it own terms.[52] Her return to Door-darshan in early 2000 showed both its plans to improve its per-formance in this area and her expectation that it would be able to do so.

Doordarshan also has a strong hand to play as a regional news provider, particularly in areas where there are no competing satellite services. Interviews with leading newspaper editors and politicians in Assam established that the Guwahati station of Doordarshan is regarded as essential viewing. 'They said they just could not afford to miss it.... Doordarshan, with all its limitations, was the best source of news on their own state, which was the most important area of their curiosity.'[53] It also provided the best mix of news—local, national and global. Satellite media were regarded as useful for international news, wildlife, science and entertainment. But there was a general consensus that 'Assam's concerns were not properly reflected in national and global media, in television, radio and print.' Though Doordarshan and AIR are essentially monopoly suppliers of Assamese broadcasting, they have the infrastructure and the manpower to improve their services to other regions and localities, providing they can be harnessed to that end. However, they face stiff competition from Star TV, which has attracted some of Doordarshan's good regional reporters and has already achieved high standards in this field.

RESEARCHING THE VIEWERS AND LISTENERS

The arrival of the private channels brought a great increase in market research. Pressure from advertisers meant they had to know whether people were watching or not. Media planning to meet this need meant new questions being asked. Market research generated more information about the audience, to the benefit of the industry as a whole. The state channels had earlier been the only available choice for the advertiser as well as the only vehicle for public service broadcasting. In the new multi-channel environment in India, Doordarshan by virtue of its reach still enjoyed a major advantage for advertisers promoting low value consumer goods. But the information from Doordarshan's own market research department seemed to be largely discounted by the agencies responsible for media planning.[54]

Common standards for gathering information about audiences would increase the range of information available and reduce its duplication. It might also eliminate widely divergent estimates from different parts of the industry. For example, in Pakistan, government and private research companies give very different figures for TV viewership.

In some countries, lack of research information stands in the way of a scientific approach to the definition of public service objectives. PTV has no research department at all, though it does commission surveys from outside agencies. Sri Lankan state broadcasters are also poorly staffed in this vital field, despite the intensity of the competition they face.

One weakness of research for satellite channels is that it concentrates largely on the urban middle class. Even if it is shared, it is of limited value in defining the needs of rural audiences. It is important, therefore, that any common approach goes beyond the immediate objectives of the commercial channels to explore issues of relevance to public broadcasting.

There is a great deal of expertise in Doordarshan and AIR in audience research and the range of sources they draw on for information has been geographically and numerically wider than the commercial research organisations. But Doordarshan has resisted joining a common system of ratings, which could be a standard for the broadcasting industry. Researchers in the commercial sector regret this. While the state broadcaster represents a majority of television viewers, this detachment is perhaps understandable, but if a common agenda could be agreed, it might help to promote a wider understanding of what viewers and listeners require. This could both influence the development of public broadcasting and involve the commercial sector in the consideration of a wider range of needs.

SETTING PROGRAMME AND QUALITY STANDARDS

In all television systems, the regulation of programme standards presents practical difficulties of implementation. It also gives grounds for an ideological argument in which the criteria of quality are disputed. For the free marketeer, quality is a matter of someone's opinion, of which the only impartial arbiter is the market. The relativist dismisses quality criteria as a thinly disguised elitist conspiracy. At an academic level, a debate on the shifting values and dynamics of popular culture is an insecure basis for judging programmes or programme schedules. But the relativist argument about the quality of television has not won the day in Europe, and broadcasters in South Asia would not be setting themselves up as opponents of diversity and plurality in setting standards for their own media.

Programme standards can be regulated in a negative way, as governments already do. Guidelines can be set as to the type of programming expected: educational, informational and cultural. But quality is not an abstract or bureaucratic concept. It arises from perceptions of what has been done and what can be done. It is a product of a climate in which creativity is encouraged. It is dependent, almost by definition, on a high degree of autonomy. Public service broadcasters have to justify their strategies not by their prospectus but by the quality of their programmes. Watchability is a part of the test, but popularity should not be achieved by appealing to the lowest common denominator. The benchmark is the programme that has something to communicate and does so in an interesting way.

The setting of quality standards is both a regulatory function and a proper role for a public broadcaster. Technical specifications have to be set by a body authorised by the state, to allow the manufacturers of radio and TV sets and dealers to know what market they are operating in. They may be subject to international negotiation, which is the prerogative of a state, or in a free market they may be pre-empted by proprietary technology. Public broadcasting institutions in turn have an important role to play in setting standards of technical excellence, as well as quality criteria for programmes.

THE PRIVATE SECTOR AND THE PUBLIC INTEREST

The extent to which private channels might be willing to accept public service obligations is rightly questioned. But when public service objectives are seen as an obligation to provide quality programming, to cater to a wide variety of tastes, and to promote debate about relevant social issues, they can be seen as common to both public and private broadcasters. Among the Indian channels only TVi, or Business India TV as it was originally called, started with public service ideals and maintained them despite the financial problems that closed the station in 1999. The priorities of most Hindi satellite channels lay elsewhere, but they have not excluded public interest objectives.

Sony Entertainment TV, which started with the single-minded objective of ensuring its presence on prime band in India's all-important cable systems, presents itself as highly receptive to whatever regulatory controls may be required. In contrast to Star TV, Sony avoids active and public lobbying on broadcasting issues but acknowledges that it can make its views known through Japanese diplomatic channels. Its chief executive, Kunal Das Gupta, points out that the Japanese broadcasting scene is much more regulated than India's is ever likely to be. Socially relevant broadcasting is very much on Sony's agenda, part of what Das Gupta calls their 'developmental process'. They are 'seriously looking at programmes which will deal with issues'.[55]

Bhaskar Majumdar, a senior executive of Zee Telefilms (the content-providing company for Zee TV) argued that most private broadcasters would be willing to submit to a requirement that they should keep a time for public service broadcasting. It could be a slot of a defined period, perhaps two hours a day. But he argued that for it to happen a clear distinction should be made between public and private broadcasting, in the kind of programmes that they put on and the advertising that they aim for. For a private channel to talk of public service broadcasting there must be a 'a level-playing field'. In other words, there should be comparable obligations on the part of other private broadcasters and reciprocal understanding on part of the public broadcaster.[56]

The core of this argument is that the public service broadcaster should opt out of popular entertainment programming. But state broadcasters would not feel justified in giving up the revenue that a popular programme with a national terrestrial audience can attract. As long as cable and satellite are accessible only to a minority of television set owners, it is acknowledged that the terrestrial audience has a right to entertainment programmes. A further argument is that to abandon entertainment would mean a neglect of popular culture on the part of the state broadcaster. It would exclude it from the opportunity to play a role in an aspect of contemporary society that the television medium serves especially well.

There has been much criticism of the extent to which public broadcasters have been revising their programme concepts and formats in the interest of raising advertising revenues, both in India and Sri Lanka. The opposite trend has been less credited—the extent to which private channels have sensed an audience saturation with the sameness of film-based programmes and have sought to enlarge and enrich their schedules. In Sri Lanka, Maharaja TV, TNL and Swarnavahini have developed some programmes, in current affairs particularly, with a clear public service remit. In some respects, they are judged to have been more successful in this field than the state broadcasters.

One problem in suggesting that private television channels should accept public service obligations is the bad name given to the concept by fifty years of state control. As one example among many, in 1993, the human rights organisation Article 19 concluded after interviews with the chairmen of Sri Lanka's state-owned broadcasting institutions that there was little concept of public service broadcasting in any of them. The chairmen rejected the argument that there was a need, as an instrument of democratic monitoring, to broadcast informed debate and criticism about government policy. Sri Lanka broadcasting was seen as 'too young' at that time to cover such debates.[57] Over the next seven years, these attitudes had to be revised, as competitors entered the market and began to hold politicians and others to account.

Some private television channels are resistant to the idea that they should be required to shoulder public service requirements for these kinds of historic reasons. According to Kalanidhi Maran of Sun TV, 'the moment something comes with the tag of public service broadcasting, it is viewed as propaganda. And most of the time, it remains propaganda. By being a sensitive, responsive broadcaster, one can do public service broadcasting more efficiently.'[58] Rajat Sharma, a prominent television presenter and chairman of Independent Media, takes the same view. He says private channels 'should not be required to assume obligations which prevent them from making money. Quality thresholds cannot be enforced.'[59]

Experience elsewhere suggests, however, that unless commercial channels are required by contract or licence to broadcast a wider range of programmes than the immediate demands of profitability require, then they are unlikely to do so. In Britain, the decision in 1990 to dilute previous quality criteria for commercial franchises has provided powerful evidence that the free market cannot be relied upon to provide the kind of quality and choice of programmes that even its advocates expect.[60] The same issue has emerged in a different form in Australia, where the ability of powerful commercial broadcasters to ignore public service obligations is undermining efforts to promote a more diversified media to replace the old model of centralised political control.[61] Here too the absence of ground rules for the commercial sector stands in the way of the achievement of wider objectives.

Though the commercial ethos, which determines the character and content of the new satellite channels, is closest to the North American broadcasting model, what is less well known is that public service broadcasting in the USA is designed to cater only for those needs which are not deemed to be met by the commercial broadcasters. Though widely accessible, its audience is small—only 2 per cent of the population. In that tradition, broadcasting in the public interest is not part of the mainstream, nor can it aspire to set standards of programme quality to which the commercial broadcasters can be compared.[62] Though the new free market in broadcasting in South Asia has proved liberating for entrepreneurs and programme makers alike after years of stultifying state control, it is questionable whether such a model is appropriate in the longer term in a region where the state and state broadcasters have traditionally acknowledged, in the interests of health, education and development at least, a responsibility to all citizens.

MARKET AND CHOICE

Intervention may be required to provide what the free market fails to provide. A committee set up in Sri Lanka to advise on the reform of laws affecting media freedom in 1996 warned that while media diversity was important, 'granting licences to private broadcasters should not be viewed as a substitute for ensuring the pluralism and independence of public-funded broadcasting'.[63] This is a clear rejection of the neo-liberal view which identifies all competitive provision for the consumer as a public service. But it does not mean that there is a fundamental conflict between the free market and public service objectives and ideals.

So far, South Asian states have viewed the licensing of competition for the state sector as a largely commercial exercise and have not used their powers as regulators to provide for quality or diversity. They have been more keen on ensuring what is not broadcast than what is. In the Indian draft Broadcasting Bill of 1997 the conditions for a licence included taste and decency provisions.

They also required impartiality and accuracy, both in news and in discussing social, political or public policy issues. There were no specific programme quality criteria. In Sri Lanka, an applicant for a television licence has to demonstrate technical, financial and professional qualifications. There is some attempt to check the financial viability of a proposal and the kinds of programmes that are planned, though precisely what criteria are applied is not clear. Applications have to be passed through the minister, the state television corporation and the telecommunications department. Bangladesh requires programmes on a licensed TV or radio station to meet professional and technical standards. In none of these countries is there an established or independent mechanism for monitoring or reporting on programme quality.

Public interest broadcasting in South Asia's multi-channel media environment is increasingly under threat. This is not just because the state broadcasters' loss of monopoly has given audiences a choice. That is not a threat, but a benefit. It is because there has been a failure to examine and redefine what it means in the new environment. Such a review should include not only the role of the state channels and their responses to the new technologies, but the role and programme output of the private channels as well and the expectations that the public legitimately have of them. The private channels' contribution to the media environment is itself a matter of public interest. It should not be judged on commercial criteria alone.

NOTES AND REFERENCES

1. Cf. J.G. Blumler (1992), *Television and the Public Interest*, cited in Karol Jakubowicz (1997), 'Public Service Broadcasting and Democracy', paper presented at an international seminar on Public Broadcasting and Editorial Independence: Strengthening Democratic Voices, Tampere, Finland, 16–18 June 1997.
2. See A. Smith (1989), 'The Public Interest', *Intermedia*, Vol. 17, No. 2, p. 23, quoted in K. Jakubowicz, 'Public Service Broadcasting and Democracy' (1997).
3. Samuel Brittan, quoted in Curran and Seaton (1991), *Power without Responsibility*, p. 337.
4. Armand Mattelart and Michele Mattelart (1992), *Rethinking Media Theory*, p. 72.
5. Sohail Hashmi, Delhi, June 1998.
6. George Verghese, The Radhanath Rath Memorial Lecture, Cuttack, 12 February 1999, in *Mainstream Annual* 1999.

7. Dr. Mohan Singh Sainju, Kathmandu, May 1998.
8. Nilanjana Gupta (1998), *Switching Channels*, pp. 88–89.
9. Abhijit Pathak, Delhi, July 1998.
10. Indrajit Lahiri, Delhi, May 1998.
11. Chandan Mitra, Delhi, July 1998.
12. Dr. T. Nannan, Chennai, May 1998.
13. *Peacock Committee Report* 1986, cited in Curran and Seaton (1991), *Power without Responsibility*, p. 341.
14. S.S. Gill, Delhi, January 1999.
15. *McKinsey Quarterly* (1997), No. 1.
16. Tabassum Inamdar, Mumbai, May 1998.
17. J.S. Kohli, Mumbai, May 1998.
18. Anjali Monteiro, Mumbai, May 1998.
19. Veena Das, Delhi, July 1998.
20. Nalaka Gunawardene, Colombo, July 1998.
21. This account of the activities of the Centre is drawn from their publications and their website: www.viewersforum.com.
22. Akhila Sivadas, Delhi, by telephone, April 2000.
23. Javed Jabbar, Issue paper for seminar organised by the Citizen's Media Commission of Pakistan on Democratic Governance and Freedom of Electronic Media, Islamabad, 14 February 1998.
24. Cf. V.R. Gadgil, Delhi, June 1998.
25. S.S. Gill, Delhi, January 1999. This charge was vigorously denied by Arun Jaitley, Minister of Information and Broadcasting in the BJP government elected in 1999.
26. Pramod Mahajan, Delhi, April 1999.
27. S.S. Gill, Delhi, January 1999.
28. Professor Malini Bhattacharya, Calcutta, June 1998.
29. Report on Prasar Bharati (Nitish Sengupta Committee), Ministry of Information and Broadcasting, Government of India, August 1996, p. 30.
30. Siddhartha Ray, Delhi, May 1998.
31. Ex-servicemen, Balajipuram, Mathura, June 1998.
32. Report of the Sen Committee (1996). See also, Chapter 8, p. 269.
33. The valuation was that of the Ministry of Information and Broadcasting, cited in Saibal Dasgupta, 'Profile of Doordarshan and All India Radio', commissioned for the Media South Asia Project, June 1998.
34. Kali Prasad, Delhi, March 1998.
35. Ram Borgaonkar, Latur, May 1998.
36. Ratikanta Mohapatra, Cuttack, September 1998.
37. Mallika and Mrinalani Sarabhai, Ahmedabad, April 1998.
38. Dr. Kiran Seth, Director, Society for the Promotion of Indian Classical Music and Culture among Youth (SPIC-MACAY), Delhi, June 1998.
39. Kelucharan Mohapatra, Cuttack, September 1998.
40. Anita Ratnam, Chennai, December 1999.
41. Professionals, Ahmedabad, May 1998.
42. Sevanti Ninan (1995), *Through the Magic Window*, p. 60.
43. Rajdeep Sardesai (1999), 'Don't Blink. You're on TV: Television has Rewritten the Rules for News Coverage, *Gentleman*, June, pp. 66–67.

44. According to this study the projection of personalities on television 'has perhaps become the single most important and influential factor in public perception of candidates and their parties'. Media Advocacy Group (1998), *General Elections 1998: Assessing the Role of Television*, April.
45. S.S. Gill, Delhi, January 1999; Rahul Dev, Delhi, July 1998.
46. For information on NICNET see National Informatics Centre website www.nic.in.
47. Rahul Dev, Delhi, July 1998.
48. Sumit Banerjee, Calcutta, May 1998.
49. Arvind Das, Delhi, June 1998.
50. M.J. Akbar, Delhi, June 1998.
51. Chandan Mitra, Delhi, June 1998.
52. Mrinal Pande, Delhi, January 1999.
53. Subir Bhaumik, Survey in Assam, commissioned for the Media South Asia Project, August 1998.
54. A senior media planner for Lever Bros explained this on the grounds that it was a 'fundamental issue in market research...that such an audience measurement should not be conducted by a media owner.' Irfan Khan, Mumbai, April 1998.
55. Kunal Dasgupta, Mumbai, April 1998.
56. Bhaskar Majumdar, Mumbai, May 1998.
57. Article 19, *Reform at Risk: Continuing Censorship in Sri Lanka*, March 1997, pp. 37–40.
58. Kalanidhi Maran, Chennai, November 1999.
59. Rajat Sharma, Delhi, July 1998.
60. According to two experts on British broadcasting 'the effect of active regulation of commercial broadcasting before 1990 had been to create pockets of space in which some broadcast staff had considerable freedom to make important programmes. These pockets are becoming smaller, and less insulated.' See James Curran and Colin Leys 'Media and the Decline of Liberal Corporatism in Britain', in Curran and Park (2000), *De-westernising Media Studies*, p. 231.
61. Marcus Breen (1996), 'Australia: Broadcasting, Policy and Information Technology', in Marc Raboy (ed.), *Public Broadcasting in the 21st Century*, pp. 126–27.
62. Cf. Michael Tracey (1996), 'The United States, PSB, and the Limitations of a Mainstream Alternative' in Marc Raboy (ed.), *Public Broadcasting in the 21st Century*, p. 162.
63. Report of the committee to advise on the reform of laws affecting media freedom (chaired by R.W. Goonesekara), Colombo, 27 May 1996.

Eleven

AGENDAS FOR CHANGE

South Asia has undergone a remarkable media revolution over the past ten years. Within less than a decade, the state has become only one player among many, its broadcasting services in many cases derided by the middle class and its assured audiences increasingly located beyond the urban limits where cable systems have not yet reached. The average middle class viewer in the larger Indian cities now has access to forty or fifty channels and the state media have had to fight a rearguard action to try to maintain their position.

This transformation has been almost wholly unregulated. Unlike in Iran, China or Malaysia, South Asian governments have neither attempted to ban these developments nor have they provided an adequate legislative framework to deal with the new realities. In many South Asian countries, it has been pressure from the cable operators, who had set up their systems in a sort of legal limbo and wanted to see them regularised, which has been the main spur to legislation rather than the activities of governments themselves. Even where governments have acted, they have done so mainly for defensive reasons. They have been slow to acknowledge that the new situation required a comprehensive rethink of broadcasting policy.

National broadcasting authorities, faced with the superior entertainment on offer on channels like Zee or Sony, have presided over a massive commercialisation of their own output as a means of retaining audiences, neglecting other kinds of programmes in the process. Where Doordarshan led, other national TV stations have since followed, including even Pakistan TV, which earlier had a much more conservative cultural agenda.

In our own soundings across South Asia, we have found plenty of disappointment that national broadcasters have not responded more creatively to the challenge of the satellite age. In some walks of public life, there is a feeling that nothing very positive can be expected of them. Among the general public, however, we have found a larger constituency for them than the popularity of the satellite channels might lead one to expect. There is a recognition that national broadcasters have a special role to play if they can overcome the problems of ethos, organisation and funding which they face. There is also a recognition that the state, whatever its shortcomings, has to play a more creative regulatory role if the public interest is to be safeguarded in the new commercial environment. This conclusion draws on the many exchanges we have had with discussion groups and with individuals. It does not offer a blue print for future policy—that has to emerge as a result of political debate and public pressures within individual countries—but a contribution to the process of rethinking which is already under way.

CONSUMING THE SATELLITE REVOLUTION

We have identified through our discussion groups in each country a far more critical public awareness of what is on offer than media entrepreneurs themselves sometimes imagine. There is a wide welcome for better entertainment and sports programmes, international news programmes, the sense of participation encouraged by quiz programmes and talent shows, the less deferential tone, the greater sense of social inclusiveness and the promise of a better material life inherent in the promotion of new products and lifestyles. But there are also concerns about taste and decency, some of them expressed most strongly among the working class. There are worries, particularly outside the metropolitan cities, that some programmes are encouraging permissiveness and the breakdown of the family. The educated, and particularly educated women, are more concerned that popular serials are reinforcing old stereotypes. There is a reassuring awareness of the commercial motivations of the channel proprietors and annoyance at the scope and intrusiveness of advertising. There is a demand for greater reflection of local culture and local issues and for better programmes in regional languages. There are special concerns about the impact of the new media on children.

Such concerns are expressed much more vocally among academics and performing artists, producers and directors. Almost all of them are worried that commercialisation of the media is shrinking the space for innovation, for the reflection of minority interests or for what might be called 'high culture'. If the public is more articulate in reacting to what it sees, these professionals lay more stress on what has not found space in the satellite schedules: the paucity of educational programmes and documentaries, the neglect of the performing arts, the absence of commissioned plays, the avoidance of controversy except where it was likely to add to the audience, and lack of space for debating serious issues other than politics.

THE SATELLITE REVOLUTION AND THE PUBLIC INTEREST

One principal concern that emerges from the book is that the state broadcasters in their anxiety to defend their audiences against satellite competition are divesting themselves of their responsibility to the whole nation. They are in effect allowing the terms of competition to be set by channels like Zee TV or Sun TV, whose main purpose is to secure commercial returns and whose programmes for that reason aim at the largest possible audiences. This competitive spur has produced many positive results. After years of monopoly, many South Asian state broadcasters had become dull and predictable, and their services in the field of entertainment have improved considerably in the new environment. We would argue, however, that moving towards a situation in which the electronic media are entirely commercial in their funding and approach would be a mistake for South Asia, where despite the growth of the middle class and its attractiveness to international business, there are serious problems of development, of health, education and welfare, which need to be addressed by the media among other institutions. The idea that the electronic media is primarily for entertainment and that people can obtain information on other subjects elsewhere is increasingly deployed by middle class South Asians, but the region is not as media-rich as such views might imply. In fact, rural South Asia, which accounts for well over 60 per cent of the population, is for the most part media-impoverished.

Of a number of possible scenarios for the future, the most likely on present trends would see the state sector carrying on more or less as it is at the moment, preserved as a voice for government, offering similar programming in all areas but news and current affairs management, while relying for its revenues on a shrinking mass audience beyond the reach of cable networks. Our preferred scenario, however, would involve the reform of the state sector, a clearer definition of its objectives, preserving an entertainment function but reasserting the need for a range of other activities as well. These include playing a greater role in articulating a sense of community, acting as a counterpoise to the commercially driven mass media and offering diversity and innovation and a greater voice for the public at different levels of society in debating the issues of the day. The realisation of such a vision, however, would require a re-appraisal of the role of the state in the management of radio and television and a willingness to use them for more creative public purposes.

CONFUSION OVER THE ROLE OF GOVERNMENT

One of the problems in tackling these issues is the fact that South Asian governments have found it difficult to distinguish between their role as regulators and their role as broadcasters. Whereas in sectors such as telecommunications, some governments have successfully privatised previously state-controlled industries and set up systems of regulation which have been accepted as fair by the industry as a whole, in the broadcasting sector the reluctance of governments to give up control of the state broadcasting media has held up progress on these regulatory questions. On the one hand, there seems to have been an assumption in most countries that autonomy for the state-controlled media is an essential pre-requisite for establishing a new regulatory framework; on the other, the unwillingness of governments to take that step, despite promises to do so in several countries, has stymied progress in regulating the industry as a whole. The climate of economic liberal-isation has created an expectation that government controls will be lifted or moderated in the media as in other walks of life. But the realities of power in South Asian democracies have proved very resistant to change. There is a growing awareness that a comprehensive rethink of media policy is necessary, but it has been slow in taking legislative shape. Policy initiatives have often turned out to be mere window dressing. Not surprisingly, governments have put their own political interests first.

India's experience with the Prasar Bharati Bill is the best example of liberal intentions which were never quite translated into effect. India also illustrates the tenacity of the centralised state in confronting the new media market. Despite the fact that many satellite channels are operating services in competition with those on Doordarshan, the state has refused to licence terrestrial competition with the state-controlled media. Concessions to media liberalisation have been minimal, though new ground was broken in 1999 with the decision to license independent FM radio stations.

Sri Lanka, unlike India, has diversified its terrestrial media. It now has a multiplicity of TV channels and radio stations, all independent of the government media, with their own transmission facilities. But Chandrika Kumaratunga's government ignored recommendations by high-powered committees for the establishment of an autonomous corporation regulated by a new independent Broadcasting Authority. Faced with a hostile press and lack of cross-party support for its constitutional proposals to resolve the Tamil crisis, it came to see continued control of Rupavahini and the Sri Lanka Broadcasting Corporation as central to getting its message across.

Pakistan and Bangladesh—states with less well established track records of media diversity—have trailed behind India and Sri Lanka in implementing liberal media policies. Pakistan's elected governments showed no sign of licensing terrestrial competition for PTV in the 1990s and in the months before the military takeover in 1999 media diversity was actually reduced in response to the challenge of Indian satellite channels. In Bangladesh, a new terrestrial television station was licensed but on terms which, at least initially, sought to maintain government control of the news agenda.

In almost all these countries, governments have resisted licensing private news and current affairs broadcasts, despite competition from satellite channels. Pakistan's STN was required to relay PBC bulletins, though it was also allowed to re-broadcast BBC and CNN. The tender document for the new Bangladeshi TV channel specified the relaying of Bangladesh TV and radio bulletins and the proper marking of important national events, though Ekushey TV was subsequently permitted to launch its own news and current affairs programmes. India's licensing of independent FM stations specifically excluded news broadcasts. Nepal's FM stations operate under similar restrictions. Sri Lanka was well ahead of the rest of the region in breaking the shackles of state control in this important area, though even its government has substantial reserve powers on security issues.

Do restrictions of this kind make sense in a world where some viewers now have access to fifty satellite channels and newspapers enjoy freedom to print comment and opinion? Many politicians, in India and particularly in neighbouring countries, think they do. The economics of satellite competition mean that India is the main market focus; very few international channels are interested enough in India's neighbours to be generating regular news about those countries. For managers of the electronic media in Pakistan or Bangladesh, therefore, retaining a state monopoly on news and current affairs ensures that there is no real competition where it counts most—in the detailed reporting of politics in that particular country. In India, the logic is less compelling, with Star TV providing 24-hour coverage of elections and Zee's Alpha channels providing regional news bulletins. However, even in India, satellite TV is still an essentially urban phenomenon, except in a few states. Given the enormous importance of the rural voter in all these countries, an incumbent government retains a distinct advantage if it controls the media with the widest reach.

It is only a matter of time, however, before satellite viewing extends to rural areas; indeed the wealthy already have dishes wherever they live, even in remote Baluchistan, and community viewing is widespread. Failure to take stock and to legislate for the new situation will only leave more time for the commercialisation of state broadcasting and the longer the trend continues the greater will be the difficulty in establishing a viable public interest role for the media in future. Recent experience has demonstrated clearly the value of the market in widening media choice in particular areas of broadcasting. But the states' responses have betrayed a lack of clear thinking, both about the future role of the state sector and about what can legitimately be required of commercial broadcasters in serving wider public needs.

WHY WAIT FOR AUTONOMY?

There are plenty of critics of the state sector who would argue that the only way it can become effective is by making it autonomous, removing it from the direct control of government and giving it the freedom to play its role more impartially and independently as an instrument of the whole society and not just of the party in power. However, even in the most liberal South Asian countries, the implementation of such a model has proved difficult to achieve. India may be moving slowly towards a political consensus which would take control of broadcasting out of the hands of politicians, but there is still considerable resistance to it, particularly in influential national parties like the Congress and the BJP.

Given the polarised nature of politics in many South Asian countries and the evident obstacles to the creation of autonomous institutions, it may make sense as a first step to attempt to achieve a measure of greater public accountability for national and commercial broadcasters without attempting a radical restructuring of the status quo. This could take the form initially of consultation within the industry over the development of a national media policy to which both sectors would subscribe. Such a policy might cover such issues as questions of taste and decency, provision of programmes for particular sectors of the community, common standards for advertising and for media training and proficiency, agreed approaches for measuring audiences, and the creation of mechanisms for responding to public criticism and suggestions. Such acceptance of self-regulation could help to resolve some of the issues which concern media professionals and their relations with the public, and could act as a charter for both public and private broadcasters in their relations with government. Whether or not government ultimately retains control of the national broadcasters, the acceptance of industry-wide norms in such fields could act as a restraint on ministerial highhandedness.

The development of such a media policy has already been mooted in Sri Lanka, where the virtually unregulated growth of the commercial sector has thrown up all sorts of problems which are not susceptible to existing methods of supervision and control. It will soon be needed in Bangladesh. In India's case, draft proposals for a new regulatory system failed to find acceptance with the satellite sector, but a new basis of agreement is urgently needed.

HARNESSING THE MARKET

Beyond such voluntary agreements, one theoretically attractive way forward would be for the state by legislation to require broadcasters—of whatever description—to provide a minimum of public interest programming and to set certain quality standards, compliance with which would be essential for the renewal of licensing arrangements.

Internationally, there is a wide range of approaches to public accountability for broadcasters. In western Europe, European Union directives on broadcasting have so far had only limited influence, principally in the field of the impact of broadcasting on children. In Germany, which has a predominantly decentralised structure of public broadcasting, the courts have developed sophisticated concepts with regard to programme standards, and have had a major influence in defining legal standards and obligations.[1] Britain's own tradition of public service broadcasting is long and its reputation both for independence and for delivering quality broadcasting arguably high. But the credibility of the BBC has been founded more on conventions than legal safeguards, and is vulnerable to political pressure.

Outside Europe, Canada imposes common obligations for national content and cultural compatibility on public and private broadcasters alike. In Canada too, methods of public accountability have been advocated which involve feedback direct from audiences to the broadcasters rather than through appointed institutions. In Latin America, community radio and TV have long been a successful part of the broadcasting scene, with governments licensing non-profit and non-partisan stations defined by their social purposes rather than the market or their political affiliation. At an international level, the objective of the Southern African Broadcasting Association (SABA)—to reflect the interests and concerns of the citizens of its member states—seems relevant to the needs of broadcasters and audiences in the South Asian region.[2]

Though quality thresholds of different kinds have been established successfully in a number of countries, they are obviously more difficult to implement where satellite broadcasters are apparently beyond the arm of the law, uplinking from other countries and not operating within a national legal framework. Satellite broadcasters would seem to be in a strong bargaining position for these reasons, though they do need to have a working relationship with their main target territories and will even submit to government regulation if other objectives are met. Rupert Murdoch's concern to establish the Star network as one friendly to India and his willingness to accept Indian government censorship as a price worth paying for the establishment of DTH shows that the Indian government would have considerable leverage in negotiating such issues, if it chose to use it. So far, however, beyond bilateral negotiations with individual channels, the Indian government has apparently made no effort to develop such a strategy.

Moving towards the acceptance of a common jurisdiction is undoubtedly complicated. The draft Indian Broadcasting Bill of 1997 attempted to achieve this by requiring all satellite broadcasters to uplink from India and to accept tough, indeed what were regarded as unworkable, terms for doing so. The refusal of international broadcasters like Star to agree to become majority-owned Indian companies brought progress to a standstill, though some of the Indian-owned channels were subsequently given permission to uplink from India to give them an advantage and to increase pressure on others. There is a good deal to play for on both sides in resolving these issues and any eventual compromise could also be extended to cover other matters of concern. One positive sign is that Zee and Sony have said they might be willing to produce more 'public interest' programming if other broadcasters, particularly Doordarshan, were bound by the same conditions.

Extending such agreements to India's neighbours would be less easy. In Pakistan, Bangladesh or Nepal, the issues are very different anyway; their problems are with the Indian focus of the satellite channels as much as with the subject matter. Their governments might be willing to participate in South Asia-wide discussions about questions of taste and decency—and the widening of that discussion could in itself contribute to the pressures on satellite channels—but persuading satellite channels aiming at the Indian market that they should do more to cover India's neighbours and be more sensitive to uses of their channels as extensions of Indian foreign policy would be more difficult, as coverage of the Kargil hostilities showed. South Asian public opinion has no effective means of making itself felt at the moment, though there is scope for the creation of new networks for this purpose. Satellite channels are unlikely to invest in reflecting wider regional realities until advertisers can deliver their goods more easily across South Asian borders. There is a growing awareness of 'South Asian' audiences, particularly outside the region, where Indians and Pakistanis form part of the same subscription markets. But in South Asia itself, it is the Indian market which dictates the programme content. For India's neighbours—and the viewers in those countries—the most effective response to the new media environment, therefore, lies in putting their own houses in order.

QUESTIONS OF FINANCE

Sources of finance for broadcasting do affect the terms of competition, even if publicly funded broadcasters remain as interested as their rivals in attracting mass audiences. In countries like Britain or Australia, a licence fee levied annually on all television set owners has provided public broadcasters with greater security in serving wider objectives. However, in South Asia, this method of funding inherited from British days has suffered from the same problems as income tax and other taxes. Not only are taxes politically unpopular, they have also proved notoriously difficult to collect.

Because the licence fee has accounted for a smaller and smaller proportion of television finances, several state broadcasters are now facing criticism for taking money through both licence fees and advertisements and for offering the same kind of programmes as their commercial competitors. In India, where the implications of total dependence on advertising revenues have become clearer since the inception of Prasar Bharati, one option being canvassed is a once-for-all tax on TV sets at the time of purchase as a means of providing an alternative source of funding for public interest programmes. It is not regarded as practical politics to re-impose the TV licence system, but there is an acceptance that without other sources of funding Prasar Bharati will not be able to meet its wider obligations. Moreover, though there might be a possibility of legislating for commercial broadcasters to meet certain minimal public service obligations, this could never extend to the full range of a public broadcaster's responsibilities; that would require alternative sources of funding, whether from direct taxation or state subsidy.

This has already become a significant issue in public debate in India. It has also been ventilated in Sri Lanka, where Rupavahini is now competing with many commercial channels. It is less of an issue in Pakistan, Bangladesh or Nepal because competition between state and private sector is more restricted. But in all countries, without a solution of this financial conundrum, broadcasting in the public interest will not survive in any relevant form.

REFORMING THE STATE SECTOR

In the battle for audiences and revenues, the state sector's superior reach has enabled it to hold its own against its satellite competitors, despite losses of audience in urban areas. However, the knee-jerk recourse to soap opera as a commercial saviour seems to indicate a loss of nerve among its managers. Doordarshan's decision to commission programmes from the private sector brought benefits not only to the schedules but to the media as a whole, but the failure to involve staff in the process of change led to serious demoralisation. The fact that so many of the private channels rely on former Doordarshan staff is a clear indication that they do not lack talent. What was needed was a new vision for the state sector which would put that talent to good effect, but it took a long time to emerge.

The judgement that the Doordarshan staff were incapable of rising to the satellite challenge was in part true. But that was a judgement as much about the organisation as about the people. The state broadcaster suffered from a variety of serious problems which made it difficult for staff to cut through the red tape and respond flexibly and independently to the new situation. These included: over-manning and inefficiency, often as a result of the exercise of political patronage and the appointment of unqualified persons; over-concentration of responsibility at the top, resulting in overburdened managers and a lack of initiative at producer level; failures of recruitment (in some cases, state broadcasters had not recruited new production staff for years); poor training; inadequate salaries; low budgets and out of date equipment.

Problems of over-centralisation also impeded the work of Doordarshan's regional managers, who were faced with tough competition from satellite channels, particularly in the South. The co-ordination at all-India level of such functions as transfers, recruitment, finance and other matters, has worked against effective regional broadcasting, with station directors deprived of real authority in important areas of their work. The system was designed to respond rapidly to central directives but it discouraged the kind of autonomy which is necessary for responsive programme making.

Doordarshan's bureaucratic problems are shared by most other South Asian broadcasters, who will have to address them with equal urgency as competition begins to bite. In Sri Lanka, where state broadcasters face the most severe domestic competition, they have already embarked on substantial staff reductions as a means of reducing their costs. Other state broadcasters are clear that over-staffing—sometimes by a factor of 50 per cent—is a problem that needs tackling. But staff worries about sacrificing the security of their employment are a significant obstacle to reform.

Beyond the problems of cost-cutting, there is a need for a redistribution of revenue to serve wider purposes. Rupavahini has taken one important step to increase programme diversity by launching a second terrestrial channel dedicated to sport, programmes for minorities and relays of the Discovery channel. India has invested in a range of satellite alternatives, though it has yet to provide the resources to make them effective. Equally necessary is the creation of a new broadcasting ethos which reduces bureaucracy and frees the producer to make programmes in the public interest without fear of government retribution. This requires the creation of a less centralised administration in which responsibility and budgets are lodged at the level of production units. Such a reform, however, would require a change in the state's attitude towards the way broadcasting is managed, which would not be easy to achieve.

THE CASE FOR DECENTRALISATION

In all South Asian countries, broadcasting is a central subject and national control extends right down to the output of individual radio stations in remote parts of the country. It is an extraordinary fact that no provincial or regional government in South Asia has had any right to license radio or television stations, despite the fact that states like Uttar Pradesh in India or Punjab in Pakistan are responsible for the health, education and agricultural development of larger numbers of people than most of the world's nation states. On Indian terrestrial television, prime time throughout the country, except in Tamil Nadu, has been devoted to Hindi programmes, which naturally creates resentment among speakers of the country's important regional languages. In Pakistan, major regional languages like Pashto, Baluchi and Sindhi have enjoyed very limited space on PTV and there has been as much reflection of regional culture through the medium of Urdu as directly in these languages. Sri Lanka's civil war has added to the problems of providing a viable television service in Tamil, and many Sri Lankan Tamils have had to be satisfied with relays of programmes designed for Indian audiences. Nepal TV has made some concessions to regional languages since 1990, but mostly in the field of translated news bulletins.

Traditionally, the political case against decentralisation has been argued in terms of the fragility of the nation state. Fears that substantial ethnic minorities like the Tamils in Sri Lanka, the Punjabis in India or the Sindhis in Pakistan will misuse decentralised powers to demand separate statehood have resulted in tight control from the centre, which has arguably exacerbated already difficult situations.

Satellite television offered a way of challenging these centralising ideologies, most immediately and most comprehensively in South India. The result, however, has been quite contrary to the fears of the centralisers. Southern satellite TV has in fact contributed to a greater sense of Indian federalism and has done so without the fulfilment of age-old predictions of fissiparous tendencies and threats to India's unity. The experience has shown that the creation of appropriate media channels for the expression of regional cultures offers a way of cementing a better sort of Indian unity. Indeed, it provides an argument for a more decentralised approach by the state itself.

It cannot be claimed that satellite television in the South is solely responsible for a more federal spirit; the way had been prepared by economic progress, by the emergence of strong regional political parties and by their involvement in coalition governments at the centre. However, southern satellite TV has constituted a very different scale of response to regional culture and concerns than anything offered by Doordarshan and has highlighted the huge gap which exists between supply and demand in this important area.

Doordarshan's decision to create its own regional satellite services, taken as part of the state's initial response to the satellite revolution, was an innovative recognition of the way technology was changing the context of media management. However, the regional channels have been very much a second priority for Doordarshan and have mainly found favour with the older generation for their diet of black and white movies and regional news bulletins. Moreover, being centrally managed, these channels suffer from the same problems of bureaucratic inertia and cautiousness which affect the whole organisation.

With the launch of Zee's Alpha channels aimed at regional audiences, Doordarshan's regional strategy came under pressure in the North as well as the South. It still retains very large audiences in the rural areas throughout India, but the experience in the South indicates a continuing erosion of support, not just in the large cities but among the regional middle class in the smaller towns as well. Doordarshan's dilemma is that failure to review its regional policies seems likely to further the process of marginalisation. Only a more genuinely regional approach and greater decentralisation of responsibility within the organisation can reverse the trend. But Prasar Bharati has not so far made any real impact in this important area.

These are also important issues in Pakistan, Bangladesh and Nepal, where national broadcasting policies have been challenged by the working of the satellite TV market, the massive popularity of Zee TV and the spread of a new kind of 'Hindigenised' South Asian popular culture. In Pakistan, which has its own problems finding a balance between centre and regions, PTV has attempted to combat Indian cultural influences by improving programmes in the national language—a counter-strategy which has actually reinforced existing centralising trends.

Arguing the case for the decentralisation of broadcasting for India's neighbours may seem like missing the main point.

However, the experience of South India would seem to validate a different view: that decentralisation is in fact a means of strengthening national cultural defences rather than weakening them. In a globalising media world, India's very large media market has dictated its own localising terms, resulting in the Indianisation of many international satellite channels. However, what is localisation for India is a new form of globalisation for Pakistan or Nepal, which would probably be more effectively countered by encouraging localisation in these countries than by any kind of head-on confrontation.

A first line of defence, as Sri Lanka has found, is to licence more terrestrial competition for the state broadcaster. This is the path which Bangladesh has also followed, with the establishment of its first commercial terrestrial channel. The advantage of such an option is that it makes the state broadcaster more competitive, sharpens its entertainment programmes and gives it a mass orientation—all services which have been provided by the satellite channels for Doordarshan and PTV—while at the same time appealing to a complete domestic television universe, which the satellite channels cannot do. Until 2000, neither India nor Pakistan, the arch-centralisers in South Asia, had licensed such competition in the television medium.

Such a strategy, however, will not serve the public interest in areas where the market is reducing choice rather than extending it. These areas include the provision of services for minorities, for special interests, for the reflection of 'high' or 'folk' culture, and the use of television or radio to serve smaller communities, for development, information or entertainment. Creating space to serve these needs requires a new willingness by the state to accept media decentralisation in principle and to fund it where necessary. This is an important challenge for South Asian nation states and one which they seem instinctively ill-prepared to tackle. Decentralisation is not just about language; it is also about greater participation. It is about encouraging democracy where it can be most effective in giving voice to public opinion and in holding politicians and others to account. Despite South Asian states' commitment to democracy, they have shown little interest in encouraging media development at this level so far.

Radio could play an important part in this process of transformation. An under-exploited medium in all South Asian countries, it offers a cheaper and more versatile way of serving communities if only it could be allowed more freedom to perform this role. In most South Asian countries, national broadcasters already have at their disposal a network of radio stations providing services in different languages. All that would be necessary to activate them would be a new vision of what they could achieve.

There are already some examples of what can be done in community radio, given the right circumstances. But the field is virtually wide open. Considering the scale of development problems in South Asia, it is remarkable that only Sri Lanka had any kind of track record in this field until the 1990s. Sri Lanka has also been more thorough in the development of commercial radio, though India is now catching up. The Sinhala radio station Sirisa has shown that after years of state monopoly, the commercial radio sector can play an important part in creating a new sense of public ownership of the airwaves.

Cable television also has the potential to contribute to the growth of a vibrant decentralised media; indeed it has already done so in some parts of India and Pakistan. But here too a choice has to be made. As cable itself witnesses a process of consolidation, with channel owners using the technology of encryption or digitisation as a means of extracting more revenue for themselves, the state has a chance to intervene to preserve some space for the local operator and the local service. So far, however, it has shown little interest in the project. India's draft Broadcasting Bill offered little encouragement to cable operators providing services to their own communities; in fact it made the provision of such services illegal.

The Internet poses a completely different level of problem for the mechanics of control. E-mail has already created new, cheaper and speedier means of communication between those with access to computers all over the world. It has also given individuals and organisations the capacity to develop their own radio and television services, something which is already taking place in a limited way and will undoubtedly expand significantly in the future. In the developing world, the Internet is currently regarded rightly as a rich person's accessory. However, if the success of India's privatised telephone services is any guide to the future, it will not be long before Internet and e-mail connections are available throughout rural areas too.

The satellite revolution in South Asia has shocked the region's various governments into a set of largely defensive initial responses, but for the longer term a more measured assessment of the forces of media globalisation is required. Old systems of centralised supervision and control look increasingly outdated and the nation state would defend its own interests more successfully if it sanctioned the use of new technologies to encourage rather than discourage greater freedom of expression and participation, greater affirmation of local and regional cultures, and greater public accountability. If it doesn't, it will happen anyway, though the state will be seen as an impediment to change and the social consequences will be less benign.

THE ROLE OF PUBLIC OPINION

The satellite revolution in South Asia has played an important role in extending the bounds of civil society and the forum for public debate. The ground was prepared in India by the growth of the middle class, its increasing importance as a market and by the winds of economic liberalisation which swept away many of the old protectionist barriers to international trade and investment. Economic progress had also made the Indian press more economically self-sufficient, less dependent on government advertising and more outspoken in its political views. The development of India's regional press—particularly in the southern and western states—mirrored the emergence of a new sort of regional politics: less hostile to Indian nationalism, more a co-partner in a new economic prosperity. However, satellite television has added a new dynamism to civil society, exploiting the powerful visual medium in offering growing numbers of cable and satellite viewers not just better entertainment but also more independent news coverage of Indian politics, a less reverential approach to authority and tradition and a more questioning, interactive and participatory style of programming.

Sri Lanka's burgeoning commercial television and radio sectors have played a similar role. The growth of independent news and current affairs, political debates, television discussions, investigative programmes and radio phone-in programmes have all added to the sense of public participation and accountability, particularly among the majority Sinhala community. In southern Sri Lanka, the licensing of terrestrial competition for state radio and TV has extended this sense of participation beyond the urban middle class into the rural areas. The north and east, because of the on-going civil war, are a different matter.

The satellite revolution has produced more complex responses in Pakistan, Bangladesh and Nepal. Cable and satellite households have welcomed the greater choice of entertainment and access to international news and documentaries. Far wider access to news and information about India has challenged old stereotypes and in normal times has helped to improve 'people-to-people' relations. Satellite reflections of India have also influenced internal debates and sometimes changed behaviour. However, the uni-directional character of the information flow has produced as many defensive as positive reactions. Fears and accusations of Indian cultural hegemony have clouded debate and provoked division. Satellite could have been a means of developing a genuinely South Asian civil society, but it has served mainly as a vehicle for the extension of Indian cultural influences. There has been no dialogue, no forum for genuine regional exchange. This is another important challenge for the future.

If the new satellite media have contributed to the development of civil society, they have done so largely on the terms of the commercial entrepreneurs. TV advertising has expanded enormously as part of this process, with media research and advertising companies enjoying exponential growth in India particularly. Public feedback on these developments has been largely confined to the columns of a small number of newspapers and the activities of non-government organisations. The print media in general, which could play a role in this area, has concentrated more on the projection of film and television stars than on media criticism.

Public broadcasters have lagged behind their commercial rivals in commissioning their own research. Many of them rely on the research of commercial companies, which until recently have focussed largely on urban areas and not on the rural viewer and listener. Television programmes have generated huge volumes of correspondence, sometimes on a scale which producers have found impossible to process, but there are few organisations representing the viewer and listener in a more systematic way.

In this book we have recorded the opinions of viewers on what they see as the positive and negative influences of the satellite media. We have traced, through the expression of individual views and group discussions, a critical awareness of where the public interest lies in particular countries and circumstances and an active desire to promote it. But we have also noted, in many parts of the region, that while people do have firm opinions on the media, they are not used to being asked for them. Often they do not believe that they have any part to play in shaping the media's future. It is not sufficient, therefore, to argue that the state has an important role to play in safeguarding the public interest. In the interests of the development of civil society, equal stress also needs to be placed on the development and reflection of public opinion on media issues.

If public opinion on media issues is relatively under-developed, what this study does show is that there are a growing number of non-governmental organisations involved in media work, whether in connection with development, education, health, or the pursuit of women's interests, and many media professionals, sociologists, and educationists in the different countries of South Asia with common interests and concerns about the way the media is developing. There is much to learn from the experiences of other South Asian countries, though as yet regional awareness is surprisingly low, except among a handful of media and development professionals. It is too early yet to talk of regional public opinion, but beyond the need to develop a more critical public opinion in individual countries the regional character of the new media also requires a regional public response. With many South Asians now watching the same programmes, those who produce them, often with only Indian audiences in mind, need to be made aware of the wider public and their reactions. As the state sector defends its patch against satellite competition, this study testifies to a wealth of critical opinion which is not currently being fed into the calculations of the broadcasters themselves. Finding means to register those opinions is an urgent priority, if the public interest is to be served more effectively.

NOTES AND REFERENCES

1. E.M. Barendt (1993), *Broadcasting Law: A Comparative Study*, pp. 19ff., 35ff. Barendt expresses the view that the public service tradition of broadcasting has survived more vigorously in Germany than in France or Italy.
2. Examples cited here draw on essays by Marc Raboy (Canada), Rafael Roncagliolo (Latin America) and Nahum Gorelick (Namibia), in M. Raboy (ed.) (1996), *Public Broadcasting for the 21st Century*.

SOURCE MATERIAL
MEDIA SOUTH ASIA PROJECT

INTERVIEWS

Bangladesh

Ahmed, Salahuddin, Dhaka, April 1998.
Ahmed, Syed Mohiuddin, Dhaka, May 1998.
Akhtar, Humayun, Dhaka, May 1998.
Akhter, Shameem, Dhaka, May 1998.
Azad, Abul Kalam, Dhaka, April 1998.
Choudhury, Geeteara S., Dhaka, March 1998; May 1998.
Chowdhury, Afsan, Chennai, January 1999.
Dring, Simon, Dhaka, May 1998.
Hamid, M., Dhaka, March 1998.
Hasan, F.R. Mahmud, Dhaka, March 1998.
Hashim, Dhaka, March 1998.
Hossain, Dr. Kamal, Dhaka, April 1998.
Husain, Anwar, Dhaka, May 1998.
Hussain, Rupak, Dhaka, March 1998.
Imam, Shami, Dhaka, May 1998.
Jameel, Dhaka, May 1998.
Jehangir, Mohammed, Dhaka, March 1998.
Kabir, Syed Borhan, Dhaka, April 1998.
Kamal, Syed Mustafa, Dhaka, May 1998.
Khan, Enayetullah (UNB), Dhaka, March 1998.
Khan, Enayetullah (Holiday), Dhaka, March 1998.
Khan, Nawazish Ali, Dhaka, May 1998.
Kunugi, June, Dhaka, June 1998.
Mahmud, A.S., Dhaka, April 1998.
Majid, Humayun, Dhaka, May 1998.
Majumdar, Ramendu, Dhaka, May 1998.
Maleka Begum, Dhaka, April 1998.
Mamoon, Prof. Muntassir, Dhaka, May 1998.

Munshi, A.F.M. Fakhrul Islam, Dhaka, May 1998.
Mutsuddi, Chinmoy, Dhaka, March 1998.
Polash, A. Chowdhury, Dhaka, March 1998.
Rahman, Shafikur, Dhaka, April 1998.
Rahman, Mahbubur, Dhaka, March 1998.
Rahman, Mahfuzur, Dhaka, March 1998.
Raju, Dhaka, March 1998.
Rashid, Parveen, Dhaka, April 1998.
Reza, Farid, Dhaka, February 1998.
Wahab, Amir, Dhaka, June 1998.
Zaker, Aly, Dhaka, April 1998.
Zaki, Syed Salahuddin, Dhaka, March 1998.

India

Adhikari, Markand, Mumbai, July 1998.
Akbar, M.J., Delhi, June 1998.
Anand, Anita, Delhi, June 1998.
Andrew, Father Joe, Chennai, November 1999.
Ansari, Tariq, Mumbai, July 1998.
Arasu, Dr. V., Chennai, November 1999.
Arulmozhi, Chennai, December 1999.
Bahl, Raghav, Delhi, June 1998.
Banerjee, Sumit, Calcutta, May 1998.
Banerjee, Ananya, Calcutta, April 1998.
Banerjee, T.K., Mumbai, July 1998.
Bapat, Ram, Mumbai, August 1998.
Barua, Nabakanta, Guwahati, May 1998.
Barua, Paresh (by telephone), May 1998.
Barua, Prasanta, Guwahati, May 1998.
Barua, Jahna, Guwahati, May 1998.
Baskaran, S.T., Chennai, February 1998.
Basu, Siddharth, Delhi, July 1998.
Bernard, Rabi, Chennai, May 1998.
Bezboruah, D.N., Guwahati, May 1998.
Bhagwat, Dr. Vidyut, Pune, August 1998.
Bhattacharya, Prof. Malini, Calcutta, June 1998.
Bhattacharya, Prof. Mihir, Calcutta, July 1998.
Bhattacharya, Rinki Roy, Mumbai, April 1998.
Bhaumik, Dr. Someshwar, Calcutta, August 1998.

Bijapurkar, Rama, Mumbai, March 1998.
Biswas, A.K., Calcutta, May 1998.
Bora, Phatak Chandra, Guwahati, May 1998.
Borgohain, Nirupama, Guwahati, May 1998.
Borgohain, Homen, Guwahati, May 1998.
Bose, Dr. Vijayalakshmi, Delhi, June 1998.
Bose, P.K., Calcutta, May 1998.
Broacha, Cyrus, Mumbai, July 1998.
Butalia, Pankaj, Delhi, July 1998.
Bwismutiary, S.K., Guwahati, May 1998.
Chakraborty, D., Delhi, May 1998.
Chakravarti, Dr. Amit, Calcutta, March 1998.
Chandrasekhar, Dr. B.S., Delhi, December 1997.
Chatterjee, Manas, Calcutta, May 1998.
Chatterjee, Somnath, Calcutta, May 1998.
Chattopadhya, Subroto, Calcutta, July 1998.
Chattopadhyaya, Shilu, Calcutta, March 1998.
Contractor, Behram, Mumbai, May 1998.
Dabholkar, Alaka, Mumbai, April 1998.
Daimary, Ranjan (by telephone), May 1998.
Dandavate, Mrs. M., Delhi, July 1998.
Dandavate, Madhu, Delhi, July 1998.
Das, Atul, Mumbai, May 1998.
Das, Dr. Biswajit, Delhi, June 1998.
Das, Prof. Veena, Delhi, July 1998.
Das, Arvind, Delhi, June 1998.
Das, Biswanath, Bhubaneswar, May 1998.
Dasgupta, Kalyanashish, Calcutta, May 1998.
Das Gupta, Abhijit, Calcutta, May 1998.
Das Gupta, Kunal, Mumbai, April 1998.
Dayal, Rajeshwar, Delhi, November 1997; March 1998.
Deka, Kanaksen, Guwahati, May 1998.
Dev, Rahul, Delhi, July 1998.
Dharkar, Anil, Mumbai, February 1998.
Diwaker, B., Delhi, June 1998.
Dwivedhi, Chandraprakash, Mumbai, May 1998.
Eapen, Dr. K.E., Bangalore, February 1998.
Eashwar, Sucharita S., Bangalore (by telephone), November 1999.
Fernandes, Vivian, Delhi, June 1998.
Fuller, Julles, Mumbai, June 1998.

Gadgil, V.N., Delhi, July 1998.
Gandhioke, Sabeena, Delhi, June 1998.
George, Father, Calcutta, April 1998.
Ghose, Bhaskar, Delhi, February 1998, January 1999.
Ghose, Sohini, Delhi, June 1998.
Gill, S.S., Delhi, January 1999.
Gogoi, Promode Kumar, Guwahati, May 1998.
Gokhale, Shanta, Mumbai, April 1998.
Gopal, M.S., Chennai, February 1998.
Gore, Dr. Neelam, Pune, August 1998.
Gupta, R.K., Bhubaneshwar, May 1998.
Gupta, Urmila, Delhi, June 1998.
Gupta, Shekhar, Delhi, July 1998.
Hashmi, Sohail, Delhi, June 1998.
Hoskote, Ranjit, Mumbai, July 1998.
Hussein, Mahommed Irteja,Varanasi, June 1998.
Inamdar, Tabassum, Mumbai, June 1998.
Irani, C.R., Calcutta, March 1998.
Iyer, Narain, Mumbai, April 1998.
Jain, Rajive, Delhi, May 1998.
Jalan, Mallika, Calcutta, May 1998.
Jayastree, Chennai, May 1998.
Jena, Manipadma, Bhubaneshwar, May 1998.
Jog, Dr. Pramod, Pune, April 1998.
Joses, George, Mumbai, May 1998.
Joshi, Manohar Shyam, Delhi, June 1998.
Joshi, Prof. P.C., Delhi, August 1998.
Kak, Sanjay, Delhi, June 1998.
Kakati, Satis, Guwahati, May 1998.
Kant, Ravi, Mumbai, July 1998.
Kapoor, Dr. Bhadrinath, Varanasi, June 1998.
Karnik, Kiran, Delhi, June 1998.
Kastoori, Vijay, Mumbai, June 1998.
Kazmi, Nikhat, Delhi, June 1998.
Kejriwal, O.P., Delhi, January 1999.
Kenkre, Damu, Mumbai, May 1998.
Ketkar, Kumar, Mumbai, February 1998.
Khan, Irfan, Mumbai, April 1998.
Khanna, Amit, Mumbai, March 1998.

Khanna, Sunil, Delhi, April 1998.
Kidwai Prof. H.R., Delhi. June 1998.
Kidwai, Sabina, Delhi. June 1998.
Kocherry, Thomas, Delhi, April 1998.
Kohli, Jagjit Singh, Mumbai, April 1998.
Kripalu, Sukanya, Mumbai, June 1998.
Krishna Dr. Sunita, Delhi, April 1998.
Krishnaswamy, Dr. S., Chennai, May 1998.
Kulkarni, Pratima, Mumbai, April 1998.
Kumar, Dr. Satish, Varanasi, June 1998.
Kumar, Sashi, Chennai, February/May 1998.
Kumar, P.R., Chennai, May 1998.
Kumar, Prof. Keval, Pune, March 1998.
Kumari, Dr. Abhilasha, Delhi, June 1998.
Lahiri, Indrajit, Delhi, May 1998.
Lal, Prof. Ananda, Calcutta, July 1998.
Lele, M.P., Delhi, January 1999.
Lulla, Sunil, Mumbai, April 1998.
Madhvani, Meenakshi, Mumbai, March 1998.
Mahajan, Pramod, Delhi, April 1999.
Mahapatra, Aditya, Bhubaneshwar, May 1998.
Maharaj, Pandit Kishan, Varanasi, June 1998.
Maharaj, Srivatsa Goswami, Brindaban, July 1998.
Majumdar, Bhaskar, Mumbai, May 1998.
Malan, Chennai, December 1999.
Malhotra, Iqbal, Delhi, June 1998.
Malhotra, Sudip, Mumbai, April 1998.
Malik, Amita, Delhi, July 1998.
Mall, Sam, Delhi, June 1998.
Maloo, Sunil, Mumbai, May 1998.
Mandal, G.C., Calcutta, March 1999.
Mansukhani, Ashok, Mumbai, May 1998.
Maran, Kalanidhi, Chennai, November 1999.
Mehta, Vinod, Delhi, June 1998.
Memon, Ayaz, Mumbai, August 1998.
Mirza, Saeed, Mumbai, June 1998.
Mishra, Radha, Mumbai, March 1998.
Mitra, Chandan, Delhi, June 1998.
Mitra, Dr. Ashok, Calcutta, March 1998.
Mohanta, Prafulla Kumar, Guwahati, May 1998.

Mohapatra, Kelucharan, Cuttack, September 1998.
Mohapatra, Ratikanta, Cuttack, September 1998.
Monteiro, Anjali, Mumbai, May 1998.
Moorthy, Ravi, Mumbai, June 1998.
Mukherjee, Jasojit, Calcutta, May 1998.
Mukherjee, Prof. Hiren, Calcutta, March 1998.
Mukherjee, Rudrangshe, Calcutta, March 1998.
Mukherjee, Soma, Calcutta, May 1999.
Nanda,Vinta, Mumbai, July 1999.
Nandy, Ashis, Delhi, January 1999.
Nandy, Pritish, Mumbai, May 1998.
Nannan, Dr. T.K., Chennai, May 1998.
Naqvi, Mukhtar Abbas, Delhi, September 1998.
Narayanmoorthy, P., Delhi, February 1998.
Natarajan, Chennai, May 1998.
Navalkar, Pramod, Mumbai, June 1998.
Nihalani, Govind, Mumbai, April 1998.
Padamsee, Alyque, Mumbai, April 1998.
Padgaonkar, Dilip, Delhi, June 1998.
Pande, Mrinal, Delhi, January 1999.
Panja, Ajit, Calcutta, May 1998.
Panneerselvan, A.S., London, December 1999.
Pathak, Dr. Abhijit, Delhi, July 1998.
Patwardhan, Vasant, Pune, August 1998.
Phadke, Y.D., Mumbai, June 1999.
Prasad, Anuradha, Delhi, June 1998.
Prasad, Kali, Delhi, March 1998.
Purokayashta, Kabindra, Guwahati, May 1998.
Raadhu, Chennai, May 1998.
Raghuvanshi, Manoj, Delhi, July 1998.
Raja, D., Delhi, July 1998.
Rajadhyaksha, Mukta, Mumbai, April 1998.
Rajendran, Viduthalai, Chennai, January 2000.
Ram, N., Chennai, February 1998; December 1999.
Ramananda, Vimala, Chennai, May 1998.
Ramchandran, Yogesh, Mumbai, April 1998.
Ramnarayan, Gowri, Chennai, November 1999.
Ranade, Dr. Ashok, Mumbai, June 1998.
Rao, Dr. N. Bhaskara, Delhi, June 1998.
Ratnam, Anita, Chennai, November 1999.

Raut, Neena, Mumbai, August 1998.
Ray, Siddhartha, Delhi, May 1998.
Reddy, Jaipal, Delhi, July 1998.
Rege, Sharmila, Pune, August 1998.
Rongpi, Jayanta, Guwahati, May 1998.
Roy, Sudeshna, Calcutta, July 1998.
Sadhu, Arun, Pune, April 1998.
Saikia, Hemoprabha, Guwahati, May 1998.
Samuel, John, Pune, July 1998.
Sarabhai, Mallika, Ahmedabad, May 1998.
Sarabhai, Mrinalani, Ahmedabad, May 1998.
Sarkar, Aveek, Calcutta, March 1998.
Sarma K.S., Delhi, January 1999.
Sayani, Ameen, Mumbai, February1998.
Screwvala, Ronnie, Mumbai, April 1998.
Sen, Ashish, Bangalore, February 1998.
Sen, Indrani, Calcutta, May 1998.
Sen, Kankan M., Calcutta, May 1998.
Sengupta, Dr. Bhawani, Delhi, December 1997.
Seth, Dr. Kiran, Delhi, June 1998.
Shah, Vipul, Mumbai, July 1999.
Shanbag, Sunil, Mumbai, April 1998.
Shankar, Mamata, Calcutta, August 1998.
Shankaracharya of Benares, Varanasi, June 1998.
Sharma, Rajat, Delhi, July 1998.
Sharma, Col. K.K., Delhi, April 1998.
Sharma, Ramesh, Delhi, June 1998.
Sharma, Dr. Mahesh Chandra, Delhi, July 1998.
Sharma, S.N., Delhi, June 1998.
Sharma, Mrs. Roop, Delhi, April 1998.
Shidore, Jayashree, Pune, March 1998.
Shorey, K.D., Mumbai, June 1998.
Shukla, Rajiv, Delhi, June 1998.
Singh, K. Bikram, Delhi, June 1998.
Singh, Malvika, Delhi, July 1998.
Singh, Prof. Yogendra, Delhi, June 1998.
Sinha Roy, Arrow, Mumbai, May 1998.
Sivadas, Akhila, Delhi, April 1998; April 2000.
Sodhi, Justice, Delhi, April 1998.
Sopariwala, Dorab R., Mumbai, July 1998.

Sriram, D., Mumbai, May 1998.
Srivastava, Durga Prasad, Lamai village, Varanasi, June 1998.
Surana, Ashok, Calcutta, May 1998.
Swaminathan, Savithri, Mumbai, June 1998.
Swamy, Sunder K., Chennai, May 1998.
Tendulkar, Vijay, Mumbai, May 1998.
Thadani, Ramesh, Mumbai, April 1998.
Thawani, Harish, Mumbai, March 1998.
Thiruvenkatam, Vijaya, Chennai, February 1998.
Tripathi, Pravin, Mumbai, June 1998.
Tully, Sam, Mumbai, April 1998.
Upendra, P., Delhi, July 1998.
Vaidya, Nitin, Mumbai, November 1999.
Vajpeyi, Ashok, Delhi, July 1998.
Venkataraman, S.V., Chennai, February 1998.
Venkatesan, Prof., Chennai, December 1999.
Verghese, B.G., Delhi, June 1998.
Vishwanathan, Hima, Mumbai, May 1998.
Wadkar, Alkar, Pune, April 1998.
Yadav, Prof. J.S., Delhi, July 1998.

Nepal

Bhattarai, Binod, Kathmandu, March 1998.
Bista, Hem Bahadur, Kathmandu, May 1998.
Chakravarty, Joydeb, Kathmandu, May 1998.
Dixit, Kanak Mani, Kathmandu, May 1998; July 1998.
Dixit, Kunda, Kathmandu (by telephone), February 2000.
Gautam, Narayan Kumar, Kathmandu, May 1998.
Ghimire, Durga, Kathmandu, May 1998.
Gyawali, Dipak, Kathmandu, May 1998.
Jha, Sushil Kant, Kathmandu, March 1998.
Joshi, Rupa , Kathmandu May 1998
Koirala, Bharat D., Kathmandu, March 1998.
Lama, Sangeetha, Kathmandu, March 1998.
Mathur, Piyush, Kathmandu, May 1998.
Onta, Pratyush, Kathmandu, May 1998.
Pant, Raghuji, Kathmandu, May 1998.
Rana, Bandana, Kathmandu, May 1998.
Sainju, Dr. Mohan Man, Kathmandu, May 1998.

Shah, Jamim, Kathmandu, May 1998.
Shah, Neer, Kathmandu, March 1998.
Sharma, Durga Nath, Kathmandu, March 1998.
Sharma, Shailendra Raj, Kathmandu, May 1998.
Singh, S.P., Kathmandu, June 1999.
Sirohiya, Kailash, Kathmandu, May 1998.
Sthapit, Keshab, Kathmandu, May 1998.
Thapa, Chiran, Kathmandu, March 1998.

Pakistan

Ahmad, Mahmood, Islamabad, January 1999.
Ahmed, Dr. Anees, Islamabad, March 1999.
Ahmed, H. Aftab, Lahore, November 1997; January 1999.
Ahmed, Khaled, Lahore, January 1999.
Ahmed, Khalid, Karachi, July 1998.
Ahmed, Nisar, Islamabad, January 1999.
Ahmed, Syed Rashid, Karachi, March 1998.
Ali, Zubair, Karachi, December 1997; May 1998.
Anand, Satish, Karachi, May 1998.
Ansari, Javed, Karachi, February 1998.
Arif, Iftikhar, Islamabad, March 1999.
Asghar, Hamid, Peshawar, June 1999.
Aslam, Imran, Karachi, December 1997; May 1998.
Aslam, Talat, Karachi, July 1998.
Azhar, Aslam, Islamabad, November 1997; March 1998; May 1998.
Azim, Akhtar Viqar, January 1999.
Baig, Mirza, Karachi, May 1998.
Baluch, Ataullah, Quetta, August 1998.
Baluch, Enayat, Islamabad, March 1998.
Baluch, Sami, Karachi, August 1998.
Bari, Farzana, Islamabad, March 1999.
Bilgrami, Jafer, Islamabad, May 1998.
Bokhari, Farhan, Islamabad, November 1997; May 1998.
Chhapra, Abdul Hameed, Karachi, May 1998.
Gauhar, Altaf, Islamabad, January 1999.
Gilani, Ijaz Shafi, Islamabad, January 1999.
Gilani, Uzma, Lahore, May 1998.
Gul, Agha Sajjad, Lahore, May 1998.
Haroon, Hameed, Karachi, December 1997.

Hasan, Prof. Mehdi, Lahore, May 1998.
Hasan, Dr. Mubashir, Lahore, May 1998.
Hashmi, Moneeza, Lahore, May 1998.
Hashmi, Mehmood, Lahore, May 1998.
Hashmi, S.H., Karachi, December 1997.
Hassan, Khalid, Lahore, May 1998.
Hussain, Mushahid, Islamabad, January 1999.
Hyder, Khursheed, Karachi, December 1998.
Ismat, Zubeida, Peshawar, August 1998.
Jabbar, Javed, Karachi, March 1997; December 1997; March 1998;
    London, April 2000.
Jabeen, Nusrat, Quetta, August 1998.
Javed, Mian Mohammed, Islamabad, May 1998.
Kaka Khail, Dr. Shahjehan, Peshawar, August 1998.
Kamal, Dr. Altamash, Karachi, December 1997; May 1998.
Kazi, Shahida, Karachi, March 1997.
Khan, Laila, Islamabad, January 1999.
Khan, Nisar Mohamed, Peshawar, June 1999.
Khan, Nighat Said, Karachi, November 1997.
Khan, Taher A., Karachi, November 1997; May 1998.
Khoso, Ayub, Quetta, August 1998.
Kirmani, Sheema, Karachi, July 1990.
Lodhi, Maleeha, Islamabad, May 1998.
Malik, Mahommed, Islamabad, March 1998.
Malik, Shahid, Lahore, May 1998.
Mahmood, Anwar, Islamabad, January 1999.
Mehmood, Shahzad, Lahore, July 1998.
Mirza, Sanjar, Lahore, May 1998.
Mirza, Tahir, Lahore, May 1998.
Mohsin, Sabih, Karachi, March 1998.
Mojiz, Gulrez, Lahore, November 1997.
Naheed, Kishwar, Islamabad, February 1999.
Naqvi, M.B., Karachi, May 1998.
Naseer, Jehanzeb, Karachi, May 1998.
Nasir, Agha, Islamabad, March 1997; May 1998; January 1999.
Noorani, Asif, Karachi, December 1998.
Parvez, Shaukat, Islamabad, January 1999.
Qazi, Mohammed Usman, Quetta, August 1998.
Qureshi, Manzoor, Karachi, August 1998.

Qureshi, Maulana Yusuf, Peshawar, August 1998.
Rehman, I.A., Lahore, May 1998.
Rind, Haroon, Karachi, August 1998.
Rizvi, Abid, Quetta, August 1998.
Saeed, Tariq, Peshawar, August 1998; June 1999.
Sahir, Fakir Hussain, Peshawar, August 1998.
Saiyid, Amera, Islamabad, November 1997.
Sarwar, Ijaz, Islamabad, March 1998; May 1998.
Shahid, Farida, Lahore, November 1997.
Shaikh, Raana, Islamabad, June 1998.
Sherjan, Faisal, Karachi, May 1998.
Syed, Raana, Islamabad, November 1997; April 2000.
Yazdani, S. Gulrez, Islamabad, May 1998.
Zaidi, Farhad, Islamabad, December 1997.

Sri Lanka

Amunugama, Sarath, Colombo, May 1998.
Bakmeewewa, Narada, Colombo, July 1998.
Banda, Ranaweera, Colombo, August 1998.
Bastian, Sunil, Colombo, December 1998.
Boyle, Sharmini, Kathmandu, September 1998.
David, M.J. R., Kathmandu, September 1998.
De Silva, Nihal, Colombo, December 1997.
De Silva, Maleec Calyaneratne, Colombo, September 1998.
Dias, Asoka, Colombo, December 1998.
Gunasekara, H.M., Colombo, March 1998.
Gunasekara, Lakshman, Colombo, December 1997.
Gunasekera, D.E.W., Colombo, March 1998.
Gunawardena, Victor, Colombo, March 1998.
Gunawardena, A.J., Colombo, June 1998.
Gunawardene, Nalaka, Colombo, July 1998.
Guruge, Vasanth, Colombo, March 1998.
Ironside, Graham, Colombo, March 1998.
Ismail, Jezima, Colombo, December 1998.
Jayaratne, Tilak, Colombo, March 1998.
Jayasinghe, M.G., Anuradhapura, August 1998.
Jayasinghe, Amal, Colombo, December 1997.
Jayasuriya, Shevanthi, Colombo, April 1998.

Jhalagama, Tennekoon, Anuradhapura, August 1998.
Karunathillake, P.G., Colombo, May 1998.
Menike, Biso, Kandy, May 1998.
Mylavaganam, K., Kandy, May 1998.
Pathirana, Damayanthi, Colombo, November 1999.
Peiris, Janadasa, Colombo, March 1998.
Peiris, Prof. G.H., Kandy, August 1998.
Perera, M.J., Colombo, March 1998.
Perera, Shirley, Colombo, March 1998.
Rajakaruna, Anoma, Colombo, September 1998.
Rajakarunanayake, Sunethra, Colombo, May 1998.
Ratnasinghe, P., Colombo, April 1998.
Rupasinghe, Ranjit, Anuradhapura, August 1998.
Samaranayake, Ajith, Colombo, June 1998.
Samerasinghe, Prof. S.W.R. de A., Kandy, August 1998.
Saravanamuttu, Paikiasothy, Colombo, December 1997.
Senanayake, Deepthi, Colombo, July 1998.
Senaratne, Rosmand, Colombo, May 1998.
Sooriyabandara, Chandana, Colombo, May 1998.
Thilillainathan, S., Colombo, June 1998.
Thiruchandran, Selvy, Colombo, May 1998.
Tilakaratne, Asanga, Colombo, November 1998.
Visvanathan, S., Colombo, March 1998.
Weeratunge, Neel, Matara, May 1998.
Wickramasinghe, Maithree, Colombo, October 1998.
Wickramesinghe, Shan, Colombo, March 1998; November 1999.
Wickremetunge, Raine, Colombo, October 1998.
Wijemanne,Livy, Colombo, December 1997.
Wijesinghe, Nimal, Anuradhapura, August 1998.
Wijewickreme, Ranjit, Anuradhapura, August 1998.

FOCUS GROUP DISCUSSIONS AND DISTRICT SURVEYS

In addition to individual interviews we carried out two other types of exercises—small-scale surveys and focus group discussions—to sample opinion among a wider range of the public served by the South Asian television channels.

Where both the survey and group discussions were carried out, the exercises were closely linked. In India, Nepal, Pakistan, Bangladesh and Sri Lanka, members of the Media South Asia Project team conducted a total of approximately 110 group discussions. In India, these were conducted in seven states and the capital, New Delhi, by the following people: Maharashtra and Gujarat in western India (by Deepa Bhatia in Mumbai, Pune and Ahmedabad and Nilu Damle in Latur district), Uttar Pradesh and Madhya Pradesh in northern India (by Nilu Damle in Varanasi district, by Saibal Das Gupta and Md. Firoz in Delhi, and by Mahesh Pande in Bhopal), West Bengal (by Anuradha Mukherjee), Assam (by Subir Bhaumik), and Tamil Nadu (by Pritham Chakravarthy in Chennai and K. Babu in Madurai). In Bangladesh, they were held in Dhaka and Jamalpur (by Afsan Chowdhury). In Nepal, they were held in two towns in the terai and two towns in the hills as well as in the capital Kathmandu (by Deepak Thapa). The Sri Lankan discussion groups were held in Colombo and in Matara district (by Santhini Jayawardena). The groups were selected with a view to being able to draw some comparisons and contrasts across South Asia between people from similar social and economic categories. The aim throughout was to sample qualitative opinion and not to draw statistical comparisons. The methodology was broadly based on guidelines for focus group discussions followed in other social surveys in South Asia.

The group discussion is widely seen as a convenient and economical way to gather opinion on a variety of issues. The method is especially relevant when the information requires probing and interaction, and the expression of unquantifiable and essentially subjective opinions and value judgements. Discussion groups were mostly conducted by the team members themselves, with assistance, or by others under their direct supervision. Most discussion groups were drawn from six categories: 1) Home makers, 2) Professionals, 3) Children, 4) Students, 5) Older people, and 6) Labourers. In Sri Lanka and Bangladesh, discussions were held with two additional categories: 7) Development workers and 8) Cultural conservatives.

The same categories were also employed in a number of small-scale sample surveys which were conducted in different districts across South Asia. The purpose of these surveys was to test opinion away from the big cities, in smaller towns and some villages.

The Indian districts chosen were Latur in Maharashtra, Varanasi in Uttar Pradesh and Madurai in Tamil Nadu. A further three surveys were carried out in Jamalpur district in Bangladesh, Matara district in Sri Lanka and Rawalpindi district in Pakistan. No district survey was conducted in Nepal, though discussions took place in three differing locations: the plains, the hills and the Kathmandu Valley. Except in Madurai, the surveys were carried out at different levels in each district: the district town, a smaller town and a village. Though formal group discussions were held in the district towns, in smaller towns and villages more informal soundings were carried out. Interviews were also conducted with social workers, teachers, journalists, and with shopkeepers and service providers with special insight into consumer and cultural trends. The aim was to test and validate the findings of group discussions. The result aimed at in each case was a series of reports based on observations and interviews. Special attention was paid to attitudes among women and issues facing women in South Asia.

The discussion groups normally included about ten participants. They focussed cn the following selected areas with appropriate emphasis according to the character of the groups: 1) Language, 2) Dress, 3) Sports, 4) Music, 5) Consumption, 6) Social and family relationships, 7) Impact on women and children, 8) Cultural practices, and 9) Use of radio and television. A questionnaire on basic listening habits was used in some, but not all, cases as a supplementary means of assessing individual views.

BANGLADESH

Focus Group Discussions

1)	University students, Dhaka	February 1998
2)	Home makers, Dhaka	February 1998
3)	Development workers, Dhaka	March 1998
4)	Professionals, Dhaka	March 1998
5)	Political activists, Dhaka	March 1998
6)	Religious conservatives, Dhaka	March 1998
7)	Home makers, Jamalpur	June 1998
8)	Young males, Jamalpur	June 1998
9)	Children, Jamalpur	June 1998
10)	Older people, Jamalpur	June 1998

11) Cultural and social activists, Jamalpur   June 1998
12) Social conservatives, Jamalpur   June 1998
Note: For social conservatives five independent interviews were conducted and then the information was put together.

District Surveys
1) A survey was organised by Afsan Chowdhury in the Dhaka area in February 1998. It involved a simple checklist interview of a hundred households with both TV and cable. Despite the small sampling size, the results were in line with the findings of advertising and research agencies.
2) A survey of opinion in Jamalpur district took place in June 1998. It employed the same questionnaire and methodology as the Dhaka survey.

INDIA

Western India

Focus Group Discussions

13) Students, M K College, Mumbai Commerce Division	May 1998
14) Students, Gujarati-speaking Ahmedabad	May 1998
15) Students, St. Xavier's College, Mumbai	July 1999
16) Students, Chanakya School, Pune	August 1998
17) Children, Pune Bal Bhavan, Pune	March 1998
18) Children, Bombay Scottish, Mumbai	May 1998
19) Children, Sunderban, Ahmedabad	May 1998
20) Professionals, Bank employees, Ahmedabad	May 1998
21) Professionals, Mumbai	July 1998
22) Professionals, Pune	August 1998
23) Home makers, Satellite Road, Ahmedabad	May 1998
24) Home makers, Marathi speaking, Mumbai	August 1998
25) Lower middle class home makers, Pune	August 1998

Women, Lower Income Groups

26) Hadapsar, Pune	March 1998
27) Padavnagar, Pune	August 1998
28) Ramdeo Nagar, Ahmedabad	May 1998
29) Millat Nagar, Ahmedabad	May 1998

30)	Mixed labourers, Wagharis, Ahmedabad	May 1998
31)	Senior citizens, Ahmedabad	May 1998
32)	Men and women over 50, Ahmedabad	May 1998
33)	Senior citizens, Mumbai	August 1998
34)	Senior citizens, Pune	August 1998

Latur District Survey

A district survey was conducted by Nilu Damle in selected areas of Maharashtra in April–May 1998. The survey was closely inte-- grated with group discussions and interviews with individuals representing the occupational and social categories identified by the project as of special interest. Small-scale surveys, group discussions and personal interviews were carried out in Latur District, specifically in Latur town, Udgeer town and Ekurka village.

Separate interviews were conducted in Latur town with teachers, a linguist, a beautician, a theatre person, an orthodox Hindu, a Muslim preacher, a tailor, a hairdresser, shop keepers, two cable operators and a music teacher. In Udgeer, individual interviews were conducted with a social scientist, a college principal, a beauty parlour owner, TV set dealers, cable operators, cassette shop owners, a librarian, a police officer, a social worker, a tailor, and dress shop owners. In Ekurka village, individual interviews were conducted with children and young people.

Latur District Focus Group Discussions

35)	Professional women, Latur District	April 1998
36)	Working-class families, Gayatri Nagar, Latur	April 1998
37)	Professionals, Latur	April 1998
38)	College students, Latur	April 1998
39)	Teachers, Udgeer,	April 1998
40)	Middle-aged men and women, Udgeer	April 1998
41)	Children, Udgeer	April 1998
42)	Working-class men and women, Udgeer	April 1998
43)	Group of men, Ekurka village	April 1998
44)	Group of women, Ekurka village	April 1998

Northern India

Focus Group Discussions

45)	Ex-servicemen, Balajipuram, Mathura	June 1998
46)	Social workers, Trilokpuri, Delhi	July 1998

47) Schoolchildren at pottery workshop, New Delhi June 1998
48) Professionals, Bhopal   June 1998
49) Students, Bhopal   June 1998
50) University teachers, Bhopal   June1998
51) University teachers, Delhi   June 1998

Varanasi District Survey
As in Maharashtra, the small-scale survey in Varanasi was closely integrated with group discussions and interviews with individuals representing selected occupational and social categories. The three levels of investigation were Varanasi town, Chiraigaon, an intermediate level urban settlement, and Lamai village. In Varanasi, group discussions covered most of the relevant issues. Individual interviews were also conducted with proprietors of dress shops, cosmetics and toiletries shops, and with Siti Cable production staff. In Chiraigaon, some group discussions were held. In Lamai there were interviews with individuals and small mixed groups which included people of different ages from different walks of life.

Varanasi District Focus Group Discussions
52) Home makers, Varanasi   June 1998
53) Boatmen, Varanasi   June 1998
54) Professionals, Varanasi   June 1998
55) Students, Varanasi   June 1998
56) Muslims of Farukhi Nagar, Varanasi   June 1998
57) Home makers, Chiraigaon   June 1998
58) Students, Chiraigaon   June 1998
59) Professionals, Chiraigaon   June 1998

Eastern and North Eastern India

Focus Group Discussions
60) Women professionals, Calcutta   March 1998
61) Schoolchildren-1 (Classes 7–9), Calcutta   May 1998
62) Schoolchildren-2 (Classes 7–9), Calcutta   May 1998
63) College students, Calcutta   May 1998
64) Home makers, Calcutta   May 1998
65) Young executives (male and female), Calcutta   May 1998
66) Students, Guwahati   May 1998
67) Students, Silchar   May 1998

Note: Discussions were conducted in Calcutta, Shantiniketan and Hooghly District with approximately a hundred individuals, including music shop owners, beauty parlour owners, boutique owners and designers, domestic helps, restaurant owners and operators, shop owners in the bazaars, Montessori teachers, school teachers, college professors, farmers and farmers' wives, journalists, social workers and NGO workers, politicians, cable operators, home makers, older people, and younger girls and boys.

In Orissa informal discussions were held with household members with a cable TV connection and with NGO sector workers in Bhubaneshwar.

In Assam, interviews were conducted with seventeen leading Assamese editors, politicians, writers, poets, and a filmmaker during visits to Assam in May 1998, and with some of them for a second time in August 1998; opinion-formers such as college and university teachers, government officials and company executives were also interviewed. Prominent Assamese underground rebel leaders were interviewed by telephone from Calcutta. Group discussions with students were held at the Regional Institute of Journalism in Guwahati and the Regional Engineering College in Silchar.

South India

Focus Group Discussions

68)	Children, Chennai	November 1999
69)	Teenagers, Chennai	November 1999
70)	Professionals-1, Chennai	November 1999
71)	Professionals-2, Chennai	November 1999
72)	Home makers, Chennai	November 1999
73)	Senior citizens-1, Chennai	November 1999
74)	Senior citizens-2, Chennai	November 1999
75)	Labourers, Chennai	November 1999
76)	Film and TV professors and students-1 Chennai	December 1999
77)	Film and TV students-2, Chennai	January 2000
78)	Professionals-1, Madurai	November 1999
79)	Professionals-2, Madurai	November 1999
80)	Home makers/elders mixed, Madurai	November 1999
81)	College students, Madurai	November 1999
82)	Labourers, Madurai	November 1999

NEPAL

Focus Group Discussions

83)	Schoolchildren, Pokhara	September 1998
84)	Young men, Tansen Hills	September 1998
85)	College students, Biratnagar	June 1999
86)	School children, Birgunj	June 1999
87)	Mixed group, Lokhantali Kathmandu Valley	May 1998
88)	Professionals, Birgunj	June 1999
89)	Working men, Biratnagar	June 1999
90)	Home makers, Biratnagar	June 1999
91)	Schoolchildren, Kathmandu	March 1998

PAKISTAN

Focus Group Discussions

92)	Women activists, Islamabad	May 1998
93)	Home makers, Karachi	June 1998
94)	Professionals, Karachi	June 1998
95)	Labourers, Karachi	December 1998
96)	Schoolchildren, Rawalpindi	January 1999
97)	College students, Islamabad	January 1999

Rawalpindi District Survey

A survey was carried out between mid-May and mid-June 1998. The three localities chosen for the survey were Westridge, a colony in Rawalpindi for serving and retired army officers, Ilyas Colony, a colony for middle ranking government employees, and Saidpur, a village close to the capital, Islamabad. A random survey of fifty households was taken from each area. The sample included equal numbers of men and women who were further categorised into students, business people, government employees, home makers and labourers. Every tenth household in each area was taken and people were asked to co-operate in the survey and be part of a group or focus group discussions. A questionnaire focused on reactions to available radio and TV channels. Open-ended questions sought information on viewers' perception of the programmes and influence of the different channels.

SRI LANKA

Focus Group Discussions

98)	Schoolchildren (Ages 10–16)	
	Boralesgamuwa, Colombo	April 1998
99)	University students, Colombo	June 1998
100)	Home makers, Colombo	June 1998
101)	Development workers, Colombo	July 1998
102)	Professionals, Colombo	September 1998
103)	Children (13–16 years), Matara	May 1998
104)	Traders and technicians, Matara	May 1998
105)	Home makers, Matara	May 1998
106)	Professionals, Matara	May 1998
107)	Teachers, Matara	May 1998
108)	Students, Matara	May 1998
109)	Labourers, Matara	May 1998
110)	Development workers, Matara	June 1998

Matara District Survey

In Sri Lanka, a small-scale survey was carried out in Puhulwella, Matara District. The survey was carried out over four days through a questionnaire and discussions (in small groups) in the Puhulwella 'town' centre and in the surrounding neighbourhood. The discussions were held after the responses to the questionnaire were obtained; not all the people involved in the discussions had responded to the questionnaire.

The questionnaire was completed by seventy-two people in ten categories: children, unemployed youth, home makers, small entrepreneurs, paddy-growing farmers, government employees, elders/conservatives, businessmen, rubber estate labourers.

REPORTS COMMISSIONED FOR THE MEDIA SOUTH ASIA PROJECT, 1998–1999

Ahmar, Tasneem, District survey in Rawalpindi, June 1998.
Ahmar, Tasneem, Media Profile of Pakistan, December 1998.
Babu, K., District survey in Madurai, December 1999.
Bhatia, Deepa, Cultural dimensions of the satellite revolution, July 1998.

Bhatt, Mayank, The new media market, July 1998.

Bhaumik, Subir, Media Profile of North East India, May 1998.

Bhaumik, Subir, Survey in Assam, August 1998.

Chakravarty, Pritham, Cable networking and satellite television in south Chennai, September 1999.

Chowdhury, Afsan, District survey in Jamalpur, June 1998.

Chowdhury, Afsan, Media Profile of Bangladesh, July 1998.

Damle, Nilu, District surveys in Latur and Benares, May and June 1998.

Dasgupta, Saibal, Profile of Doordarshan and All India Radio, June 1998.

David, M.J.R., Community broadcasting in Sri Lanka, December 1999.

Firoz, Md., Media Profile of India, June 1998.

Jayawardena, Santhini, Media Profile of Sri Lanka, October 1998.

Jayawardena, Santhini, District survey in Matara, July 1998.

Memon, M.F., Cable networks in Karachi, December 1998.

Mukherjee, Anuradha, Media Profile of West Bengal and Orissa, July 1998.

Panneerselvan, A.S., Note on satellite TV in Tamil Nadu, December 1999.

Ramaseshan, Lata, Television Profile of South India, March 1999.

ARTICLES AND DOCUMENTS

The authors and members of the Media South Asia Project research team have drawn on information from published and unpublished sources: government commission reports, government orders, proposals and files; annual reports of the state broadcasting organisations; audit reports; advertising strategy papers; market analysis and market tracking reports; internal government reviews; regulatory documents for radio and TV; private sector proposals for broadcasting; brochures, books and fliers of the private and public sector; company and institutional websites; published studies; private submissions and unpublished papers; articles in specialist journals; reports in newspapers and journals; and transcripts of broadcast programmes. Publications and unpublished sources cited or consulted in the preparation of the book include the following.

Official Records and Publications

All India Radio, 1996, *All India Radio Report, 1996*, AIR, New Delhi.
————, 1997, *All India Radio Report, 1997*, AIR, New Delhi.
British Library, India Office Records, Information Department IOR/L/I/1.

L/I/1/445 File 223/1	Correspondence on Broadcasting in India, 1932–35
L/I/1/446 File 223/7	Broadcasting in the Indian States, 1926–29
L/I/1/672 File 462/10L	British Political Warfare Machinery 1942–44
L/I/1/958 File 462/57GG	War Cabinet Committee on Broadcasting 1944–45.
L/I/1/967 File 462/57R	Government of India Long Term Plans on the Development of Broadcasting.
L/I/1/973 File 462/57X	Opening of All India Radio Peshawar 1942
L/I/1/440 File 217/8	Radio SEAC, Ceylon.

BBC Monitoring Online, 'Government Committed to Funding Expansion of National Broadcaster', Text of Report in the Bhutanese Official Newspaper *Kuensel* website, 26 February 2000.
Doordarshan, 1995, *Electronic Media in the Tribal Areas*, Audience Research Unit, New Delhi.
————, 1996, *Doordarshan 1996*, Audience Research Unit, Prasar Bharati, New Delhi.
————, 1997, *Doordarshan 1997*, Audience Research Unit, Prasar Bharati, New Delhi.
————, 1997, *Television and Satellite Television in Rural India*, Audience Research Unit, New Delhi.
————, *Doordarshan 1998*, Audience Research Unit, Prasar Bharati, New Delhi.
Government of Bangladesh, 1997, *Report of the Autonomy Commission for Radio and TV* (in Bengali), Dhaka.
Government of India, 1966, Report of the Committee on Broadcasting and Information Media (Chanda Committee), Ministry of Information and Broadcasting, New Delhi.

Government of India, 1977, *White Paper on Misuse of Mass Media during the Internal Emergency*, prepared on the basis of the report of an inquiry conducted by K.K. Dass under the direction of the Government of India and other material available to the Government, PDIB-25(E)/7600 (August), Controller of Publications, New Delhi.

————, 1996, *National Media Policy*, A Working Paper Submitted by the Sub-committee of the Consultative Committee of the Ministry of Information and Broadcasting, New Delhi.

————, 1996, *Prasar Bharati Act 1990*, New Delhi.

————, 1996, *Proposed Broadcasting Bill*, Draft and Press Release (19–20 December), New Delhi.

————, 1996, *Report on Prasar Bharati* (Nitish Sengupta Committee), Ministry of Information and Broadcasting, New Delhi.

————, 1996, *Report of the Expert Committee on the Marketing of Commercial Time of AIR and DD* (Siddhartha Sen Committee), Ministry of Information and Broadcasting, New Delhi.

————, 1977, *Pursuit: Jhabua Development Communications Project*, DECU/ISRO, Ahmedabad.

Government of Pakistan, 1978, *White Paper on Misuse of Media*, Rawalpindi.

Government of Sri Lanka, 1966, *Report of the Commission on Broadcasting and Information*, Colombo.

Government of Sri Lanka, 1972, *Report of the Commission of Inquiry on the Ceylon Broadcasting Corporation*, Colombo.

————, 1996, *Report of the Committee to Advise on the Reform of Laws Affecting Media Freedom* (Chaired by R.W. Goonesekera), Colombo.

Pakistan Broadcasting Corporation, 1998, *Performance and Achievement*, Rawalpindi.

Other Reports, Articles and Private Submissions

Abu-Lughod, Lila, 1993, 'Finding a Place for Islam: Egyptian Television Serials and the National Interest', *Public Culture*, Vol. 5, No. 3.

————, 1995, 'The Objects of Soap Opera: Egyptian Television and the Cultural Politics of Modernity', in Daniel Miller (ed.), *Worlds Apart*, Routledge, London.

Agrawal, Binod C., 1999, 'Balancing Business and Social Responsibility in Broadcasting', AMIC/CBA seminar paper, April, New Delhi.

Ahmed, Syed Rashid, n.d., 'Speech on the Fiftieth Anniversary of the Lahore Station of Radio Pakistan', Lahore.

——, n.d., 'Broadcasting Structures in Pakistan'.

All India Joint Action Council (AIJAC), 1992, Submission on Prasar Bharati, New Delhi.

AMIC/CBA Conference, 1998, 'Thriving in a Diverse Broadcasting Environment', Conference Papers, Singapore, 20–21 February.

Ammirati Puris Lintas(APL), 1999 *Media Guide India*, June.

Anant Productions, 1999, *Amaanat*, Concept Paper.

Article 19, 1991, *Freedom of Expression and Information in Sri Lanka*.

——, 1994, *An Agenda for Change: The Right to Freedom of Expression in Sri Lanka*, October.

——, 1997, *Reform at Risk: Continuing Censorship in Sri Lanka*, March.

Asia Business News, 1997, Regional Television in Asia, Singapore.

Asia Cable and Satellite Directory Annual 1996, Cornerstone Associates, Hong Kong.

Asia Communication Handbook 1998, AMIC, Singapore.

Asian Mass Communications Bulletin (AMCB), 1998, Vol. 28, No. 1, Kuala Lumpur meeting, December 1997.

——, 1998, 'Thriving in a Diverse Broadcasting Environment', 1998, Public Broadcasters' Meeting, Singapore, 20–21 February, Vol. 28, No. 2.

Asian Media Information and Communication Centre (AMIC), 1997, 'Newspapers in Asia: Media and Culture', *Media Asia*, Vol. 24, No. 1.

——, 1997, 'Telecommunications Broadcasting', *Media Asia*, Vol. 24, No. 2.

——, 1997, *Media Asia* (AMIC Conference Issue), Vol. 24, No. 3.

——, 1999, 'Public Service Broadcasting', *Media Asia*, Vol. 26, No. 2.

Bajpai, Shailaja, 1999, 'Culture and Television', *Seminar*, 475, March.

Balaji Telefilms, 1999, *Hum Paanch*, Concept Note.

Basu, Rathikant, 2000, 'TV circa 2010', *The Hindustan Times*, 1 January.

Source Material 415

Bhasin, Usha and Singhal, Arvind, 1998, 'Participatory Approaches to Message Design: Jeevan Saurabh—A Pioneering Radio Serial in India for Adolescents', *Media Asia*, Vol. 25, No. 1.

Bhasin, Ritu, 1996, 'Children and Viewing', *Communicator*, July–September.

Biernatzki, William E.S.J., 1997, 'Globalisation of Communication', *Communication Research Trends*, Vol. 17, No. 1.

Bijapurkar, Rama, Valentine, Virginia and Alexander, Monty, 1995, 'Charting the Future of Cultural Markets', Paper delivered at the 47th European Social Marketing Research (ESOMAR) Congress, Davos, Switzerland, 11–14 September 1994, in *ESOMAR Congress Handbook 1994*, pp. 143–62.

Boyd-Barrett, J.O., 1982, 'Cultural Dependency and the Mass Media', in Michael Gurevitch, Tony Bennett, James Curran and Janet Woollacott (eds), *Culture, Society and the Media*, Methuen, London.

Breen, Marcus, 1996, 'Australia: Broadcasting, Policy and Information Technology', in Marc Raboy (ed.), *Public Broadcasting for the 21st Century*, University of Luton Press, Luton.

Burman, Rachna, *The Times of India*, 11 May 1999.

Business India, 1998, Anniversary Issue, Mumbai.

Business World, 1995, 'The Entertainment Industry: A Survey', January.

———, 1999, 'Goodnight DD: Good Morning Sat', 22 January–6 February.

———, 2000, 'It's Showtime Folks', 10 January.

Cable Operators Federation of India, 'Memorandum Against the Broadcasting Bill', Press Release, 18 November 1997.

Cable Waves, 1997, 'Indian Copyright Act', 1–15 November.

———, 1997, 'All India Media Reach NRS(1995) and NRS (1997)', 16–31 March.

———, 1997, 'English Channels Viewership', 16–31 May.

———, 1997, 'A Regulator too Many: Prasar Bharati Act', 16–31 July.

———, 1997, 'DD Penetration of Rural India', 1–15 August.

———, 1997, 'Audience for Niche Channels', 1–15 November.

———, 1997, 'FM Radio', 16–30 November.

———, 1997, 'From Hope to Despair: Developments in Indian Broadcasting Industry', 16–31 December.

Cable Waves, 1998, 'Viewership Share of Different Programme Genres', 1–15 January.

———, 1998, *Directory of Indian Broadcasting Industry*, 2nd edition, Delhi.

———, 1999, 'Indian Regulators Ready to Address Issue of Convergence', 16–30 November.

Cable Quest, 1997, 'Broadcasting Its Future in India: Subhash Chandra of Zee TV', Vol. 4, No. 1, April.

———, 1997, 'Operators Unhappy with the Broadcast Bill', Vol. 4, No. 1, April.

———, 1997, 'Cable TV Hardware Industry', Vol. 4, No. 9, April.

———, 1997, 'Cable Anger of Varanasi Siti Cable Franchisees', Vol. 4, No. 9, April.

———, 1999, 'Amending Broadcasting Bill Need of the Hour', Vol. 6, No. 9, December.

Cable Television Networks (Regulation) Ordinance 1994, 1995, Universal Book Traders, New Delhi.

Centre for Media Studies, 1998, 'Children and Television', A Round Table, 21 November, New Delhi.

Centre for Policy Alternatives, 1997, Workshop on 'Satellite Broadcasting: Legal Challenges', Sri Lanka Foundation Institute, 30 October, Colombo.

Chakravarty, Rangan and Gooptu, Nandini, 2000, 'Imagination: The Media, Nation and Politics in Contemporary India', in Hallam, Elizabeth, and Street, Brian (eds), *Cultural Encounters: Representing Otherness*, Routledge, London.

Chakravarty, Nikhil, 1997, 'Jaipal Reddy Redesigns Prasar Bharati', *Mainstream*, Vol. XXXV, No. 49, 8 November.

Chandra, Subhash, 2000, 'Intelligence on the Idiot Box', *The Hindustan Times*, 1 January.

Chitnis, E.V., 1983, 'TV Creativity for Rural Growth', *India International Centre Quarterly*, Vol. 10, No. 2, June.

Crawley, William, 1996, 'Air Wars: Competition and Control in India's Electronic Media', *Contemporary South Asia*, Vol. 5, No. 3, November.

———, 1998, 'Autonomy: Means to an End', Paper at AMIC/CBA Conference on Public Service Broadcasting, Singapore, 20–21 February.

———, 1999, 'Public Service Broadcasting: Sustainability in the New Media Order', *Media Asia*, Vol. 26, No. 2.

Das, Veena, 1995, 'On Soap Opera: What Kind of Anthropological Object Is It?', in Daniel Miller (ed.), *Worlds Apart*, Routledge, London.

Dawn, Karachi, 'Tuesday Review', 5–11 March 1996.

———, Karachi, 'Review', 29 October–4 November, 1998.

Dhanraj, Deepa, 1994, 'A Critical Focus' in Joseph, Ammu and Sharma, Kalpana (eds), *Whose News? The Media and Women's Iissues*, Sage Publications, New Delhi.

Eashwar, Sucharita and Mathew, Philip, 1998, 'What Works for Radio? The Indian Experience', *Voices*, Bangalore.

Economic Times, New Delhi, 'Sri Adhikari Bros', 18 June 1998.

Economist Intelligence Unit, 1997, *Pakistan Business Report*, 1st Quarter, Hong Kong.

ETV Channel 21, 1998, 'Ekushey Television Proposal', 21 February.

Exhibitions India, 1997, BCS India 97/CommsIndia 97, *Broadcasting Cable and Satellite Conference Publication*, Delhi, 9–11 December.

Exhibitions India, 1997, *Communications Today*, Delhi, November–December.

Farmer, Victoria, 1997, 'Accretion, Accommodation and Transformation: Governance of Mass Media in India', Paper delivered at seminar organised by the Centre for the Advanced Study of India, New Delhi, November.

Federation of Indian Chambers of Commerce and Industry (FICCI), 1997, National Conference on 'Strategies for Development of Entertainment Electronics Information and Broadcasting', Background Paper, New Delhi, 24 June.

Fernando, E.S.T., 1990, 'Mahaweli Community Radio', in Wickrama, S. (ed.), *Mahaweli Development Plan*, Government of Sri Lanka, Colombo.

Firoz, Md., 1997, 'Communication, Values and Advent of Star TV in India: A Sociological Study of Social and Cultural Impact in the Delhi Metropolis', Unpublished paper.

Friedrich Ebert Stiftung/Ford Foundation, 1995, Viewing Habits of Delhi Teenagers, New Delhi.

Gentleman, 1999, Interview with Alyque Padamsee, Mumbai, February.

———, 1999, 'Inside Media Manipulation', articles by A.G. Noorani, Sashi Kumar, Rajdeep Sardesai and Subhanjan Sarkar, Mumbai, June.

Ghosh, Avik, 1983, 'TV Films or Alternative Television Programming for Social Change and Development', *Communicator*, January.

Gilani, Ijaz, 1995, The Satellite Revolution: Implications for Marketing and Media Research, Conference Presentation, Gallup Business Research Bureau of Pakistan, Karachi.

———, 1997, 'Media Scenario of Pakistan', Gallup Profile of Pakistan Series, (chapter for *Asian Handbook of Communications*, AMIC, Singapore).

Goswami, Onkar, 1998, 'The Wasted Years', *Business India*, 9–22 March.

Gunasekara, Lakshman, 1998, 'Freedom of Expression and Media Freedom in Sri Lanka', in *State of Human Rights 1998*, Law and Society Trust, Colombo.

Gunawardena, Victor, 1996, 'More Responsive and Responsible Media', Unpublished manuscript, ICES, Kandy.

Gupta, Arun K. and Jain, Nisha, 1998, 'Gender Mass Media and Social Change: A Case Study of TG Commercials', *Media Asia*, Vol. 25, No. 1.

Habermas, Jurgen, 1992, Further Reflections on the Public Sphere, in Calhoun, Craig (ed.), *Habermas and the Public Sphere*, MIT Press, Cambridge.

Hasan, K., 1998, 'Bangladesh National Media Survey 1998', ORG-MARG-QUEST Ltd, Dhaka, Sponsored by Bangladesh Centre for Communication Programmes, Johns Hopkins University, Social Marketing Company and UNICEF.

Hesmondhalgh, Desmond, 1998, 'Globalisation and Cultural Imperialism: A Case Study of the Music Industry, in R. Kiely and P. Marfleet, *Globalisation and the Third World*, Routledge, London.

Hewage, W., 1990, Experiences in Field Production, Paper presented in the regional workshop on South Asian Community Broadcasting, Kandy.

Himal South Asia, 'Orbital Junk', June 1996.

Hina, Farzana, 1993, 'PTV Peshawar Role in Islamisation', University of Peshawar, Dept. of Journalism Thesis.

Hukill, Mark A., 1998, 'Structures of Television in Singapore', *Media Asia*, Vol. 25, No. 1.

Indica Research Private Ltd, 1997, 'Project Akarshan-IV: Presentation Text for Evaluation of *Star Yaar Kalaakar* (Sony TV), Mumbai.

Jabbar, Javed, 1993, 'Communications Ethics from a South Asian Viewpoint', Observations at an AMIC Seminar in Colombo, in Javed Jabbar, 1999, *The Global City*, Royal Book Company, Karachi.

———, 1997, 'An Overview of Advertising in Pakistan', Paper for conference on 'A Celebration of Advertising' organised by The British Council, Karachi, 15 September.

———, 1998, 'Issues', Paper for seminar on 'Democratic Governance and Freedom of Electronic Media' organised by Citizen's Media Commission of Pakistan, Islamabad, 14 February.

Jakubowicz, Karol, 1997, 'Public Service Broadcasting and Democracy', Paper presented at seminar on 'Public Broadcasting and Editorial Independence: Strengthening Democratic Voices' in Tampere, Finland, 16–18 June.

Jeffrey, Robin, 1997, 'Indian Language Newspapers', Articles in *Economic and Political Weekly*, January–March (Hindi, 18 January; Bengali, 25 January, Telugu, 1 February, Tamil, 8 February; Gujarati, 15 February; Marathi, 22 February; Punjabi, 1–8 March; Oriya, 15 March; Kannada, 22 March)

Jian Wang, 1997, 'Global Media and Cultural Change', *Media Asia*, Vol. 24, No. 1.

Joshi, S.R., Joshi, Hansa, Trivedi, Bela and Hashmi, Jawaid N., 1995, *Effects Study: Role of Television in Rural Areas*, DECU/ISRO, Bangalore.

Joshi, S.R., and Bhatia, B.S. 1997, *Broadcasting in India*, ISRO, Bangalore.

Juneau, Pierre, 1998, 'Public Broadcasting and National Culture', UNESCO Interministerial Conference, Stockholm, 19 March–2 April.

Kaifu, Kazuo, 1997, NHK Internationalization, Market Deregulation and Digitization, NHK Broadcasting Culture and Research Institute (BCRI), Autumn.

Karnik, Kiran, 1993, 'Satellite and Cable TV Invasion: Its Socio-Economic Impact', *Mass Media*, New Delhi.

Kohli, J.S., 1995, 'Interactive Round Table, Progress and Plans for the Future', C&S Development Policy and Regulation, India, Cable and Satellite International Summit, 18–20 October, New Delhi.

Krishnan, Srinivas, 1998, 'Music TV (MTV India) and Channel V Comparison', *Business Standard*, 21 April.

Krishnaswamy Associates Pvt. Ltd., 1995, '31st Anniversary Brochure', Madras.

Lall, Bhuvan, 1999, *Screen International*, London, 8 October.

Lipschutz, R., 1992, 'Reconstructing World Politics: The Emergence of Global Civil Society, *Millennium: Journal of International Studies*, Vol. 21, No.3.

Lloyds Securities, India, 1995, Research Sector Study, Mumbai.

Madhyam Communications, 1993, 'Report on the Consultation on New Communication Technologies: Possibilities and Problems', Bangalore, 18–20 March.

Madhyam, 1996, 'Media Policy and Nation Building', Vol. XI, No. 2.

————, 1997, 'Communicating for Peace and Justice', Vol. XII, No. 1.

McCaughan, Dave, 1997, 'Hanging Out: Real Media Issues for Asian Youth', McCann-Erickson Asia Pacific Occasional Paper.

Martin-Barbero, J., 1988, 'Communication from Culture: The Crisis of the Nations and the Emergence of the Popular, *Media, Culture and Society*, Vol. 10.

Media Advocacy Group, 1994, 'People's Perception: Obscenity and Violence on the Small Screen', Study sponsored by the National Commission for Women, New Delhi.

————, 1997, 'The Audience Speaks: Building a Consumer Forum', New Delhi.

————, 1998, 'A Study of Television and Election 1998: An Analysis of News Bulletins and Current Affairs Programmes (Interim Report)', New Delhi, April.

Media Development—Journal of the World Association of Christian Communication, 1999, 'Key Issues of Global Communications', Vol. 2.

Media Matters, 1998, A Monthly for Media and Development Communication, Colombo, March.

Mehta, Hemant, 1995, 'Aiming for the Pie in the Sky: The Role of Research', Session Paper and Presentation Points, Indian Market Research Bureau.

Mitra, Ananda, 1993, 'Television and the Nation: Doordarshan's India', *Media Asia*, Vol. 20, No. 1.

Monteiro, Anjali, 1998, 'Official Television and Unofficial Fabrications of the Self: The Spectator as Subject, in Ashis Nandy (ed.), *The Secret Politics of Our Desires*, Delhi.

Monteiro, Anjali and Jayasankar, K.P., 2000, 'Between the Normal and the Imaginary: The Spectator Self, the Other and Satellite

Television in India', in Hagen, I. and Washo, J. (eds), *Consuming Audiences: Production and Reception in Media Research*, Hampton Press, London.

MTV Youth Marketing Forum, 1998, 'Making a Brand of Youth Relevant: MTV and Brand Equity', Mumbai, 20 February.

MTV Research Report, 1999, 'Tuning in to Indian Youth, Part II', Mumbai.

N.G. Productions, 1999, *Saans*, A brief sketch.

NAMEDIA, 1986a, 'Vision for Indian Television: Report of a Feedback Project: Indian Television Today and Tomorrow', New Delhi.

————, 1986b, *Free Flow of Information in South Asia: A Study for UNESCO*, UNESCO, New Delhi.

NCAER Publications, National Council of Applied Economic Research, New Delhi.

————, 1996, *Indian Market Demographics*, edited by S.L. Rao.

————, 1998, *Indian Market Demographics*, edited by I. Natarajan.

NCAER, 1998, *The Very Rich Whitebook: A Study of Super Affluent Indian Consumers*, New Delhi.

National Readership Survey 1997, India.

National Readership Survey 1999, India.

Natarajan, I. (ed.), 1998, *Indian Market Demographics*, NCAER, New Delhi.

Ninan, Sevanti, 1998, 'History of Indian Broadcasting Reform', in Price, Monroe E. and Verhulst, Stefaan G. (eds), *Broadcasting Reform in India*, Oxford University Press, New Delhi.

Noorani, A.G., 1997, 'Sri Lanka's TV', *The Statesman*, Delhi, 10–11 June.

Orient McCann Erickson, 1997, *Pakistan Advertising Scene*, Orient Advertising (Pvt) Ltd., Karachi.

Outlook, 'The World's Last Shangri-La (Bhutan), 14 June 1999, www.outlookindia.com.

Padgaonkar D., Rao, N. Bhaskara and Verghese, B.G., 1995, 'Broadcasting as a Public Service: An Approach Paper, Unpublished.

Page, David, 1998, 'South Asian Media in a Globalising World', Paper delivered at a conference on 'The Impact of Globalisation on Asia' organised by the Heinrich Boll Foundation, Karachi, 27 February–1 March.

————, 1998, 'Public Broadcasting in the Cable Age', Paper delivered to the Panos Public Service Broadcasting Workshop, Kathmandu, 20–22 September.

Parakrama, Arjuna, 1997, 'Television News Reporting as the Means of Mainstreaming of public Perceptions', *Media Monitor*, Vol. 1, No. 2, December.

Prasad, Nandini, 1996, 'Media Policy and Women's Issues', in Gupta, V. S. and Dayal, R., *National Media Policy*, Concept Publishing, New Delhi.

Rai, Sharita, 1996 'Women and Media', in Gupta, V.S. and Dayal, R., *National Media Policy*, New Delhi.

Rajagopal, Arvind, 1993, 'The Rise of National Programming: The Case of Indian Television', *Media, Culture and Society*, Vol. 15.

Rao, N. Bhaskara, 1997, 'An Outline of the Proposed Autonomous Broadcasting Services Bill', Discussion paper, Centre for Media Studies, Delhi.

————, 1995, 'Mass Media and Market Communication: Perspectives into 2020', Centre for Media Studies, New Delhi.

————, n.d., 'The Mass Communication Environment: The Indian Scene', Conference paper.

Reports and Articles on Broadcasting, 1995–2000
India: *Asian Age, Business Standard, Business World, Economic Times, Hindu, Hindustan Times, Indian Express, India Today, Outlook, Pioneer, Seminar, Statesman, Times of India*
Pakistan: *The Muslim, The News, Dawn, The Nation, Friday Times, Herald, Newsline, Nawa-i-waqt*
Bangladesh: *Daily Sangbad*
Nepal: *Himal*
Sri Lanka: *Daily News, Island, Lanka Guardian, Observer, Sunday Times, Sunday Leader*

Rishi, Vibha, 1999, Presentation at the MTV Youth Forum, Mumbai, January.

Rudolph, Lloyd I., 1992, 'The Media and Cultural Politics', *Economic and Political Weekly* , 11 July.

Rupavahini, Journal of the Sri Lanka Rupavahini Corporation, July 1998.

Sagarmatha Radio: Project Proposal 1997, Kathmandu.

Samarajiva, Rohan, 1994, 'The Problem of Credibility', *Lanka Guardian*, Vol.16, No. 23, 1 April.

Samarasinghe, S.W.R. de A., 1997, 'Reading, Listening and Watching: A National Sample Survey of the Sri Lankan News Media', in Peiris, G.H. (ed.), *Studies on the Press in Sri Lanka and South Asia*, International Centre for Ethnic Studies, Kandy.

Satellite & Cable TV, 1997, 'Focus INSAT-2D', Delhi, 10 November.
————, 1997, 'Digital TV is Coming', Delhi, 10 December.
————, 1998, Cable and Satellite in Rural India', Delhi, 10 March.
————, 1998, Digital Channels over India', Delhi, 10 February.
————, 1998, 'Star TV goes Digital', Delhi, 10 January.
Sekhar, K., 1999, 'Emergence of Religious and Regional Language Programming in Indian TV: Some Perspectives', *Media Asia*, Vol. 26, No. 1.
Sen, Amartya, 1998, 'Culture, Freedom and Independence', in *UNESCO World Culture Report*.
Sengupta, Subir and Frith, Katherine T., 1997, 'Multinational Corporation Advertising and Cultural Imperialism', *Asian Journal of Communication*, Vol. 7, No. 1.
Sharma, Roop, 1995, 'Multi Channel Television in India', Cable Operators Federation of India, Delhi.
Sinclair, John, 1997, 'The Business of International Broadcasting: Cultural Bridges and Barriers, *Asian Journal of Communication*, Vol. 7, No. 1.
Sinha, Ajay, n.d., *Hasratein*, Director's note and synopsis.
Sinha, Arbind and Parmar, K.M., 1995, *Insat Effects Study: Television and Rural Life: A Closer Look*, DECU/ISRO, Bangalore.
SIRIUS Marketing and Social Research Ltd., 1998, A Proposal for a BTV Advertisement Audit: Continuous Monitoring of All Commercials Appearing on Bangladesh Television', Dhaka, May.
SLBC, 1985, *Mahaweli Community Radio: Audience Survey Report*, Colombo.
SLRC, 1997, *15 Years of Continuing Excellence*, Sri Lanka Rupavahini Corporation, Colombo.
Smith, Anthony D., 1989, 'The Public Interest', *Intermedia*, Vol. 17, No. 2, June–July.
Sri Lanka Foundation Institute, 1995, 'Devolution Proposals: A Way Forward', Colombo, 10 August.
SRL Fact File Survey, Research Lanka Pvt Ltd, January 1998.
Star TV, 'Satellite Television Code of Practice on Programme Standards' as at 1 August 1996.
Television Asia, *Satellite and Cable Annual Guide 1999–2000*, Singapore.
Thapar, Romila, 1991, 'A Historical Perspective on the Story of Rama', in Gopal S. (ed.), *Anatomy of a Confrontation*, Penguin, New Delhi.

Thomas, Pradip N., 1993, 'Broadcasting and the state in India: Towards Relevant Alternatives', *Gazette*, Vol. 51.

————, 1999, 'Trading the Nation: Multinational Negotiations and the Fate of Communications in India', *Gazette*, Vol. 61 Nos. 3–4.

Thussu, Daya Kishan, 1999, 'Privatising the Airwaves: The Impact of Globalisation on Broadcasting in India', *Media, Culture and Society*, Vol. 21.

Turner/CNNI, 1997–98, Publicity and Press Releases, Hong Kong.

————, undated, 'The DD-CNNI partnership', CNN Executive Abstract.

Verghese, B.G., 1999, 'Media and society', *Mainstream Annual*, Radhanath Rath Memorial Lecture, Cuttack, 12 February.

Videazimut and Cendit, 1994, 'New Technologies and the Democratisation of Audiovisual Communication: Their Impact, Implications and Appropriation of New Technologies of Communication, International Symposium, New Delhi, 9–12 February.

Vidyarthi, Indrani, 1999, 'The Millennium Generation Speaks... Direct Dil Se', Presentation on behalf of ORG-MARG to the MTV Youth Forum, Mumbai, January.

Voices, 1996, 'Bangalore Declaration on Radio', Bangalore, September.

————, 1996, 'Consultation on Media Policy and Community Radio 1996', Workshop Report by Shangon Das Gupta, Bangalore, December.

————, 1997, 'Telephone for All: Privilege or Basic Right?', Vol. 1, No. 3, Bangalore.

————, 1999, 'Community Radio and Governance', Background paper.

Watagedera, Sugath, 1998, 'Rupavahini Ruva Guna', *Rupavahini Journal*, SLRC, July.

Wijesinha, 1990, 'Experiences in Interviewing', Paper presented in the regional workshop on 'South Asian Community Broadcasting', Kandy.

Wildermuth, Norbert, 1998, 'Global Going Local: Fighting for the Indian TV Audiences', in Hjarvard, Stig and Tufte, Thomas, *Audio Visual Media in Transition, Yearbook of the Department of Film and Media Studies*, University of Copenhagan, Copenhagen.

Zee Telefilms, *Annual Report 1996–97*, Mumbai.

Zee TV publicity releases.
ZeeTV website: *www.zeetelevision.com*

BOOKS

Abercrombie, Nicholas, 1996, *Television and Society*, Polity Press, Cambridge.

Acharya, A.N., 1987, *Television in India*, Manas Publication, New Delhi.

Anderson, Benedict, 1983, *Imagined Communities*, Verso, London.

Appadurai, Arjun (ed.), 1986, *The Social Life of Things: Commodities in Cultural Perspective*, Cambridge University Press, Cambridge.

Appadurai, A., 1997, *Modernity at Large: Cultural Dimensions of Globalisation*, Oxford University Press, Delhi.

Appadurai, A., Breckenridge, C. and Merol, A. (eds), 1995, *Consuming Modernity: Public Culture in South Asia*, University of Minnesota Press, Minneapolis.

Babb, Lawrence A. and Wadley, Susan S. (eds), 1997, *Media and the Transformation of Religion in South Asia*, Motilall Banarsidass, Delhi.

Bagadikian, B., 1992, *The Media Monopoly*, Beacon Press, Boston.

Barendt, E.M., 1995, *Broadcasting Law: A Comparative Study*, Clarendon, Oxford.

Barker, Chris, 1997, *Global Television: An Introduction*, Blackwell, Oxford.

Baskaran, S. Theodore, 1981, *The Message Bearers: The Nationalist Politics and the Entertainment Media in South India 1880–1945*, Cre-A, Madras.

Bassnett, Susan (ed.), 1997, *Studying British Cultures: An Introduction*, Routledge, London.

Bhatt, S.C., 1994, *Satellite Invasion*, Gyan Publication, New Delhi.

Bhattacharya, Vivek, 1976, *Communication in a Global Village*, Chetna, New Delhi.

Blumler J.G. (ed.), 1992, *Television and the Public Interest: Vulnerable Values in Western European Broadcasting*, Sage, London.

Bochner, Stephen (ed.), 1983, *Cultures in Contact: Studies in Cross-cultural Interaction*, Pergamon Press, Oxford.

Bokhari, Zulfiqar Ali, 1998, *Sar Guzisht*, Global Publishing, Lahore.

Bourdieu, Pierre, 1998, *On Television and Journalism*, Pluto Press, London.

Boyd-Barrett, Oliver and Rantanen, Terhi (eds), 1998, *The Globalisation of News*, Sage, London.

Brosius, C. and Butcher, M. (eds), 1999, *Image Journeys: Audio-visual Media and Cultural Change in India*, Sage, New Delhi.

Butler, Rex, 1999, *Jean Baudrillard: The Defence of the Real*, Sage, London.

Cable, Vincent and Distler, Catherine, 1995, *Global Superhighways: The Future of International Telecommunications Policy*, RIIA, London.

Cairncross, Frances, 1997, *The Death of Distance: How the Communications Revolution Will Change Our Lives*, Orion, London.

Calhoun, Craig (ed.), 1992, *Habermas and the Public Sphere*, MIT Press, Cambridge, Mass.

Carey, James W., 1992, *Communication as Culture: Essays on Media and Society*, Routledge, London.

Chakravarty, Sumita, 1993, *National Identity in Indian Popular Cinema 1947–87*, University of Texas, Austin.

Chakravarty, Suhas, 1997, *Press and Media: The Global Dimensions*, Kanishka, Delhi.

Chatterji, P.C., 1998, *The Adventure of Indian Broadcasting: A Philosopher's Autobiography*, Konark Publishers, New Delhi.

———, 1991, *Broadcasting in India, (2nd edition, revised and updated)*, Sage, New Delhi.

Chomsky, Noam and Herman, E., 1988, *Manufacturing Consent*, Pantheon Books, New York.

Christian, Clifford and Traber, Michael, (eds), 1997, *Communication Ethics and Universal Values*, Sage, London.

Clarke, Arthur C., 1979, *The View from Serendib*, Pan Paperbacks, London.

Cohn, Bernard S., 1997, *Colonialism and its Forms of Knowledge: The British in India*, Oxford University Press, Delhi.

Collins, R, Garnham N. and Locksley G., 1988, *The Economics of Television: UK Case*, Sage, London.

Curran, James and Park, Myung-Jin, (eds), 2000, *De-westernising Media Studies*, Routledge, London.

Curran, James and Seaton, Jean 1991, *Power without Responsibility: The Press and Broadcasting in Britain (4th edition), (5th edition 1997)*, Routledge, London.

Curran, J., Smith, A. and Wingate, B.P. (eds), 1987, *Impacts and Influences: Essays on Media and Power in the Twentieth Century*, Methuen, London.

Damle, Nilu, 2000, *Tele-vartan*, Akshar Prakashan, Mumbai.

Desai, M.V., and Ninan, Sevanti (eds), 1996, *Beyond those Headlines: Insiders on the Indian Press*, The Media Foundation, New Delhi.

Desai, M.V., 1977, *Communication Policies in India*, Paris, UNESCO.

Dixit, Kunda, 1997, *Dateline Earth: Journalism as if the Planet Mattered*, IPS, Pasig City, Philippines.

Dizard, Wilson P., 1982, *The Coming of the Information Age*, New York, Longman.

Featherstone, Mike, 1995, *Undoing Culture: Globalism, Postmodernism and Identity*, Sage, London.

Fielden, Lionel, 1960, *The Natural Bent*, Andre Deutsch, London.

Fiske, J., 1987, *Television Culture*, Methuen, London.

French, David and Richards, Michael (eds), 1996, *Contemporary Television: Eastern Perspectives*, Sage, New Delhi.

Friedrich Ebert Stiftung (ed.), 1997, *Media and Critical Issues of Democracy*, Friedrich-Ebert-Stiftung (FES), Islamabad.

Fukuyama, Francis, 1992, *The End of History and the Last Man*, Free Press, New York.

Garnham, Nicholas, 1994, *Capitalism and Communication*, Sage, London.

Gauhar, Altaf, 1994, *Ayub Khan: Pakistan's First Military Ruler*, Sang-e-Meel Publications, Lahore.

Gazdar, Mushtaq, 1997, *Pakistan Cinema 1947–1997*, Oxford University Press, Karachi.

Golding, Peter and Harris, Phil (eds), 1997, *Beyond Cultural Imperialism: Globalisation, Communication and the New Information Order*, Sage, London.

Gopal, Sarvepalli (ed.), 1991, *Anatomy of a Confrontation: The Babri Masjid-Ram Janmabhumi Issue.* Penguin Books, New Delhi.

Gunasekara, H.M., 1997, *Media as Bridge Maker: Coordinating Group for Studies on South Asian Perspectives (2nd edition)*, FES, Colombo.

Gunawardena, Victor, 1993, *Press as Promoter*, FES, Colombo.

Gupta, Nilanjana, 1998, *Switching Channels: Ideologies of Television in India*, Oxford University Press, Delhi.

Gupta, Partha Sarathi, 1995, *Radio and the Raj (S.G. Deuskar Lectures on Indian History and Culture,1988)*, K.P. Bagchi and Co., Calcutta.

Gupta, V.S. and Dayal, Rajeshwar (eds), 1995, *Rural Press: Problems and Prospects*, AMIC/FES, Delhi.

————, 1996, *National Media Policy*, AMIC/FES, Concept Publishing, New Delhi.

Gurevitch, Michael, Bennett, Tony, Curran, James and Woollacott, Janet (eds), 1995, *Culture, Society and the Media*, Routledge, London.

Habermas, Jurgen, 1987, *The Philosophical Discourse of Modernity*, MIT Press, Cambridge, Massachusetts.

————, 1996, *The Structural Transformation of the Public Sphere*, Blackwell, Oxford.

Hachten, William A. and Hachten, Harva, 1993, *The Growth of Media in the Third World: African Failures Asian Successes*, Iowa State University Press, Ames, Iowa.

Hagen, I. and Wasko, J. (eds), 2000, *Consuming Audiences: Production and Reception in Media Research*, Hampton Press, London.

Hale, Julian, 1975, *Radio Power: Propaganda and International Broadcasting*, Paul Elek, London.

Hallam, Elizabeth, and Street, Brian (eds), 2000, *Cultural Encounters: Representing Otherness*, Routledge, London.

Hamelink, Cees J., 1994, *The Politics of World Communication*, Sage, London.

Herman, Edward S. and Chomsky, Noam, 1994, *Manufacturing Consent: The Political Economy of the Media*, Vintage Books, London.

Herman, Edward S. and McChesney Robert, W., 1997, *The Global Media: New Missionaries of Global Capitalism*, Cassell, London.

Hoggart, Richard, 1995, *The Way We Live Now*, Pimlico, London.

Hossain, Dr. Kamal, 1997, *The Right to a Culture of Tolerance: Report by the Commonwealth Human Rights Advisory Commission*, Commonwealth Human Rights Initiative, New Delhi.

Hower, David, 1996, *Cross-cultural Consumption: Global Markets and Local Realities*, Routledge, London.

Jabbar, Javed, 1999, *The Global City*, Royal Book Company, Karachi.

Jabbar, Javed and Qazi Faez, Isa (eds), 1997, *Mass Media Laws and Regulations in Pakistan*, AMIC, Singapore.

Jeffrey, Robin, 2000, *India's Newspaper Revolution: Capitalism, Politics and the Indian Language Press*, Hurst, London.

Joseph, Ammu and Sharma, Kalpana (eds), 1994, *Whose News? The Media and Women's Issues*, Sage, New Delhi.

Kaifu, Kazuo, 1997, *Internationalization, Market Deregulation and Digitization*, NHK (BCRI), Tokyo.

Kaplan, E. Kann, 1989, *Rocking Around the Clock: Music Television, Post-Modernism and Consumer Culture*, Routledge, London.

Karunanayake, Nandana, 1990, *Broadcasting in Sri Lanka: Potential and Performance*, Centre for Media and Policy Studies, Sri Lanka.

Khilnani, Sunil, 1997, *The Idea of India*, Penguin, New Delhi.

Kiely, Ray and Marfleet, Phil, 1998, *Globalisation and the Third World*, Routledge, London.

Kulathilaka, C. de S.A., n.d., *Survey of Mahaweli Community Music Recordings*, SLBC, Colombo.

Kumar, Prem, 1988, *The Television Industry in India: Market Structure, Conduct and Performance*, Deep and Deep Publishers, New Delhi.

Laiq, Jawid, 1996, *The Western Media in Asia: Globalisation and Resistance*, Just World Trust, Penang.

Lamb, Robert, 1997, *The Bigger Picture: A Survey of the Audio-visual Landscape 1997–2000*, TVE-UNICEF, New York.

Lee, Philip (ed.), 1995, *The Democratisation of Communication*, University of Wales Press, Cardiff.

Lerner, D., 1958, *The Passing of Traditional Society*, Free Press, New York.

Lury, Celia, 1996, *Consumer Culture*, Polity Press, Cambridge.

Luthra, H.R., 1986, *Indian Broadcasting*, Government of India, Delhi.

Madras Institute of Development Studies, 1997, *Tamil Cinema: History, Culture, Theory*, Workshop, 15–19 August, Chennai.

Mallick, Ross, 1998, *Development Ethnicity and Human Rights in South Asia*, Sage, New Delhi.

Mansell, Gerard, 1982, *Let Truth be Told: 50 years of BBC External Broadcasting*, Weidenfeld and Nicolson, London.

Manuel, Peter, 1993, *Cassette Culture*, University of Chicago Press, Chicago.

Masani, Mehra, 1985, *Broadcasting and the People*, National Book Trust, New Delhi.

Mathur, J.C. and Neurath, Paul, 1959, *An Indian Experiment in Farm Radio Forums*, UNESCO, Paris.

Mattelart, Armand, 1979, *Multinational Corporations and the Control of Culture*, Harvester Press, Brighton.

———, 1994, *Mapping World Communication: War, Progress, Culture (English translation)*, University of Minnesota Press, Minneapolis.

Mattelart, Armand and Mattelart, Michele, 1992, *Rethinking Media Theory*, University of Minnesota, Minneapolis.

———, 1998, *Theories of Communication: A Short Introduction (English translation)*, Sage, London.

Mcluhan, M., 1967, *The Medium is the Message*, Bantam Books, New York.

McQuail, Denis, 1994, *Mass Communication Theory: An Introduction (3rd edition)*, Sage, London.

Melkote, Srinivas R., Shields, Peter and Agrawal, Binod C. (eds), 1998, *International Satellite Broadcasting in South Asia: Political Economic and Cultural Implications*, University Press of America Inc., Lanham.

Miller, Daniel (ed.), 1995, *Worlds Apart: Modernity through the Prism of the Local*, Routledge, London.

Miller, Daniel, 1987, *Material Culture and Mass Consumption*, Basil Blackwell, Oxford.

Mitra, Ananda, 1993, *Television and Popular Culture in India*, Sage, New Delhi.

Mohammadi, Ali (ed.), 1997, *International Communication and Globalisation*, Sage, London.

Moragas, Spa Miquel de and Garitoanandia, Carmelo (eds), 1995, *Decentralisation in the Global Era: Television in the Regions, Nationalities and Smaller Countries of the European Union*, John Libbey, London.

Morley, David, 1992, *Television Audiences and Cultural Studies*, Routledge, London.

Morley, David and Robins, Kevin, 1995, *Spaces of Identity: Global Media, Electronic Landscapes and Cultural Boundaries*, Routledge, London.

Mullick, K.S., 1974, *Tangled Tapes*, Sterling Publishers, Delhi.

Nandy, Ashish (ed.), 1998, *The Secret Politics of our Desires: Innocence, Culpability and Indian Popular Cinema*, Oxford University Press, Delhi.

Nasr, Abu and Hoque, Md Gaziul (eds), 1992, *Mass Media Laws and Regulations in Bangladesh* AMIC, Singapore.

Neuman, W. Russell, 1991, *The Future of the Mass Audience*, Cambridge University Press, Cambridge.

Niazi, Zamir, 1986, *The Press in Chains*, Karachi Press Club, Karachi.

———, 1992, *The Press Under Siege*, Karachi Press Club, Karachi.

Niazi, Zamir, 1994, *The Web of Censorship,* Oxford University Press, Karachi.

Ninan, Sevanti, 1995, *Through the Magic Window: Television and Change in India,* Penguin Books, Delhi.

Pandian, M.S.S., 1992, *The Image Trap: M.G. Ramachandran in Film and Politics,* Sage, New Delhi.

Partasarathy, Rangaswami, 1994, *Here is the News! Reporting for the Media,* Sterling, Delhi.

Pasha, A.R., 1997, *Community Radio: The Voice of the People,* Voices, Bangalore.

Peiris, G.H. (ed.), 1997, *Studies on the Press in Sri Lanka and South Asia,* International Centre for Ethnic Studies, Kandy.

Pervez, Nasreen, 1998, *Pakistan TV Drama and Social Change,* Dept. of Mass Communication, Karachi University.

Pokhrel, Gokul Prasad and Koirala, Bharat Dutta (eds), 1995, *Mass Media Laws and Regulations in Nepal,* AMIC, Singapore.

Poster, Mark, 1995, *The Second Media Age,* Polity Press, Cambridge and Blackwell, Oxford.

Prasad, M. Madhava, 1998, *Ideology of the Hindi Film: A Historical Construction,* Oxford University Press, Delhi.

Price, Monroe E., 1995, *Television, The Public Sphere, and National Identity,* Clarendon, Oxford.

Price, Monroe E. and Verhulst, Stefaan G., (eds), 1998, *Broadcasting Reform in India; Media Law from a Global Perspective,* Oxford University Press, Delhi.

Pujitha-Gunawardena, C.L., 1990, *This is Colombo Calling,* Perali Publishers, Colombo.

Raboy, Marc (ed.), 1996, *Public Broadcasting for the 21st Century,* University of Luton Press, Luton.

Rahman, Tariq, 1998, *Language and Politics in Pakistan,* Oxford University Press, Karachi.

Ray, Samirendra N., 1995, *Communication in Rural Development: A Public Policy Perspective,* IIAS, Simla.

Sadanandan, Nair and White, Shirley A. (eds), 1993, *Perspectives of Development Communication,* Sage, New Delhi.

Sardar, Ziauddin, 1998, *Postmodernism and the Other: The New Imperialism of Western Culture,* Pluto Press, London.

Saxena, Gopal, 1996, *Television in India: Changes and Challenges,* Vikas, Delhi.

Schiller, H.I., 1976, *Communication and Cultural Domination*, N.V. International Service and Art Press, White Plain.

Schramm, W. and Lerner, Daniel J., 1964, *Mass Media and National Development*, Stanford University Press, Stanford.

Schramm, W. and Roberts, D.F. (eds), 1976, *Communication and Change: The Last Ten Years*, University Press of Hawaii, Honolulu.

Selvakumaran, N. and Edrisinha, Rohan, 1995, *Mass Media Laws and Regulations in Sri Lanka*, AMIC, Singapore.

Sen, Jahar, 1992, *India and Nepal: Some Aspects of Culture Contact*, IIAS, Simla.

Senadhira, Sugeeswara P., 1996, *Under Siege: Mass Media in Sri Lanka*, Segment Books, New Delhi.

Shah, Amrita, 1997, *Hype Hypocrisy and Television in Urban India*, Vikas, Delhi.

Shankar, V., 1974, *My Reminiscences of Sardar Patel*, vol. 1, Macmillan, Delhi.

Sinclair, John, Jacka, Elizabeth and Cunningham, Stuart (eds), 1996, *New Patterns in Global Television: Peripheral Vision*, Oxford University Press, Oxford.

Singh, B.P., 1998, *India's Culture: The State, the Arts and Beyond*, Oxford University Press, Delhi.

Singh, Yogendra, 1993, *Social Change in India: Crisis and Resilience*, Har Anand Publication, New Delhi.

Singhal, Arvind and Rogers, Everett M., 1989, *India's Information Revolution*, Sage, New Delhi.

Smith, Anthony D., 1980, *The Geopolitics of Information*, Faber and Faber, London.

Sokal, Alan and Bricmont, Jean, 1998, *Intellectual Impostures*, Profile Books, London.

Sreberny-Mohammadi, Annabelle, Winseck, D., McKenna J. and Boyd-Barrett, O., 1997, *Media in Global Context: A Reader*, Arnold, London.

Srinivas, M.N., 1972, *Social Change in Modern India*, University of California Press, Stanford.

———, 1991, *India: Social Structure*, Hindustan Publications, New Delhi.

Stevenson, Robert L., 1988, *Communication, Development and the Third World: The Global Politics of Information*, University Press of America, New York.

Swingewood, A., 1997, *The Myth of Mass Culture*, Macmillan, London.

Thakur, Ramesh, 1996, *The Government and Politics of India*, Macmillan, London.

Thapa, Bhekh B. and Sharma, Kul Shekhar, 1996, *Mass Media and Democratisation: Country Study on Nepal*, Institute for Integrated Development Studies (IIDS), Kathmandu.

Thiruchandran, Selvy, 1997, *Ideology, Caste, Class and Gender*, Vikas, Delhi.

Tomlinson, John, 1991, *Cultural Imperialism: A Critical Introduction*, Pinter, London.

Tunstall, Jeremy, 1996, *Newspaper Power: The New National Press in Britain*, Clarendon Press, Oxford.

Tunstall, J. and Palmer, M. (eds), 1991, *Media Moguls*, Routledge, London.

UNESCO, 1998, *World Culture Report 1998*, UNESCO, Paris.

Unnikrishnan, Namita and Bajpai, Shailaja, 1996, *The Impact of Television Advertising on Children*, Sage, New Delhi.

Valbuena, V.T., 1988, *The Mahaweli Community Radio Project: An Evaluation*, AMIC, Singapore.

Varma, Pavan K., 1998, *The Great Indian Middle Class*, Viking, Delhi.

Venkateswaran K.S. (ed.), 1993, *Mass Media Laws and Regulations in India*, AMIC, Singapore.

Wenham, Brian (ed.), 1982, *The Third Age of Broadcasting*, Faber and Faber, London.

Wickrama, S., (ed.) 1990, *Mahaweli Development Plan*, Government of Sri Lanka, Colombo.

Williams, Raymond, 1977, *Marxism and Literature*, Oxford University Press, Delhi.

———, 1983, *Towards 2000*, Chatto and Windus/Hogarth Press, London.

Williams, Raymond (ed. by Ederyn Williams), 1975, *Television: Technology and Cultural Form*, Fontana, London.

Wijemanne, Livy, 1998, *A Broadcaster Looks Back*, Unpublished manuscript, Colombo.

Yadav, J.S., 1984, *Politics of News: Third World Perspectives*, Concept, New Delhi.

INDEX

in early history of Indian broad-
casting 38–43; viewership 123–27
BBDO 134
Benares (see Varanasi)
Benares Hindu university 157, 170
Bengali advertising market 196, 199,
201, 286
Bengali cinema (see cinema)
Bengali culture 58, 148, 152, 193ff,
199–201, 224ff, 326
Bengali language (see language)
Bengali middle class (see middle
class)
Bengali satellite channels 24, 82, 88,
193, 198–201, 217, 219–20, 224,
228–29; see also ATN and DD7
Bernard, Rabi 214–15
Bhagwat, Vidyut 168–69
Bhanubhakta 231
Bharatiya Janata Party (BJP) 79, 188,
207, 353, 368; and the arts 145–
46; and the development of radio
273, 324; and the issue of broad-
casting autonomy 272–73, 318,
350–51, 376
Bhatia, Deepa 180
Bhatt, Mayank 136
Bhattacharya, Malini 195, 197
Bhattarai, Binod 330
Bhaumik, Subir 152, 369
Bhutan 12, 288
Bhutto, Benazir 242, 274–75, 277, 320
Bhutto, Zulfiqar Ali 55
Bidwai, Praful 111
Bihar 102, 103, 215
Bijapurkar, Rama 141–42, 146, 166–
67, 181
Binaca Geet Mala 50
Binodon Bichitra 224, 310
Biratnagar 19–20, 230, 231
Birgunj 161, 171, 230, 231, 233
Bista, Hem Bahadur 287–88
BITV(see Business India TV)
BJP (see Bharatiya Janata Party)
Bokhari, Ahmed Shah 41–42, 46
Bokhari, Ashfak 234
Bokhari, Zulfiqar A. 41–42, 47
Bold and the Beautiful, The 77

Bollywood 54, 79, 97, 105, 152–55,
175, 186, 194, 202, 230, 234, 346;
contrasted with satellite TV 152–
53, 155; in Nepal 230–31; its
popularity in Bangladesh 223–25;
in Pakistan 97, 234–37; its role in
popularising satellite TV 68, 78,
80, 89, 92, 122, 158–61, 179, 185–
86, 223ff, 234ff, 253; in Sri Lanka
250, 252, 257; see also cinema
Bombay 35–36, 43, 46, 49–51, 54–55,
66, 78–82, 89, 105, 124, 134–35,
147, 153, 159, 200, 225–26, 228,
235, 267, 310, 319; see also Mumbai
Bon Jovi, Jon 189
borders 25, 55, 114, 135, 157, 223, 342;
cross-border advertising 129, 131–
32, 379; cross-border media influences 20, 30, 46, 61, 88, 106, 158,
200–01, 229, 234–35; cross-border
trade 83, 379
Borgaonkar, Ram 356
Bose, P.K. 199
Brayne, Frederick 37
Britain (UK) 23, 35, 44, 48–49, 148,
192, 292, 343, 348, 365, 377, 379
Britannia India 104
British American Tobacco 132
British Broadcasting Corporation (see
BBC)
Brittan, Samuel 340
Broacha, Cyrus 150
broadcasters
    assassination of 64; as civil ser-
    vants 42–43, 46–47, 315, 318, 381;
    community broadcasters 329,
    331–32, 334; early Indian broad-
    casters 41–42; for Radio Ceylon
    49; in Sri Lanka 254, 257;
broadcasting
    broadcasting and community
    302–38; broadcasting legislation
    82, 96, 264–67, 272–73, 290–91,
    370, 377; evolution of a centralised
    system 38–40; funding 36, 279,
    294–95, 313, 323, 351–53, 379; his-
    tory in south Asia 35ff; impact of
    the Second World War 44–46;

ABOUT THE AUTHORS

William Crawley and **David Page** have shared an interest in South Asia since their student days. They worked together in the BBC World Service for over twenty years. They are currently co-directors of the Media South Asia Project, which is based at the Institute of Development Studies at Sussex University in the UK.

William Crawley joined the BBC in 1970 and worked as a scriptwriter, commentator and editor. From 1986, he was head of the BBC Eastern Service, broadcasting to South and West Asia and to Burma. Since leaving the BBC, he has worked as a media consultant for the Commonwealth Broadcasting Association in Sri Lanka and Bangladesh. He has written a number of articles and book reviews on South Asian history, politics and broadcasting.

David Page joined the BBC Eastern Service in 1972, where he worked as a producer and editor of programmes broadcast to South Asia and Afghanistan. After leaving the BBC, he served as the media training coordinator for the European Union's Med Media programme. He has lectured on South Asian politics at Oxford and London universities. He is the author of *Prelude to Partition*, a study of Muslim politics in India before independence.

ABOUT THE DOCUMENTARY FILM

As part of the Media South Asia Project, Nupur Basu, a television journalist and award-winning documentary film maker from India, was commissioned to produce a film which explores the same themes as the book.

Nupur Basu filmed in different regions of India and Pakistan, and in Bangladesh, Sri Lanka and Nepal, interviewing over 200 people, including media owners and managers, television producers, government officials, academics, representatives of NGOs and members of the public. She worked with film crews from all five countries. The filming was mostly carried out in 2000.

The film is intended both for general distribution and for use in media studies as a counterpart to the book. It is being distributed by Television Trust for the Environment, a non-profit making organisation that works globally to promote the use of audio and visual media to discuss development issues.

Within the Asia-Pacific region, inquiries about broadcast and non-broadcast copies should be directed to:

TVE Asia Pacific Regional Office,
24, First lane, Koswatte Road,
Nawala, Sri Lanka.
Telephone: 00 94 1 877 808
Fax: 00 94 74 403 443
E-mail: tve_sl@sri.lanka.net or sletp@eureka.lk

Inquiries from elsewhere may be addressed to:

TVE Distribution, TVE International,
Prince Albert Road,
London NW1 4RZ.
Telephone 00 44 207 586 5526
Fax: 00 44 207 586 4866
E-mail: tve-dist@tve.org.uk